D1451444

HOLT McDOUGAL

South and East Asia and the Pacific

Christopher L. Salter

HOLT McDOUGAL

HOUGHTON MIFFLIN HARCOURT

Author

Dr. Christopher L. Salter

Dr. Christopher L. "Kit" Salter is Professor Emeritus of geography and former Chair of the Department of Geography at the University of Missouri. He did his undergraduate work at Oberlin College and received both his M.A. and Ph.D. degrees in geography from the University of California at Berkeley.

Dr. Salter is one of the country's leading figures in geography education. In the 1980s he helped found the national Geographic Alliance network to promote geography education in all 50 states. In the 1990s Dr. Salter was Co-Chair of the National Geography Standards Project, a group of distinguished geographers who created *Geography for Life* in 1994, the document outlining national standards in geography. In 1990 Dr. Salter received the National Geographic Society's first-ever Distinguished Geography Educator Award. In 1992 he received the George Miller Award for distinguished service in geography education from the National Council for Geographic Education. In 2006 Dr. Salter was awarded Lifetime Achievement Honors by the Association of American Geographers for his transformation of geography education.

Over the years, Dr. Salter has written or edited more than 150 articles and books on cultural geography, China, field work, and geography education. His primary interests lie in the study of the human and physical forces that create the cultural landscape, both nationally and globally.

Printed in the U.S.A.

ISBN-13 978-0-547-48485-3

1 2 3 4 5 6 7 8 9 10 0914 19 18 17 16 15 14 13 12 11 10

4500263433 ^ B C D E F G

Reviewers

Academic Reviewers

Elizabeth Chako, Ph.D.
Department of Geography
The George Washington University

Altha J. Cravey, Ph.D.
Department of Geography
University of North Carolina

Eugene Cruz-Uribe, Ph.D.
Department of History
Northern Arizona University

Toyin Falola, Ph.D.
Department of History
University of Texas

Sandy Freitag, Ph.D.
Director, Monterey Bay History and Cultures Project
Division of Social Sciences
University of California, Santa Cruz

Oliver Froehling, Ph.D.
Department of Geography
University of Kentucky

Reuel Hanks, Ph.D.
Department of Geography
Oklahoma State University

Phil Klein, Ph.D.
Department of Geography
University of Northern Colorado

B. Ikubolajeh Logan, Ph.D.
Department of Geography
Pennsylvania State University

Marc Van De Mieroop, Ph.D.
Department of History
Columbia University
New York, New York

Christopher Merrett, Ph.D.
Department of History
Western Illinois University

Thomas R. Paradise, Ph.D.
Department of Geosciences
University of Arkansas

Jesse P. H. Poon, Ph.D.
Department of Geography
University at Buffalo–SUNY

Robert Schoch, Ph.D.
CGS Division of Natural Science
Boston University

Derek Shanahan, Ph.D.
Department of Geography
Millersville University
Millersville, Pennsylvania

David Shoenbrun, Ph.D.
Department of History
Northwestern University
Evanston, Illinois

Sean Terry, Ph.D.
Department of Interdisciplinary Studies, Geography and Environmental Studies
Drury University
Springfield, Missouri

Educational Reviewers

Dennis Neel Durbin
Dyersburg High School
Dyersburg, Tennessee

Carla Freel
Hoover Middle School
Merced, California

Tina Nelson
Deer Park Middle School
Randallstown, Maryland

Don Polston
Lebanon Middle School
Lebanon, Indiana

Robert Valdez
Pioneer Middle School
Tustin, California

Teacher Review Panel

Heather Green
LaVergne Middle School
LaVergne, Tennessee

John Griffin
Wilbur Middle School
Wichita, Kansas

Rosemary Hall
Derby Middle School
Birmingham, Michigan

Rose King
Yeatman-Liddell School
St. Louis, Missouri

Mary Liebl
Wichita Public Schools USD 259
Wichita, Kansas

Jennifer Smith
Lake Wood Middle School
Overland Park, Kansas

Melinda Stephani
Wake County Schools
Raleigh, North Carolina

Contents

Available @

hmhsocialstudies.com

- Facts About the World
- Regions of the World Handbook
- Standardized Test-Taking Strategies
- Economics Handbook

HISTORY™ is the leading destination for revealing, award-winning, original non-fiction series and event-driven specials that connect history with viewers in an informative, immersive and entertaining manner across multiple platforms. HISTORY is part of A&E Television Networks (AETN), a joint venture of Hearst Corporation, Disney/ABC Television Group and NBC Universal, an award-winning, international media company that also includes, among others, A&E Network™, BIO™, and History International™.

HISTORY programming greatly appeals to educators and young people who are drawn into the visual stories our documentaries tell. Our Education Department has a long-standing record in providing teachers and students with curriculum resources that bring the past to life in the classroom. Our content covers a diverse variety of subjects, including American and world history, government, economics, the natural and applied sciences, arts, literature and the humanities, health and guidance, and even pop culture.

The HISTORY website, located at **www.history.com**, is the definitive historical online source that delivers entertaining and informative content featuring broadband video, interactive timelines, maps, games, podcasts and more.

"We strive to engage, inspire and encourage the love of learning..."

Since its founding in 1995, HISTORY has demonstrated a commitment to providing the highest quality resources for educators. We develop multimedia resources for K–12 schools, two- and four-year colleges, government agencies, and other organizations by drawing on the award-winning documentary programming of A&E Television Networks. We strive to engage, inspire and encourage the love of learning by connecting with students in an informative and compelling manner. To help achieve this goal, we have formed a partnership with Houghton Mifflin Harcourt.

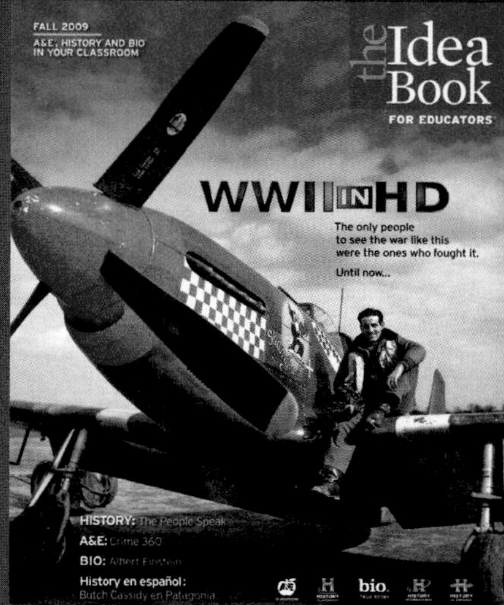

The Idea Book for Educators

Classroom resources that bring the past to life

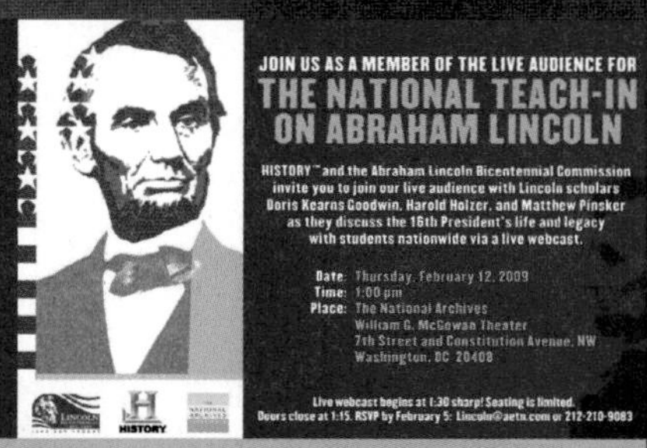

Live webcasts

HISTORY Take a Veteran to School Day

In addition to premium video-based resources, **HISTORY** has extensive offerings for teachers, parents, and students to use in the classroom and in their in-home educational activities, including:

- ***The Idea Book for Educators*** is a biannual teacher's magazine, featuring guides and info on the latest happenings in history education to help keep teachers on the cutting edge.

- **HISTORY Classroom (www.history.com/classroom)** is an interactive website that serves as a portal for history educators nationwide. Streaming videos on topics ranging from the Roman aqueducts to the civil rights movement connect with classroom curricula.

- **HISTORY email newsletters** feature updates and supplements to our award-winning programming relevant to the classroom with links to teaching guides and video clips on a variety of topics, special offers, and more.

- **Live webcasts** are featured each year as schools tune in via streaming video.

- **HISTORY Take a Veteran to School Day** connects veterans with young people in our schools and communities nationwide.

In addition to **HOUGHTON MIFFLIN HARCOURT**, our partners include the *Library of Congress*, the *Smithsonian Institution*, *National History Day*, *The Gilder Lehrman Institute of American History*, the *Organization of American Historians*, and many more. HISTORY video is also featured in museums throughout America and in over 70 other historic sites worldwide.

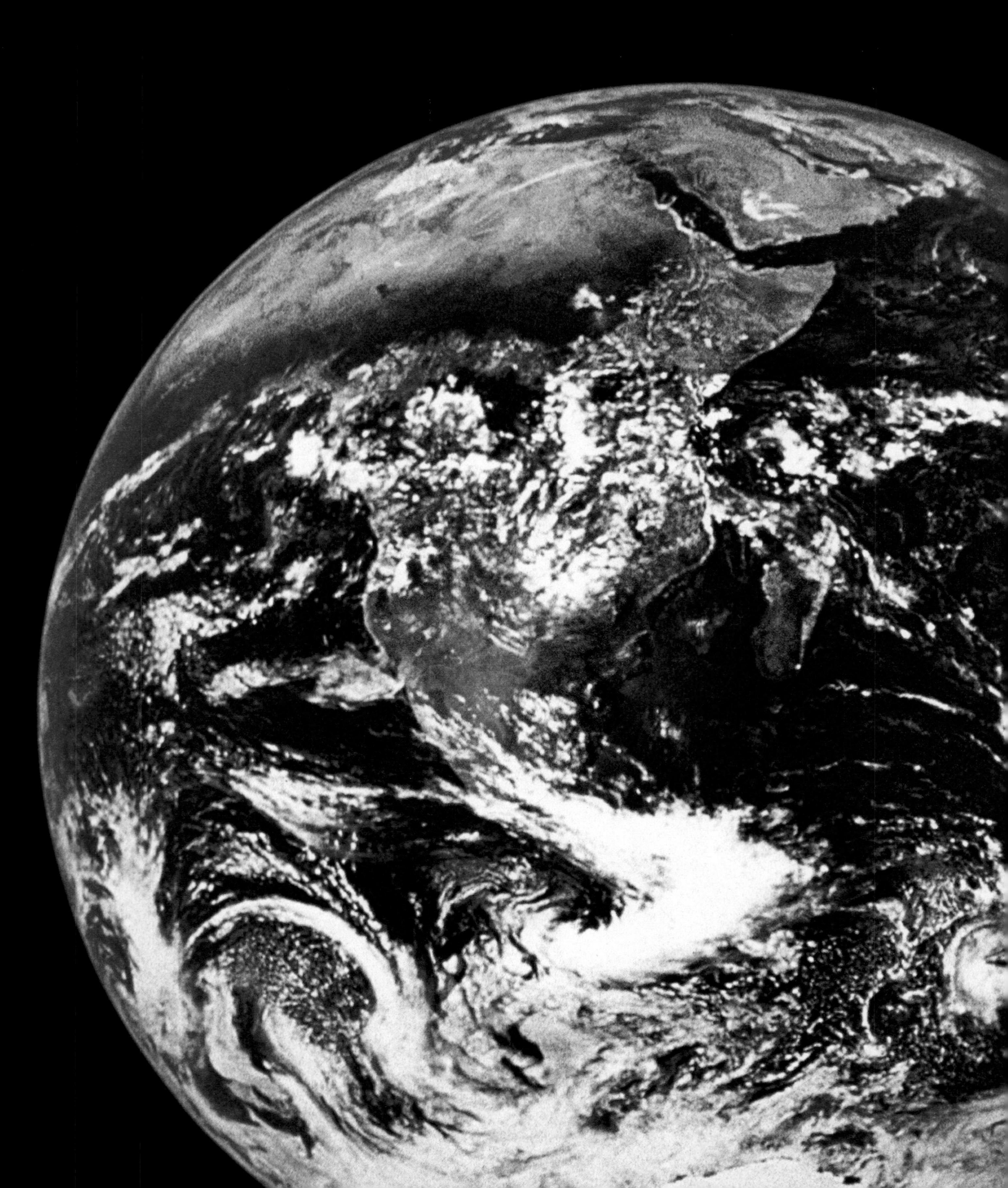

Geography and Map Skills Handbook

Contents

Throughout this textbook, you will be studying the world's people, places, and landscapes. One of the main tools you will use is the map—the primary tool of geographers. To help you begin your studies, this Geography and Map Skills Handbook explains some of the basic features of maps. For example, it explains how maps are made, how to read them, and how they can show the round surface of Earth on a flat piece of paper. This handbook will also introduce you to some of the types of maps you will study later in this book. In addition, you will learn about the different kinds of features on Earth and about how geographers use themes and elements to study the world.

hmhsocialstudies.com INTERACTIVE MAPS

Geography Skills With map zone geography skills, you can go online to find interactive versions of the key maps in this book. Explore these interactive maps to learn and practice important map skills and bring geography to life.

You can access all of the interactive maps in this book through the Interactive Student Edition at

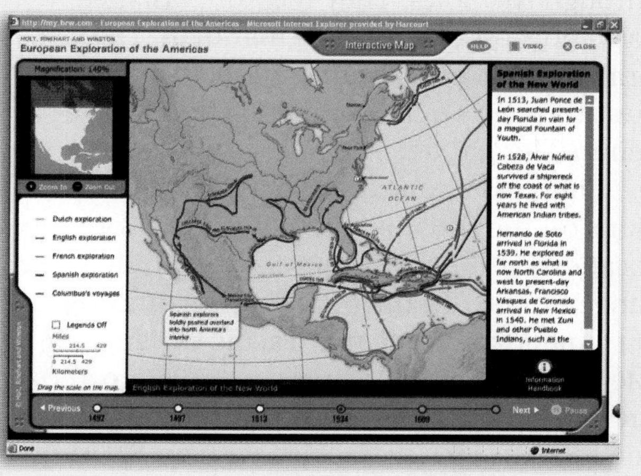

Mapping the Earth

Using Latitude and Longitude

A **globe** is a scale model of the Earth. It is useful for showing the entire Earth or studying large areas of Earth's surface.

To study the world, geographers use a pattern of imaginary lines that circles the globe in east-west and north-south directions. It is called a **grid**. The intersection of these imaginary lines helps us find places on Earth.

The east-west lines in the grid are lines of **latitude**, which you can see on the diagram. Lines of latitude are called **parallels** because they are always parallel to each other. These imaginary lines measure distance north and south of the **equator**. The equator is an imaginary line that circles the globe halfway between the North and South Poles. Parallels measure distance from the equator in **degrees**. The symbol for degrees is °. Degrees are further divided into **minutes**. The symbol for minutes is ´. There are 60 minutes in a degree. Parallels north of the equator are labeled with an N. Those south of the equator are labeled with an S.

The north-south imaginary lines are lines of **longitude**. Lines of longitude are called **meridians**. These imaginary lines pass through the poles. They measure distance east and west of the **prime meridian**. The prime meridian is an imaginary line that runs through Greenwich, England. It represents 0° longitude.

Lines of latitude range from 0°, for locations on the equator, to 90°N or 90°S, for locations at the poles. Lines of longitude range from 0° on the prime meridian to 180° on a meridian in the mid-Pacific Ocean. Meridians west of the prime meridian to 180° are labeled with a W. Those east of the prime meridian to 180° are labeled with an E. Using latitude and longitude, geographers can identify the exact location of any place on Earth.

Lines of Latitude

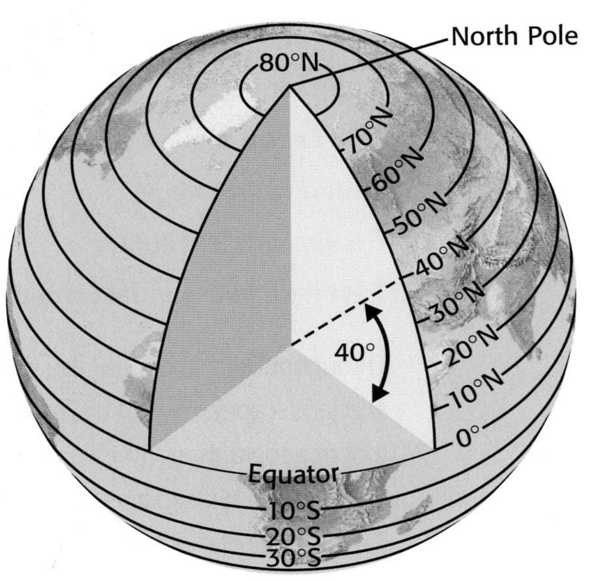

Lines of Longitude

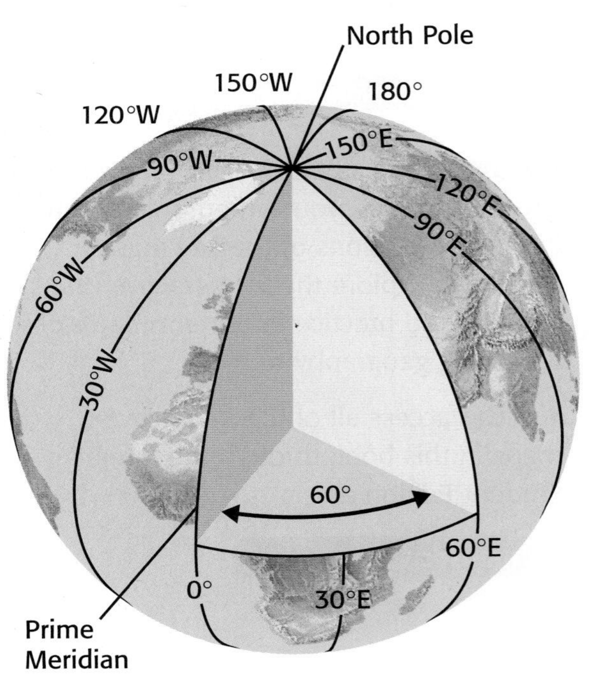

The equator divides the globe into two halves, called **hemispheres**. The half north of the equator is the Northern Hemisphere. The southern half is the Southern Hemisphere. The prime meridian and the 180° meridian divide the world into the Eastern Hemisphere and the Western Hemisphere. Look at the diagrams on this page. They show each of these four hemispheres.

Earth's land surface is divided into seven large landmasses, called **continents**. These continents are also shown on the diagrams on this page. Landmasses smaller than continents and completely surrounded by water are called **islands**.

Geographers organize Earth's water surface into major regions too. The largest is the world ocean. Geographers divide the world ocean into the Pacific Ocean, the Atlantic Ocean, the Indian Ocean, and the Arctic Ocean. Lakes and seas are smaller bodies of water.

Northern Hemisphere

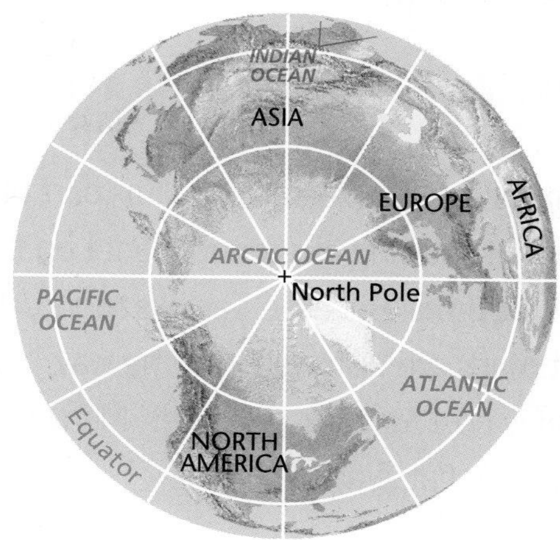

Southern Hemisphere

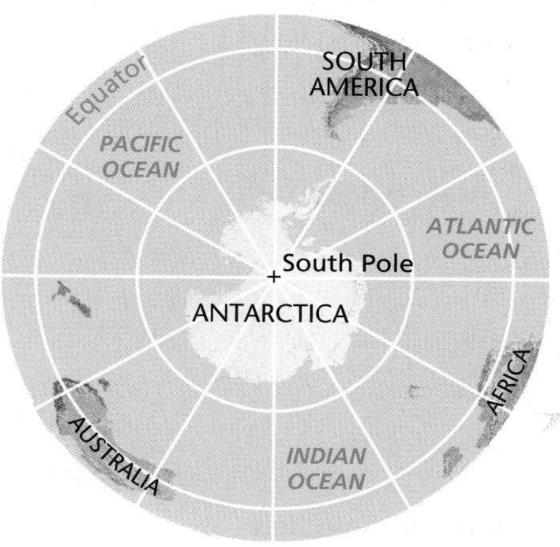

Western Hemisphere

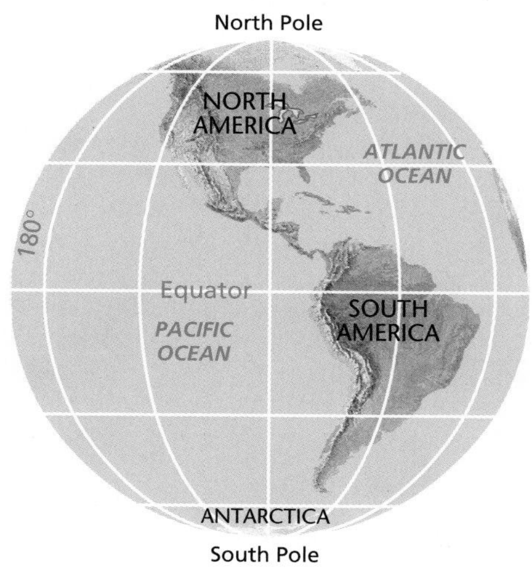

Eastern Hemisphere

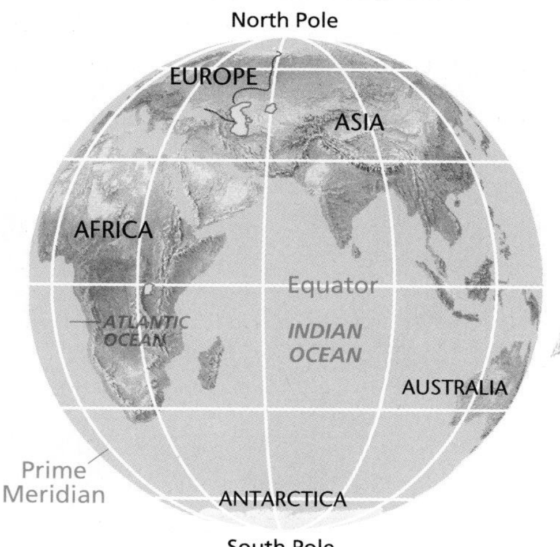

Mapmaking

Understanding Map Projections

A **map** is a flat diagram of all or part of Earth's surface. Mapmakers have created different ways of showing our round planet on flat maps. These different ways are called **map projections**. Because Earth is round, there is no way to show it accurately on a flat map. All flat maps are distorted in some way. Mapmakers must choose the type of map projection that is best for their purposes. Many map projections are one of three kinds: cylindrical, conic, or flat-plane.

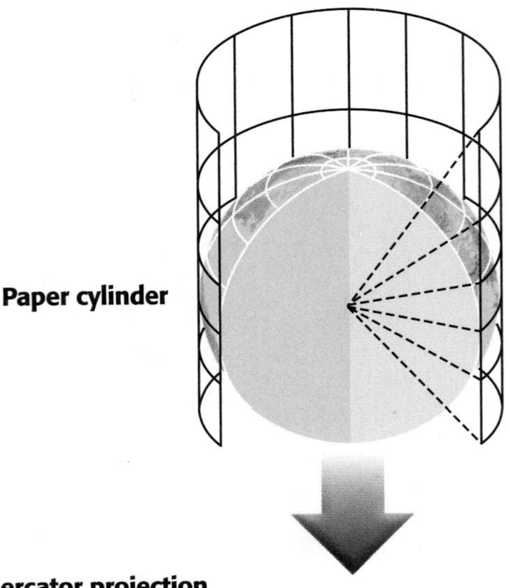

Cylindrical Projections

Cylindrical projections are based on a cylinder wrapped around the globe. The cylinder touches the globe only at the equator. The meridians are pulled apart and are parallel to each other instead of meeting at the poles. This causes landmasses near the poles to appear larger than they really are. The map below is a Mercator projection, one type of cylindrical projection. The Mercator projection is useful for navigators because it shows true direction and shape. However, it distorts the size of land areas near the poles.

Mercator projection

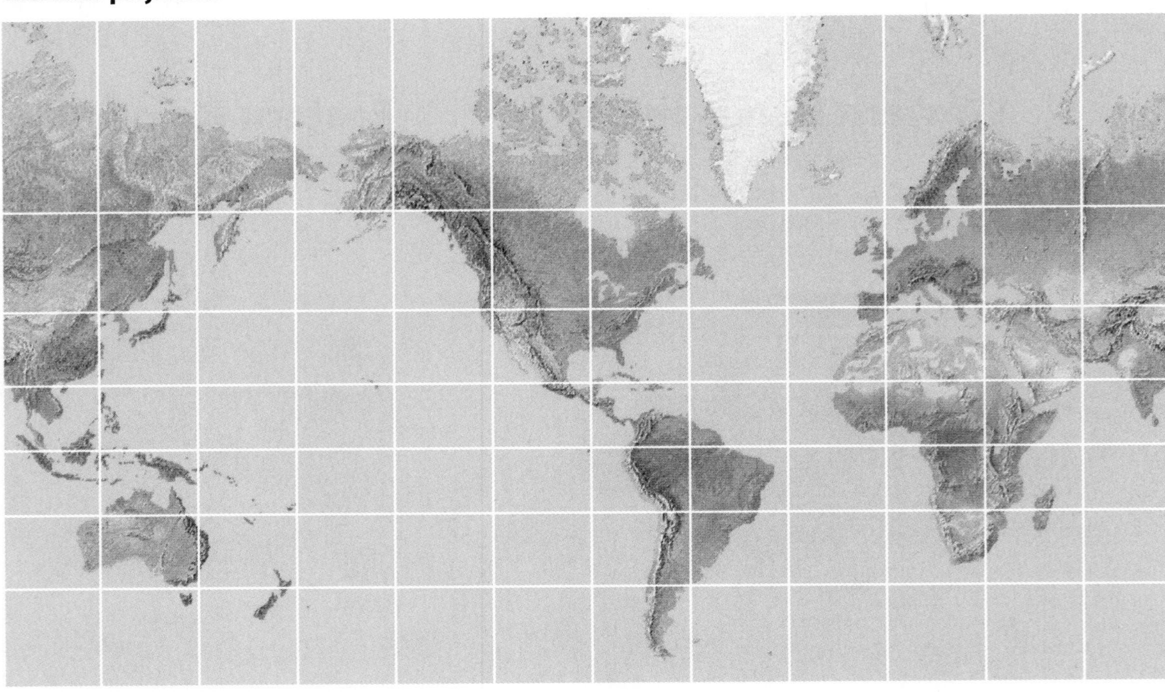

Conic Projections

Conic projections are based on a cone placed over the globe. A conic projection is most accurate along the lines of latitude where it touches the globe. It retains almost true shape and size. Conic projections are most useful for showing areas that have long east-west dimensions, such as the United States.

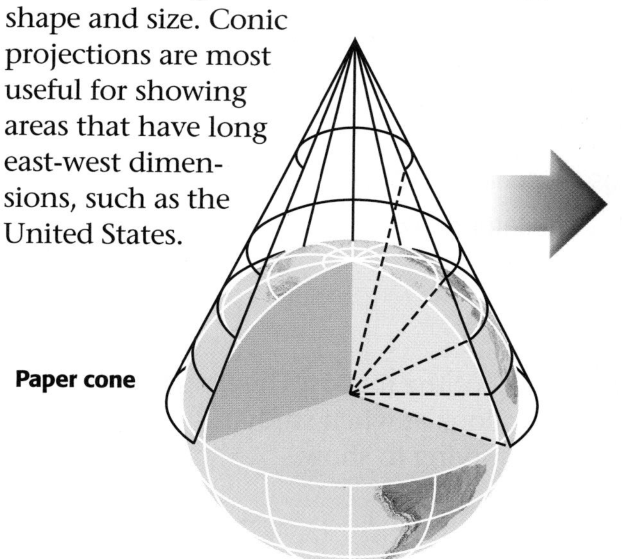

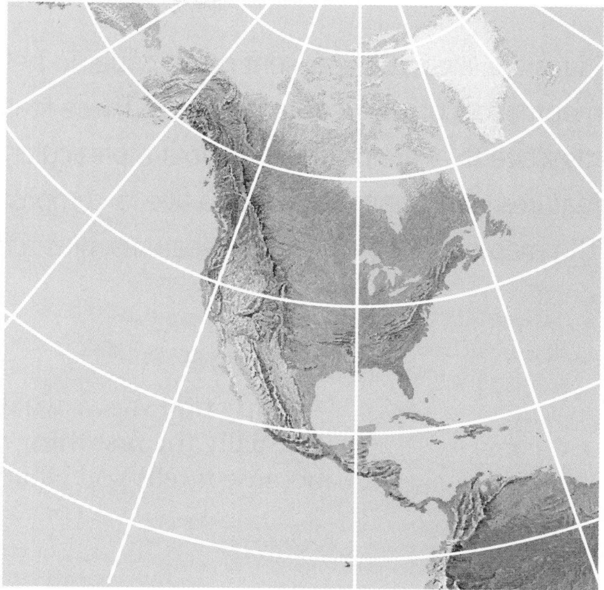

Conic projection

Flat-plane Projections

Flat-plane projections are based on a plane touching the globe at one point, such as at the North Pole or South Pole. A flat-plane projection is useful for showing true direction for airplane pilots and ship navigators. It also shows true area. However, it distorts the true shapes of landmasses.

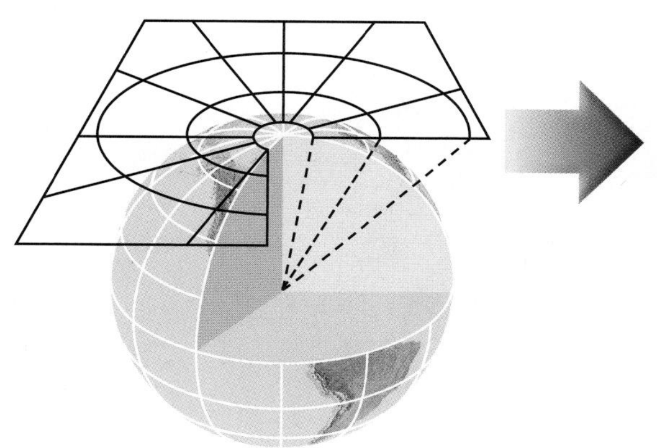

Flat-plane projection

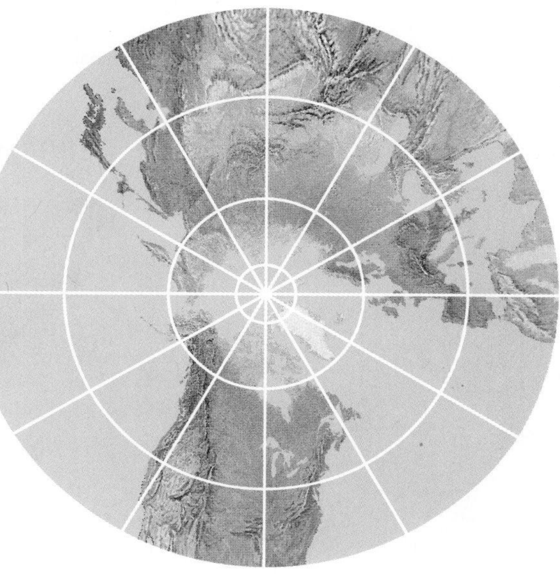

Map Essentials

How to Read a Map

Maps are like messages sent out in code. To help us translate the code, mapmakers provide certain features. These features help us understand the message they are presenting about a particular part of the world. Of these features, almost all maps have a title, a compass rose, a scale, and a legend. The map below has these four features, plus a fifth—a locator map.

1 Title

A map's **title** shows what the subject of the map is. The map title is usually the first thing you should look at when studying a map, because it tells you what the map is trying to show.

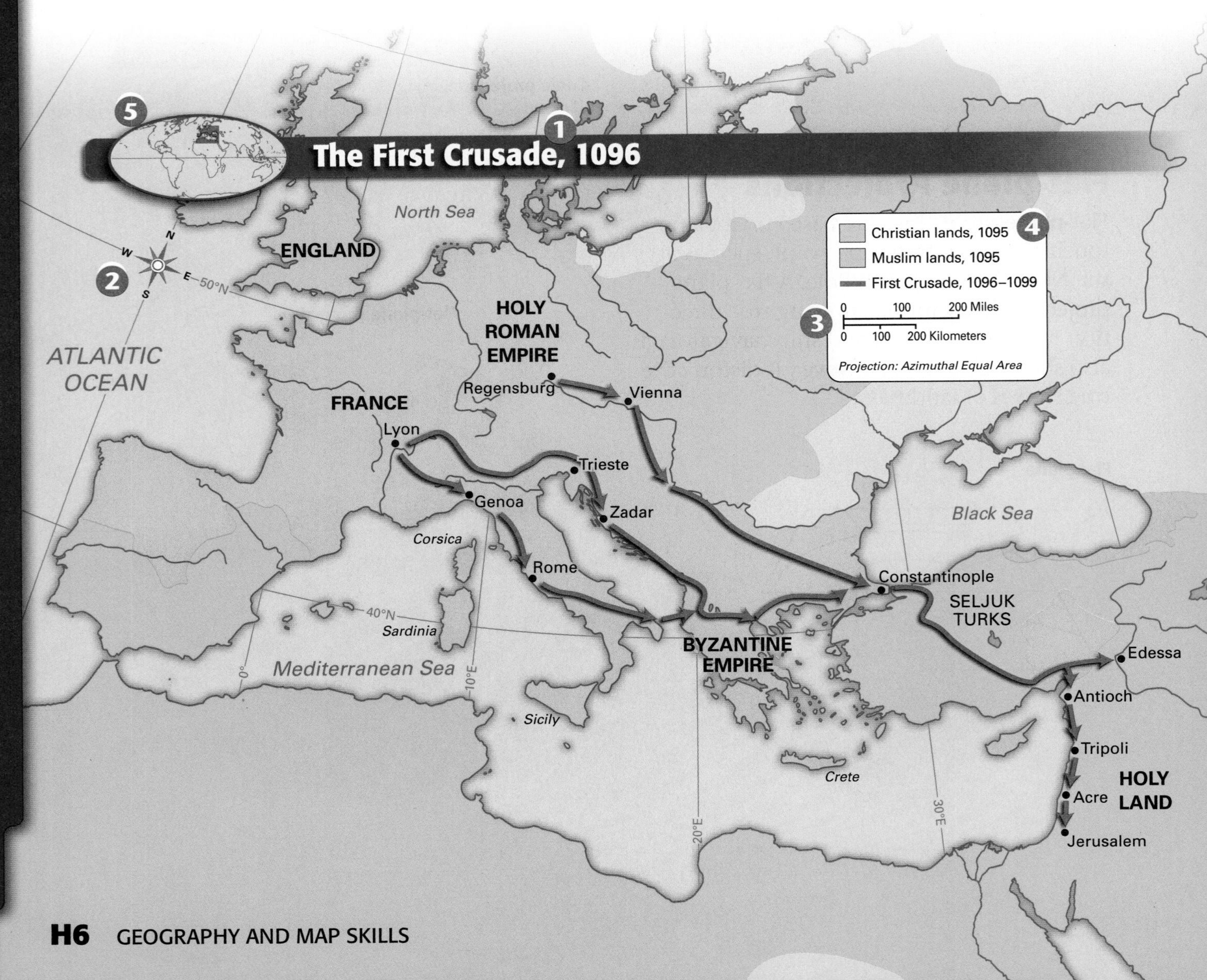

❷ Compass Rose

A directional indicator shows which way north, south, east, and west lie on the map. Some mapmakers use a "north arrow," which points toward the North Pole. Remember, "north" is not always at the top of a map. The way a map is drawn and the location of directions on that map depend on the perspective of the mapmaker. Most maps in this textbook indicate direction by using a compass rose. A **compass rose** has arrows that point to all four principal directions.

❸ Scale

Mapmakers use scales to represent the distances between points on a map. Scales may appear on maps in several different forms. The maps in this textbook provide a **bar scale**. Scales give distances in miles and kilometers.

To find the distance between two points on the map, place a piece of paper so that the edge connects the two points. Mark the location of each point on the paper with a line or dot. Then, compare the distance between the two dots with the map's bar scale. The number on the top of the scale gives the distance in miles. The number on the bottom gives the distance in kilometers. Because the distances are given in large intervals, you may have to approximate the actual distance on the scale.

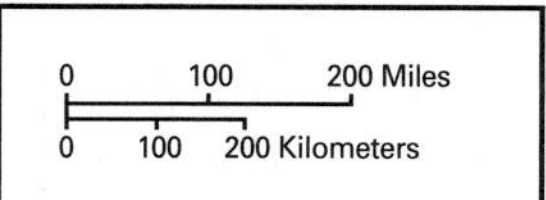

❹ Legend

The **legend**, or key, explains what the symbols on the map represent. Point symbols are used to specify the location of things, such as cities, that do not take up much space on the map. Some legends show colors that represent certain features like empires or other regions. Other maps might have legends with symbols or colors that represent features such as roads. Legends can also show economic resources, land use, population density, and climate.

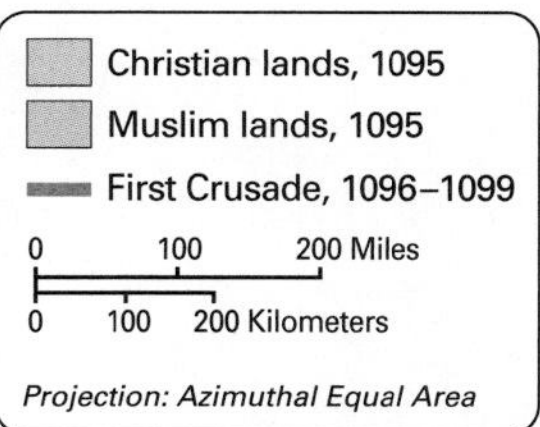

❺ Locator Map

A **locator map** shows where in the world the area on the map is located. The area shown on the main map is shown in red on the locator map. The locator map also shows surrounding areas so the map reader can see how the information on the map relates to neighboring lands.

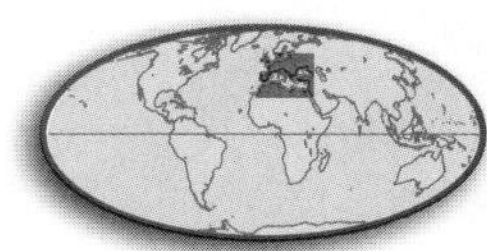

Working with Maps

Using Different Kinds of Maps

As you study the world's regions and countries, you will use a variety of maps. Political maps and physical maps are two of the most common types of maps you will study. In addition, you will use special-purpose maps. These maps might show climate, population, resources, ancient empires, or other topics.

Political Maps

Political maps show the major political features of a region. These features include country borders, capital cities, and other places. Political maps use different colors to represent countries, and capital cities are often shown with a special star symbol.

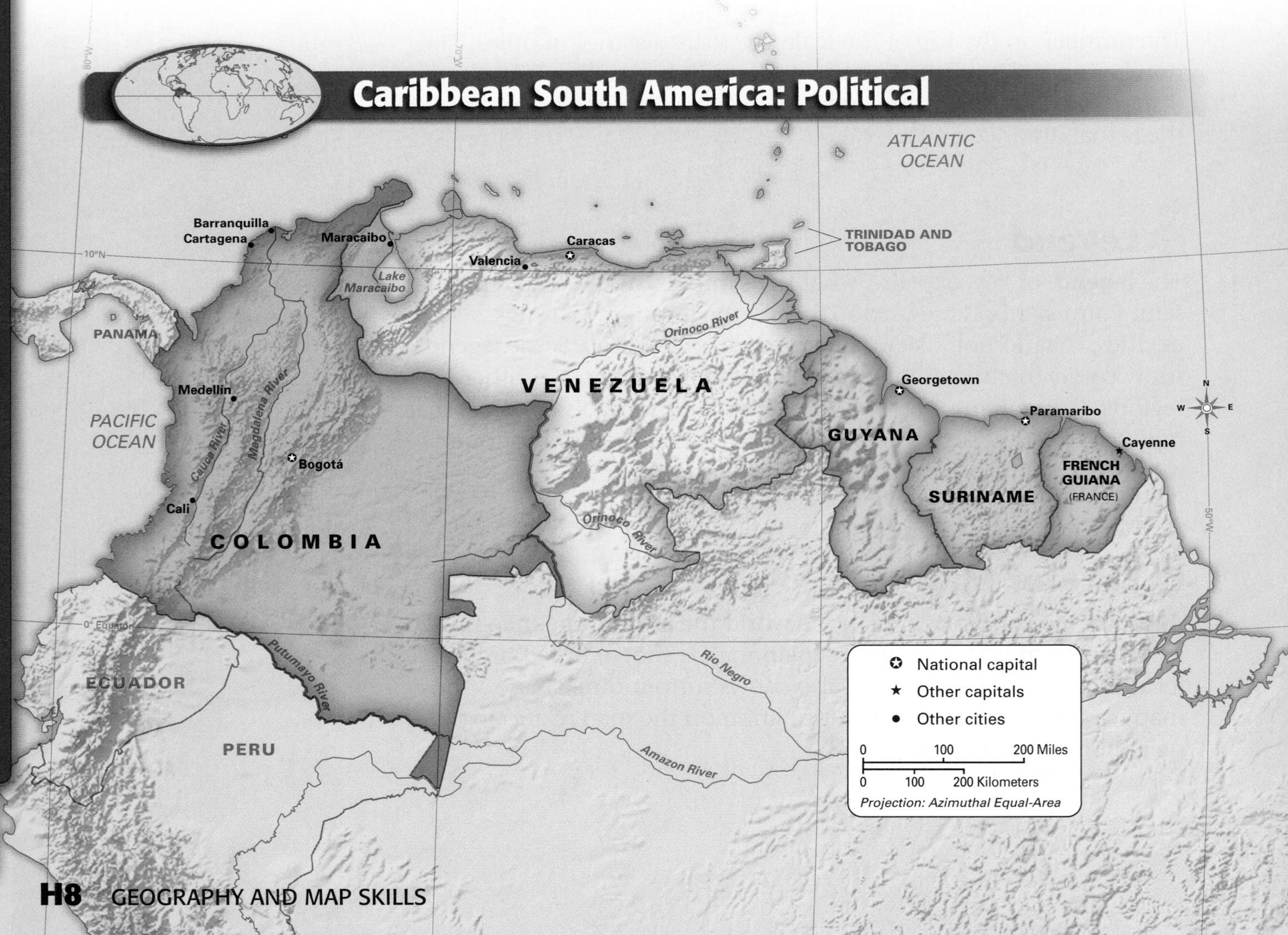

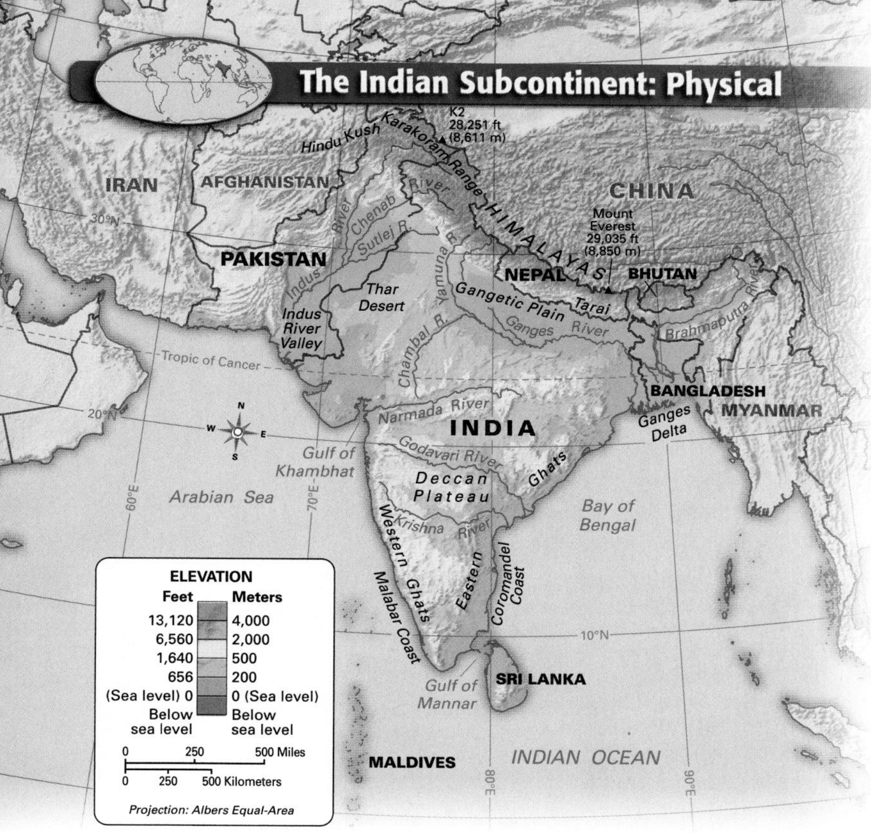

Physical Maps

Physical maps show the major physical features of a region. These features may include mountain ranges, rivers, oceans, islands, deserts, and plains. Often, these maps use different colors to represent different elevations of land. As a result, the map reader can easily see which areas are high elevations, like mountains, and which areas are lower.

Special-Purpose Maps

Special-purpose maps focus on one special topic, such as climate, resources, or population. These maps present information on the topic that is particularly important in the region. Depending on the type of special-purpose map, the information may be shown with different colors, arrows, dots, or other symbols.

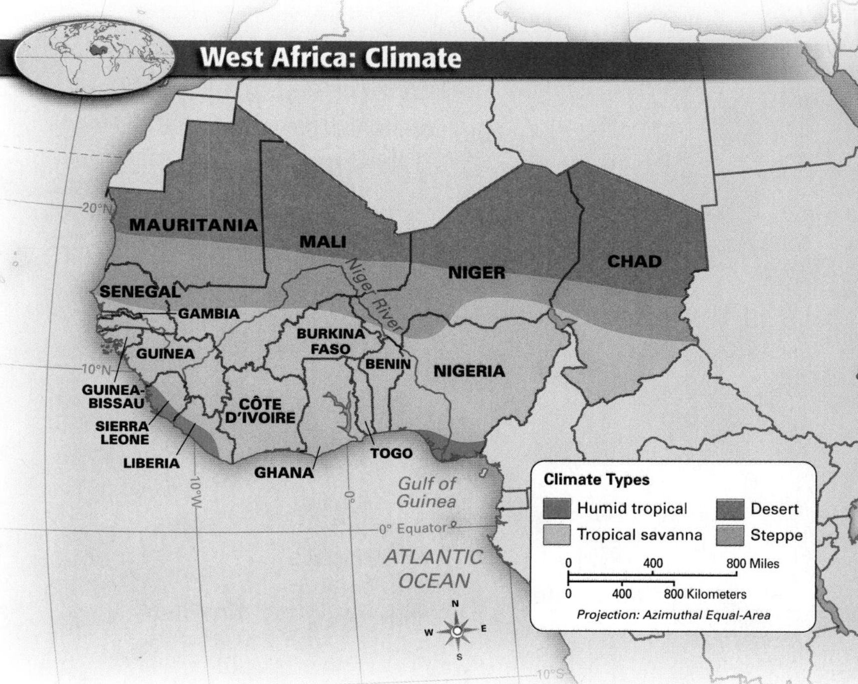

Using Maps in Geography The different kinds of maps in this textbook will help you study and understand geography. By working with these maps, you will see what the physical geography of places is like, where people live, and how the world has changed over time.

GEOGRAPHY AND MAP SKILLS

Geographic Dictionary

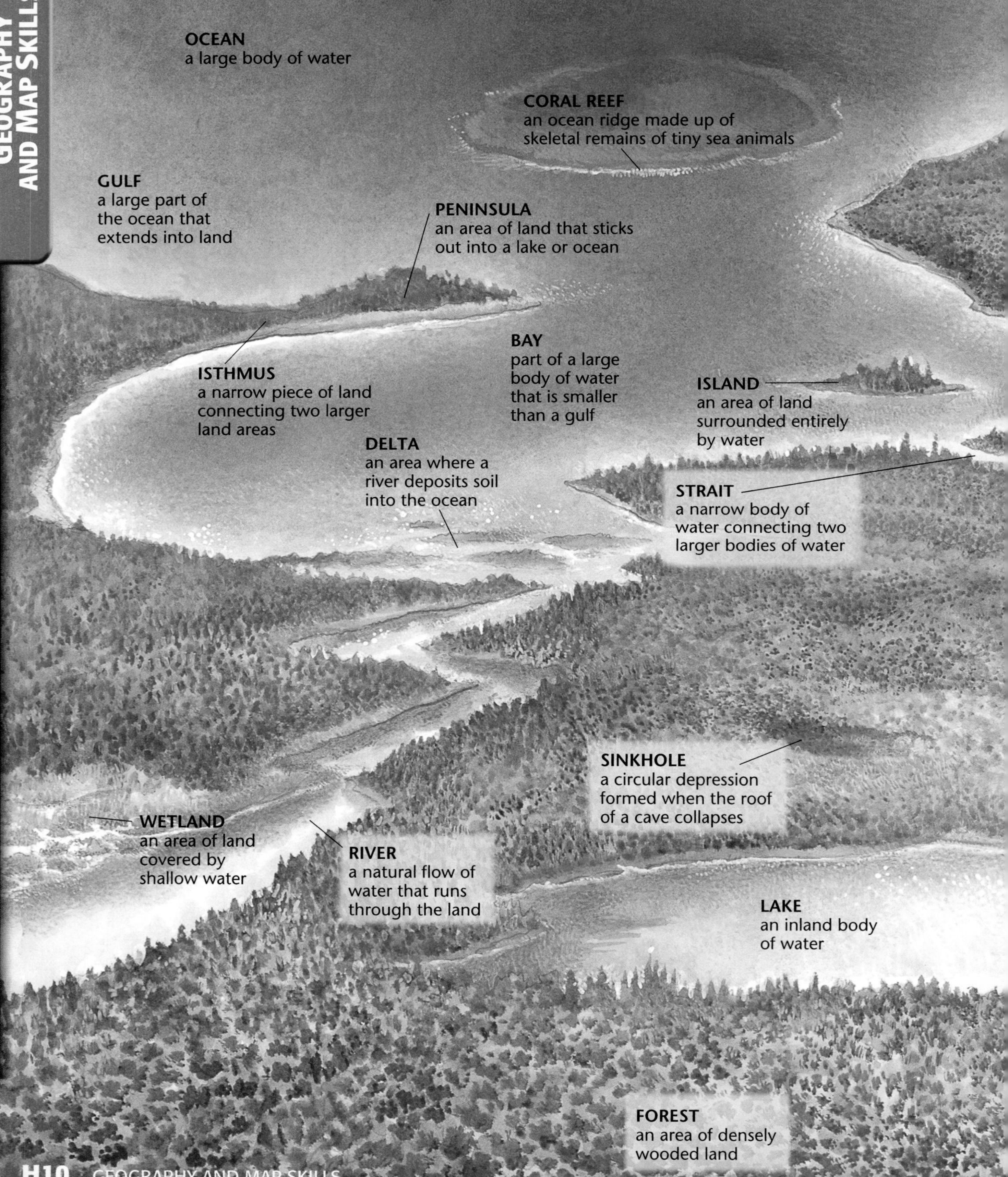

GEOGRAPHY AND MAP SKILLS

OCEAN
a large body of water

CORAL REEF
an ocean ridge made up of skeletal remains of tiny sea animals

GULF
a large part of the ocean that extends into land

PENINSULA
an area of land that sticks out into a lake or ocean

ISTHMUS
a narrow piece of land connecting two larger land areas

BAY
part of a large body of water that is smaller than a gulf

ISLAND
an area of land surrounded entirely by water

DELTA
an area where a river deposits soil into the ocean

STRAIT
a narrow body of water connecting two larger bodies of water

SINKHOLE
a circular depression formed when the roof of a cave collapses

WETLAND
an area of land covered by shallow water

RIVER
a natural flow of water that runs through the land

LAKE
an inland body of water

FOREST
an area of densely wooded land

COAST
an area of land near the ocean
MOUNTAIN
an area of rugged land that generally rises higher than 2,000 feet
VALLEY
an area of low land between hills or mountains
VOLCANO
an opening in Earth's crust where lava, ash, and gases erupt
CANYON
a deep, narrow valley with steep walls
GLACIER
a large area of slow-moving ice
HILL
a rounded, elevated area of land smaller than a mountain
PLAIN
a nearly flat area
DUNE
a hill of sand shaped by wind
OASIS
an area in the desert with a water source
DESERT
an extremely dry area with little water and few plants
PLATEAU
a large, flat, elevated area of land

Themes and Essential Elements of Geography

by Dr. Christopher L. Salter

To study the world, geographers have identified 5 key themes, 6 essential elements, and 18 geography standards.

"How should we teach and learn about geography?" Professional geographers have worked hard over the years to answer this important question.

In 1984 a group of geographers identified the 5 Themes of Geography. These themes did a wonderful job of laying the groundwork for good classroom geography. Teachers used the 5 Themes in class, and geographers taught workshops on how to apply them in the world.

By the early 1990s, however, some geographers felt the 5 Themes were too broad. They created the 18 Geography Standards and the 6 Essential Elements. The 18 Geography Standards include more detailed information about what geography is, and the 6 Essential Elements are like a bridge between the 5 Themes and 18 Standards.

Look at the chart to the right. It shows how each of the 5 Themes connects to the Essential Elements and Standards. For example, the theme of Location is related to The World in Spatial Terms and the first three Standards. Study the chart carefully to see how the other themes, elements, and Standards are related.

The last Essential Element and the last two Standards cover The Uses of Geography. These key parts of geography were not covered by the 5 Themes. They will help you see how geography has influenced the past, present, and future.

5 Themes of Geography

Location The theme of location describes where something is.

Place Place describes the features that make a site unique.

Regions Regions are areas that share common characteristics.

Movement This theme looks at how and why people and things move.

Human-Environment Interaction People interact with their environment in many ways.

6 Essential Elements

18 Geography Standards

I. The World in Spatial Terms

1. How to use maps and other tools
2. How to use mental maps to organize information
3. How to analyze the spatial organization of people, places, and environments

II. Places and Regions

4. The physical and human characteristics of places
5. How people create regions to interpret Earth
6. How culture and experience influence people's perceptions of places and regions

III. Physical Systems

7. The physical processes that shape Earth's surface
8. The distribution of ecosystems on Earth

IV. Human Systems

9. The characteristics, distribution, and migration of human populations
10. The complexity of Earth's cultural mosaics
11. The patterns and networks of economic interdependence on Earth
12. The patterns of human settlement
13. The forces of cooperation and conflict

V. Environment and Society

14. How human actions modify the physical environment
15. How physical systems affect human systems
16. The distribution and meaning of resources

VI. The Uses of Geography

17. How to apply geography to interpret the past
18. How to apply geography to interpret the present and plan for the future

READING SOCIAL STUDIES

Become an Active Reader

Did you ever think you would begin reading your social studies book by reading about *reading*? Actually, it makes better sense than you might think. You would probably make sure you knew some soccer skills and strategies before playing in a game. Similarly, you need to know something about reading skills and strategies before reading your social studies book. In other words, you need to make sure you know whatever you need to know in order to read this book successfully.

Tip #1

Read Everything on the Page!

You can't follow the directions on the cake-mix box if you don't know where the directions are! Cake-mix boxes always have directions on them telling you how many eggs to add or how long to bake the cake. But, if you can't find that information, it doesn't matter that it is there.

Likewise, this book is filled with information that will help you understand what you are reading. If you don't study that information, however, it might as well not be there. Let's take a look at some of the places where you'll find important information in this book.

The Chapter Opener
The chapter opener gives you a brief overview of what you will learn in the chapter. You can use this information to prepare to read the chapter.

The Section Openers
Before you begin to read each section, preview the information under What You Will Learn. There you'll find the main ideas of the section and key terms that are important in it. Knowing what you are looking for before you start reading can improve your understanding.

Boldfaced Words
Those words are important and are defined somewhere on the page where they appear—either right there in the sentence or over in the side margin.

Maps, Charts, and Artwork
These things are not there just to take up space or look good! Study them and read the information beside them. It will help you understand the information in the chapter.

Questions at the End of Sections
At the end of each section, you will find questions that will help you decide whether you need to go back and re-read any parts before moving on. If you can't answer a question, that is your cue to go back and re-read.

Questions at the End of the Chapter
Answer the questions at the end of each chapter, even if your teacher doesn't ask you to. These questions are there to help you figure out what you need to review.

Tip #2

Use the Reading Skills and Strategies in Your Textbook

Good readers use a number of skills and strategies to make sure they understand what they are reading. In this textbook you will find help with important reading skills and strategies such as "Visualizing," and "Understanding Fact and Opinion."

We teach the reading skills and strategies in several ways. Use these activities and lessons and you will become a better reader.

- First, on the opening page of every chapter we identify and explain the reading skill or strategy you will focus on as you work through the chapter. In fact, these activities are called "Focus on Reading."
- Second, as you can see in the example at right, we tell you where to go for more help. The back of the book has a reading handbook with a full-page practice lesson to match the reading skill or strategy in every chapter.

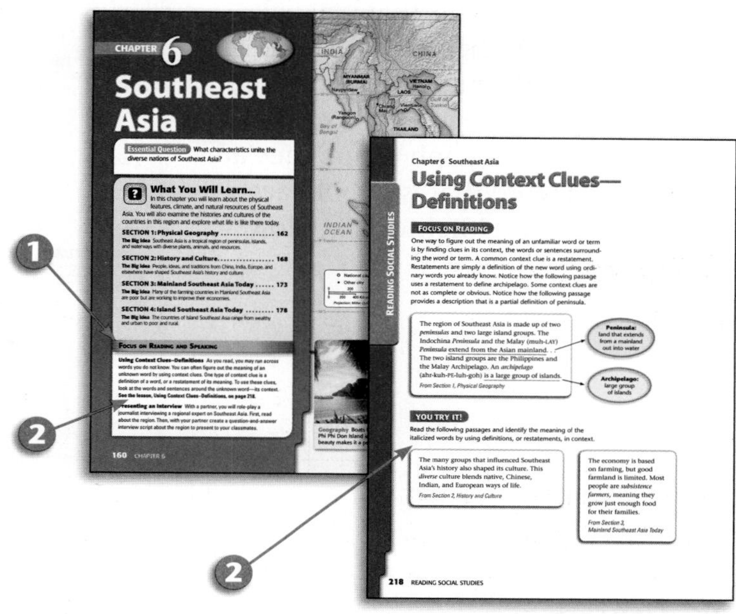

CHAPTER 6
Southeast Asia

Chapter 6 Southeast Asia

Using Context Clues—Definitions

FOCUS ON READING

One way to figure out the meaning of an unfamiliar word or term is by finding clues in its context, the words or sentences surrounding the word or term. A common context clue is a restatement. Restatements are simply a definition of the new word using ordinary words you already know. Notice how the following passage uses a restatement to define archipelago. Some context clues are not as complete or obvious. Notice how the following passage provides a description that is a partial definition of peninsula.

The region of Southeast Asia is made up of two *peninsulas* and two large island groups. The Indochina *Peninsula* and the Malay (muh-LAY) *Peninsula* extend from the Asian mainland. . . The two island groups are the Philippines and the Malay Archipelago. An *archipelago* (ahr-kuh-PE-luh-goh) is a large group of islands.
From Section 1, Physical Geography

Peninsula: land that extends from a mainland out into water

Archipelago: large group of islands

YOU TRY IT!

Read the following passages and identify the meaning of the italicized words by using definitions, or restatements, in context.

The many groups that influenced Southeast Asia's history also shaped its culture. This *diverse* culture blends native, Chinese, Indian, and European ways of life.
From Section 2, History and Culture

The economy is based on farming, but good farmland is limited. Most people are *subsistence farmers*, meaning they grow just enough food for their families.
From Section 3, Mainland Southeast Asia Today

218 READING SOCIAL STUDIES

- Third, we give you short practice activities and examples as you read the chapter. These activities and examples show up in the margin of your book. Again, look for the words, "Focus on Reading."

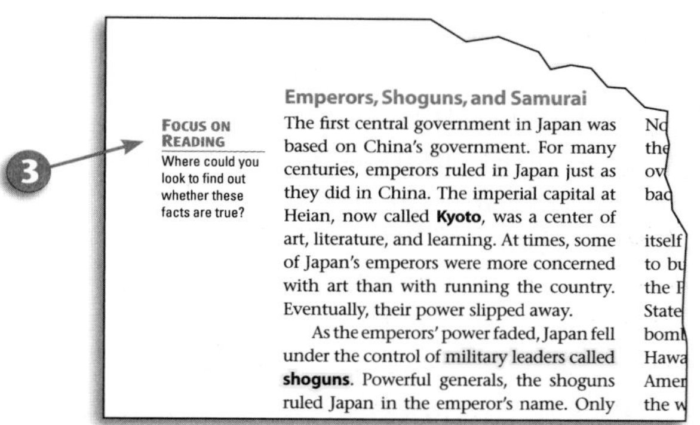

FOCUS ON READING
Where could you look to find out whether these facts are true?

Emperors, Shoguns, and Samurai

The first central government in Japan was based on China's government. For many centuries, emperors ruled in Japan just as they did in China. The imperial capital at Heian, now called **Kyoto**, was a center of art, literature, and learning. At times, some of Japan's emperors were more concerned with art than with running the country. Eventually, their power slipped away.

As the emperors' power faded, Japan fell under the control of military leaders called **shoguns**. Powerful generals, the shoguns ruled Japan in the emperor's name. Only

- Finally, we provide another practice activity in the Chapter Review at the end of every chapter. That activity gives you one more chance to make sure you know how to use the reading skill or strategy.

FOCUS ON READING AND WRITING

Understanding Fact and Opinion *Decide whether each of the following statements is a fact or an opinion.*

22. Japan would be a great place to live.
23. Japan is an island country.
24. North Korea should give up communism.
25. The Koreas should reunify.

Writing Your Five-Line Poem *Use your notes and the instructions below to create your poem.*

26. Review your notes and decide on a topic to write about. Remember that your poem should describe one image or picture—an object, a place, etc.—from Japanese or Korean culture.

The first three lines of your poem should describe the object or place you have chosen.

Tip #3

Pay Attention to Vocabulary

It is no fun to read something when you don't know what the words mean, but you can't learn new words if you only use or read the words you already know. In this book, we know we have probably used some words you don't know. But, we have followed a pattern as we have used more difficult words.

- First, at the beginning of each section you will find a list of key terms that you will need to know. Be on the lookout for those words as you read through the section. You will find that we have defined those words right there in the paragraph where they are used. Look for a word that is in boldface with its definition highlighted in yellow.

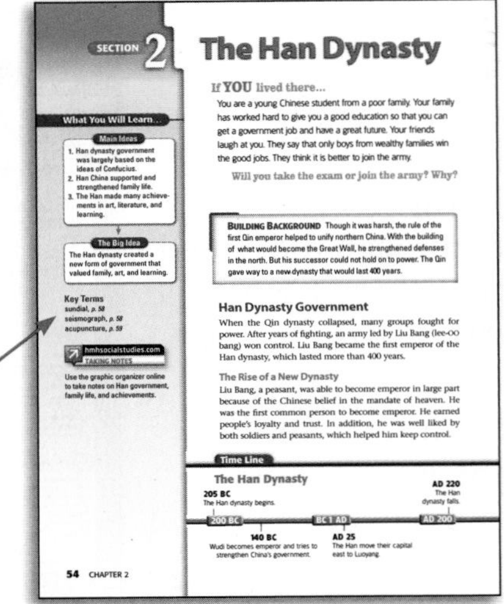

SECTION 2

The Han Dynasty

What You Will Learn...

Main Ideas

1. Han dynasty government was largely based on the ideas of Confucius.
2. Han China supported and strengthened family life.
3. The Han made many achievements in art, literature, and learning.

The Big Idea

The Han dynasty created a new form of government that valued family, art, and learning.

Key Terms
sundial, *p. 58*
seismograph, *p. 58*
acupuncture, *p. 59*

hmhsocialstudies.com
TAKING NOTES

Use the graphic organizer online to take notes on Han government, family life, and achievements.

If YOU lived there...

You are a young Chinese student from a poor family. Your family has worked hard to give you a good education so that you can get a government job and have a great future. Your friends laugh at you. They say that only boys from wealthy families win the good jobs. They think it is better to join the army.

Will you take the exam or join the army? Why?

BUILDING BACKGROUND Though it was harsh, the rule of the first Qin emperor helped to unify northern China. With the building of what would become the Great Wall, he strengthened defenses in the north. But his successor could not hold on to power. The Qin gave way to a new dynasty that would last 400 years.

Han Dynasty Government

When the Qin dynasty collapsed, many groups fought for power. After years of fighting, an army led by Liu Bang (lee-OO bang) won control. Liu Bang became the first emperor of the Han dynasty, which lasted more than 400 years.

The Rise of a New Dynasty

Liu Bang, a peasant, was able to become emperor in large part because of the Chinese belief in the mandate of heaven. He was the first common person to become emperor. He earned people's loyalty and trust. In addition, he was well liked by both soldiers and peasants, which helped him keep control.

Time Line

The Han Dynasty

205 BC
The Han dynasty begins.

200 BC

140 BC
Wudi becomes emperor and tries to strengthen China's government.

BC 1 AD

AD 25
The Han move their capital east to Luoyang.

AD 200

AD 220
The Han dynasty falls.

54 CHAPTER 2

1

Bangladesh

Bangladesh is a small country about the same size as the state of Wisconsin. Despite its small size, Bangladesh's population is almost half the size of the U.S. population. As a result, it is one of the world's most densely populated countries with some 3,018 people per square mile (1,165 per square km). The capital and largest city, **Dhaka** (DA-kuh), is home to more than 13 million people. Overcrowding is not limited to urban areas, however. Rural areas are also densely populated.

Flooding is one of Bangladesh's biggest challenges. Many circumstances cause these floods. The country's many streams and rivers flood annually, often damaging farms and homes. Summer monsoons also cause flooding. For example, massive flooding in 2004 left more than 25 million people homeless. It also destroyed schools, farms, and roads throughout the country.

ACADEMIC VOCABULARY
circumstances conditions that influence an event or activity

Nepal

The small kingdom of Nepal also faces many challenges today. Its population is growing rapidly. In fact, the population has more than doubled in the last 30 years. **Kathmandu** (kat-man-DOO), the nation's capital and largest city, is troubled by overcrowding and poverty. Thousands have moved to Kathmandu in search of jobs and better opportunities. As a result of population growth and poor resources, Nepal is one of the world's least-developed nations.

Nepal also faces environmental threats. As the population grows, more and more land is needed to grow enough food. To meet this need, farmers clear forests to create more farmland. This deforestation causes soil erosion and harms the wildlife in the region. Nepal's many tourists add to the problem as they use valuable resources and leave behind trash.

Bhutan

Bhutan is a small mountain kingdom that lies in the Himalayas between India and China. Because of the rugged mountains, Bhutan has been isolated throughout much of its history. This isolation limited outside influences until the 1900s, when Bhutan's king established ties first with Great Britain and later with India. By the mid-1900s Bhutan had ended its long isolation. Efforts to modernize Bhutan resulted in the construction of new roads, schools, and hospitals.

Today Bhutan continues to develop economically. Most Bhutanese earn a living as farmers, growing rice, potatoes, and

Nepal
Many of Nepal's people live in the rugged Himalayas and earn a living herding animals.

102 CHAPTER 3

2

- Second, when we use a word that is important in all classes, not just social studies, we define it in the margin under the heading Academic Vocabulary. You will run into these academic words in other textbooks, so you should learn what they mean while reading this book.

Tip #4

Read Like a Skilled Reader

You won't be able to climb to the top of Mount Everest if you do not train! If you want to make it to the top of Mount Everest then you must start training to climb that huge mountain.

Training is also necessary to become a good reader. You will never get better at reading your social studies book—or any book for that matter—unless you spend some time thinking about how to be a better reader.

Skilled readers do the following:

1. They preview what they are supposed to read before they actually begin reading. When previewing, they look for vocabulary words, titles of sections, information in the margin, or maps or charts they should study.
2. They get ready to take some notes while reading by dividing their notebook paper into two parts. They title one side "Notes from the Chapter" and the other side "Questions or Comments I Have."
3. As they read, they complete their notes.
4. They read like **active readers**. The Active Reading list below shows you what that means.
5. Finally, they use clues in the text to help them figure out where the text is going. The best clues are called signal words. These are words that help you identify chronological order, causes and effects, or comparisons and contrasts.

   Chronological Order Signal Words: *first, second, third, before, after, later, next, following that, earlier, subsequently, finally*

   Cause and Effect Signal Words: *because of, due to, as a result of, the reason for, therefore, consequently, so, basis for*

   Comparison/Contrast Signal Words: *likewise, also, as well as, similarly, on the other hand*

READING SOCIAL STUDIES

Active Reading

There are three ways to read a book: You can be a turn-the-pages-no-matter-what type of reader. These readers just keep on turning pages whether or not they understand what they are reading. Or, you can be a stop-watch-and-listen kind of reader. These readers know that if they wait long enough, someone will tell them what they need to know. Or, you can be an active reader. These readers know that it is up to them to figure out what the text means. Active readers do the following as they read:

Predict what will happen next based on what has already happened. When your predictions don't match what happens in the text, re-read the confusing parts.

Question what is happening as you read. Constantly ask yourself why things have happened, what things mean, and what caused certain events. Jot down notes about the questions you can't answer.

Summarize what you are reading frequently. Do not try to summarize the entire chapter! Read a bit and then summarize it. Then read on.

Connect what is happening in the section you're reading to what you have already read.

Clarify your understanding. Be sure that you understand what you are reading by stopping occasionally to ask yourself whether you are confused by anything. Sometimes you might need to re-read to clarify. Other times you might need to read further and collect more information before you can understand. Still other times you might need to ask the teacher to help you with what is confusing you.

Visualize what is happening in the text. In other words, try to see the events or places in your mind. It might help you to draw maps, make charts, or jot down notes about what you are reading as you try to visualize the action in the text.

SOCIAL STUDIES WORDS

Social Studies Words

As you read this textbook, you will be more successful if you learn the meanings of the words on this page. You will come across these words many times in your social studies classes, like geography and history. Read through these words now to become familiar with them before you begin your studies.

Social Studies Words

WORDS ABOUT TIME

AD	refers to dates after the birth of Jesus
BC	refers to dates before Jesus's birth
BCE	refers to dates before Jesus's birth, stands for "before the common era"
CE	refers to dates after Jesus's birth, stands for "common era"
century	a period of 100 years
decade	a period of 10 years
era	a period of time
millennium	a period of 1,000 years

WORDS ABOUT THE WORLD

climate	the weather conditions in a certain area over a long period of time
geography	the study of the world's people, places, and landscapes
physical features	features on Earth's surface, such as mountains and rivers
region	an area with one or more features that make it different from surrounding areas
resources	materials found on Earth that people need and value

WORDS ABOUT PEOPLE

anthropology	the study of people and cultures
archaeology	the study of the past based on what people left behind
citizen	a person who lives under the control of a government
civilization	the way of life of people in a particular place or time
culture	the knowledge, beliefs, customs, and values of a group of people
custom	a repeated practice or tradition
economics	the study of the production and use of goods and services
economy	any system in which people make and exchange goods and services
government	the body of officials and groups that run an area
history	the study of the past
politics	the process of running a government
religion	a system of beliefs in one or more gods or spirits
society	a group of people who share common traditions
trade	the exchange of goods or services

Academic Words

What are academic words? They are important words used in all of your classes, not just social studies. You will see these words in other textbooks, so you should learn what they mean while reading this book. Review this list now. You will use these words again in the chapters of this book.

Academic Words

abstract	expressing a quality or idea without reference to an actual thing
circumstances	conditions that influence an event or activity
concrete	specific, real
consequences	effects of a particular event or events
criteria	rules for defining
effect	the results of an action or decision
efficient	productive and not wasteful
element	part
establish	to set up or create
function	work or perform
incentive	something that leads people to follow a certain course of action
influence	change, or have an effect on
innovation	a new idea, method, or device
motive	a reason for doing something
policy	rule, course of action
process	a series of steps by which a task is accomplished
role	part of function
values	ideas that people hold dear and try to live by

Academic Words features provide definitions for important terms that will help you understand social studies content.

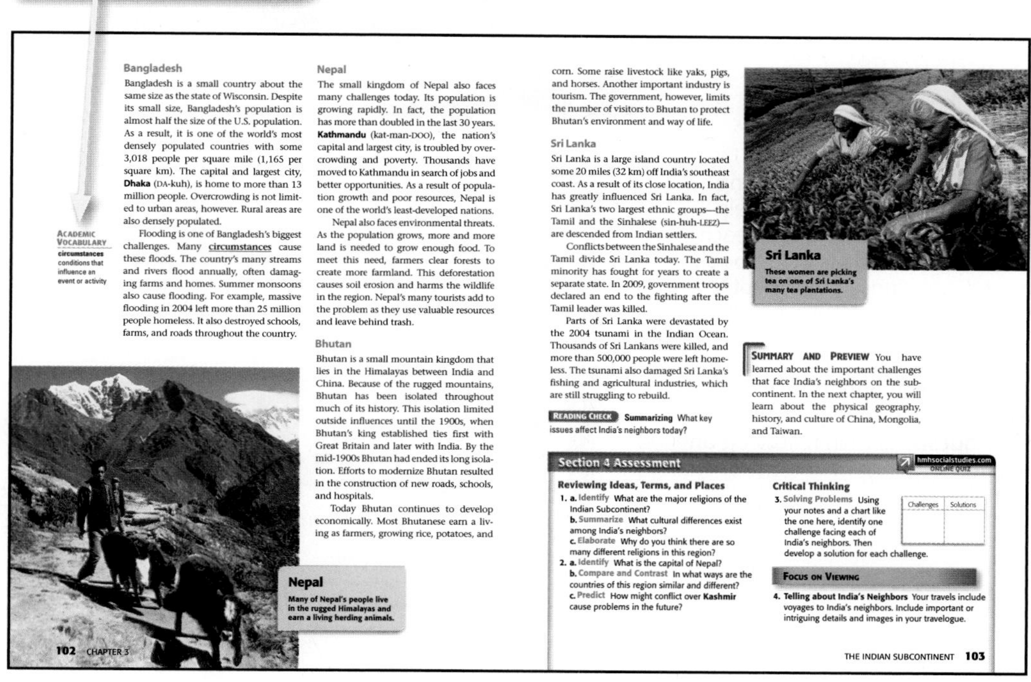

Bangladesh

Bangladesh is a small country about the same size as the state of Wisconsin. Despite its small size, Bangladesh's population is almost half the size of the U.S. population. As a result, it is one of the world's most densely populated countries with some 3,018 people per square mile (1,165 per square km). The capital and largest city, **Dhaka** (DA-kuh), is home to more than 13 million people. Overcrowding is not limited to urban areas, however. Rural areas are also densely populated.

Flooding is one of Bangladesh's biggest challenges. Many circumstances cause these floods. The country's many streams and rivers flood annually, often damaging farms and homes. Summer monsoons also cause flooding. For example, massive flooding in 2004 left more than 25 million people homeless. It also destroyed schools, farms, and roads throughout the country.

ACADEMIC VOCABULARY
circumstances conditions that influence an event or activity

Nepal

The small kingdom of Nepal also faces many challenges today. Its population is growing rapidly. In fact, the population has more than doubled in the last 30 years. **Kathmandu** (kat-man-DOO), the nation's capital and largest city, is troubled by overcrowding and poverty. Thousands have moved to Kathmandu in search of jobs and better opportunities. As a result of population growth and poor resources, Nepal is one of the world's least-developed nations.

Nepal also faces environmental threats. As the population grows, more and more land is needed to grow enough food. To meet this need, farmers clear forests to create more farmland. This deforestation causes soil erosion and harms the wildlife in the region. Nepal's many tourists add to the problem as they use valuable resources and leave behind trash.

Bhutan

Bhutan is a small mountain kingdom that lies in the Himalayas between India and China. Because of the rugged mountains, Bhutan has been isolated throughout much of its history. This isolation limited outside influences until the 1900s, when Bhutan's king established ties first with Great Britain and later with India. By the mid-1900s Bhutan had ended its long isolation. Efforts to modernize Bhutan resulted in the construction of new roads, schools, and hospitals.

Today Bhutan continues to develop economically. Most Bhutanese earn a living as farmers, growing rice, potatoes, and corn. Some raise livestock like yaks, pigs, and horses. Another important industry is tourism. The government, however, limits the number of visitors to Bhutan to protect Bhutan's environment and way of life.

Nepal Many of Nepal's people live in the rugged Himalayas and earn a living herding animals.

Sri Lanka

Sri Lanka is a large island country located some 20 miles (32 km) off India's southeast coast. As a result of its close location, India has greatly influenced Sri Lanka. In fact, Sri Lanka's two largest ethnic groups—the Tamil and the Sinhalese (sin-huh-LEEZ)—are descended from Indian settlers.

Conflicts between the Sinhalese and the Tamil divide Sri Lanka today. The Tamil minority has fought for years to create a separate state. In 2009, government troops declared an end to the fighting after the Tamil leader was killed.

Parts of Sri Lanka were devastated by the 2004 tsunami in the Indian Ocean. Thousands of Sri Lankans were killed, and more than 500,000 people were left homeless. The tsunami also damaged Sri Lanka's fishing and agricultural industries, which are still struggling to rebuild.

READING CHECK **Summarizing** What key issues affect India's neighbors today?

Sri Lanka These women are picking tea on one of Sri Lanka's many tea plantations.

SUMMARY AND PREVIEW You have learned about the important challenges that face India's neighbors on the subcontinent. In the next chapter, you will learn about the physical geography, history, and culture of China, Mongolia, and Taiwan.

Section 4 Assessment

hmhsocialstudies.com ONLINE QUIZ

Reviewing Ideas, Terms, and Places

1. a. Identify What are the major religions of the Indian Subcontinent?
   b. Summarize What cultural differences exist among India's neighbors?
   c. Elaborate Why do you think there are so many different religions in this region?
2. a. Identify What is the capital of Nepal?
   b. Compare and Contrast In what ways are the countries of this region similar and different?
   c. Predict How might conflict over **Kashmir** cause problems in the future?

Critical Thinking

3. Solving Problems Using your notes and a chart like the one here, identify one challenge facing each of India's neighbors. Then develop a solution for each challenge.

Challenges	Solutions

FOCUS ON VIEWING

4. **Telling about India's Neighbors** Your travels include voyages to India's neighbors. Include important or intriguing details and images in your travelogue.

102 CHAPTER 3

THE INDIAN SUBCONTINENT 103

Making This Book Work for You

Studying geography will be easy for you with this textbook. Take a few minutes now to become familiar with the easy-to-use structure and special features of your book. See how it will make geography come alive for you!

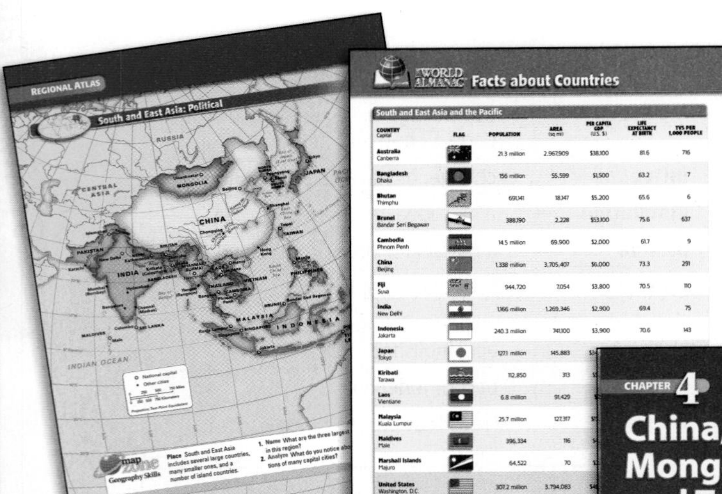

Your book begins with a satellite image, a regional atlas, and a table with facts about each country. Use these pages to get an overview of the region you will study.

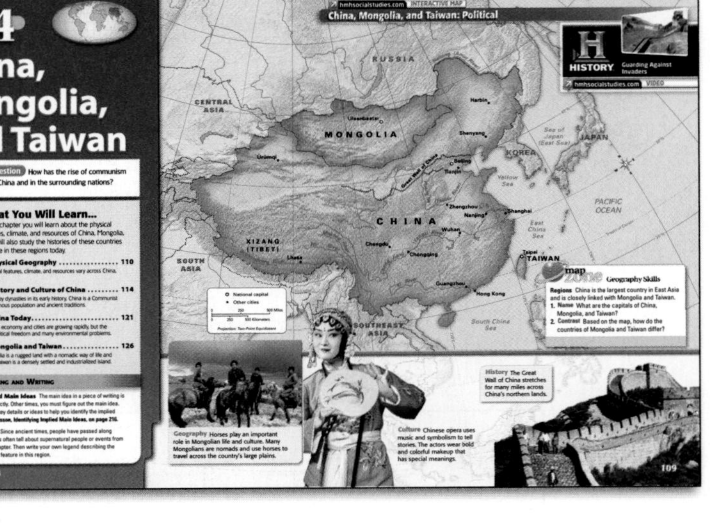

Chapter

Each chapter includes an introduction, a Social Studies Skills activity, Chapter Review pages, and a Standardized Test Practice page.

Reading Social Studies Chapter reading lessons give you skills and practice to help you read the textbook. More help with each lesson can be found in the back of the book. Margin notes and questions in the chapter make sure you understand the reading skill.

Social Studies Skills The Social Studies Skills lessons give you an opportunity to learn, practice, and apply an important skill. Chapter Review questions then follow up on what you learned.

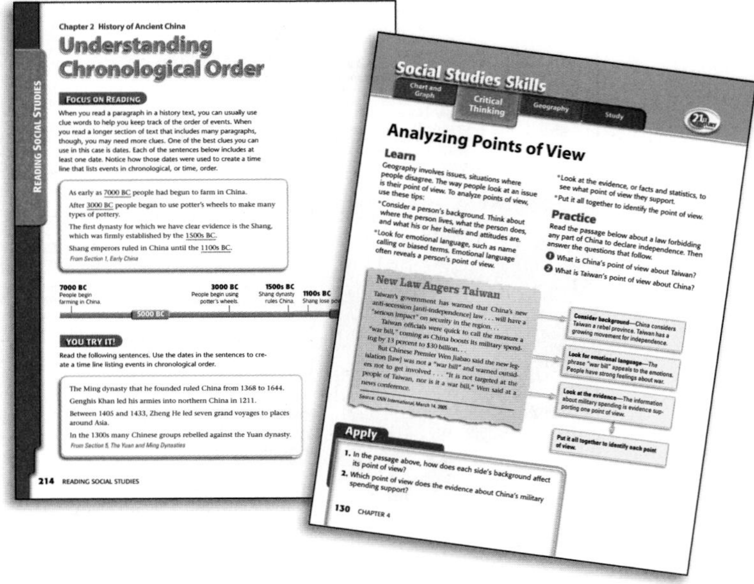

Section

The section opener pages include Main Ideas, an overarching Big Idea, and Key Terms and Places. In addition, each section includes these special features.

If YOU Lived There . . . Each section begins with a situation for you to respond to, placing you in a place that relates to the content you will be studying in the section.

Building Background Building Background connects what will be covered in each section with what you already know.

Short Sections of Content The information in each section is organized into small chunks of text that you can easily understand.

Taking Notes Suggested graphic organizers help you read and take notes on the important ideas in the section.

SECTION 3

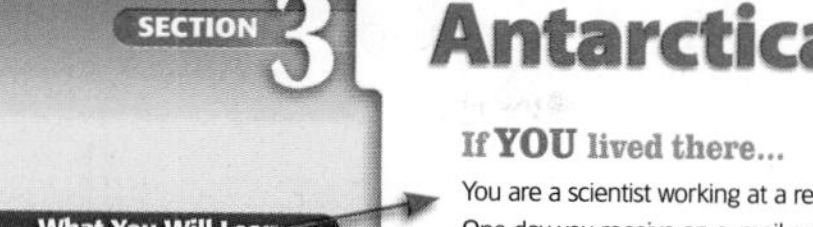

Antarctica

What You Will Learn...

Main Ideas

1. Freezing temperatures, ice, and snow dominate Antarctica's physical geography.
2. Explorations in the 1800s and 1900s led to Antarctica's use for scientific research.
3. Research and protecting the environment are key issues in Antarctica today.

The Big Idea

Antarctica's unique environment has made it an important site for research.

Key Terms and Places

ice shelf, *p. 203*
icebergs, *p. 203*
Antarctic Peninsula, *p. 203*
polar desert, *p. 203*
ozone layer, *p. 204*

hmhsocialstudies.com TAKING NOTES

Use the graphic organizer online to take notes on Antarctica's physical geography, early exploration, and issues today.

If YOU lived there...

You are a scientist working at a research laboratory in Antarctica. One day you receive an e-mail message from a friend. She wants to open a company that will lead public tours through Antarctica so people can see its spectacular icy landscapes and wildlife. Some of your fellow scientists think that tours are a good idea, while others think that they could ruin the local environment.

What will you tell your friend?

BUILDING BACKGROUND Antarctica, the continent surrounding the South Pole, has no permanent residents. The only people there are scientists who research the frozen land. For many years, people around the world have debated the best way to use this frozen land.

Physical Geography

In the southernmost part of the world is the continent of Antarctica. This frozen land is very different from any other place on Earth.

The Land

Ice covers about 98 percent of Antarctica's 5.4 million square miles (14 million square km). This ice sheet contains more than 90 percent of the world's ice. On average the ice sheet is more than 1 mile (1.6 km) thick.

Penguins live in the icy waters around Antarctica, a continent almost completely covered in ice.

Although many rajas were related, they didn't always get along. Sometimes rajas joined forces before fighting a common enemy. Other times, however, rajas went to war against each other. In fact, Aryan groups fought each other nearly as often as they fought outsiders.

Language

The first Aryan settlers did not read or write. Because of this, they had to memorize the poems and hymns that were important in their culture, such as the Vedas. If people forgot these poems and hymns, the works would be lost forever.

The language in which these Aryan poems and hymns were composed was **Sanskrit**, the most important language of ancient India. At first, Sanskrit was only a spoken language. Eventually, however, people figured out how to write it down so they could keep records. These Sanskrit records are a major source of information about Aryan society. Sanskrit is no longer widely spoken today, but it is the root of many modern South Asian languages.

READING CHECK **Identifying** What source provides much of the information we have about the Aryans?

Aryan Migrations

map zone Geography Skills

Movement The Aryans migrated to India.
1. **Read the Map** In what general direction did the Aryans travel?
2. **Analyze** Why do you think the Aryans entered India where they did?

SUMMARY AND PREVIEW The earliest civilizations in India were centered in the Indus Valley. In the next section, you will learn about a new religion that developed in the Indus Valley after the Aryans settled there—Hinduism.

Section 1 Assessment

hmhsocialstudies.com ONLINE QUIZ

Reviewing Ideas, Terms, and Places

1. a. **Recall** Where did the Harappan civilization develop?
   b. **Explain** Why did the Harappans make contact with people far from India?
2. a. **Identify** What was **Mohenjo Daro**?
   b. **Analyze** What is one reason that scholars do not completely understand some important parts of Harappan society?
3. a. **Identify** Who were the Aryans?
   b. **Contrast** How was Aryan society different from Harappan society?

Critical Thinking

4. **Summarizing** Using your notes, list the major achievements of India's first two civilizations. Record your conclusions in a diagram like this one.

Early Indian Achievements
Harappan society
Aryan society

FOCUS ON WRITING

5. **Illustrating Geography and Early Civilizations** This section described two possible topics for your poster—geography and early civilizations. Which of them is more interesting to you? Write down some ideas for a poster about that topic.

HISTORY OF ANCIENT INDIA 21

Reading Check Questions end each section of content so you can check to make sure you understand what you just studied.

Summary and Preview The Summary and Preview connects what you studied in the section to what you will study in the next section.

Section Assessment Finally, the section assessment boxes make sure that you understand the main ideas of the section. We also provide assessment practice online!

Scavenger Hunt

Are you ready to explore the world of geography? ***Holt McDougal: South and East Asia and the Pacific*** is your ticket to this exciting world. Before you begin your journey, complete this scavenger hunt to get to know your book and discover what's inside.

On a separate sheet of paper, fill in the blanks to complete each sentence below. In each answer, one letter will be in a yellow box. When you have answered every question, copy these letters in order to reveal the answer to the question at the bottom of the page.

1. According to the Table of Contents, the title of Chapter 5 is Japan and the _ _ _ _ _ _.

2. The section that begins on page 100 is called India's _ _ _ _ _ _ _ _ _. What chapter is this section in?

3. According to the Geographic Dictionary on page H11, an area of land near the ocean is a _ _ _ _ _.

4. Look up the term Grand Canal in the English and Spanish Glossary. The third word of the definition is _ _ _ _ _ _ _.

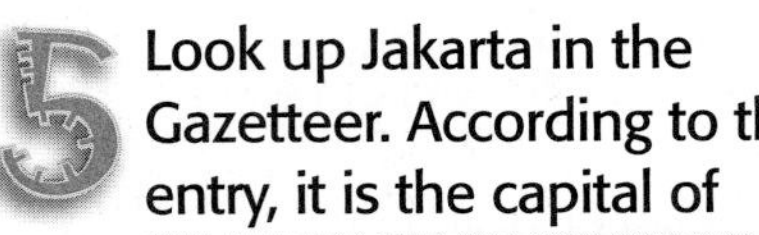

5. Look up Jakarta in the Gazetteer. According to the entry, it is the capital of _ _ _ _ _ _ _ _ _.

6. The Geography and History feature on pages 194–195 is called _ _ _ _ _ _ _ _ the Pacific.

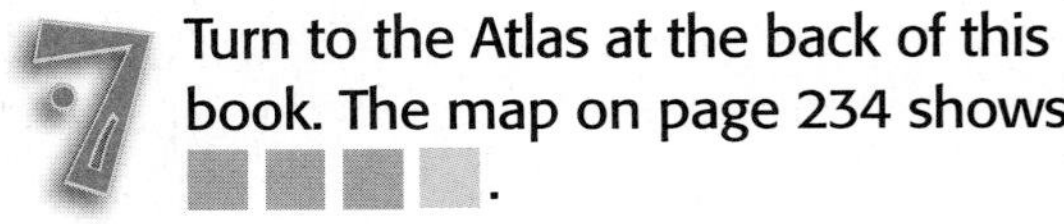

7. Turn to the Atlas at the back of this book. The map on page 234 shows _ _ _ _.

8. The Reading Social Studies skills lesson on page 219 will teach you about Drawing _ _ _ _ _ _ _ _ _ _ _.

Fact!

One of the most powerful volcanic eruptions in history occurred in Indonesia in 1883. This eruption caused the loudest noise ever recorded by human beings and was heard thousands of miles away. What was the name of the volcano that erupted?

_ _ _ _ _ _ _ _

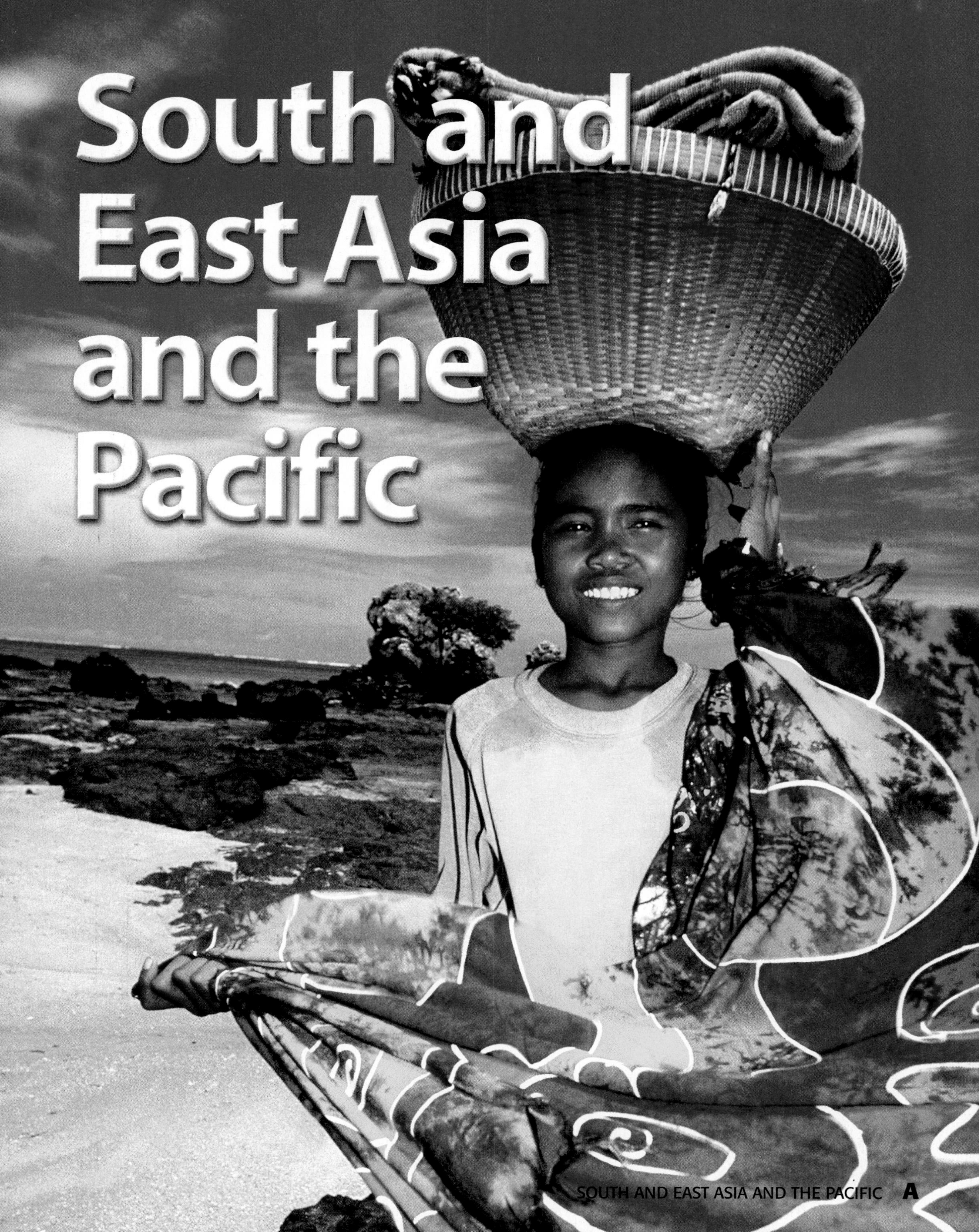

South and East Asia and the Pacific

Himalayas

The highest mountain range in the world, the Himalayas, separates the Indian Subcontinent from the rest of Asia.

The Outback

About 75 to 80 percent of Australia is covered by the Outback, a dry interior region of ancient rocks and plains.

South and East Asia and the Pacific

Rain Forest

The rich green color of Southeast Asia is caused by tropical rain forests. They are home to rare animals like the orangutan, found only in this region.

Explore the Satellite Image

Towering mountains, dense rain forests, and dry plains are all features of this large region in Asia and the Pacific. What other physical features can you see in this satellite image?

The Satellite's Path

>44'56.08<

>>>>>>>>>>>665.00'87<

567.476.348

+355

+799

+803

+996

456.094.

South and East Asia: Physical

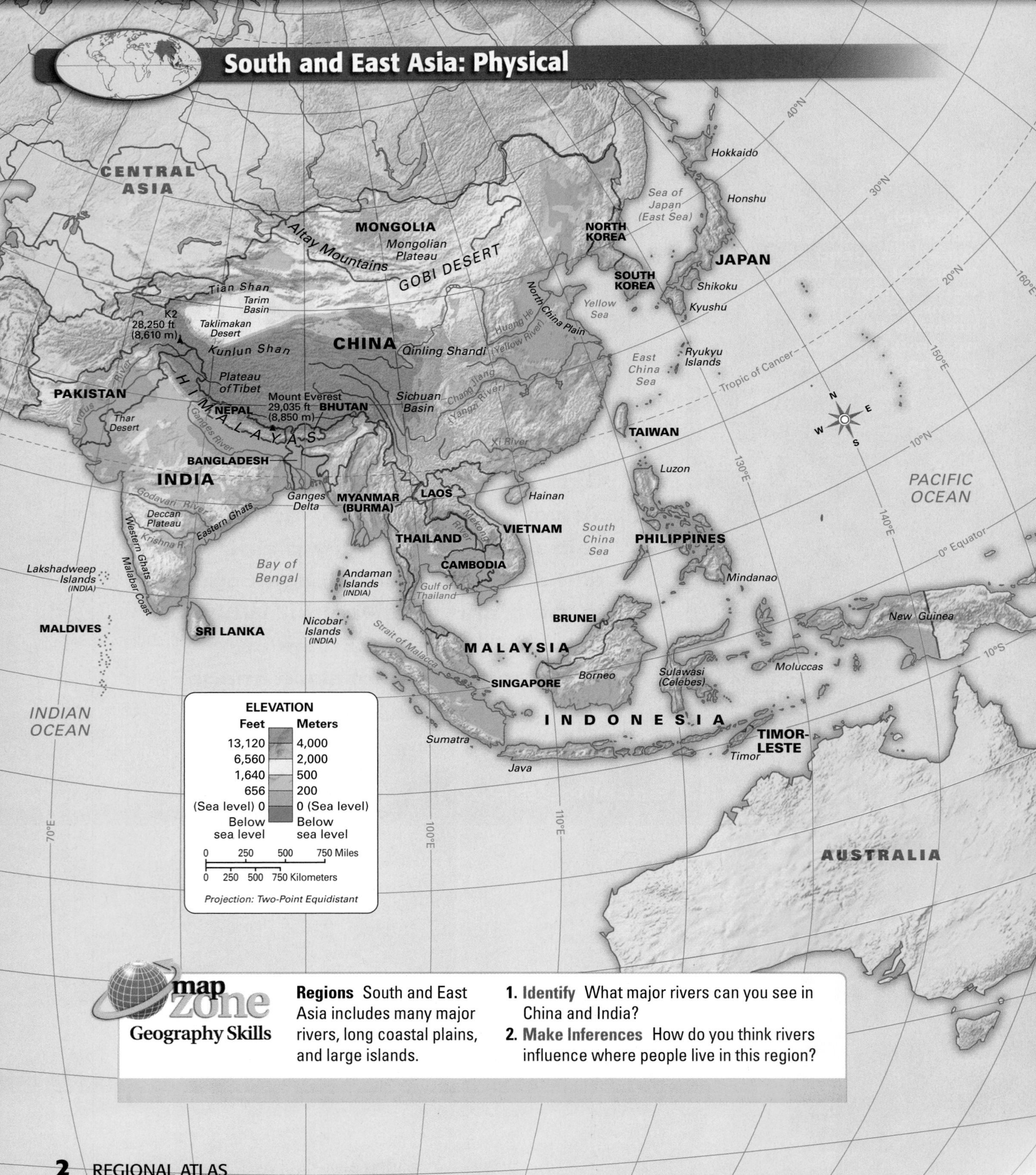

map zone
Geography Skills

Regions South and East Asia includes many major rivers, long coastal plains, and large islands.

1. **Identify** What major rivers can you see in China and India?
2. **Make Inferences** How do you think rivers influence where people live in this region?

South and East Asia and the Pacific

THE WORLD ALMANAC®
Facts about the World

Geographical Extremes: South and East Asia

Longest River	Chang Jiang (Yangzi River), China: 3,450 miles (5,552 km)
Highest Point	Mount Everest, Nepal/China: 29,035 feet (8,850 m)
Lowest Point	Turpan Depression, China: 505 feet (154 m) below sea level
Highest Recorded Temperature	Turpan Depression, China 118°F (48°C)
Wettest Place	Mawsynram, India: 467.4 inches (1,187.2 cm) average precipitation per year
Largest Country	China: 3,705,407 square miles (9,596,960 square km)
Smallest Country	Maldives: 116 square miles (300 square km)
Largest Rain Forest	Indonesia: 386,000 square miles (999,740 square km)
Strongest Earthquake	Off the coast of Sumatra, Indonesia, on December 26, 2004: Magnitude 9.1

Mount Everest

hmhsocialstudies.com

Size Comparison: The United States and South and East Asia

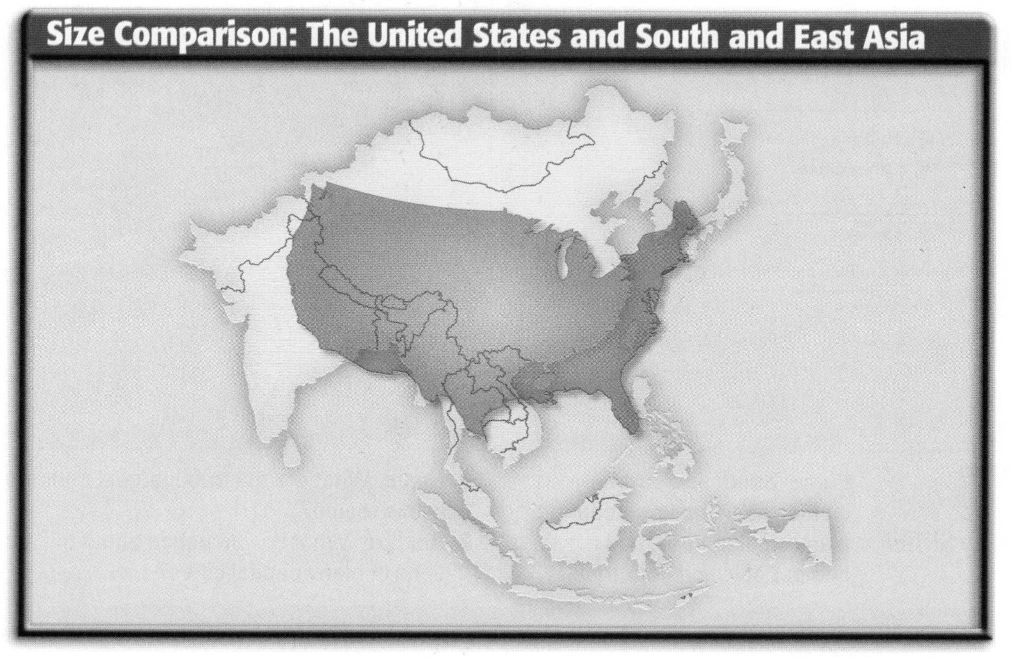

South and East Asia: Political

map zone
Geography Skills

Place South and East Asia includes several large countries, many smaller ones, and a number of island countries.

1. **Name** What are the three largest countries in this region?
2. **Analyze** What do you notice about the locations of many capital cities?

South and East Asia and the Pacific

South and East Asia: Population

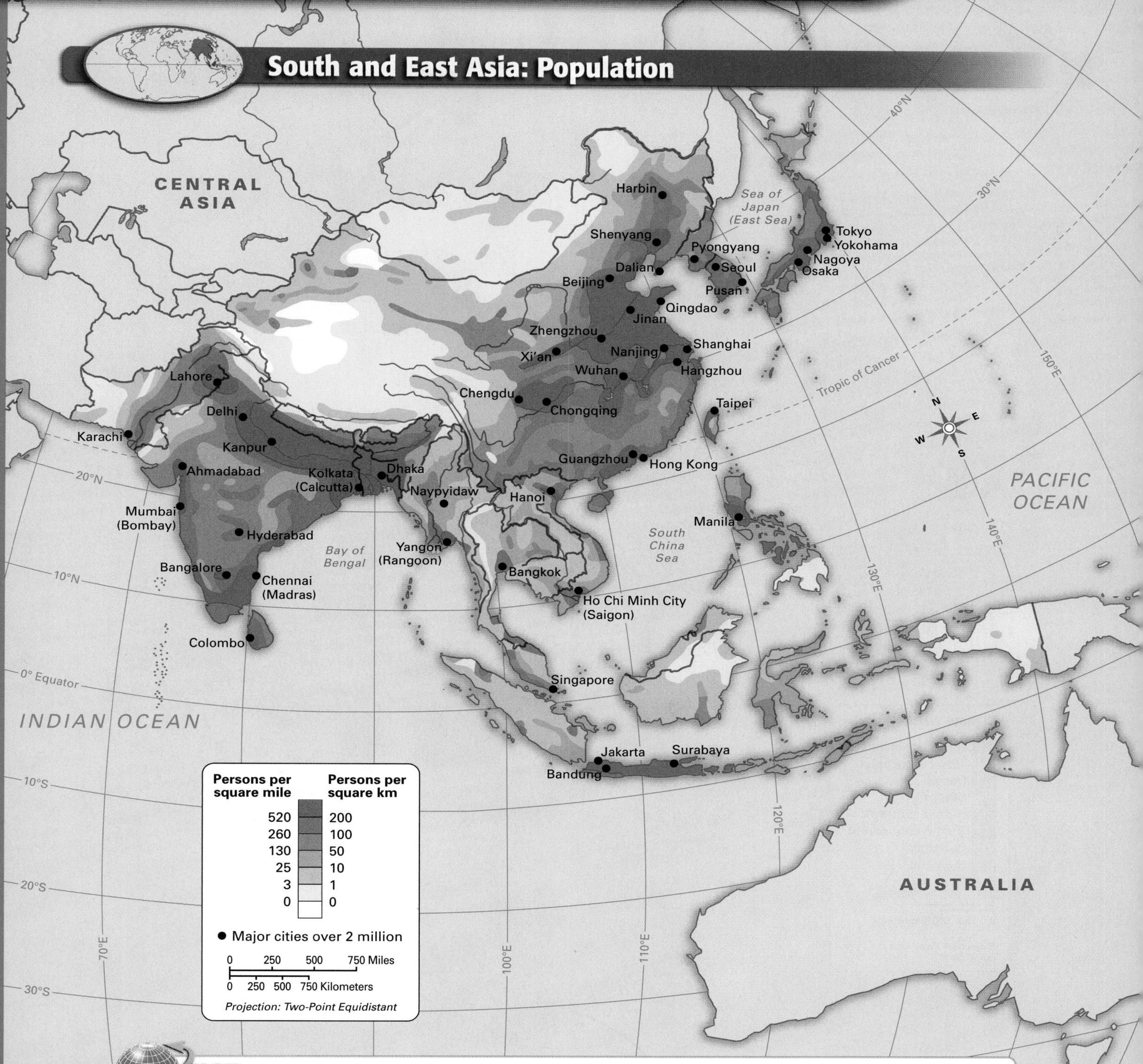

CENTRAL ASIA

Harbin
Sea of Japan (East Sea)
Tokyo
Yokohama
Nagoya
Osaka
Shenyang
Pyongyang
Seoul
Dalian
Beijing
Pusan
Qingdao
Jinan
Zhengzhou
Shanghai
Xi'an
Nanjing
Hangzhou
Wuhan
Tropic of Cancer
Chengdu
Chongqing
Taipei
Lahore
Delhi
Karachi
Kanpur
Guangzhou
Hong Kong
PACIFIC OCEAN
20°N
Ahmadabad
Kolkata (Calcutta)
Dhaka
Naypyidaw
Hanoi
Mumbai (Bombay)
Manila
Hyderabad
Bay of Bengal
Yangon (Rangoon)
South China Sea
Bangalore
Chennai (Madras)
Bangkok
10°N
Ho Chi Minh City (Saigon)
Colombo
0° Equator
Singapore
INDIAN OCEAN
Jakarta
Surabaya
Bandung
10°S
20°S
AUSTRALIA
30°S
40°N
30°N
150°E
140°E
130°E
120°E
110°E
100°E
70°E

Persons per square mile	Persons per square km
520	200
260	100
130	50
25	10
3	1
0	0

● Major cities over 2 million

0 250 500 750 Miles

0 250 500 750 Kilometers

Projection: Two-Point Equidistant

map zone Geography Skills

Regions This region has very large populations.

1. **Name** Based on the map, which two countries do you think have the largest populations?

2. **Compare** Compare this map to the physical map. How does China's physical geography relate to its population patterns?

South and East Asia: Climate

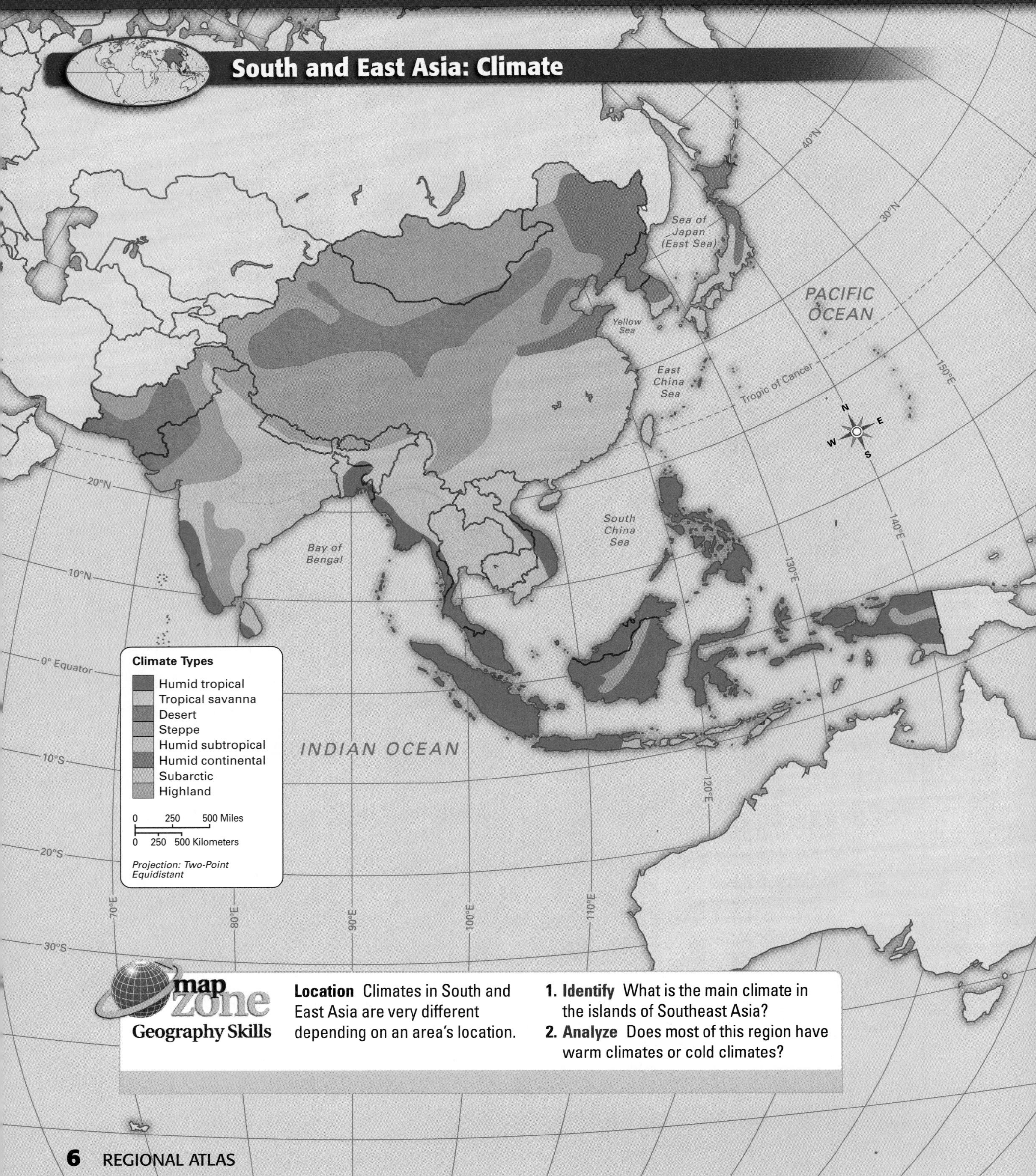

map zone Geography Skills

Location Climates in South and East Asia are very different depending on an area's location.

1. **Identify** What is the main climate in the islands of Southeast Asia?
2. **Analyze** Does most of this region have warm climates or cold climates?

South and East Asia and the Pacific

map zone Geography Skills

Human-Environment Interaction
People have converted much of this region to farmland. South and East Asia is also rich in resources.

1. **Locate** In which part of China is commercial farming found?
2. **Explain** Why do you think interior parts of Asia have only limited economic activity?

The Pacific World: Physical

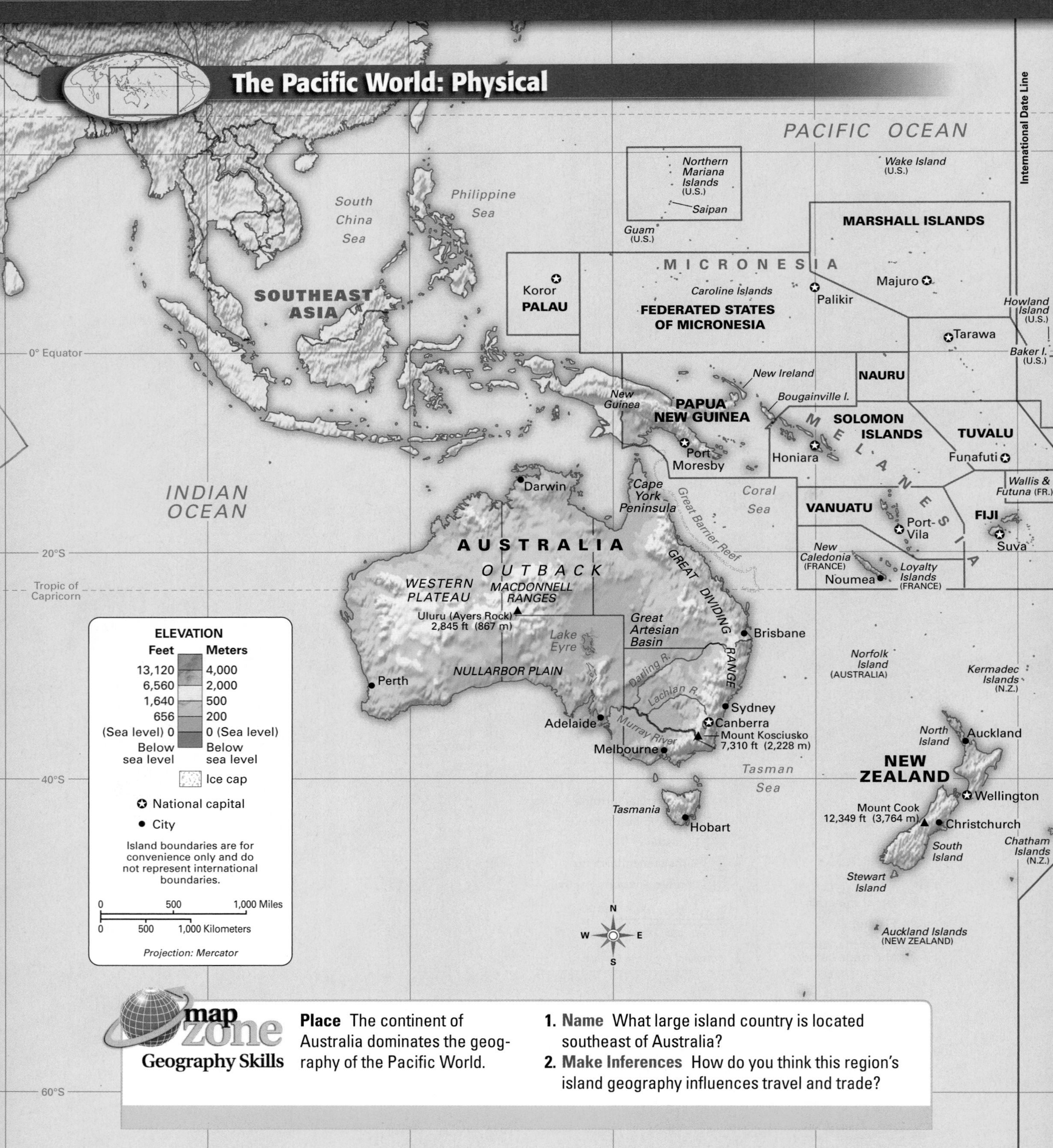

Place The continent of Australia dominates the geography of the Pacific World.

1. **Name** What large island country is located southeast of Australia?
2. **Make Inferences** How do you think this region's island geography influences travel and trade?

South and East Asia and the Pacific

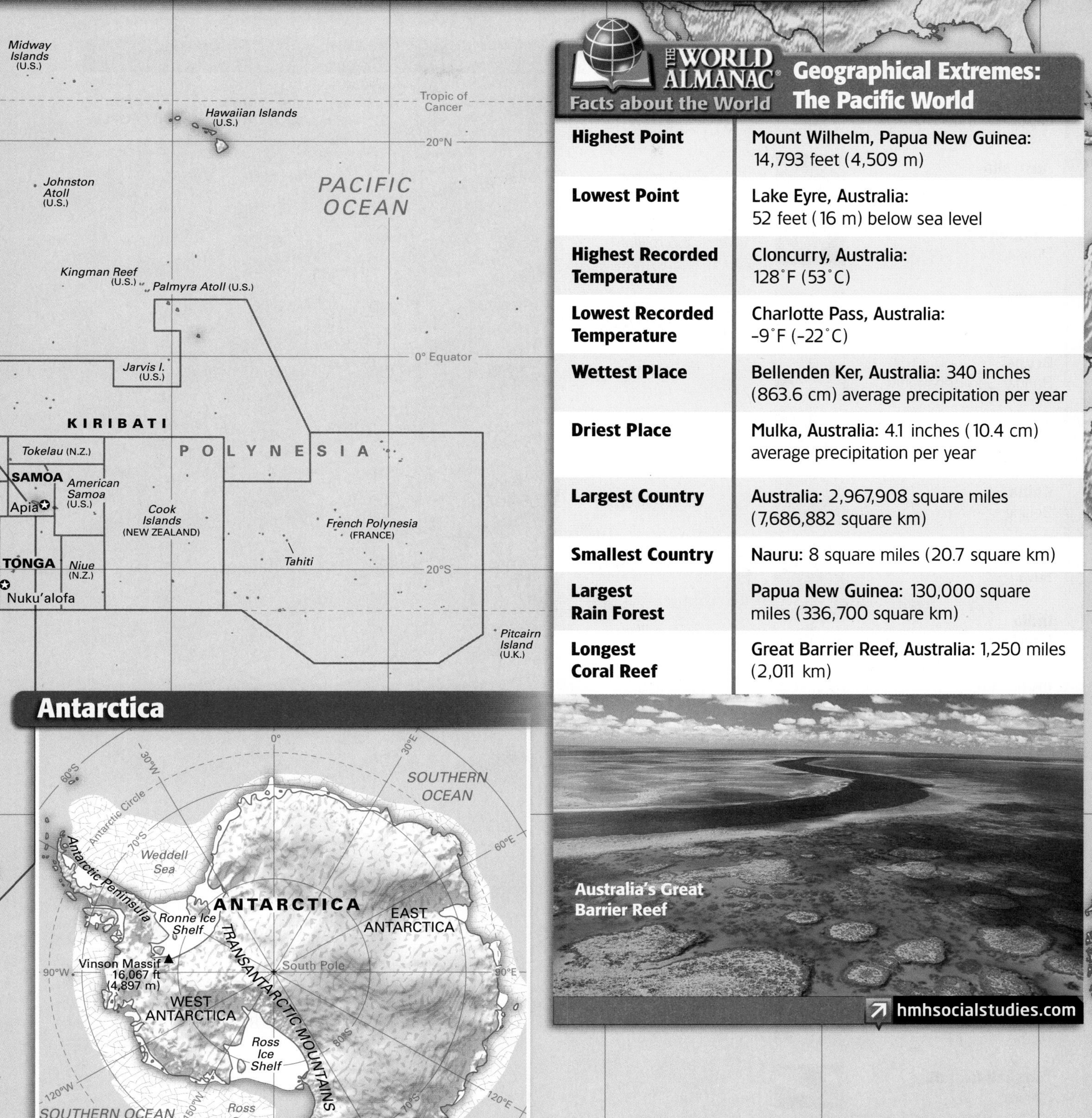

THE WORLD ALMANAC® Facts about the World

Geographical Extremes: The Pacific World

Highest Point	Mount Wilhelm, Papua New Guinea: 14,793 feet (4,509 m)
Lowest Point	Lake Eyre, Australia: 52 feet (16 m) below sea level
Highest Recorded Temperature	Cloncurry, Australia: 128°F (53°C)
Lowest Recorded Temperature	Charlotte Pass, Australia: -9°F (-22°C)
Wettest Place	Bellenden Ker, Australia: 340 inches (863.6 cm) average precipitation per year
Driest Place	Mulka, Australia: 4.1 inches (10.4 cm) average precipitation per year
Largest Country	Australia: 2,967,908 square miles (7,686,882 square km)
Smallest Country	Nauru: 8 square miles (20.7 square km)
Largest Rain Forest	Papua New Guinea: 130,000 square miles (336,700 square km)
Longest Coral Reef	Great Barrier Reef, Australia: 1,250 miles (2,011 km)

Australia's Great Barrier Reef

hmhsocialstudies.com

South and East Asia and the Pacific

COUNTRY Capital	FLAG	POPULATION	AREA (sq mi)	PER CAPITA GDP (U.S. $)	LIFE EXPECTANCY AT BIRTH	TVS PER 1,000 PEOPLE
Australia Canberra		21.3 million	2,967,909	$38,100	81.6	716
Bangladesh Dhaka		156 million	55,599	$1,500	63.2	7
Bhutan Thimphu		691,141	18,147	$5,200	65.6	6
Brunei Bandar Seri Begawan		388,190	2,228	$53,100	75.6	637
Cambodia Phnom Penh		14.5 million	69,900	$2,000	61.7	9
China Beijing		1,338 million	3,705,407	$6,000	73.3	291
Fiji Suva		944,720	7,054	$3,800	70.5	110
India New Delhi		1,166 million	1,269,346	$2,900	69.4	75
Indonesia Jakarta		240.3 million	741,100	$3,900	70.6	143
Japan Tokyo		127.1 million	145,883	$34,000	82.2	719
Kiribati Tarawa		112,850	313	$5,300	63	23
Laos Vientiane		6.8 million	91,429	$2,100	56.4	10
Malaysia Kuala Lumpur		25.7 million	127,317	$15,200	73.1	174
Maldives Male		396,334	116	$4,400	73.8	38
Marshall Islands Majuro		64,522	70	$2,500	70.6	NA
United States Washington, D.C.		307.2 million	3,794,083	$46,900	78.2	844

COUNTRY Capital	FLAG	POPULATION	AREA (sq mi)	PER CAPITA GDP (U.S. $)	LIFE EXPECTANCY AT BIRTH	TVS PER 1,000 PEOPLE
Micronesia, Federated States of Palikir		107,434	271	$2,200	70.4	20
Mongolia Ulaanbaatar		3 million	603,909	$3,200	67.4	58
Myanmar (Burma); Yangon (Rangoon) Naypyidaw		48 million	261,970	$1,200	63	7
Nauru No official capital		14,019	8	$5,000	63.9	1
Nepal Kathmandu		28.6 million	54,363	$1,100	60.9	6
New Zealand Wellington		4.2 million	103,738	$28,000	80.2	516
North Korea Pyongyang		22.7 million	46,541	$1,800	72.3	55
Pakistan Islamabad		176.2 million	310,403	$2,500	64.1	105
Palau Koror		20,800	177	$8,100	70.7	98
Papua New Guinea Port Moresby		6 million	178,704	$2,200	65.6	13
Philippines Manila		98 million	115,831	$3,300	70.5	110
Samoa Apia		219,998	1,137	$4,800	71.3	56
Singapore Singapore		4.7 million	268	$51,500	81.8	341
Solomon Islands Honiara		595,613	10,985	$1,900	73.2	16
South Korea Seoul		48.5 million	38,023	$27,600	78.8	364
United States Washington, D.C.		307.2 million	3,794,083	$46,900	78.2	844

Facts about Countries

COUNTRY Capital	FLAG	POPULATION	AREA (sq mi)	PER CAPITA GDP (U.S. $)	LIFE EXPECTANCY AT BIRTH	TVS PER 1,000 PEOPLE
Sri Lanka Colombo		21.3 million	25,332	$4,300	74.8	102
Taiwan Taipei		23 million	13,892	$31,100	77.6	327
Thailand Bangkok		65.9 million	198,457	$8,400	72.6	274
Timor-Leste Dili		1.1 million	5,743	$2,300	67	NA
Tonga Nuku'alofa		120,898	289	$4,600	70.1	61
Tuvalu Funafuti		12,373	10	$1,600	68.6	9
Vanuatu Port-Vila		218,519	4,710	$4,600	63.2	12
Vietnam Hanoi		87 million	127,244	$2,800	71.1	184
United States Washington, D.C.		307.2 million	3,794,083	$46,900	78.2	844

Palm trees along the coast of Tonga

ANALYSIS SKILL **ANALYZING TABLES**

1. Which five countries in this region have the highest per capita GDPs? How do they compare to the per capita GDP of the United States?
2. Compare the life expectancy and number of TVs per 1,000 people in Japan and Kiribati. What might this comparison indicate about life in the two countries?

hmhsocialstudies.com

Population Giants

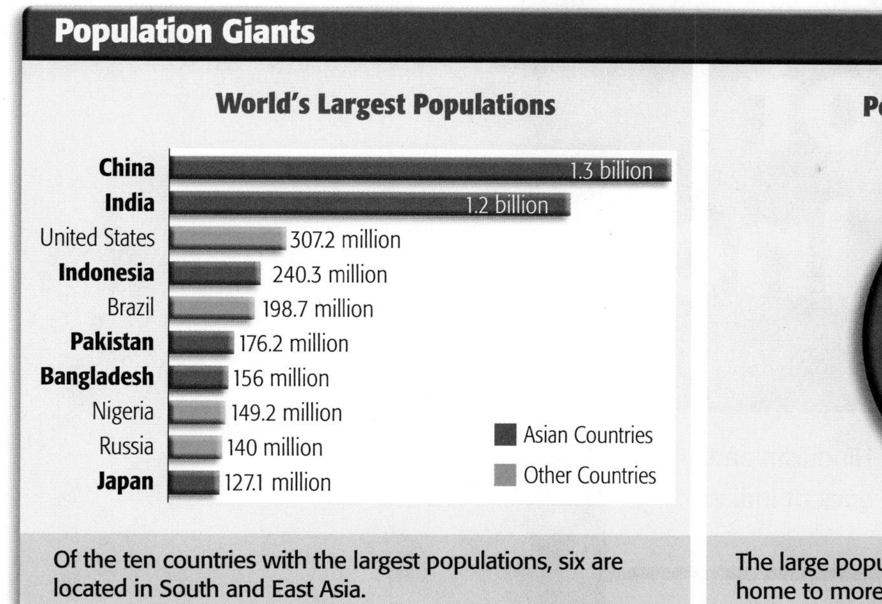

Of the ten countries with the largest populations, six are located in South and East Asia.

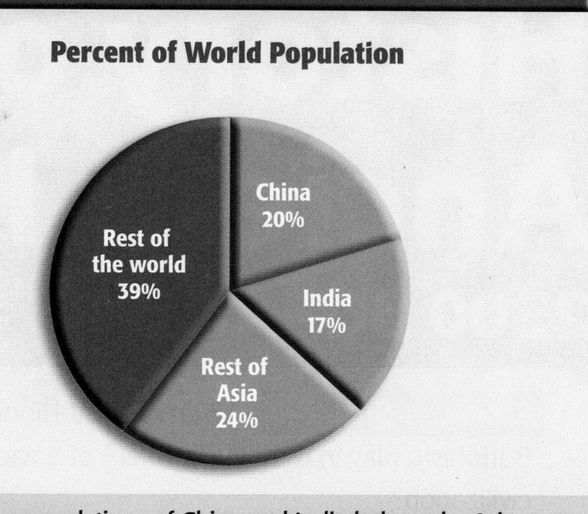

The large populations of China and India help make Asia home to more than 60 percent of the world's people.

Economic Powers

Japan

- World's third-largest economy
- $746.5 billion in exports
- Gross Domestic Product $4.3 Trillion
- Major exports: transportation equipment, cars, semiconductors, electronics

Japan is one of the most technologically advanced countries and is a leading producer of hi-tech goods.

China

- World's second-largest economy
- $1.4 trillion in exports
- Gross Domestic Product $8 Trillion
- Major exports: machinery and electronics, clothing, plastics, furniture, toys

China is an emerging economic powerhouse with a huge population and a fast growing economy.

ANALYSIS SKILL **ANALYZING VISUALS**

1. Which two countries have the largest populations?
2. What kinds of exports help make Japan and China economic powers?

CHAPTER 1

History of Ancient India
2300 BC–AD 500

Essential Question What role did Hinduism and Buddhism play in the development of ancient Indian civilization?

What You Will Learn...

In this chapter you will learn about the ancient civilization and powerful empires of India, the birthplace of two major world religions—Hinduism and Buddhism.

Focus on Reading and Writing

Sequencing When you read, it is important to keep track of the sequence, or order, in which events happen. Look for dates and other clues to help you figure out the proper sequence. **See the lesson, Sequencing, on page 213.**

Creating a Poster Ancient India was the home of amazing cities, strong empires, and influential religions. As you read this chapter, think about how you could illustrate one aspect of Indian culture in a poster.

30°N

20°N

10°N

40°E

60°E

map zone

Geography Skills

Location Ancient Indian civilization began in the Indus Valley and gradually spread through India.

1. **Read the Map** What two cities were located on the Indus River?
2. **Interpret** Based on the icons on this map, how do you think Indian civilization expanded?

Early India The first civilization in India, the Harappans, were skilled builders and artists.

Hinduism A major world religion, Hinduism, developed in India. In this photo, Hindus bathe in the sacred river Ganges.

Buddhism India was also the birthplace of another religion, Buddhism. Buddhist temples like this one at Ajanta are found all over India.

SECTION 1

Early Indian Civilizations

What You Will Learn...

Main Ideas

1. Located on the Indus River, the Harappan civilization also had contact with people far from India.
2. Harappan achievements included a writing system, city planning, and art.
3. The Aryan migration changed India's civilization.

The Big Idea

Indian civilization developed on the Indus River.

Key Terms and Places

Indus River, *p. 16*
Harappa, *p. 17*
Mohenjo Daro, *p. 17*
Sanskrit, *p. 21*

Use the graphic organizer online to take notes on India's two earliest civilizations, the Harappans and Aryans.

If YOU lived there...

You are a trader in the huge city of Mohenjo Daro. Your business is booming, as traders come to the city from all over Asia. With your new wealth, you have bought a huge house with a rooftop terrace and even indoor plumbing! This morning, however, you heard that invaders are headed toward the city. People are telling you that you should flee for your safety.

What will you miss most about life in the city?

BUILDING BACKGROUND India was home to one of the world's first civilizations. Like other early civilizations, the one in India grew up in a river valley. As archaeologists discovered, however, the society that eventually developed in India was very different from the ones that developed elsewhere.

Harappan Civilization

Imagine that you are an archaeologist. You are out in a field one day looking for a few pots, a tablet, or some other small artifact. Imagine your surprise, then, when you find a whole city!

Archaeologists working in India in the 1920s had that very experience. While digging for artifacts along the **Indus River**, they found not one but two huge cities. The archaeologists had thought people had lived along the Indus long ago, but they had no idea that an advanced civilization had existed there.

India's First Civilization

Historians call the civilization that developed along the Indus and Sarasvati Rivers the Harappan (huh-RA-puhn) civilization. The name comes from the modern city of Harappa (huh-RA-puh), Pakistan. It was near this city that the ruins of the ancient civilization were first discovered. Archaeologists currently estimate that the civilization thrived between 2300 and 1700 BC.

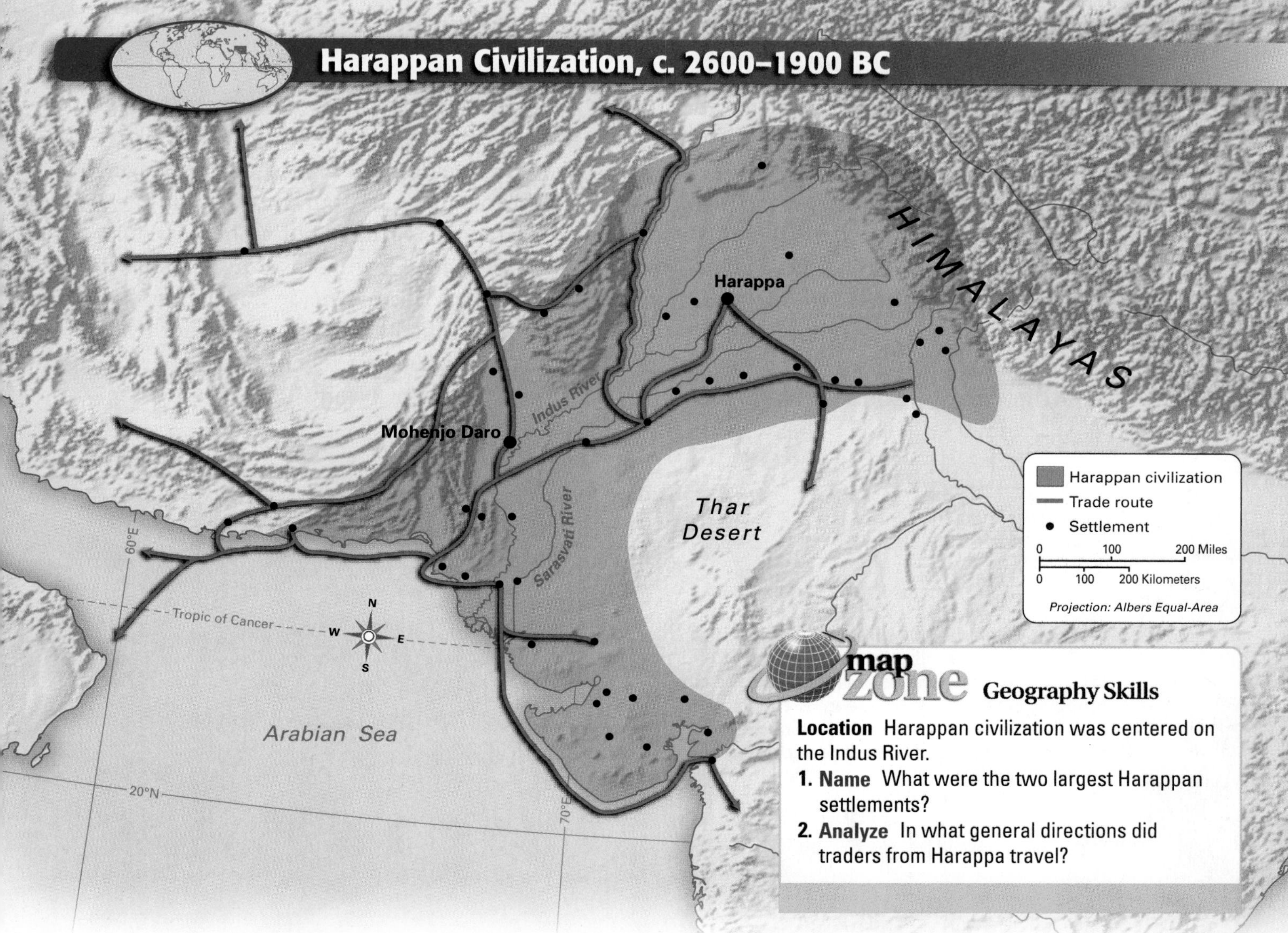

The Harappan civilization controlled large areas on both sides of the Indus River. As you can see on the map, settlements were scattered over a huge area. Most of these settlements lay next to rivers. The largest settlements were two cities, **Harappa** and **Mohenjo Daro** (mo-HEN-joh DAR-oh).

Like most other ancient societies, the Harappan civilization was dependent on agriculture. Farmers in the Indus Valley grew a variety of crops—from wheat and barley to dates and vegetables—to feed both themselves and city dwellers. They used irrigation canals to bring water from the Indus and other rivers to their fields.

Contact with Other Cultures

Although the Harappan civilization was centered on the Indus, its influence reached far beyond that area. In fact, archaeologists have found evidence that the Harappans had contact with people as far away as southern India and Mesopotamia.

Most of this contact with other cultures was in the form of trade. The Harappans traded to obtain raw materials. They then used these materials to make products such as pottery, stamps and seals, and statues.

READING CHECK **Finding Main Ideas** Where was the Harappan civilization located?

Harappan Achievements

Historians do not know much about the Harappan civilization. They think the Harappans had kings and strong central governments, but they are not sure. They also know little about Harappan religion.

Although we do not know much about how the Harappans lived, we do know that they made great achievements in many fields. Everything we know about these achievements comes from artifacts.

Writing System

The ancient Harappans developed India's first writing system. However, scholars have not yet learned to read this language. Archaeologists have found many examples of Harappan writing, but none of them is more than a few words long. This lack of long passages has made translating the language difficult. Because we cannot read what they wrote, we rely on other clues to study Harappan society.

Close-up

Life in Mohenjo Daro

Mohenjo Daro was one of the two major cities of the Harappan civilization. Located next to the Indus River in what is now Pakistan, the city probably covered one square mile. The people who lived in the city enjoyed some of the most advanced comforts of their time, including indoor plumbing.

Harappan merchants used a standard set of weights to measure goods such as precious stones.

City Planning

Most of what we have learned about the Harappans has come from studying their cities, especially Harappa and Mohenjo Daro. The two cities lay on the Indus more than 300 miles apart, but they appear to have been remarkably similar.

Both Harappa and Mohenjo Daro were well-planned cities. A close examination of their ruins shows that the Harappans were careful planners and skilled engineers.

Harappa and Mohenjo Daro were built with defense in mind. Each city stood near a towering fortress. From these fortresses, defenders could look down on the cities' carefully laid out brick streets. These streets crossed at right angles and were lined with storehouses, workshops, market stalls, and houses. Using their engineering skills, the Harappans built extensive sewer systems to keep their streets from flooding. They also installed plumbing in many buildings.

Next to the city was a huge citadel, or fortress, to guard against invasions.
The houses of Mohenjo Daro had flat roofs. People climbed to their roofs to take advantage of cooling breezes.
The city's streets were paved and well drained. They met at right angles, creating a grid pattern.

ANALYSIS SKILL ANALYZING VISUALS

What in this picture suggests that Mohenjo Daro was a well-planned city?

Artistic Achievements

In Harappan cities, archaeologists have found many artifacts that show that the Harappans were skilled artisans. For example, they have found sturdy pottery vessels, jewelry, and ivory objects.

Some of these ancient artifacts have helped historians draw conclusions about Harappan society. For example, they found a statue that shows two animals pulling a cart. Based on this statue, they conclude that the Harappans built and used wheeled vehicles. Likewise, a statue of a man with elaborate clothes and jewelry suggests that Harappan society had an upper class.

Focus on Reading

In what order did the Aryans settle lands in India?

Harappan civilization ended by the early 1700s BC, but no one is sure why. Perhaps invaders destroyed the cities or natural disasters, like floods or earthquakes, caused the civilization to collapse.

READING CHECK **Analyzing** Why do we not know much about Harappan civilization?

Harappan Art

Like other ancient peoples, the Harappans made small seals like the one below that were used to stamp goods. They also used clay pots like the one at right decorated with a goat.

Aryan Migration

Not long after the Harappan civilization crumbled, a new group appeared in the Indus Valley. These people were called the Aryans (AIR-ee-uhnz). Possibly from the area around the Caspian Sea in Central Asia, over time they became the dominant group in India.

Arrival and Spread

Many historians and archaeologists believe that the Aryans first arrived in India in the 2000s BC, probably crossing into India through mountain passes in the northwest. Over many centuries, they spread east and south into central India. From there they moved even farther east into the Ganges River Valley.

Much of what we know about Aryan society comes from religious writings known as the Vedas (VAY-duhs). These are collections of poems, hymns, myths, and rituals that were written by Aryan priests. You will read more about the Vedas later in this chapter.

Government and Society

As nomads, the Aryans took along their herds of animals as they moved. But over time, they settled in villages and began to farm. Unlike the Harappans, they did not build big cities.

The Aryan political system was also different from the Harappan system. The Aryans lived in small communities, based mostly on family ties. No single ruling authority existed. Instead, each group had its own leader, often a skilled warrior.

Aryan villages were governed by rajas (RAH-juhz). A raja was a leader who ruled a village and the land around it. Villagers farmed some of this land for the raja. They used other sections as pastures for their cows, horses, sheep, and goats.

Although many rajas were related, they didn't always get along. Sometimes rajas joined forces before fighting a common enemy. Other times, however, rajas went to war against each other. In fact, Aryan groups fought each other nearly as often as they fought outsiders.

Language

The first Aryan settlers did not read or write. Because of this, they had to memorize the poems and hymns that were important in their culture, such as the Vedas. If people forgot these poems and hymns, the works would be lost forever.

The language in which these Aryan poems and hymns were composed was **Sanskrit**, the most important language of ancient India. At first, Sanskrit was only a spoken language. Eventually, however, people figured out how to write it down so they could keep records. These Sanskrit records are a major source of information about Aryan society. Sanskrit is no longer widely spoken today, but it is the root of many modern South Asian languages.

READING CHECK **Identifying** What source provides much of the information we have about the Aryans?

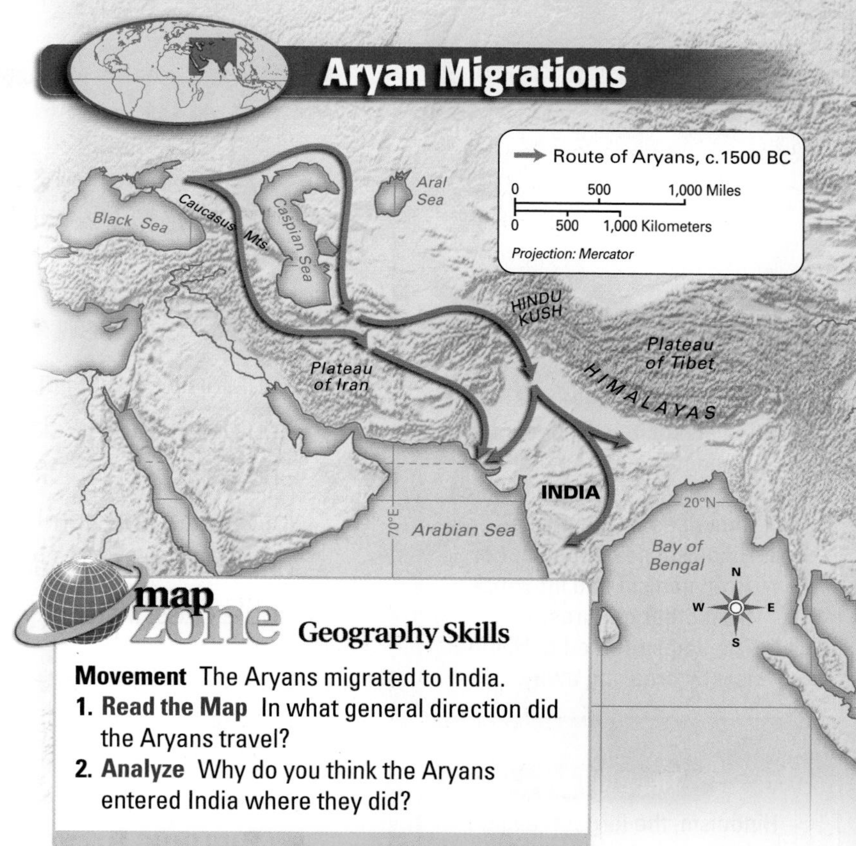

map zone Geography Skills

Movement The Aryans migrated to India.

1. **Read the Map** In what general direction did the Aryans travel?
2. **Analyze** Why do you think the Aryans entered India where they did?

SUMMARY AND PREVIEW The earliest civilizations in India were centered in the Indus Valley. In the next section, you will learn about a new religion that developed in the Indus Valley after the Aryans settled there—Hinduism.

Section 1 Assessment

hmhsocialstudies.com ONLINE QUIZ

Reviewing Ideas, Terms, and Places

1. a. **Recall** Where did the Harappan civilization develop? Along the Indus and Sarasvati rivers.
   b. **Explain** Why did the Harappans make contact with people far from India? Through
2. a. **Identify** What was **Mohenjo Daro**?
   b. **Analyze** What is one reason that scholars do not completely understand some important parts of Harappan society?
3. a. **Identify** Who were the Aryans?
   b. **Contrast** How was Aryan society different from Harappan society?

Critical Thinking

4. **Summarizing** Using your notes, list the major achievements of India's first two civilizations. Record your conclusions in a diagram like this one.

Early Indian Achievements
Harappan society
Aryan society

FOCUS ON WRITING

5. **Illustrating Geography and Early Civilizations** This section described two possible topics for your poster—geography and early civilizations. Which of them is more interesting to you? Write down some ideas for a poster about that topic.

SECTION 2

Origins of Hinduism

What You Will Learn...

Main Ideas

1. Indian society divided into distinct groups.
2. The Aryans formed a religion known as Brahmanism.
3. Hinduism developed out of Brahmanism and influences from other cultures.
4. The Jains reacted to Hinduism by breaking away.

The Big Idea

Hinduism, the largest religion in India, developed out of ancient Indian beliefs and practices.

Key Terms

caste system, *p. 23*
reincarnation, *p. 25*
karma, *p. 26*
nonviolence, *p. 27*

Use the graphic organizer online to take notes on Hinduism. Pay attention to its origins, teachings, and other religions that developed alongside it.

If YOU lived there...

Your family are skillful weavers who make beautiful cotton cloth. You belong to the class in Aryan society who are traders, farmers, and craftspeople. Often the raja of your town leads the warriors into battle. You admire their bravery but know you can never be one of them. To be an Aryan warrior, you must be born into that noble class. Instead, you have your own duty to carry out.

How do you feel about remaining a weaver?

BUILDING BACKGROUND As the Aryans came to dominate the Indus Valley, they developed a system of social classes. As their influence spread through India, so did their class system. Before long, this class system was a key part of Indian society.

Indian Society Divides

As Aryan society became more complex, their society became divided into groups. These groups were largely organized by people's occupations. Strict rules developed about how people of different groups could interact. As time passed, these rules became stricter and became central to Indian society.

The *Varnas*

According to the Vedas, there were four main *varnas*, or social divisions, in Aryan society. These *varnas* were

- Brahmins (BRAH-muhns), or priests,
- Kshatriyas (KSHA-tree-uhs), or rulers and warriors,
- Vaisyas (VYSH-yuhs), or farmers, craftspeople, and traders, and
- Sudras (SOO-drahs), or laborers and non-Aryans.

The Brahmins were seen as the highest ranking because they performed rituals for the gods. This gave the Brahmins great influence over the other *varnas*.

The Caste System

As the rules of interaction between *varnas* got stricter, the Aryan social order became more complex. In time, each of the *varnas* in Aryan society was further divided into many castes, or groups. This **caste system** divided Indian society into groups based on a person's birth, wealth, or occupation. At one time, some 3,000 separate castes existed in India.

The caste to which a person belonged determined his or her place in society. However, this ordering was by no means permanent. Over time, individual castes gained or lost favor in society as caste members gained wealth or power. On rare occasions, people could change caste.

People in the lowest class, the Sudra castes, had hard lives. After a few centuries, a fifth group developed, a group who didn't belong to any caste at all. Called untouchables because others were not supposed to have contact with them, they were seen as unclean and as social outcasts. The only jobs open to them were unpleasant ones, such as tanning animal hides and disposing of dead animals.

Caste Rules

To keep their classes distinct, the Aryans developed sutras, or guides, which listed the rules for the caste system. For example, people could not marry someone from a different class. It was even forbidden for people from one class to eat with people from another. People who broke the caste rules could be banned from their homes and their castes, which would make them untouchables. Because of these strict rules, people spent almost all of their time with others in their same class. The caste system also brought stability to Hindu society and a sense of belonging to people of each caste.

READING CHECK **Drawing Inferences** How did a person become a member of a caste?

The *Varnas*

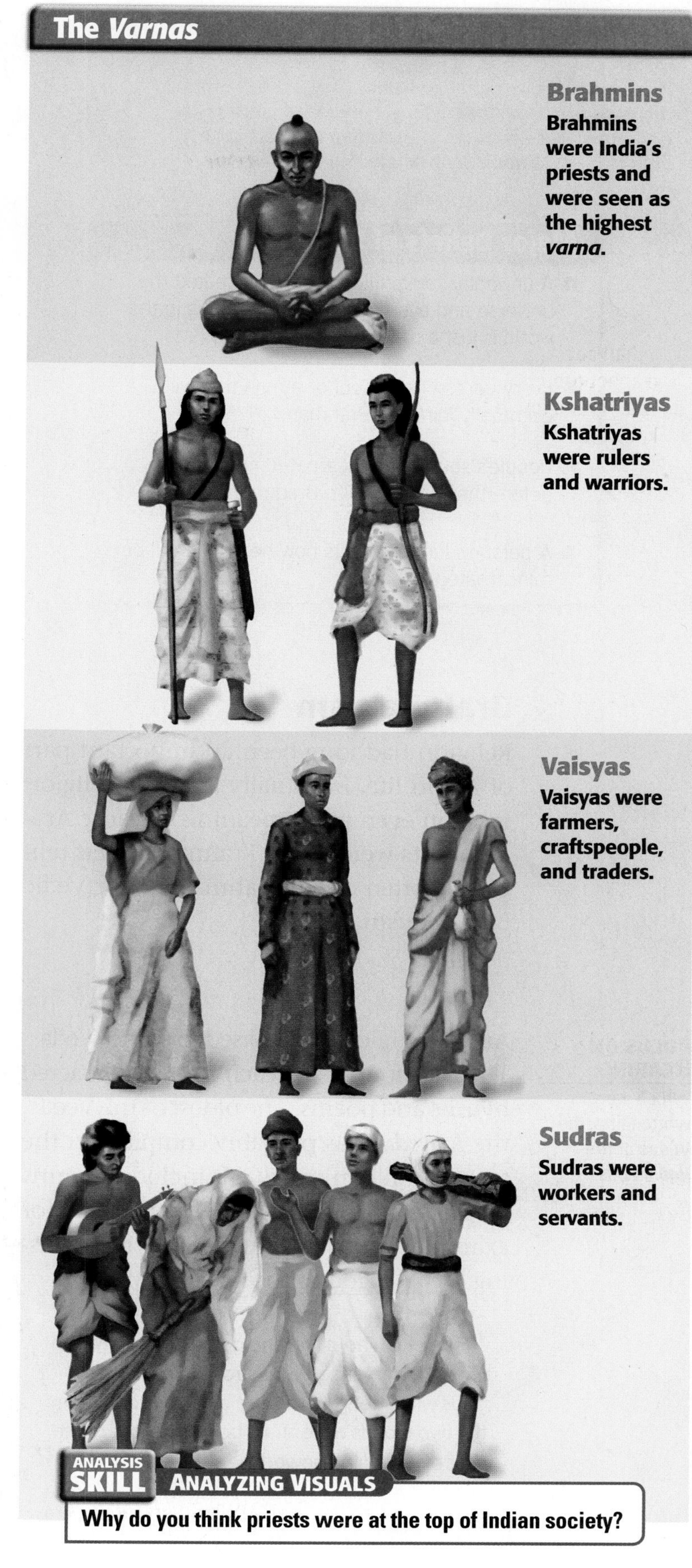

Brahmins
Brahmins were India's priests and were seen as the highest *varna*.

Kshatriyas
Kshatriyas were rulers and warriors.

Vaisyas
Vaisyas were farmers, craftspeople, and traders.

Sudras
Sudras were workers and servants.

ANALYSIS SKILL **ANALYZING VISUALS**

Why do you think priests were at the top of Indian society?

Hindu Gods and Beliefs

Hindus believe in many gods, but they believe that all the gods are aspects of a single universal spirit called Brahman. Three aspects of Brahman are particularly important in Hinduism—Brahma, Siva, and Vishnu.

Major Beliefs of Hinduism

- A universal spirit called Brahman created the universe and everything in it. Everything in the world is just a part of Brahman.
- Every person has a soul or atman that will eventually join with Brahman.
- People's souls are reincarnated many times before they can join with Brahman.
- A person's karma affects how he or she will be reincarnated.

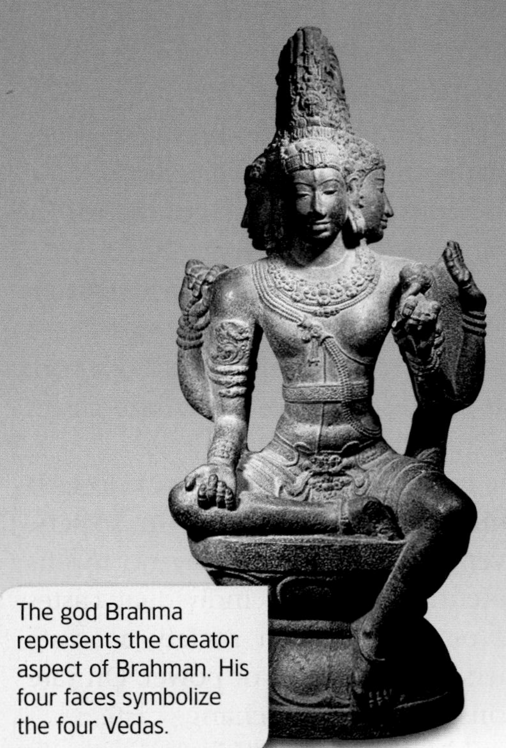

The god Brahma represents the creator aspect of Brahman. His four faces symbolize the four Vedas.

Brahmanism

Religion had long been an important part of Aryan life. Eventually in India, religion took on even more meaning. Because Aryan priests were called Brahmins, their religion is often called Brahmanism, or Vedic Brahmanism.

The Vedas

FOCUS ON READING
Which were written first, the Vedas or the Vedic texts?

Aryan religion was based on the Vedas. There are four Vedas, each containing sacred hymns and poems. The oldest of the Vedas, the *Rigveda*, was probably compiled in the second millennium BC. It includes hymns of praise to many gods. This passage, for example, is the opening of a hymn praising Indra, a god of the sky and war.

> "The one who is first and possessed of wisdom when born; the god who strove to protect the gods with strength; the one before whose force the two worlds were afraid because of the greatness of his virility [power]: he, O people, is Indra."
>
> –from the *Rigveda*, in *Reading about the World, Volume I*, edited by Paul Brians, et al

Later Vedic Texts

Over the centuries, Aryan Brahmins wrote down their thoughts about the Vedas. In time these thoughts were compiled into collections called Vedic texts.

One collection of Vedic texts describes Aryan religious rituals. For example, it describes how to perform sacrifices. Priests prepared animals, food, or drinks to be sacrificed in a fire. The Aryans believed that the fire would carry these offerings to the gods.

A second collection of Vedic texts describes secret rituals that only certain people could perform. In fact, the rituals were so secret that they had to be done in the forest, far from other people.

The final group of Vedic texts are the Upanishads (oo-PAHN-ee-shads), most of which were written by about 600 BC. These writings are reflections on the Vedas by religious students and teachers.

READING CHECK **Finding Main Ideas** What are the Vedic texts?

Siva, the destroyer aspect of Brahman, is usually shown with four arms and three eyes. Here he is shown dancing on the back of a demon he has defeated.

Vishnu is the preserver aspect of Brahman. In his four arms, he carries a conch shell, a mace, and a discus, symbols of his power and greatness.

Hinduism Develops

The Vedas, the Upanishads, and the other Vedic texts remained the basis of Indian religion for centuries. Eventually, though, the ideas of these sacred texts began to blend with ideas from other cultures. People from Persia and other kingdoms in Central Asia, for example, brought their ideas to India. In time, this blending of ideas created a religion called Hinduism, the largest religion in India today.

Hindu Beliefs

The Hindus believe in many gods. Among them are three major gods: Brahma the Creator, Siva the Destroyer, and Vishnu the Preserver. At the same time, however, Hindus believe that each god is part of a single universal spirit called Brahman. They believe that Brahman created the world and preserves it. Gods such as Brahma, Siva, and Vishnu are different aspects of Brahman. In fact, Hindus believe that everything in the world is part of Brahman.

Life and Rebirth

According to Hindu teachings, everyone has a soul, or atman. This soul holds the person's personality, those qualities that make a person who he or she is. Hindus believe that a person's ultimate goal should be to reunite that soul with Brahman, the universal spirit.

Hindus believe that their souls will eventually join Brahman because the world we live in is an illusion. Brahman is the only reality. The Upanishads taught that people must try to see through the illusion of the world. Since it is hard to see through illusions, it can take several lifetimes. That is why Hindus believe that souls are born and reborn many times, each time in a new body. This process of rebirth is called **reincarnation**.

More than 900 million people in India practice Hinduism today.

Hinduism and the Caste System

According to the traditional Hindu view of reincarnation, a person who has died is reborn in a new physical form.

The type of form depends upon his or her **karma**, the effects that good or bad actions have on a person's soul. Evil actions during one's life will build bad karma. A person with bad karma will be reborn into a lower caste, or even as a lower life-form such as an animal or a plant.

In contrast, good actions build good karma. People with good karma are born into a higher caste in their next lives. In time, good karma will bring salvation, or freedom from life's worries and the cycle of rebirth. This salvation is called *moksha*.

Hinduism taught that each person had a duty to accept his or her place in the world without complaint. This is called obeying one's dharma. People could build good karma by fulfilling the duties required of their specific caste. Through reincarnation, Hinduism offered rewards to those who lived good lives. Even untouchables could be reborn into a higher caste.

Hinduism was popular at all levels of Hindu society, through all four *varnas*. By teaching people to accept their places in life, Hinduism helped preserve the caste system in India.

Hinduism and Women

Early Hinduism taught that both men and women could gain salvation. However, like other ancient religions, Hinduism considered women inferior to men. Women were generally not allowed to study the Vedas.

Over the centuries, Hindu women have gained more rights. This change has been the result of efforts by influential Hindu leaders like Mohandas Gandhi, who led the movement for Indian independence. As a result, many of the restrictions once placed on Hindu women have been lifted.

READING CHECK **Summarizing** What factors determined how a person would be reborn?

FOCUS ON CULTURE

The Sacred Ganges

Hindus believe that there are many sacred places in India. Making a pilgrimage to one of these places, they believe, will help improve their karma and increase their chance for salvation. The most sacred of all the pilgrimage sites in India is the Ganges River in the northeast.

Known to Hindus as Mother Ganga, the Ganges flows out of the Himalayas. In traditional Hindu teachings, however, the river flows from the feet of Vishnu and over the head of Siva before it makes its way across the land. Through this contact with the gods, the river's water is made holy. Hindus believe that bathing in the Ganges will purify them and remove some of their bad karma.

Although the entire Ganges is considered sacred, a few cities along its path are seen as especially holy. At these sites, pilgrims gather to bathe and celebrate Hindu festivals. Steps lead down from the cities right to the edge of the water so people can more easily reach the river.

Summarizing Why is the Ganges a pilgrimage site?

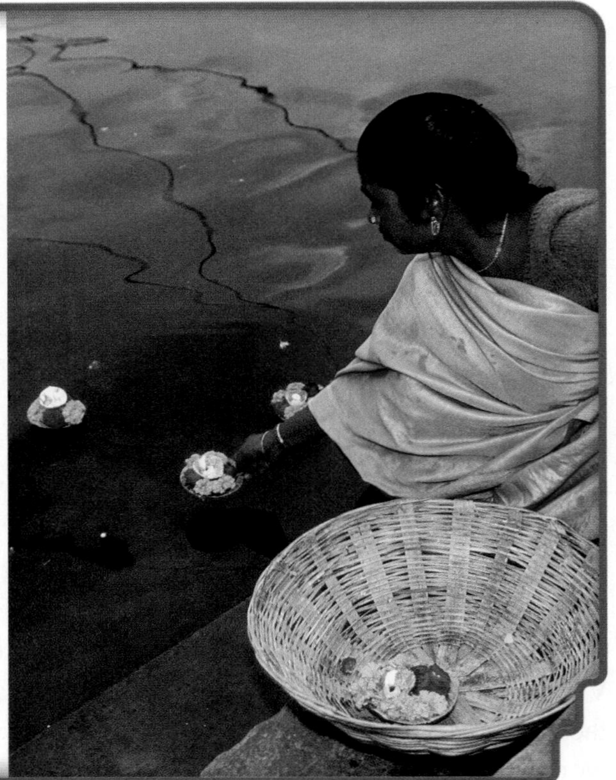

Jains React to Hinduism

Although Hinduism was widely followed in India, not everyone agreed with its beliefs. Some unsatisfied people and groups looked for new religious ideas. One such group was the Jains (JYNZ), believers in a religion called Jainism (JY-niz-uhm).

Jainism is based on the teachings of a man named Mahavira. Born into the Kshatriya *varna* in the middle of the 500s BC, he was unhappy with the control of religion by the Brahmins, whom he thought put too much emphasis on rituals. Mahavira gave up his life of luxury, became a monk, and established the principles of Jainism.

The Jains try to live by four principles: injure no life, tell the truth, do not steal, and own no property. In their efforts not to injure anyone or anything, the Jains practice **nonviolence**, or the avoidance of violent actions. The Sanskrit word for this nonviolence is *ahimsa* (uh-HIM-sah). Many Hindus also practice *ahimsa*.

The Jains' emphasis on nonviolence comes from their belief that everything is alive and part of the cycle of rebirth. Jains are very serious about not injuring or killing any creature—humans, animals, insects, or plants. They do not believe in animal sacrifice, unlike the ancient Brahmins. Because they do not want to hurt any living creatures, Jains are vegetarians. They do not eat any food that comes from animals.

READING CHECK **Identifying Points of View** Why do Jains avoid eating meat?

SUMMARY AND PREVIEW You have learned about two religions that grew in ancient India—Hinduism and Jainism. In Section 3, you will learn about a third religion that began there—Buddhism.

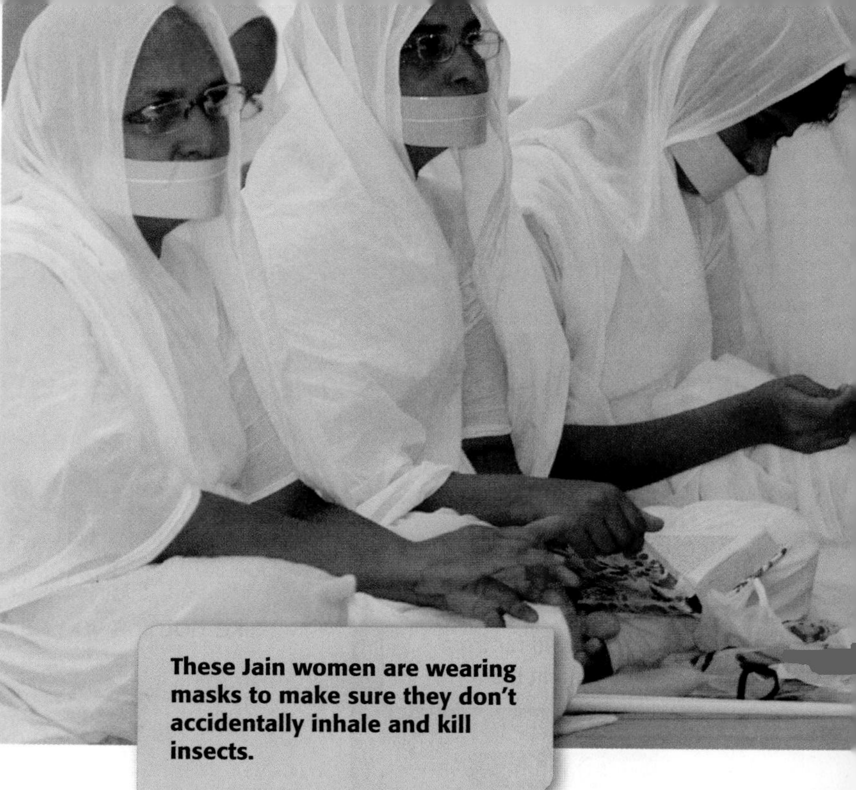

These Jain women are wearing masks to make sure they don't accidentally inhale and kill insects.

Section 2 Assessment

Reviewing Ideas, Terms, and Places

1. a. **Identify** What is the **caste system**?
   b. **Explain** Why did strict caste rules develop?
2. a. **Identify** What does the *Rigveda* include?
   b. **Analyze** What role did sacrifice play in Aryan society?
3. a. **Define** What is **karma**?
   b. **Sequence** How did Brahmanism develop into Hinduism?
   c. **Elaborate** How does Hinduism reinforce followers' willingness to remain within their castes?
4. a. **Recall** What are the four main teachings of Jainism?
   b. **Predict** How do you think the idea of **nonviolence** affected the daily lives of Jains in ancient India?

Critical Thinking

5. **Analyzing Causes** Draw a graphic organizer like this one. Using your notes, explain how Hinduism developed from Brahmanism and how Jainism developed from Hinduism.

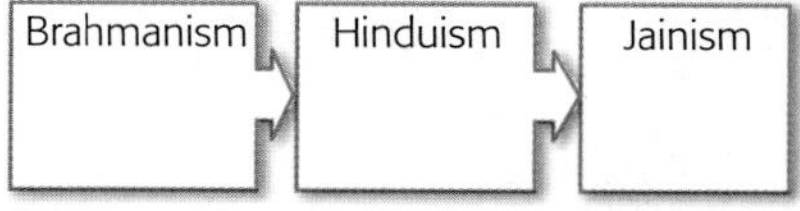

FOCUS ON WRITING

6. **Illustrating Hinduism** Now you have another possible topic for your poster. How might you illustrate a complex religion like Hinduism? What pictures would work best?

SECTION 3

Origins of Buddhism

What You Will Learn...

Main Ideas

1. Siddhartha Gautama searched for wisdom in many ways.
2. The teachings of Buddhism deal with finding peace.
3. Buddhism spread far from where it began in India.

The Big Idea

Buddhism began in India and became a major religion.

Key Terms

fasting, *p. 29*
meditation, *p. 29*
nirvana, *p. 30*
missionaries, *p. 32*

Use the graphic organizer online to take notes on the basic ideas of Buddhism and on Buddhism's spread.

If YOU lived there...

You are a trader traveling in northern India in about 520 BC. As you pass through a town, you see a crowd of people sitting silently in the shade of a huge tree. A man sitting at the foot of the tree is speaking about how one ought to live. His words are like nothing you have heard from the Hindu priests.

Will you stay to listen? Why or why not?

BUILDING BACKGROUND The Jains were not the only ones to break from Hinduism. In the 500s BC a young Indian prince attracted many people to his teachings about how people should live.

Siddhartha's Search for Wisdom

In the late 500s BC a restless young man, dissatisfied with the teachings of Hinduism, began to ask his own questions about life and religious matters. In time, he found answers. These answers attracted many followers, and the young man's ideas became the foundation of a major new religion in India.

The Quest for Answers

The restless young man was Siddhartha Gautama (si-DAHR-tuh GAU-tuh-muh). Born around 563 BC in northern India near the Himalayas, Siddhartha was a prince who grew up in luxury. Born a Kshatriya, a member of the warrior class, Siddhartha never had to struggle with the problems that many people of his time faced. However, Siddhartha was not satisfied. He felt something was missing in his life.

Siddhartha looked around him and saw how hard most people had to work and how much they suffered. He saw people grieving for lost loved ones and wondered why there was so much pain in the world. As a result, Siddhartha began to ask questions about the meaning of human life.

In this painting, Prince Siddhartha leaves his palace to search for the true meaning of life, an event known as the Great Departure. Special helpers called *ganas* hold his horse's hooves so he won't awaken anyone.

Before Siddhartha reached age 30, he left his home and family to look for answers. His journey took him to many regions in India. Wherever he traveled, he had discussions with priests and people known for their wisdom. Yet no one could give convincing answers to Siddhartha's questions.

The Buddha Finds Enlightenment

Siddhartha did not give up. Instead, he became even more determined to find the answers he was seeking. For several years, he wandered in search of answers.

Siddhartha wanted to free his mind from daily concerns. For a while, he did not even wash himself. He also started **fasting**, or going without food. He devoted much of his time to **meditation**, the focusing of the mind on spiritual ideas.

According to legend, Siddhartha spent six years wandering throughout India. He eventually came to a place near the town of Gaya, close to the Ganges River. There, he sat down under a tree and meditated. After seven weeks of deep meditation, he suddenly had the answers that he had been looking for. He had realized that human suffering comes from three things:

- wanting what we like but do not have,
- wanting to keep what we like and already have, and
- not wanting what we dislike but have.

Siddhartha spent seven more weeks meditating under the tree, which his followers later named the Tree of Wisdom. He then described his new ideas to five of his former companions. His followers later called this talk the First Sermon.

Focus on Reading
What steps did the Buddha take in his search for enlightenment?

Siddhartha Gautama was about 35 years old when he found enlightenment under the tree. From that point on, he would be called the Buddha (BOO-duh), or the "Enlightened One." The Buddha spent the rest of his life traveling across northern India and teaching people his ideas.

Reading Check **Summarizing** What did the Buddha conclude about the cause of suffering?

Teachings of Buddhism

As he traveled, the Buddha gained many followers. Many of these followers were merchants and artisans, but he even taught a few kings. These followers were the first believers in Buddhism, the religion based on the teachings of the Buddha.

The Buddha was raised Hindu, and many of his teachings reflected Hindu ideas. Like Hindus, he believed that people should act morally and treat others well. In one of his sermons, he said

> "Let a man overcome anger by love. Let him overcome the greedy by liberality [giving], the liar by truth. This is called progress in the discipline [training] of the Blessed."
>
> –The Buddha, quoted in *The History of Nations: India*

Four Noble Truths

At the heart of the Buddha's teachings were four guiding principles. These became known as the Four Noble Truths:

1. Suffering and unhappiness are a part of human life. No one can escape sorrow.
2. Suffering comes from our desires for pleasure and material goods. People cause their own misery because they want things they cannot have.
3. People can overcome their desires and ignorance and reach **nirvana**, a state of perfect peace. Reaching nirvana would free a person's soul from suffering and from the need for further reincarnation.
4. People can overcome ignorance and desire by following an eightfold path that leads to wisdom, enlightenment, and salvation.

The chart on the next page shows the steps in the Eightfold Path. The Buddha believed that this path was a middle way between human desires and denying oneself any pleasure. He believed that people should overcome their desire for material goods. They should, however, be reasonable, and not starve their bodies or cause themselves unnecessary pain.

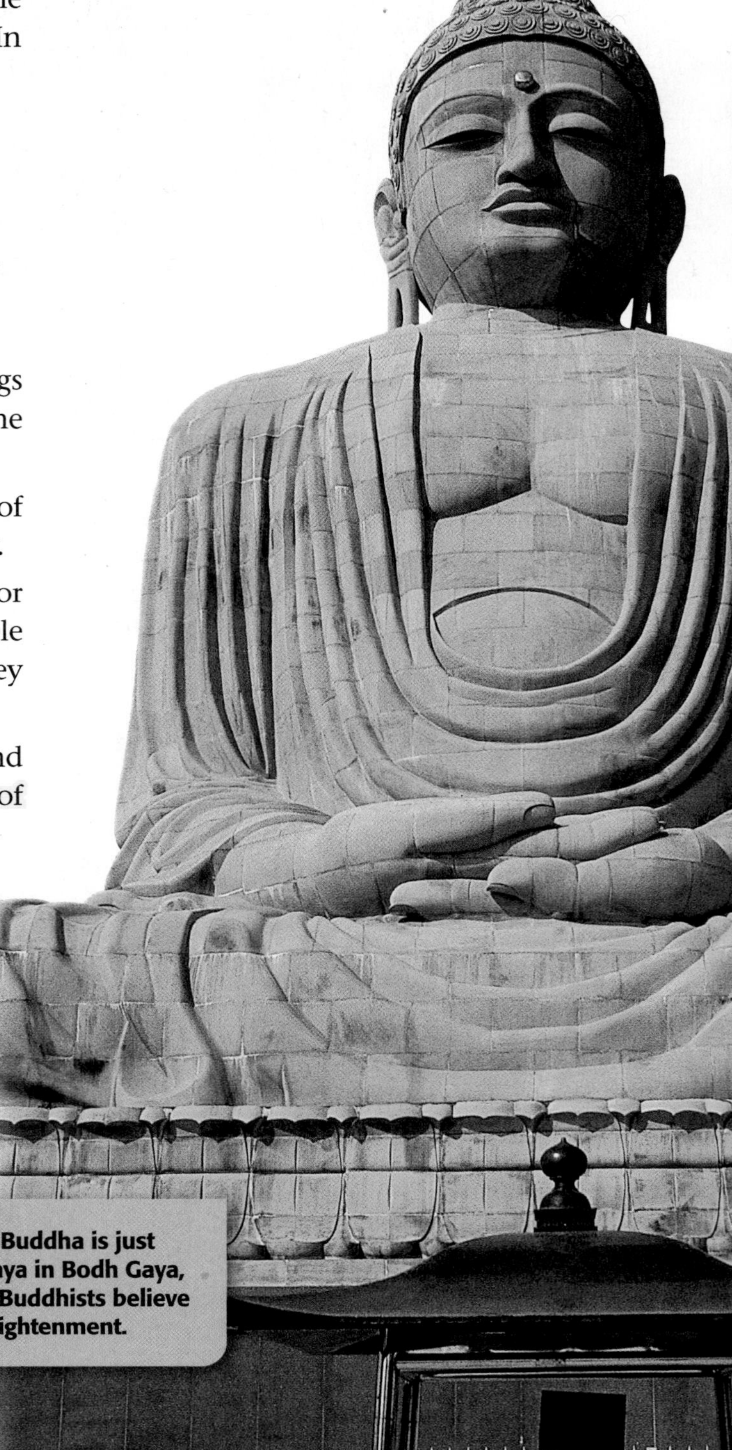

This giant statue of the Buddha is just south of the town of Gaya in Bodh Gaya, India—the place where Buddhists believe Siddhartha reached enlightenment.

The Eightfold Path

1. **Right Thought**
Believe in the nature of existence as suffering and in the Four Noble Truths.

2. **Right Intent**
Incline toward goodness and kindness.

3. **Right Speech**
Avoid lies and gossip.

4. **Right Action**
Don't steal from or harm others.

5. **Right Livelihood**
Reject work that hurts others.

6. **Right Effort**
Prevent evil and do good.

7. **Right Mindfulness**
Control your feelings and thoughts.

8. **Right Concentration**
Practice proper meditation.

Challenging Hindu Ideas

Some of the Buddha's teachings challenged traditional Hindu ideas. For example, the Buddha rejected many of the ideas contained in the Vedas, such as animal sacrifice. He told people that they did not have to follow these texts.

The Buddha challenged the authority of the Hindu priests, the Brahmins. He did not believe that they or their rituals were necessary for enlightenment. Instead, he taught that it was the responsibility of each person to work for his or her own salvation. Priests could not help them. However, the Buddha did not reject the Hindu teaching of reincarnation. He taught that people who failed to reach nirvana would have to be reborn time and time again until they achieved it.

The Buddha was opposed to the caste system. He didn't think that people should be confined to a particular place in society. He taught that every person who followed the Eightfold Path properly would reach nirvana. It didn't matter what *varna* or caste they had belonged to in life as long as they lived the way they should.

The Buddha's opposition to the caste system won him the support of the masses. Many herders, farmers, artisans, and untouchables liked hearing that their low social rank would not be a barrier to their enlightenment. Unlike Hinduism, Buddhism made them feel that they had the power to change their lives.

The Buddha also gained followers among the higher classes. Many rich and powerful Indians welcomed his ideas about avoiding extreme behavior while seeking salvation. By the time of his death around 483 BC, the Buddha's influence was spreading rapidly throughout India.

READING CHECK **Comparing** How did Buddha's teachings agree with Hinduism?

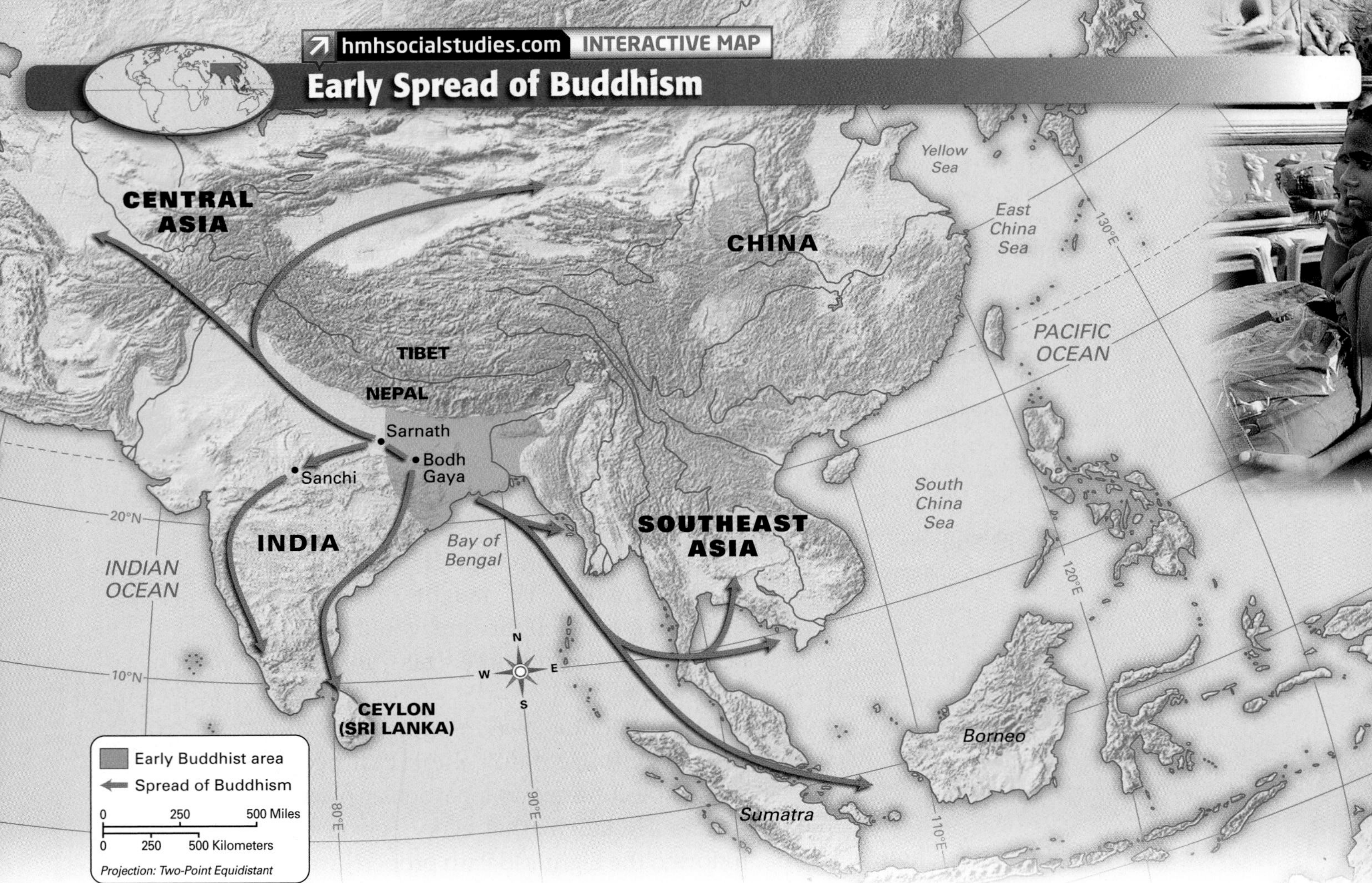

hmhsocialstudies.com
ANIMATED GEOGRAPHY
The Spread of Buddhism

Buddhism Spreads

Buddhism continued to attract followers after the Buddha's death. After spreading through India, the religion began to spread to other areas as well.

Buddhism Spreads in India

According to Buddhist tradition, 500 of the Buddha's followers gathered together shortly after he died. They wanted to make sure that the Buddha's teachings were remembered correctly.

In the years after this council, the Buddha's followers spread his teachings throughout India. The ideas spread very quickly, because Buddhist teachings were popular and easy to understand. Within 200 years of the Buddha's death, Buddhism had spread through most of India.

Buddhism Spreads beyond India

The spread of Buddhism increased after one of the most powerful kings in India, Asoka, became Buddhist in the 200s BC. Once he converted, he built Buddhist temples and schools throughout India. More importantly, though, he worked to spread Buddhism into areas outside of India. You will learn more about Asoka and his accomplishments in the next section.

Asoka sent Buddhist **missionaries**, or people who work to spread their religious beliefs, to other kingdoms in Asia. One group of these missionaries sailed to the island of Sri Lanka around 251 BC. Others followed trade routes east to what is now Myanmar and to other parts of Southeast Asia. Missionaries also went north to areas near the Himalayas.

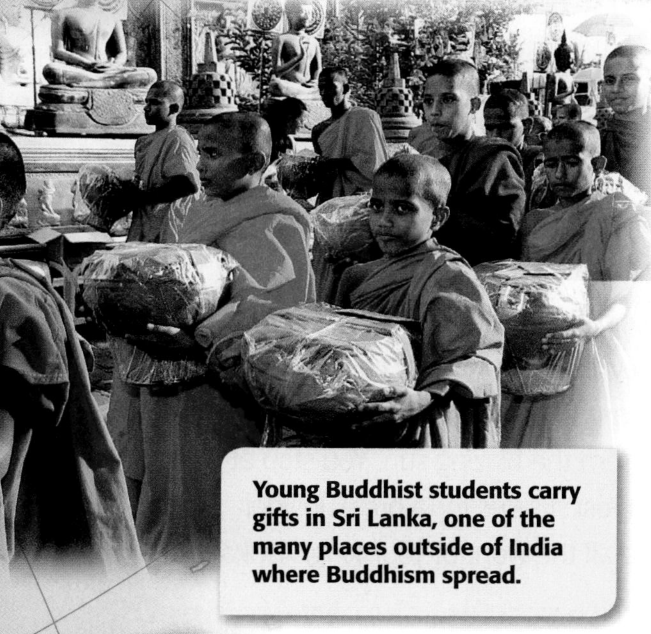

Young Buddhist students carry gifts in Sri Lanka, one of the many places outside of India where Buddhism spread.

map zone Geography Skills

Movement After the Buddha died, his teachings were carried through much of Asia.

1. **Identify** Buddhism spread to what island south of India?
2. **Interpret** What physical feature kept Buddhist missionaries from moving directly into China?

Missionaries also introduced Buddhism to lands west of India. They founded Buddhist communities in Central Asia and Persia. They even taught about Buddhism as far away as Syria and Egypt.

Buddhism continued to grow over the centuries. Eventually, it spread via the Silk Road into China, then Korea and Japan. Through their work, missionaries taught Buddhism to millions of people.

A Split within Buddhism

Even as Buddhism spread through Asia, however, it began to change. Not all Buddhists could agree on their beliefs and practices. Eventually, disagreements between Buddhists led to a split within the religion. Two major branches of Buddhism were created—Theravada and Mahayana.

Members of the Theravada branch tried to follow the Buddha's teachings exactly as he had stated them. Mahayana Buddhists, though, believed that other people could interpret the Buddha's teachings to help people reach nirvana. Both branches have millions of believers today, but Mahayana is by far the larger branch.

READING CHECK **Sequencing** How did the Buddha's teachings spread out of India?

SUMMARY AND PREVIEW Buddhism, one of India's major religions, grew more popular once it was adopted by rulers of India's great empires. You will learn more about those empires in the next section.

Section 3 Assessment

Reviewing Ideas, Terms, and Places

1. a. **Identify** Who was the Buddha, and what does the term *Buddha* mean?
   b. **Summarize** How did Siddhartha Gautama free his mind and clarify his thinking as he searched for wisdom?
2. a. **Identify** What is **nirvana**?
   b. **Contrast** How are Buddhist teachings different from Hindu teachings?
   c. **Elaborate** Why do Buddhists believe that following the Eightfold Path leads to a better life?
3. a. **Describe** Into what lands did Buddhism spread?
   b. **Summarize** What role did **missionaries** play in spreading Buddhism?

Critical Thinking

4. **Finding Main Ideas** Draw a diagram like this one. Use it and your notes to identify and describe Buddhism's Four Noble Truths. Write a sentence explaining how the Truths are central to Buddhism.

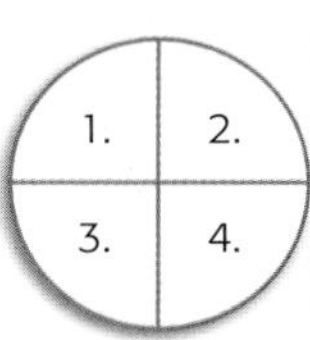

FOCUS ON WRITING

5. **Considering Indian Religions** Look back over what you've read and your notes about Hinduism. Perhaps you will want to focus your poster on ancient India's two major religions. Think about how you could design a poster around this theme.

SECTION 4

Indian Empires

What You Will Learn...

Main Ideas

1. The Mauryan Empire unified most of India.
2. Gupta rulers promoted Hinduism in their empire.

The Big Idea

The Mauryas and the Guptas built great empires in India.

Key Terms

mercenaries, *p. 34*
edicts, *p. 35*

Use the graphic organizer online to take notes about the rise and fall of ancient India's two greatest empires.

If YOU lived there...

You are a merchant in India in about 240 BC. You travel from town to town on your donkey, carrying bolts of colorful cloth. In the heat of summer, you are grateful for the banyan trees along the road. They shelter you from the blazing sun. You stop at wells for cool drinks of water and rest houses for a break in your journey. You know these are all the work of your king, Asoka.

How do you feel about your king?

BUILDING BACKGROUND For centuries after the Aryan migration, India was divided into small states. Each state had its own ruler and laws. Then, in the 300s BC, a foreign general, Alexander the Great, took over and unified part of northwestern India. Soon after Alexander departed, a strong leader united India.

Mauryan Empire Unifies India

In the 320s BC a military leader named Candragupta Maurya (kuhn-druh-GOOP-tuh MOUR-yuh) rose to power in northern India. Using an army of **mercenaries**, or hired soldiers, he seized control of the entire northern part of India. By doing so, he founded the Mauryan Empire. Mauryan rule lasted for about 150 years.

The Mauryan Empire

Candragupta Maurya ruled his empire with the help of a complex government. It included a network of spies and a huge army of some 600,000 soldiers. The army also had thousands of war elephants and thousands of chariots. In return for the army's protection, farmers paid a heavy tax to the government.

In 301 BC Candragupta decided to become a Jainist monk. To do so, he had to give up his throne. He passed the throne to his son, who continued to expand the empire. Before long, the Mauryas ruled all of northern India and much of central India as well.

Asoka

Around 270 BC Candragupta's grandson Asoka (uh-SOH-kuh) became king. Asoka was a strong ruler, the strongest of all the Mauryan emperors. He extended Mauryan rule over most of India. In conquering other kingdoms, Asoka made his own empire both stronger and richer.

For many years, Asoka watched his armies fight bloody battles against other peoples. A few years into his rule, however, Asoka converted to Buddhism. When he did, he swore that he would not launch any more wars of conquest.

After converting to Buddhism, Asoka had the time and resources to improve the lives of his people. He had wells dug and roads built throughout the empire. Along these roads, workers planted shade trees, built rest houses for travelers, and raised large stone pillars carved with Buddhist **edicts**, or laws. Asoka also encouraged the spread of Buddhism in India and the rest of Asia. As you read in the previous section, he sent missionaries to lands all over Asia.

Asoka died in 233 BC, and the empire began to fall apart soon afterward. His sons fought for power, and invaders threatened the empire. In 184 BC the last Mauryan king was killed by one of his generals. India divided into smaller states once again.

FOCUS ON READING What were some key events in Asoka's life? In what order did they occur?

READING CHECK **Finding Main Ideas** How did the Mauryans gain control of most of India?

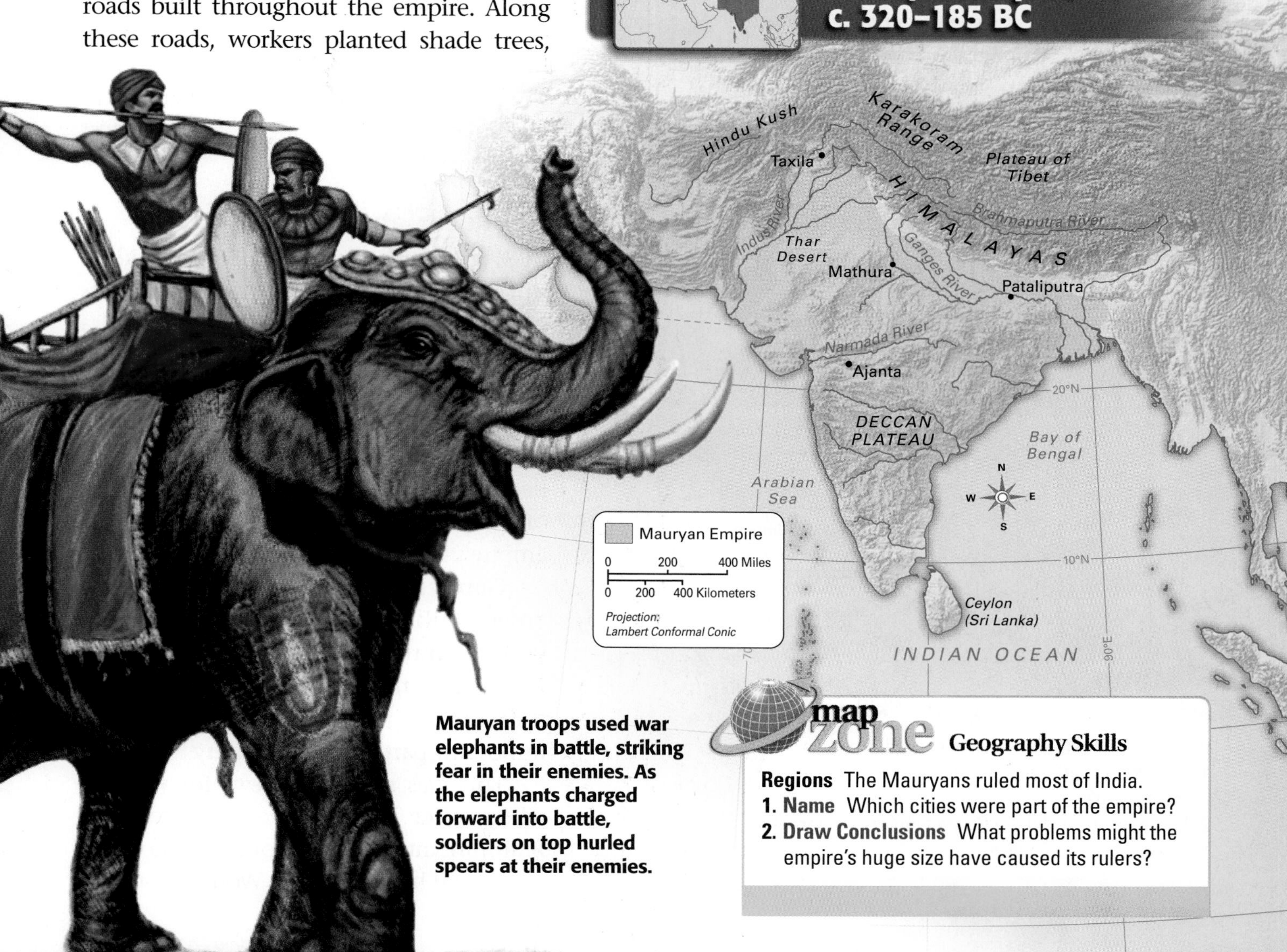

Mauryan troops used war elephants in battle, striking fear in their enemies. As the elephants charged forward into battle, soldiers on top hurled spears at their enemies.

map zone **Geography Skills**

Regions The Mauryans ruled most of India.

1. **Name** Which cities were part of the empire?
2. **Draw Conclusions** What problems might the empire's huge size have caused its rulers?

Gupta Rulers Promote Hinduism

After the collapse of the Mauryan Empire, India remained divided for about 500 years. During that period, Buddhism continued to prosper and spread in India, and so the popularity of Hinduism declined.

A New Hindu Empire

ACADEMIC VOCABULARY
establish to set up or create

Eventually, however, a new dynasty was **establish**ed in India. It was the Gupta (GOOP-tuh) dynasty, which took over India around AD 320. Under the Guptas, India was once again united, and it once again became prosperous.

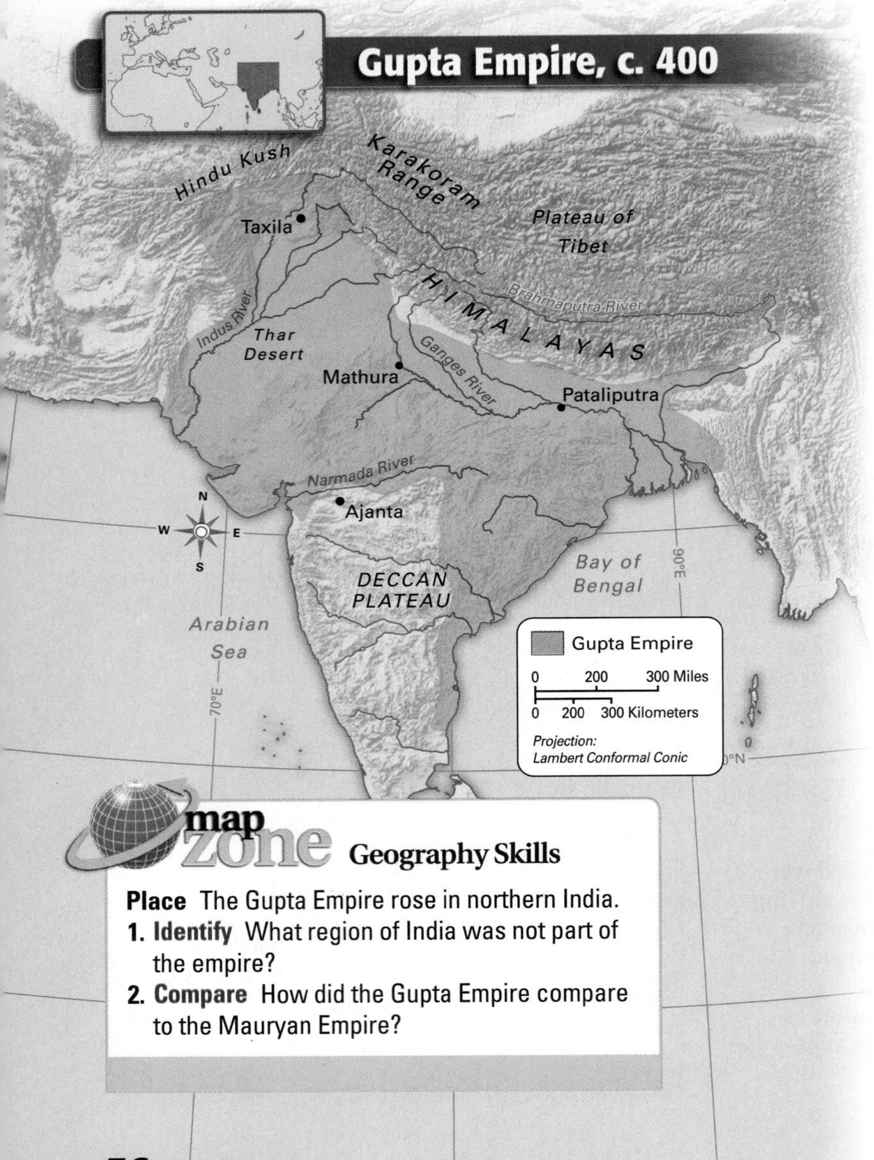

map zone Geography Skills

Place The Gupta Empire rose in northern India.

1. **Identify** What region of India was not part of the empire?
2. **Compare** How did the Gupta Empire compare to the Mauryan Empire?

The first Gupta emperor was Candra Gupta I. Although their names are similar, he was not related to Candragupta Maurya. From his base in northern India, Candra Gupta's armies invaded and conquered neighboring lands. Eventually, he brought much of the northern part of India under his control.

Indian civilization flourished under the Gupta rulers. These rulers were Hindu, so Hinduism became India's dominant religion. Gupta kings built many Hindu temples, some of which became models for later Indian architecture. They also promoted a revival of Hindu writings and worship practices.

Although they were Hindus, the Gupta rulers also supported the religious beliefs of Buddhism and Jainism. They promoted Buddhist art and built Buddhist temples. They also established a university at Nalanda that became one of Asia's greatest centers for Buddhist studies.

Gupta Society

In 375 Emperor Candra Gupta II took the throne in India. Gupta society reached its high point during his rule. Under Candra Gupta II, the empire continued to grow, eventually stretching all the way across northern India. At the same time, the empire's economy strengthened, and so people prospered. They created fine works of art and literature. Outsiders admired the empire's wealth and beauty.

Gupta kings believed the strict social order of the Hindu caste system would strengthen their rule. They also thought it would keep the empire stable. As a result, the Guptas considered the caste system an important part of Indian society.

This was not good news for women, whose roles were limited by caste rules. Brahmins taught that a woman's role was to marry and have children. Women couldn't

Gupta Art

This Gupta painting of a palace scene shows some of India's different castes. Gupta rulers supported Hinduism and the caste system.

even choose their own husbands. Parents arranged all marriages. Once married, wives had few rights. They were expected to serve their husbands. Widows had an even lower social status than other women.

Gupta rule remained strong in India until the late 400s. At that time the Huns, a group from Central Asia, invaded India from the northwest. Their fierce attacks drained the Gupta Empire of its power and wealth. As the Hun armies marched farther into India, the Guptas lost hope. By the middle of the 500s, Gupta rule had ended, and India had divided into small kingdoms yet again.

READING CHECK **Summarizing** What was the Gupta dynasty's position on religion?

SUMMARY AND PREVIEW The Mauryans and Guptas united much of India in their empires. Next, you will learn about their many achievements.

Section 4 Assessment

hmhsocialstudies.com
ONLINE QUIZ

Reviewing Ideas, Terms, and Places

1. **a. Identify** Who created the Mauryan Empire?
   b. Summarize What happened after Asoka became a Buddhist?
   c. Elaborate Why do you think many people consider Asoka the greatest of all Mauryan rulers?
2. **a. Recall** What religion did most of the Gupta rulers belong to?
   b. Compare and Contrast How were the rulers Candragupta Maurya and Candra Gupta I alike, and how were they different?
   c. Evaluate Do you think the Gupta enforcement of caste rules was a good idea? Why or why not?

Critical Thinking

3. **Categorizing** Draw a chart like this one. Fill it with facts about India's rulers.

Ruler	Dynasty	Accomplishments

FOCUS ON WRITING

4. **Comparing Indian Empires** Another possible topic for your poster could be a comparison of the Mauryan and Gupta empires. Jot down ideas on what you could show in such a comparison.

BIOGRAPHY

Asoka

How can one decision change a man's entire life?

When did he live? before 230 BC

Where did he live? Asoka's empire included much of northern and central India.

What did he do? After fighting many bloody wars to expand his empire, Asoka gave up violence and converted to Buddhism.

Why is he important? Asoka is one of the most respected rulers in Indian history and one of the most important figures in the history of Buddhism. As a devout Buddhist, Asoka worked for years to spread the Buddha's teachings. In addition to sending missionaries around Asia, he had huge columns carved with Buddhist teachings raised all over India. Largely through his efforts, Buddhism became one of Asia's main religions.

Generalizing How did Asoka's life change after he became Buddhist?

KEY EVENTS

- **c. 270 BC** Asoka becomes the Mauryan emperor.
- **c. 261 BC** Asoka's empire reaches its greatest size.
- **c. 261 BC** Asoka becomes a Buddhist.
- **c. 251 BC** Asoka begins to send Buddhist missionaries to other parts of Asia.

This Buddhist shrine, located in Sanchi, India, was built by Asoka.

Indian Achievements

SECTION 5

If YOU lived there...

You are a traveler in western India in the 300s. You are visiting a cave temple that is carved into a mountain cliff. Inside the cave it is cool and quiet. Huge columns rise all around you. You don't feel you're alone, for the walls and ceilings are covered with paintings. They are filled with lively scenes and figures. In the center is a large statue with calm, peaceful features.

How does this cave make you feel?

BUILDING BACKGROUND The Mauryan and Gupta empires united most of India politically. During these empires, Indian artists, writers, scholars, and scientists made great advances. Some of their works are still studied and admired today.

Religious Art

The Indians of the Mauryan and Gupta periods created great works of art, many of them religious. Many of their paintings and sculptures illustrated either Hindu or Buddhist teachings. Magnificent temples—both Hindu and Buddhist—were built all around India. They remain some of the most beautiful buildings in the world today.

Temples

Early Hindu temples were small, stone structures. They had flat roofs and contained only one or two rooms. In the Gupta period, though, temple architecture became more complex. Gupta temples were topped by huge towers and were covered with carvings of the god worshipped inside.

Buddhist temples of the Gupta period are also impressive. Some Buddhists carved entire temples out of mountainsides. The most famous such temples are at Ajanta and Ellora. Builders filled the caves there with beautiful paintings and sculpture.

What You Will Learn...

Main Ideas

1. Indian artists created great works of religious art.
2. Sanskrit literature flourished during the Gupta period.
3. The Indians made scientific advances in metalworking, medicine, and other sciences.

The Big Idea

The people of ancient India made great contributions to the arts and sciences.

Key Terms

metallurgy, *p. 42*
alloys, *p. 42*
Hindu-Arabic numerals, *p. 42*
inoculation, *p. 42*
astronomy, *p. 43*

Use the graphic organizer online to take notes on the achievements of ancient India.

This Hindu temple is covered with finely detailed carvings and decorations. Many individual sculptures are images of major Hindu gods, like the statue of Vishnu above.

Another type of Buddhist temple was the stupa. Stupas had domed roofs and were built to house sacred items from the life of the Buddha. Many of them were covered with detailed carvings.

Paintings and Sculpture

The Gupta period also saw the creation of countless works of art, both paintings and statues. Painting was a greatly respected profession, and India was home to many skilled artists. However, we don't know the names of many artists from this period. Instead, we know the names of many rich and powerful members of Gupta society who paid artists to create works of beauty and religious and social significance.

Most Indian paintings of the Gupta period are clear and colorful. Some of them show graceful Indians wearing fine jewelry and stylish clothes. Such paintings offer us a glimpse of the Indians' daily and ceremonial lives.

Artists from both of India's major religions, Hinduism and Buddhism, drew on their beliefs to create their works. As a result, many of the finest paintings of ancient India are found in temples. Hindu painters drew hundreds of gods on temple walls and entrances. Buddhists covered the walls and ceilings of temples with scenes from the life of the Buddha.

Indian sculptors also created great works. Many of their statues were made for Buddhist cave temples. In addition to the temples' intricately carved columns, sculptors carved statues of kings and the Buddha. Some of these statues tower over the cave entrances. Hindu temples also featured impressive statues of their gods. In fact, the walls of some temples, such as the one pictured above, were completely covered with carvings and images.

READING CHECK **Summarizing** How did religion influence ancient Indian art?

Sanskrit Literature

As you read earlier, Sanskrit was the main language of the ancient Aryans. During the Mauryan and Gupta periods, many works of Sanskrit literature were created. These works were later translated into many other languages.

Religious Epics

The greatest of these Sanskrit writings are two religious epics, the *Mahabharata* (muh-HAH-BAH-ruh-tuh) and the *Ramayana* (rah-MAH-yuh-nuh). Still popular in India, the *Mahabharata* is one of the longest literary works ever written. It is a story about a struggle between two families for control of a kingdom. Included within the story are long passages about Hindu beliefs. The most famous is called the *Bhagavad Gita* (BUG-uh-vuhd GEE-tah).

The *Ramayana,* another great epic, tells about a prince named Rama. In truth, the prince was the god Vishnu in human form. He had become human so he could rid the world of demons. He also had to rescue his wife, a princess named Sita. For centuries, characters from the *Ramayana* have been seen as models for how Indians should behave. For example, Rama is seen as the ideal ruler and his relationship with Sita as the ideal marriage.

Other Works

Writers in the Gupta period also created plays, poetry, and other types of literature. One famous writer of this time was Kalidasa (kahl-ee-DAHS-uh). His work was so brilliant that Candra Gupta II hired him to write plays for the royal court.

Sometime before 500, Indian writers also produced a book of stories called the *Panchatantra* (PUHN-chuh-TAHN-truh). The stories in this collection were intended to teach lessons. They praise people for cleverness and quick thinking. Each story ends with a message about winning friends, losing property, waging war, or some other idea. For example, the message below warns listeners to think about what they are doing before they act.

> "The good and bad of given schemes
> Wise thought must first reveal:
> The stupid heron saw his chicks
> Provide a mongoose meal."
>
> –from the *Panchatantra*, translated by Arthur William Ryder

Eventually, translations of this popular collection spread throughout the world. It became popular in countries even as far away as Europe.

READING CHECK **Categorizing** What types of literature did writers of ancient India create?

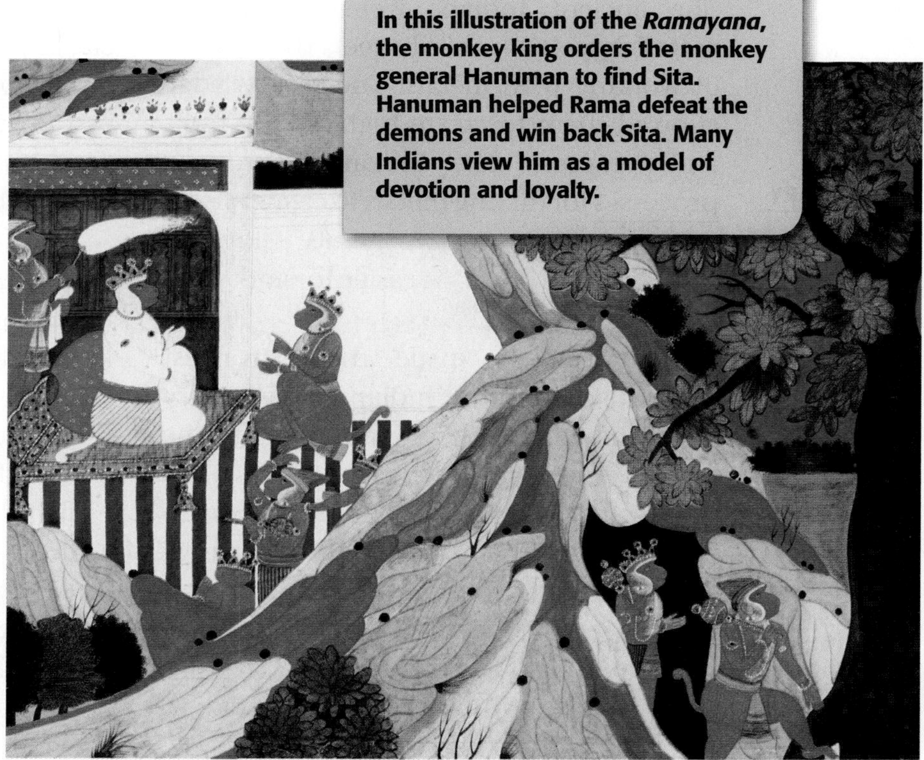

In this illustration of the *Ramayana*, the monkey king orders the monkey general Hanuman to find Sita. Hanuman helped Rama defeat the demons and win back Sita. Many Indians view him as a model of devotion and loyalty.

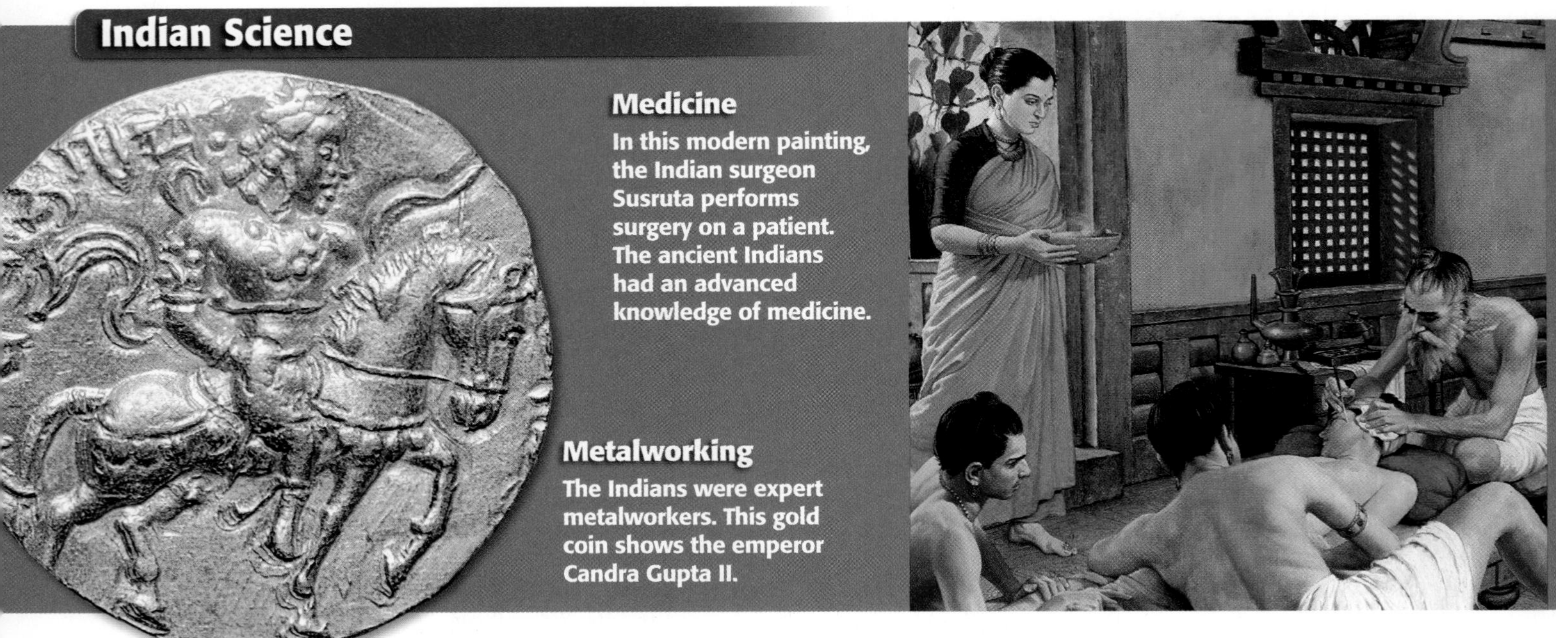

Indian Science

Medicine
In this modern painting, the Indian surgeon Susruta performs surgery on a patient. The ancient Indians had an advanced knowledge of medicine.

Metalworking
The Indians were expert metalworkers. This gold coin shows the emperor Candra Gupta II.

Scientific Advances

Indian achievements were not limited to art, architecture, and literature. Indian scholars also made important advances in metalworking, math, and the sciences.

Metalworking

The ancient Indians were pioneers of **metallurgy** (MET-uhl-uhr-jee), the science of working with metals. Their knowledge allowed them to create high-quality tools and weapons. The Indians also knew processes for mixing metals to create **alloys**, mixtures of two or more metals. Alloys are sometimes stronger or easier to work with than pure metals.

ACADEMIC VOCABULARY
process a series of steps by which a task is accomplished

Metalworkers made their strongest products out of iron. Indian iron was very hard and pure. These features made the iron a valuable trade item.

During the Gupta dynasty, metal-workers built the famous Iron Pillar near Delhi. Unlike most iron, which rusts easily, the pillar is very resistant to rust. The tall column still attracts crowds of visitors. Scholars study this column even today to learn the Indians' secrets.

THE IMPACT TODAY
People still get inoculations against many diseases.

Mathematics and Other Sciences

Gupta scholars also made advances in math and science. In fact, they were among the most skilled mathematicians of their day. They developed many of the elements of our modern math system. The very numbers we use today are called **Hindu-Arabic numerals** because they were created by Indian scholars and brought to Europe by Arabs. The Indians were also the first people to create the zero. Although it may seem like a small thing, modern math wouldn't be possible without the zero.

The ancient Indians were also very skilled in the medical sciences. As early as the AD 100s, doctors were writing their knowledge down in textbooks. Among the skills these books describe is how to make medicines from plants and minerals.

Besides curing people with medicines, Indian doctors knew how to protect them against diseases. They used **inoculation** (i-nah-kyuh-LAY-shuhn), the practice of injecting a person with a small dose of a virus to help him or her build a defense to a disease. By fighting off this small dose, the body learns to protect itself.

Mathematics

The Hindu scholar Aryabhata was a mathematician and astronomer. He wrote one of the first books on algebra about AD 500.

Astronomy

The Gupta made great advances in astronomy, despite their lack of modern devices such as telescopes. They used devices like this one from the 1700s to observe and map the stars.

ANALYSIS SKILL **ANALYZING VISUALS**

What are some areas of science that people studied in ancient India?

For people who were injured, Indian doctors could perform surgery. Surgeons repaired broken bones, treated wounds, removed infected tonsils, reconstructed broken noses, and even reattached torn earlobes! If they could find no other cure for an illness, doctors would cast magic spells to help people recover.

Indian interest in **astronomy**, the study of stars and planets, dates back to early times as well. Indian astronomers knew of seven of the nine planets in our solar system. They knew that the sun was a star and that the planets revolved around it. They also knew that the earth was a sphere and that it spun on its axis. In addition, they could predict eclipses of the sun and the moon.

READING CHECK **Finding Main Ideas** What were two Indian achievements in mathematics?

SUMMARY AND PREVIEW From a group of cities along the Indus and Sarasvati Rivers, India grew into a major empire whose people made great achievements. In the next chapter, you'll read about another civilization that experienced similar growth—China.

Section 5 Assessment

Reviewing Ideas, Terms, and Places

1. a. **Describe** What did Hindu temples of the Gupta period look like?
   b. **Analyze** How can you tell that Indian artists were well respected?
   c. **Evaluate** Why do you think Hindu and Buddhist temples contained great works of art?
2. a. **Identify** What is the *Bhagavad Gita*?
   b. **Explain** Why were the stories of the *Panchatantra* written?
   c. **Elaborate** Why do you think people are still interested in ancient Sanskrit epics today?
3. a. **Define** What is **metallurgy**?
   b. **Explain** Why do we call the numbers we use today **Hindu-Arabic numerals**?

Critical Thinking

4. **Categorizing** Draw a chart like this one. Identify the scientific advances that fall into each category below.

Metallurgy	Math	Medicine	Astronomy

Focus on Writing

5. **Highlighting Indian Achievements** List the Indian achievements you could include on a poster. Consider these topics as well as your topic ideas from earlier sections in this chapter. Choose one topic for your poster.

Comparing Maps

Learn

Maps are a necessary tool in the study of both history and geography. Sometimes, however, a map does not contain all the information you need. In those cases, you may have to compare two or more maps and combine what is shown on each.

For example, if you look at a physical map of India you can see what landforms are in a region. You can then look at a population map to see how many people live in that region. From this comparison, you can conclude how the region's landforms affect its population distribution.

Practice

Compare the two maps on this page to answer the following questions.

1. What was the northeastern boundary of the Gupta Empire? What is the physical landscape like there?
2. What region of India was never part of the Gupta Empire? Based on the physical map, what might have been one reason for this?

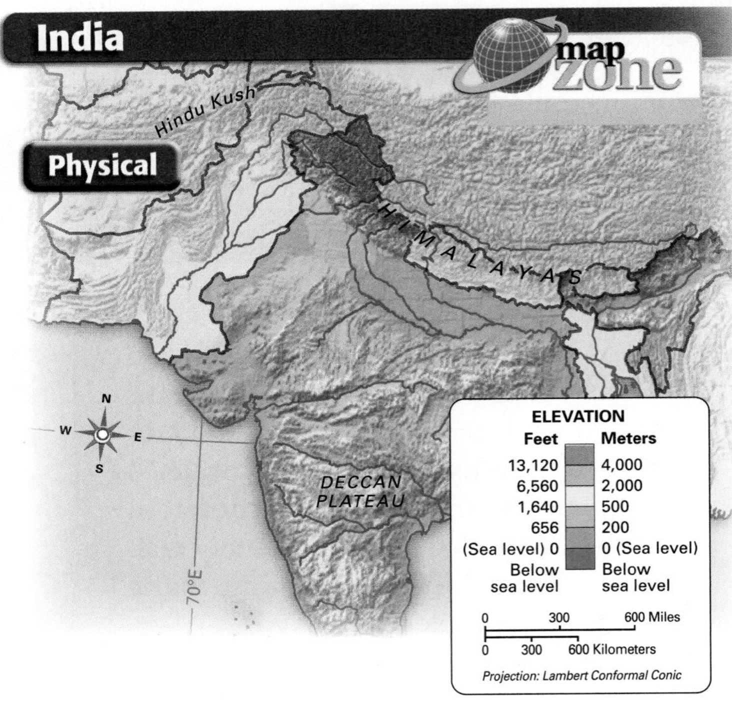

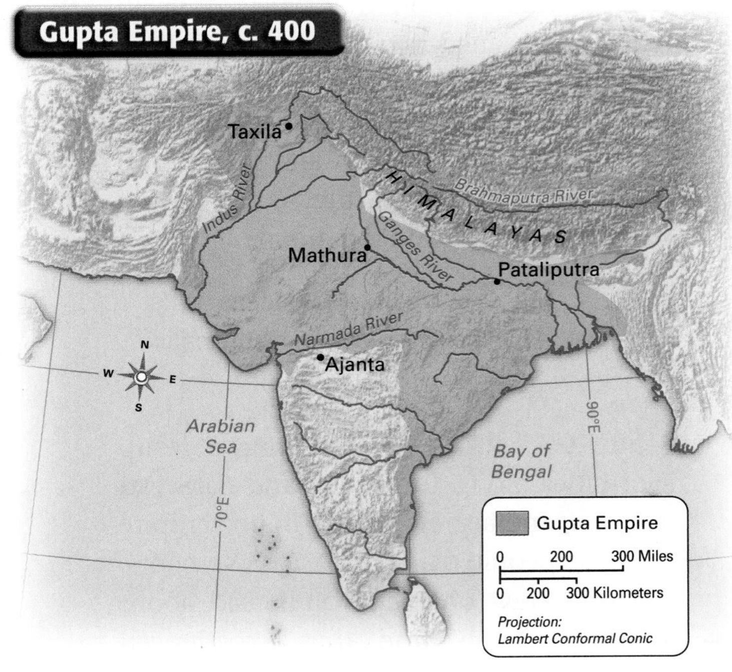

Apply

Choose two maps from this chapter or two maps from the Atlas in this book. Study the two maps and then write three questions that someone could answer by comparing them. Remember that the questions should have people look at both maps to determine the correct answers.

CHAPTER 1

Chapter Review

Geography's Impact
video series
Review the video to answer the closing question:
Do you think enlightenment is an achievable goal in today's world? Why or why not?

Visual Summary

Use the visual summary below to help you review the main ideas of the chapter.

QUICK FACTS

The Harappan civilization began in the Indus River Valley.

Hinduism and Buddhism both developed in India.

Indians made great advances in art, literature, science, and other fields.

Reviewing Vocabulary, Terms, and Places

Fill in the blanks with the correct term or name from this chapter.

1. __________ are hired soldiers.

2. A __________ is a division of people into groups based on birth, wealth, or occupation.

3. Hindus believe in __________, the belief that they will be reborn many times after death.

4. Harappa and __________ were the largest cities of the Harappan civilization.

5. The focusing of the mind on spiritual things is called __________.

6. People who work to spread their religious beliefs are called __________.

7. People who practice __________ use only peaceful ways to achieve change.

8. Indian civilization first developed in the valley of the __________.

9. A mixture of metals is called an __________.

Comprehension and Critical Thinking

SECTION 1 *(Pages 16–21)*

10. a. Describe What caused floods on the Indus River, and what was the result of those floods?

b. Contrast How was Aryan culture different from Harappan culture?

c. Elaborate In what ways was Harappan society an advanced civilization?

SECTION 2 *(Pages 22–27)*

11. a. Identify Who were the Brahmins, and what role did they play in Aryan society?

b. Analyze How do Hindus believe karma affects reincarnation?

c. Elaborate Hinduism has been called both a polytheistic religion—one that worships many gods—and a monotheistic religion—one that worships only one god. Why do you think this is so?

SECTION 3 *(Pages 28–33)*

12. a. Describe What did the Buddha say caused human suffering?

b. Analyze How did Buddhism grow and change after the Buddha died?

c. Elaborate Why did the Buddha's teachings about nirvana appeal to many people of lower castes?

SECTION 4 *(Pages 34–37)*

13. a. Identify What was Candragupta Maurya's greatest accomplishment?

b. Compare and Contrast What was one similarity between the Mauryans and the Guptas? What was one difference between them?

c. Predict How might Indian history have been different if Asoka had not become a Buddhist?

SECTION 5 *(Pages 39–43)*

14. a. Describe What kinds of religious art did the ancient Indians create?

b. Make Inferences Why do you think religious discussions are included in the *Mahabharata?*

c. Evaluate Which of the ancient Indians' achievements do you think is most impressive? Why?

Using the Internet

15. Activity: Making a Brochure In this chapter, you learned about India's early history. That history was largely shaped by India's geography. Through the online book, research the geography and civilizations of India, taking notes as you go along. Finally, use the interactive brochure template to present what you have found.

hmhsocialstudies.com

Social Studies Skills

Comparing Maps *Study the physical and population maps of South and East Asia in the Atlas. Then answer the following questions.*

16. Along what river in northeastern India is the population density very high?

17. Why do you think fewer people live in far northwestern India than in the northeast?

Map Activity

18. Ancient India On a separate sheet of paper, match the letters on the map with their correct labels.

Mohenjo Daro	Indus River
Harappa	Ganges River
Bodh Gaya	

hmhsocialstudies.com INTERACTIVE MAP

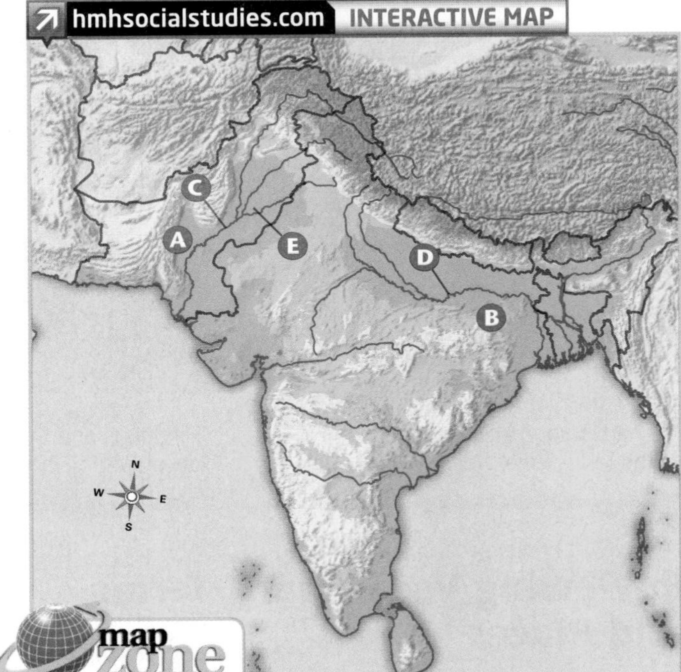

Focus on Reading and Writing

19. Sequencing Arrange the following list of events in the order in which they happened. Then write a brief paragraph describing the events, using clue words such as *then* and *later* to show the proper sequence.

- The Gupta Empire is created.
- Harappan civilization begins.
- The Aryans migrate to India.
- The Mauryan Empire is formed.

20. Designing Your Poster Now that you have a topic for your poster, it's time to create it. On a large sheet of paper or poster board, write a title that identifies your topic. Then draw pictures, maps, or diagrams that illustrate it. Next to each picture, write a short caption to identify what the picture, map, or diagram shows.

CHAPTER 1 Standardized Test Prep

DIRECTIONS: Read questions 1 through 7 and write the letter of the best response. Then read question 8 and write your own well-constructed response.

1 The earliest civilizations in India developed along which river?

A Indus
B Ganges
C Brahmaputra
D Krishna

2 The people of which *varna* in early India had the hardest lives?

A Brahmins
B Kshatriyas
C Sudras
D Vaisyas

3 What is the *main* goal of people who follow Buddhism as it was taught by the Buddha?

A wealth
B rebirth
C missionary work
D reaching nirvana

4 Which Indian ruler greatly enlarged his empire before giving up violence and promoting the spread of Buddhism?

A Candragupta Maurya
B Asoka
C Buddha
D Mahavira

5 Early India's contributions to world civilization included

A developing the world's first calendar.
B creating what is now called algebra.
C inventing the plow and the wheel.
D introducing zero to the number system.

> "From anger comes confusion;
> from confusion memory lapses;
> from broken memory understanding is lost;
> from loss of understanding, he is ruined.
>
> But a man of inner strength
> whose senses experience objects
> without attraction and hatred,
> in self control, finds serenity."
>
> –from the *Bhagavad Gita*,
> translated by Barbara Stoler Miller

6 Read the psssage above. According to this passage, what will a person find if he has inner strength and self control?

A confusion
B loss of understanding
C serenity
D anger

7 According to Hindu teachings, the universal spirit of which everything in the world is part is called

A Vishnu.
B Brahman.
C Siva.
D Buddha.

8 Writing an Expository Essay Now that you have collected your notes about ancient India, you are ready to write your expository essay. Remember, the purpose of this is to inform your reader about the history, culture, and achievements of ancient India. Review your notes and decide which information and details you wish to include in your essay. Start your essay with a statement that clearly presents your controlling idea.

CHAPTER 2

History of Ancient China

1600 BC–AD 1450

Essential Question How did the progression of ruling dynasties shape the culture of ancient China?

What You Will Learn...

In this chapter you will learn about the history and culture of ancient China. China was one of the world's early centers of civilization.

Focus on Reading and Writing

Understanding Chronological Order When you read about history, it is important to keep track of the order in which events happened. You can often use words in the text to help figure this order out. **See the lesson, Understanding Chronological Order, on page 214.**

Writing a Magazine Article You are a freelance writer who has been asked to write a magazine article about the achievements of the ancient Chinese. As you read this chapter, you will collect information. Then you will use the information to write your magazine article.

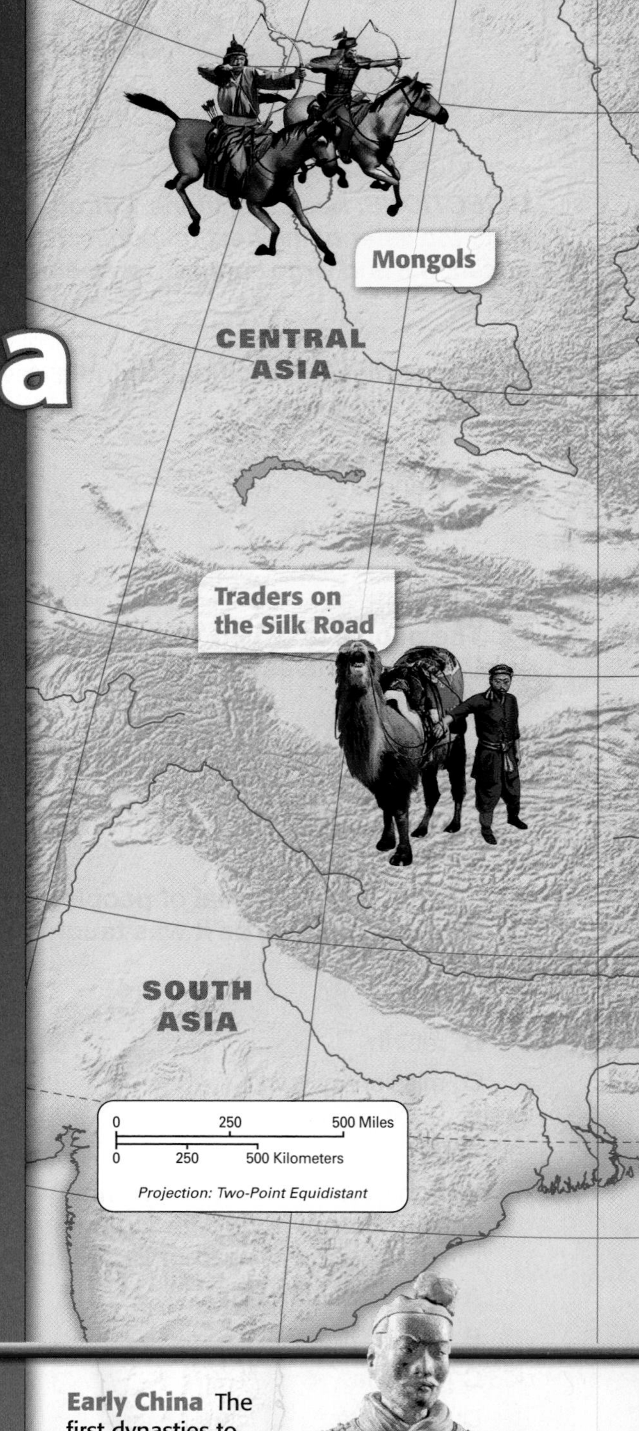

Early China The first dynasties to rule China left behind artifacts such as this clay figure of a soldier.

Ancient China, 1600 BC–AD 1450

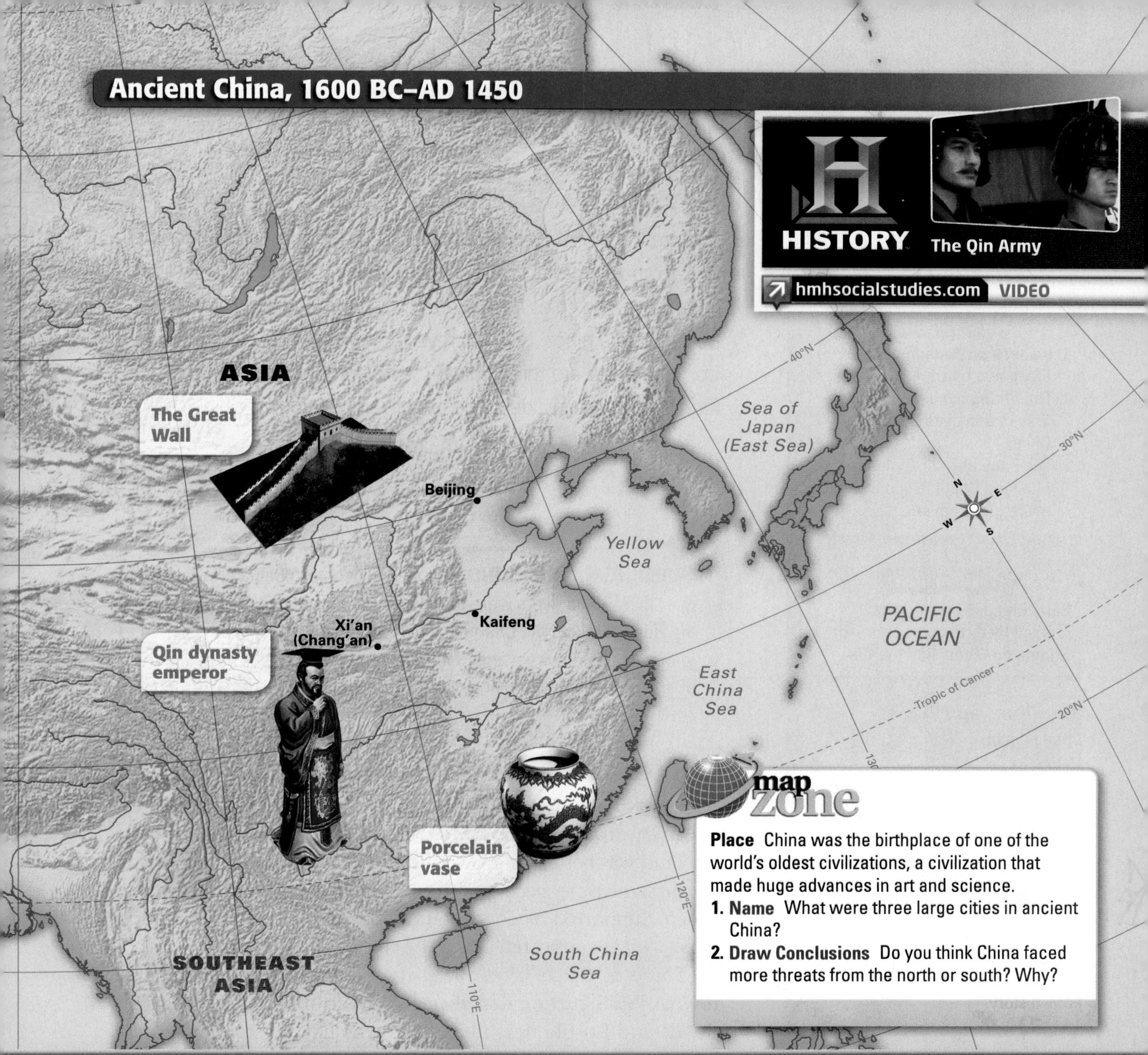

HISTORY The Qin Army

hmhsocialstudies.com VIDEO

ASIA

The Great Wall

Beijing

Sea of Japan (East Sea)

Yellow Sea

Xi'an (Chang'an)

Kaifeng

Qin dynasty emperor

PACIFIC OCEAN

East China Sea

Tropic of Cancer

Porcelain vase

SOUTHEAST ASIA

South China Sea

40°N 30°N 20°N 110°E 120°E 130°E

N E S W

map zone

Place China was the birthplace of one of the world's oldest civilizations, a civilization that made huge advances in art and science.

1. **Name** What were three large cities in ancient China?
2. **Draw Conclusions** Do you think China faced more threats from the north or south? Why?

Tang and Song Dynasties The Chinese invented many items that we still use today, including fireworks.

Yuan and Ming Dynasties During the Yuan and Ming dynasties, Beijing became China's largest city and a center of Chinese culture.

SECTION 1

Early China

What You Will Learn...

Main Ideas

1. Chinese civilization began along two rivers.
2. The Shang dynasty was the first known dynasty to rule China.
3. The Zhou and Qin dynasties changed Chinese society and made great advances.

The Big Idea

Early Chinese history was shaped by three dynasties—the Shang, the Zhou, and the Qin.

Key Terms and Places

Chang Jiang, *p. 50*
Huang He, *p. 50*
mandate of heaven, *p. 52*
Xi'an, *p. 53*
Great Wall, *p. 53*

Use the graphic organizer online to take notes on each period in China's early history.

If YOU lived there...

You are the ruler of China, and hundreds of thousands of people look to you for protection. For many years, your country has lived in peace. Large cities have grown up, and traders travel freely from place to place. Now, however, a new threat looms. Invaders from the north are threatening China's borders. Frightened by the ferocity of these invaders, the people turn to you for help.

What will you do to protect your people?

BUILDING BACKGROUND As in India, people in China first settled near rivers. Two rivers were particularly important in early China—the Huang He and the Chang Jiang. Along these rivers, people began to farm, cities grew up, and China's government was born. The head of that government was an emperor, the ruler of all China.

Chinese Civilization Begins

As early as 7000 BC people had begun to farm in China. They grew rice in the middle **Chang Jiang** Valley. North, along the **Huang He**, the land was better for growing cereals such as millet and wheat. At the same time, people domesticated animals such as pigs and sheep. Supported by these sources of food, China's population grew. Villages appeared along the rivers.

Some of the villages along the Huang He grew into large towns. Walls surrounded these towns to defend them against floods and hostile neighbors. In towns like these, the Chinese left many artifacts, such as arrowheads, fishhooks, tools, and pottery. Some village sites even contained pieces of cloth.

Over time, Chinese culture became more advanced. After 3000 BC people began to use potter's wheels to make many types of pottery. They also learned to dig water wells. As populations grew, villages spread out over larger areas in both northern and southeastern China.

READING CHECK **Analyzing** When and where did China's earliest civilizations develop?

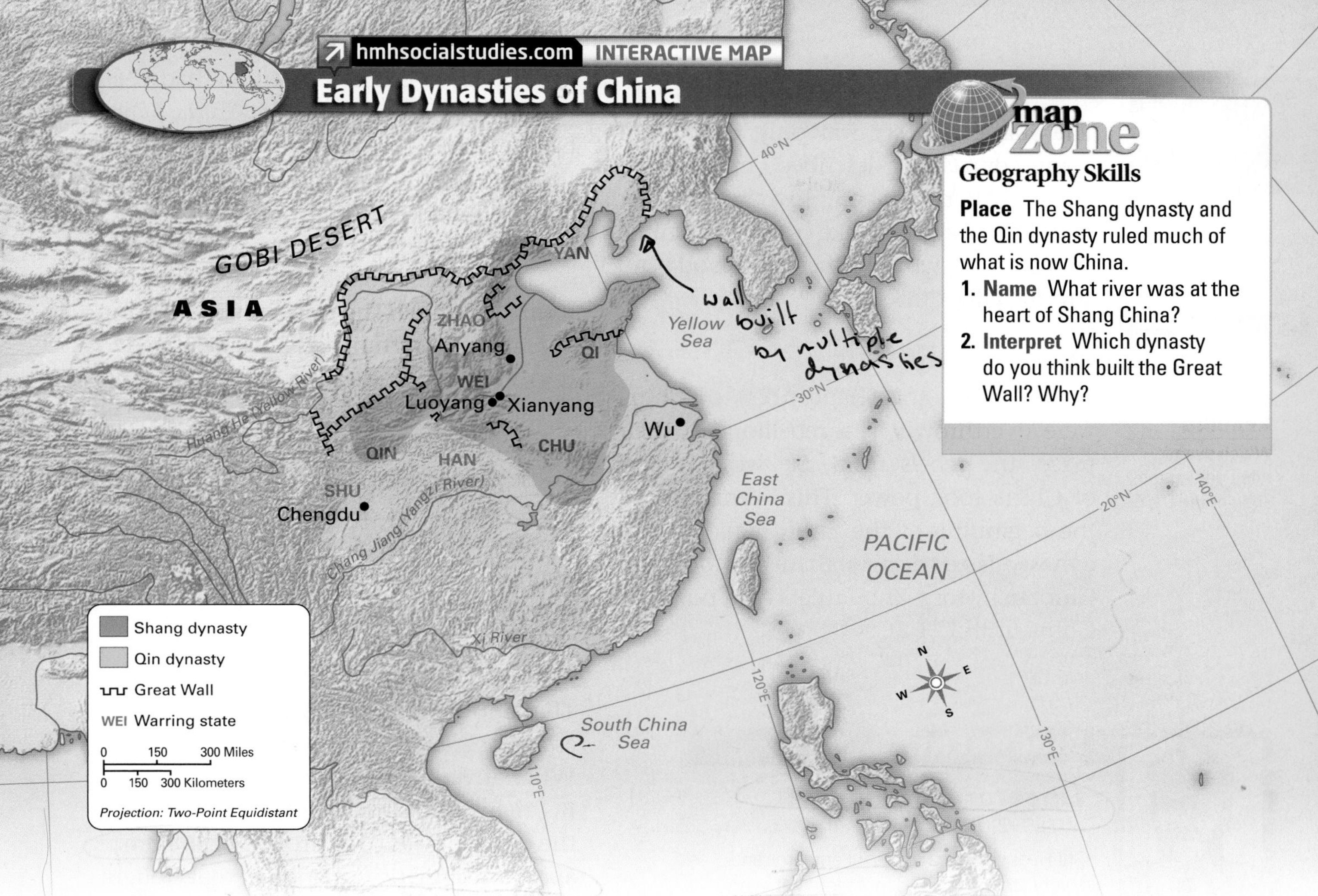

map zone

Geography Skills

Place The Shang dynasty and the Qin dynasty ruled much of what is now China.

1. **Name** What river was at the heart of Shang China?
2. **Interpret** Which dynasty do you think built the Great Wall? Why?

Shang Dynasty

As time passed, dynasties, or families, of strong rulers began to take power in China. The first dynasty for which we have clear evidence is the Shang, which was firmly established by the 1500s BC. Strongest in the Huang He Valley, the Shang ruled a broad area of northern China, as you can see on the map. Shang emperors ruled in China until the 1100s BC.

The Shang made many advances, including China's first writing system. This system used more than 2,000 symbols to express words or ideas. Although the system has gone through changes over the years, the Chinese symbols used today are based on those of the Shang period.

Many examples of Shang writing that we have found were on cattle bones and turtle shells. Priests had carved questions about the future on bones or shells, which were then heated, causing them to crack. The priests believed they could "read" these cracks to predict the future.

In addition to writing, the Shang also made other achievements. Artisans made beautiful bronze containers for cooking and religious ceremonies. They also made axes, knives, and ornaments from jade. Soldiers developed war chariots, powerful bows, and bronze armor. The Shang also invented a calendar based on the cycles of the moon.

READING CHECK **Summarizing** What were two Shang achievements?

Zhou and Qin Dynasties

VIDEO
China's Shortest Dynasty

hmhsocialstudies.com

The Shang dynasty was only the first of many dynasties described in Chinese records. After the Shang lost power, other dynasties rose up to take control of China. Two of those dynasties were the Zhou (JOH) and the Qin (CHIN).

Zhou Dynasty

FOCUS ON READING
Which dynasty ruled earlier, the Zhou or the Qin?

In the 1100s, the Shang rulers of China were overthrown in a rebellion. In their place, the rebels from the western part of China took power. This event marked the beginning of the Zhou dynasty. This dynasty lasted longer than any other in Chinese history. Zhou rulers held power in China until 771 BC.

The Zhou claimed that they had been chosen by heaven to rule China. They believed that no one could rule without heaven's permission. This idea that heaven chose China's ruler and gave him or her power was called the **mandate of heaven**.

Under the Zhou, a new political order formed in China. The emperor was at the top of society. Everything in China belonged to him, and everyone had to be loyal to him.

Emperors gave land to people in exchange for loyalty or military service. Those people who received this land became lords. Below the lords were peasants, or farmers who owned little land. In addition to growing their own food, peasants had to grow food for lords.

Warring States Period

The Zhou political system broke down as lords grew less loyal to the emperors. When invaders attacked the capital in 771 BC, many lords would not fight. As a result, the emperor was overthrown. China broke apart into many kingdoms that fought each other. This time of disorder in China is called the Warring States period.

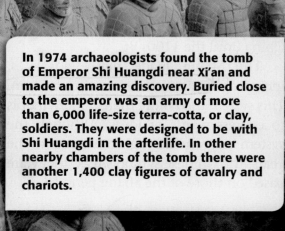

BIOGRAPHY

Emperor Shi Huangdi
(c. 259–210 BC)

Shi Huangdi was a powerful emperor and a very strict one. He demanded that everyone in China believe the same things he did. To prevent people from having other ideas, he ordered all books that did not agree with his beliefs burned. When a group of scholars protested the burning of these books, Shi Huangdi had them buried alive. These actions led many Chinese people to resent the emperor. As a result, they were eager to bring the Qin dynasty to an end.

In 1974 archaeologists found the tomb of Emperor Shi Huangdi near Xi'an and made an amazing discovery. Buried close to the emperor was an army of more than 6,000 life-size terra-cotta, or clay, soldiers. They were designed to be with Shi Huangdi in the afterlife. In other nearby chambers of the tomb there were another 1,400 clay figures of cavalry and chariots.

Qin Dynasty

The Warring States period came to an end when one state became strong enough to defeat all its rivals. That state was called Qin. In 221 BC, a king from Qin managed to unify all of China under his control and name himself emperor.

As emperor, the king took a new name. He called himself Shi Huangdi (SHEE hwahng-dee), a name that means "first emperor." Shi Huangdi was a very strict ruler, but he was an effective ruler as well. He expanded the size of China both to the north and to the south, as the map at the beginning of this section shows.

Shi Huangdi greatly changed Chinese politics. Unlike the Zhou rulers, he refused to share his power with anyone. Lords who had enjoyed many rights before now lost those rights. In addition, he ordered thousands of noble families to move to his capital, now called **Xi'an** (SHEE-AHN). He thought nobles that he kept nearby would be less likely to rebel against him.

The Qin dynasty did not last long. While Shi Huangdi lived, he was strong enough to keep China unified. The rulers who followed him, however, were not as strong. In fact, China began to break apart within a few years of Shi Huangdi's death. Rebellions began all around China, and the country fell into civil war.

Qin Achievements

Although the Qin did not rule for long, they saw great advances in China. As emperor, Shi Huangdi worked to make sure that people all over China acted and thought the same way. He created a system of laws that would apply equally to people in all parts of China. He also set up a new system of money. Before, people in each region had used local currencies. He also created a uniform system of writing that eliminated minor differences between regions.

The Qin's best known achievements, though, were in building. Under the Qin, the Chinese built a huge network of roads and canals. These roads and canals linked distant parts of the empire to make travel and trade easier.

To protect China from invasion, Shi Huangdi built the **Great Wall**, a barrier that linked earlier walls that stood near China's northern border. Building the wall took years of labor from hundreds of thousands of workers. Later dynasties added to the wall, parts of which still stand today.

SUMMARY AND PREVIEW Early Chinese history was shaped by the Shang, Zhou, and Qin dynasties. Next, you will read about another strong dynasty, the Han.

Section 1 Assessment

hmhsocialstudies.com
ONLINE QUIZ

Reviewing Ideas, Terms, and Places

1. a. **Identify** On what rivers did Chinese civilization begin?
   b. **Analyze** What advances did the early Chinese make?
2. a. **Describe** What area did the Shang rule?
   b. **Evaluate** What do you think was the Shang dynasty's most important achievement? Why?
3. a. **Define** What is the **mandate of heaven**?
   b. **Generalize** How did Shi Huangdi change China?

Critical Thinking

4. **Analyzing** Draw a chart like the one shown here. Using your notes, write details about the achievements and political system of China's early dynasties.

	Achievements	Political System
Shang		
Zhou		
Qin		

FOCUS ON WRITING

5. **Identifying Advances** The Shang, Zhou, and Qin made some of the greatest advances in Chinese history. Which of these will you mention in your magazine article? Write down some ideas.

SECTION 2

The Han Dynasty

What You Will Learn...

Main Ideas

1. Han dynasty government was largely based on the ideas of Confucius.
2. Han China supported and strengthened family life.
3. The Han made many achievements in art, literature, and learning.

The Big Idea

The Han dynasty created a new form of government that valued family, art, and learning.

Key Terms

sundial, *p. 58*
seismograph, *p. 58*
acupuncture, *p. 59*

Use the graphic organizer online to take notes on Han government, family life, and achievements.

If YOU lived there...

You are a young Chinese student from a poor family. Your family has worked hard to give you a good education so that you can get a government job and have a great future. Your friends laugh at you. They say that only boys from wealthy families win the good jobs. They think it is better to join the army.

Will you take the exam or join the army? Why?

BUILDING BACKGROUND Though it was harsh, the rule of the first Qin emperor helped to unify northern China. With the building of what would become the Great Wall, he strengthened defenses in the north. But his successor could not hold on to power. The Qin gave way to a new dynasty that would last 400 years.

Han Dynasty Government

When the Qin dynasty collapsed, many groups fought for power. After years of fighting, an army led by Liu Bang (lee-OO bang) won control. Liu Bang became the first emperor of the Han dynasty, which lasted more than 400 years.

The Rise of a New Dynasty

Liu Bang, a peasant, was able to become emperor in large part because of the Chinese belief in the mandate of heaven. He was the first common person to become emperor. He earned people's loyalty and trust. In addition, he was well liked by both soldiers and peasants, which helped him keep control.

Time Line

The Han Dynasty

205 BC The Han dynasty begins.

140 BC Wudi becomes emperor and tries to strengthen China's government.

AD 25 The Han move their capital east to Luoyang.

AD 220 The Han dynasty falls.

200 BC — BC 1 AD — AD 200

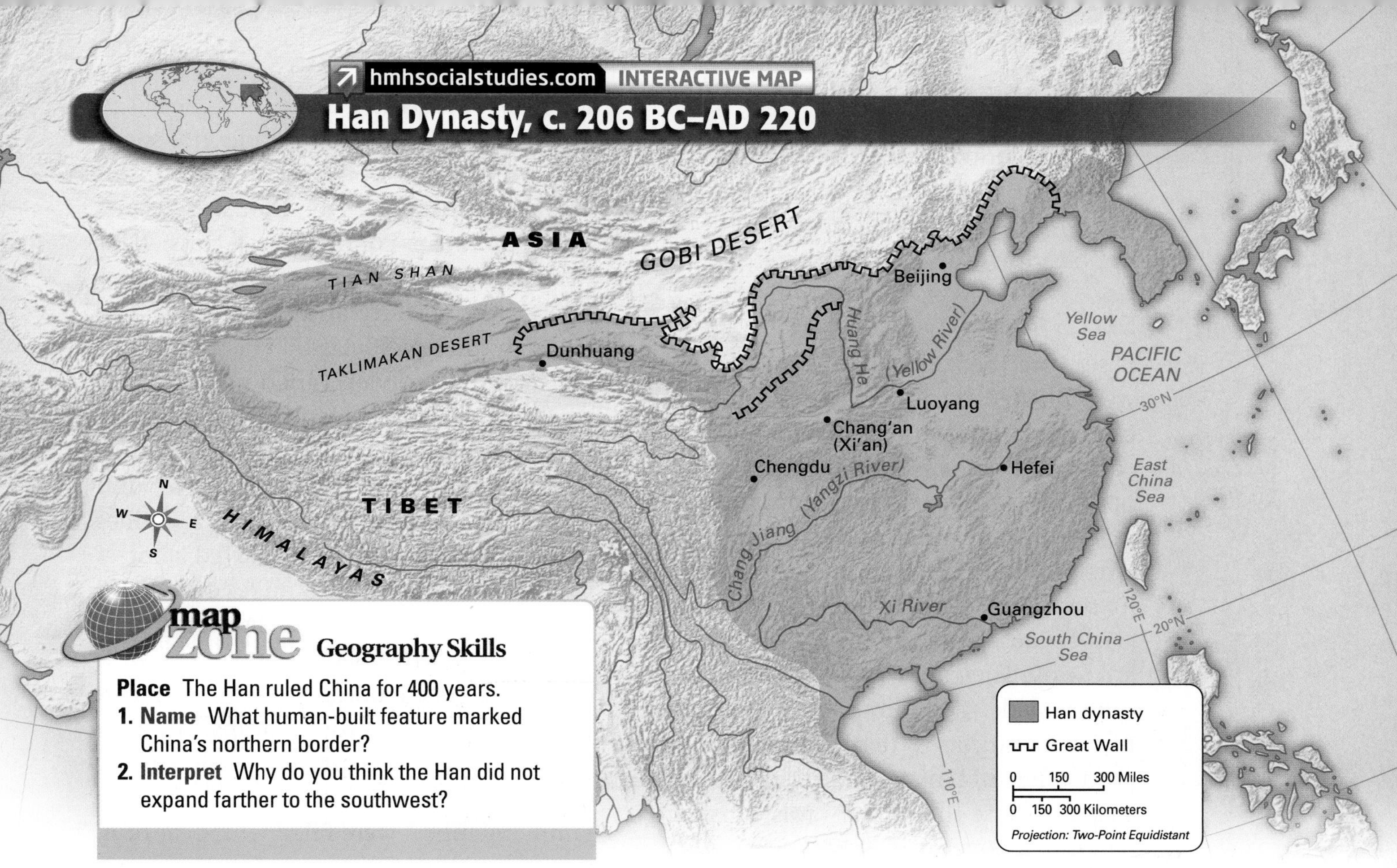

Liu Bang's rule was different from the strict government of the Qin. He wanted to free people from harsh government policies. He lowered taxes for farmers and made punishments less severe. He gave large blocks of land to his supporters.

In addition to setting new policies, Liu Bang changed the way government worked. He set up a government structure that built on the foundation begun by the Qin. He also relied on educated officials to help him rule.

Wudi Creates a New Government

In 140 BC Emperor Wudi (WOO-dee) took the throne. He wanted to create a stronger government. To do that, he took land from the lords, raised taxes, and put the supply of grain under government control. He also made Confucianism China's official government philosophy.

Confucianism is a philosophy based on the teachings of a man named Confucius. It emphasizes the importance of ethics and moral values, such as respect for elders and loyalty toward family members. Under the Han, government officials were expected to practice Confucianism. Wudi even began a university to teach Confucian ideas.

Focus on Reading

Who ruled first, Liu Bang or Wudi?

Studying Confucianism could also get a person a good job in China. If a person passed an exam on Confucian teachings, he could get a position working for the government. Not just anyone could take the test, though. The exams were only open to people who had been recommended for government service already. As a result, wealthy or influential families continued to control the government.

Reading Check **Analyzing** How was the Han government based on the ideas of Confucius?

Family Life

The Han period was a time of great social change in China. Class structure became more rigid. The family once again became important within Chinese society.

Social Classes

Based on the Confucian system, people were divided into four classes. The upper class was made up of the emperor, his court, and scholars who held government positions. The second class, the largest, was made up of the peasants. Next were artisans who produced items for daily life and some luxury goods. Merchants were the lowest class because they did not actually produce anything. They only bought and sold what others made. The military was not a class in the Confucian system. Still, joining the army offered men a chance to rise in social status because the military was considered part of the government.

This Han artifact is an oil lamp held by a servant.

Lives of Rich and Poor

The classes only divided people into social rank. They did not indicate wealth or power. For instance, even though peasants made up the second highest class, they were poor. Many merchants, on the other hand, were wealthy and powerful despite being in the lowest class.

People's lifestyles varied according to wealth. The emperor and his court lived in a large palace. Less important officials lived in multilevel houses built around courtyards. Many of these wealthy families owned large estates and employed laborers to work the land. Some families even hired private armies to defend their estates.

The wealthy filled their homes with expensive decorations. These included paintings, pottery, bronze lamps, and jade figures. Rich families hired musicians for entertainment. Even the tombs of dead family members were filled with beautiful, expensive objects.

Most people in Han China, however, did not live so comfortably. Nearly 60 million people lived in China during the Han dynasty, and about 90 percent of them were peasants who lived in the countryside. Peasants put in long, tiring days working the land. Whether it was in the millet fields of the north or in the rice paddies of the south, the work was hard. In the winter, peasants were forced to work on building projects for the government. Heavy taxes and bad weather forced many farmers to sell their land and work for rich landowners. By the last years of the Han dynasty, only a few farmers were independent.

Chinese peasants lived simple lives. They wore plain clothing made of fiber from a native plant. The main foods they ate were cooked grains like barley. Most peasants lived in small villages. Their small, wood-framed houses had walls made of mud or stamped earth.

The Importance of Family

Honoring one's family was an important duty in Han China. In this painting, people give thanks before their family shrine. Only the men can participate. The women watch from inside the house.

ANALYZING VISUALS How are these men giving thanks?

The Revival of the Family

Since Confucianism was the government's official philosophy during Wudi's reign, Confucian teachings about the family were also honored. Children were taught from birth to respect their elders. Disobeying one's parents was a crime. Even emperors had a duty to respect their parents.

Confucius had taught that the father was the head of the family. Within the family, the father had absolute power. The Han taught that it was a woman's duty to obey her husband, and children had to obey their father.

Han officials believed that if the family was strong and people obeyed the father, then they would also obey the emperor. Since the Han rewarded strong family ties and respect for elders, some men even gained government jobs based on the respect they showed their parents.

Children were encouraged to serve their parents. They were also expected to honor dead parents with ceremonies and offerings. All members of a family were expected to care for family burial sites.

Chinese parents valued boys more highly than girls. This was because sons carried on the family line and took care of their parents when they were old. On the other hand, daughters became part of their husband's family. According to a Chinese proverb, "Raising daughters is like raising children for another family." Some women, however, still gained power. They could gain influence in their sons' families. An older widow could even become the head of the family.

READING CHECK **Identifying Cause and Effect** Why did the family take on such importance during the Han dynasty?

During the Han dynasty, the Chinese made many advances in art and learning. Some of these advances are shown here.

Science

This is a model of an ancient Chinese seismograph. When an earthquake struck, a lever inside caused a ball to drop from a dragon's mouth into a toad's mouth, indicating the direction from which the earthquake had come.

Han Achievements

Han rule was a time of great achievements. Art and literature thrived, and inventors developed many useful devices.

Art and Literature

The Chinese of the Han period produced many works of art. They became experts at figure painting—a style of painting that includes portraits of people. Portraits often showed religious figures and Confucian scholars. Han artists also painted realistic scenes from everyday life. Their creations covered the walls of palaces and tombs.

Academic Vocabulary

innovation a new idea, method, or device

In literature, Han China is known for its poetry. Poets developed new styles of verse, including the *fu* style, which was the most popular. *Fu* poets combined prose and poetry to create long literary works. Another style, called *shi*, featured short lines of verse that could be sung. Many Han rulers hired poets known for the beauty of their verse.

Han writers also produced important works of history. One historian by the name of Sima Qian wrote a complete history of all the dynasties through the early Han. His format and style became the model for later historical writings.

Inventions and Advances

The Han Chinese invented one item that we use every day—paper. They made it by grinding plant fibers, such as mulberry bark and hemp, into a paste. Then they let it dry in sheets. Chinese scholars produced books by pasting several pieces of paper together into a long sheet. Then they rolled the sheet into a scroll.

The Han also made other **innovations** in science. These included the sundial and the seismograph. A **sundial** is a device that uses the position of shadows cast by the sun to tell the time of day. It was an early type of clock. A **seismograph** is a device that measures the strength of earthquakes. Han emperors were very interested in knowing

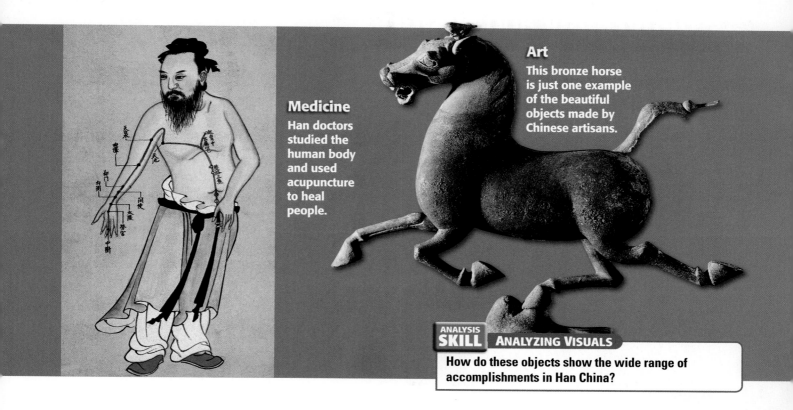

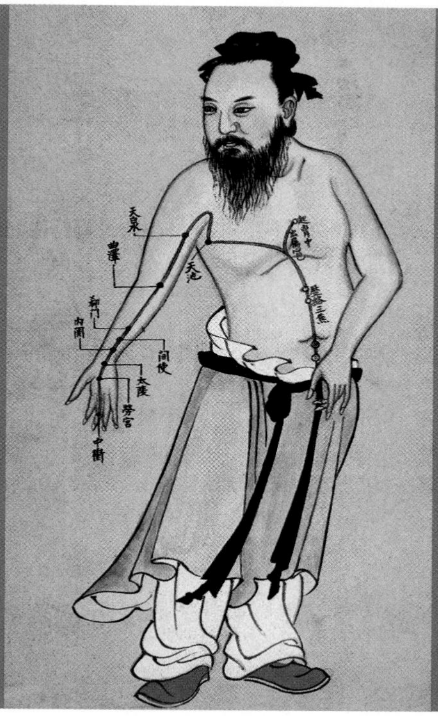

Medicine
Han doctors studied the human body and used acupuncture to heal people.

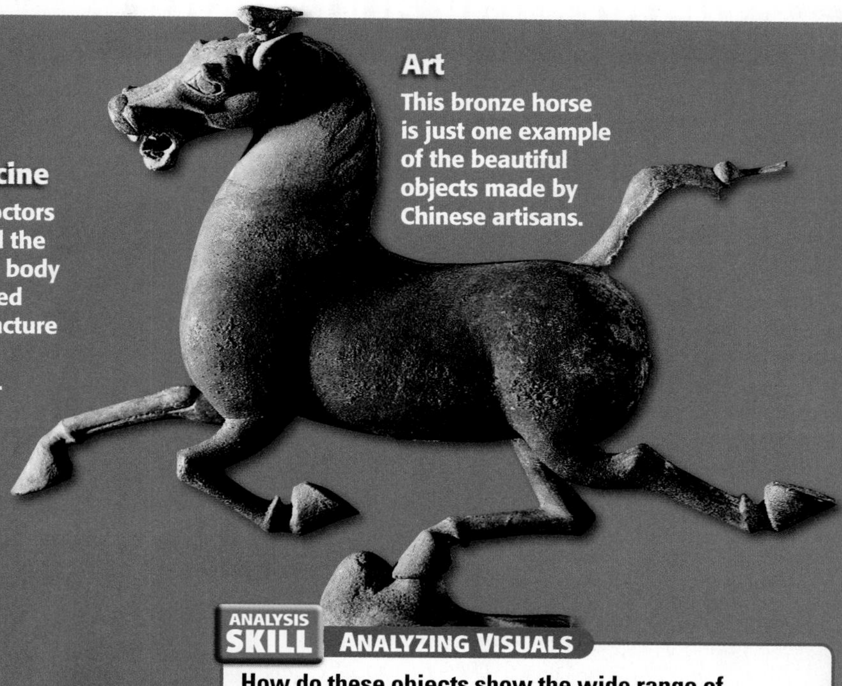

Art
This bronze horse is just one example of the beautiful objects made by Chinese artisans.

ANALYSIS SKILL **ANALYZING VISUALS**

How do these objects show the wide range of accomplishments in Han China?

about the movements of the Earth. They believed that earthquakes were signs of future evil events.

Another Han innovation, acupuncture (AK-yoo-punk-cher), improved medicine. **Acupuncture** is the practice of inserting fine needles through the skin at specific points to cure disease or relieve pain. Many Han inventions in science and medicine are still used today.

READING CHECK **Categorizing** What advances did the Chinese make during the Han period?

SUMMARY AND PREVIEW Rulers of the Han dynasty based their government on Confucianism, which strengthened family bonds in China. In addition, art and learning thrived under Han rule. In the next section you will learn about two dynasties that also made great advances, the Tang and the Song.

Section 2 Assessment

hmhsocialstudies.com ONLINE QUIZ

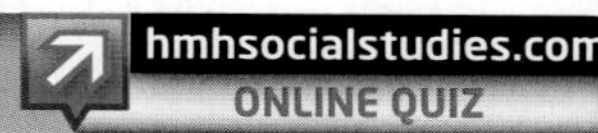

Reviewing Ideas, Terms, and People

1. a. **Identify** What is Confucianism? How did it affect the government during the Han dynasty?
   b. **Summarize** How did Emperor Wudi create a strong central government?
   c. **Evaluate** Do you think that an exam system is the best way to make sure that people are fairly chosen for government jobs? Why or why not?
2. a. **Describe** What was the son's role in the family?
   b. **Contrast** How did living conditions for the wealthy differ from those of the peasants during the Han dynasty?
3. **Identify** What device did the Chinese invent to measure the strength of earthquakes?

Critical Thinking

4. **Analyzing** Use your notes to complete this diagram about how Confucianism influenced Han government and family.

Government
↑
Confucianism
↓
Family

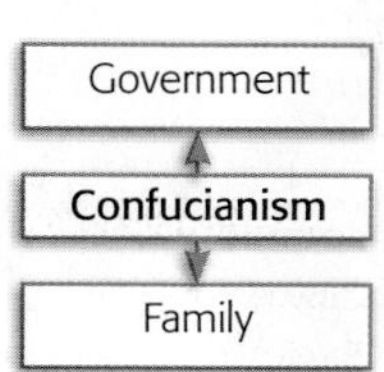

FOCUS ON WRITING

5. **Analyzing the Han Dynasty** The Han dynasty was one of the most influential in all of Chinese history. How will you describe the dynasty's many achievements in your article? Make a list of achievements you want to include.

Geography and History

The Silk Road

The Silk Road was a long trade route that stretched across the heart of Asia. Along this route, an active trade developed between China and Southwest Asia by about 100 BC. By AD 100, the Silk Road connected Han China in the east with the Roman Empire in the west.

The main goods traded along the Silk Road were luxury goods—ones that were small, light, and expensive. These included goods like silk, spices, and gold. Because they were small and valuable, merchants could carry these goods long distances and still sell them for a large profit. As a result, people in both the east and the west were able to buy luxury goods that were unavailable at home.

Goods from the West Roman merchants like this man grew rich from Silk Road trade. Merchants in the west traded goods like those you see here—wool, amber, and gold.

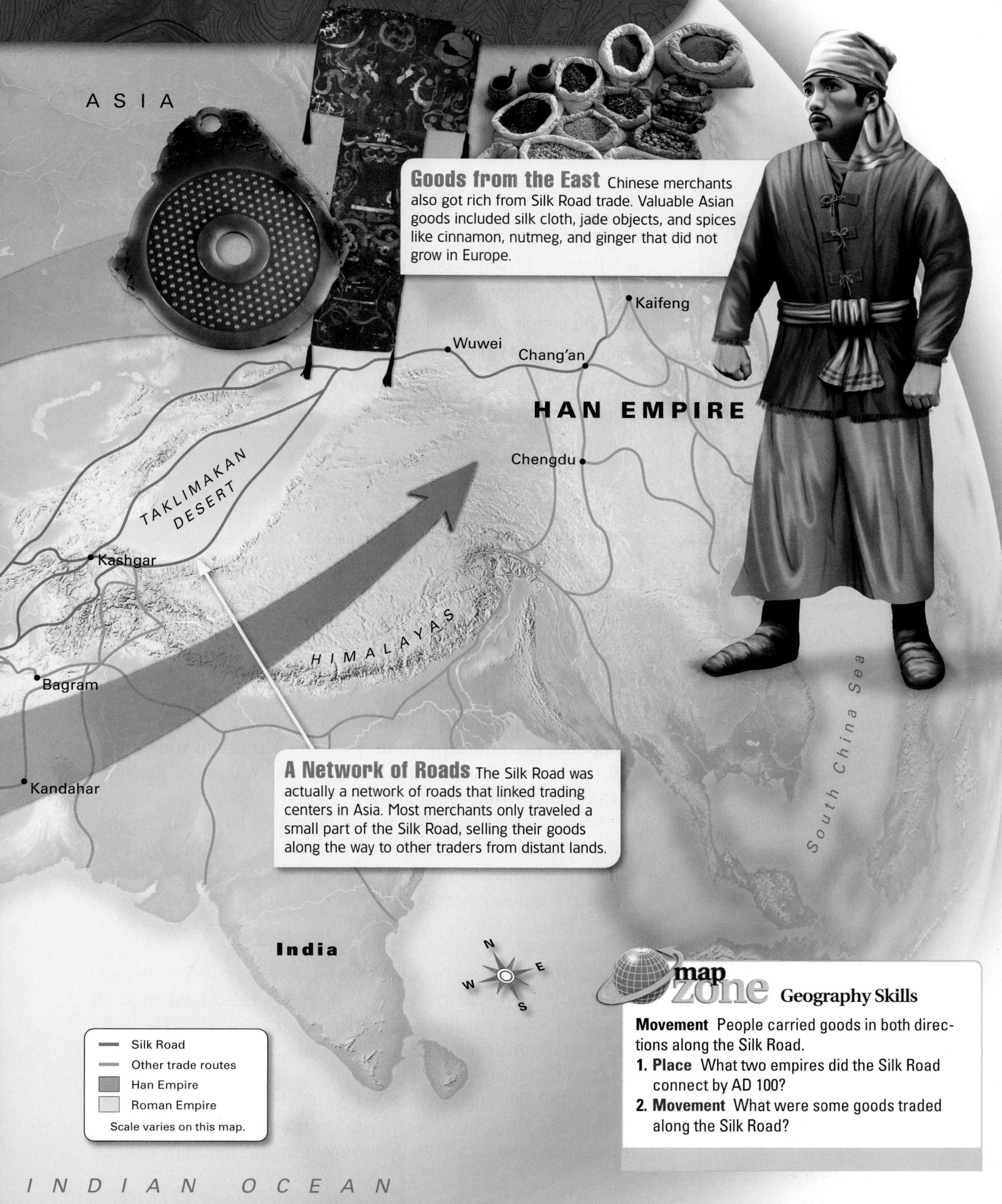
ASIA
Goods from the East Chinese merchants also got rich from Silk Road trade. Valuable Asian goods included silk cloth, jade objects, and spices like cinnamon, nutmeg, and ginger that did not grow in Europe.
Kaifeng
Wuwei
Chang'an
HAN EMPIRE
Chengdu
TAKLIMAKAN DESERT
Kashgar
HIMALAYAS
Bagram
Kandahar
A Network of Roads The Silk Road was actually a network of roads that linked trading centers in Asia. Most merchants only traveled a small part of the Silk Road, selling their goods along the way to other traders from distant lands.
South China Sea
India
N
E
W
S
Silk Road
Other trade routes
Han Empire
Roman Empire
Scale varies on this map.
INDIAN OCEAN

map zone Geography Skills

Movement People carried goods in both directions along the Silk Road.

1. **Place** What two empires did the Silk Road connect by AD 100?
2. **Movement** What were some goods traded along the Silk Road?

SECTION 3

The Sui, Tang, and Song Dynasties

What You Will Learn...

Main Ideas

1. After the Han dynasty, China fell into disorder but was reunified by new dynasties.
2. Cities and trade grew during the Tang and Song dynasties.
3. The Tang and Song dynasties produced fine arts and inventions.

The Big Idea

The Tang and Song dynasties were periods of economic, cultural, and technological accomplishments.

Key Terms and Places

Grand Canal, *p. 62*
Kaifeng, *p. 64*
porcelain, *p. 65*
woodblock printing, *p. 66*
gunpowder, *p. 66*
compass, *p. 66*

Use the graphic organizer online to take notes on the accomplishments of the Tang and Song dynasties.

If YOU lived there...

It is the year 1270. You are a rich merchant in a Chinese city of about a million people. The city around you fills your senses. You see people in colorful clothes among beautiful buildings. Glittering objects lure you into busy shops. You hear people talking—discussing business, gossiping, laughing at jokes. You smell delicious food cooking at a restaurant down the street.

How do you feel about your city?

BUILDING BACKGROUND The Tang and Song dynasties were periods of great wealth and progress. Changes in farming formed the basis for other advances in Chinese civilization.

Disorder and Reunification

When the Han dynasty collapsed, China split into several rival kingdoms, each ruled by military leaders. Historians sometimes call the time of disorder that followed the collapse of the Han the Period of Disunion. It lasted from 220 to 589.

War was common during the Period of Disunion. At the same time, however, Chinese culture spread. New groups moved into China from nearby areas. Over time, many of these groups adopted Chinese customs and became Chinese themselves.

Sui Dynasty

Finally, after centuries of political confusion and cultural change, China was reunified. The man who finally ended the Period of Disunion was a northern ruler named Yang Jian (YANG jee-EN). In 589, he conquered the south, unified China, and created the Sui (SWAY) dynasty.

The Sui dynasty did not last long, only from 589 to 618. During that time, however, its leaders restored order and began the **Grand Canal**, a canal linking northern and southern China.

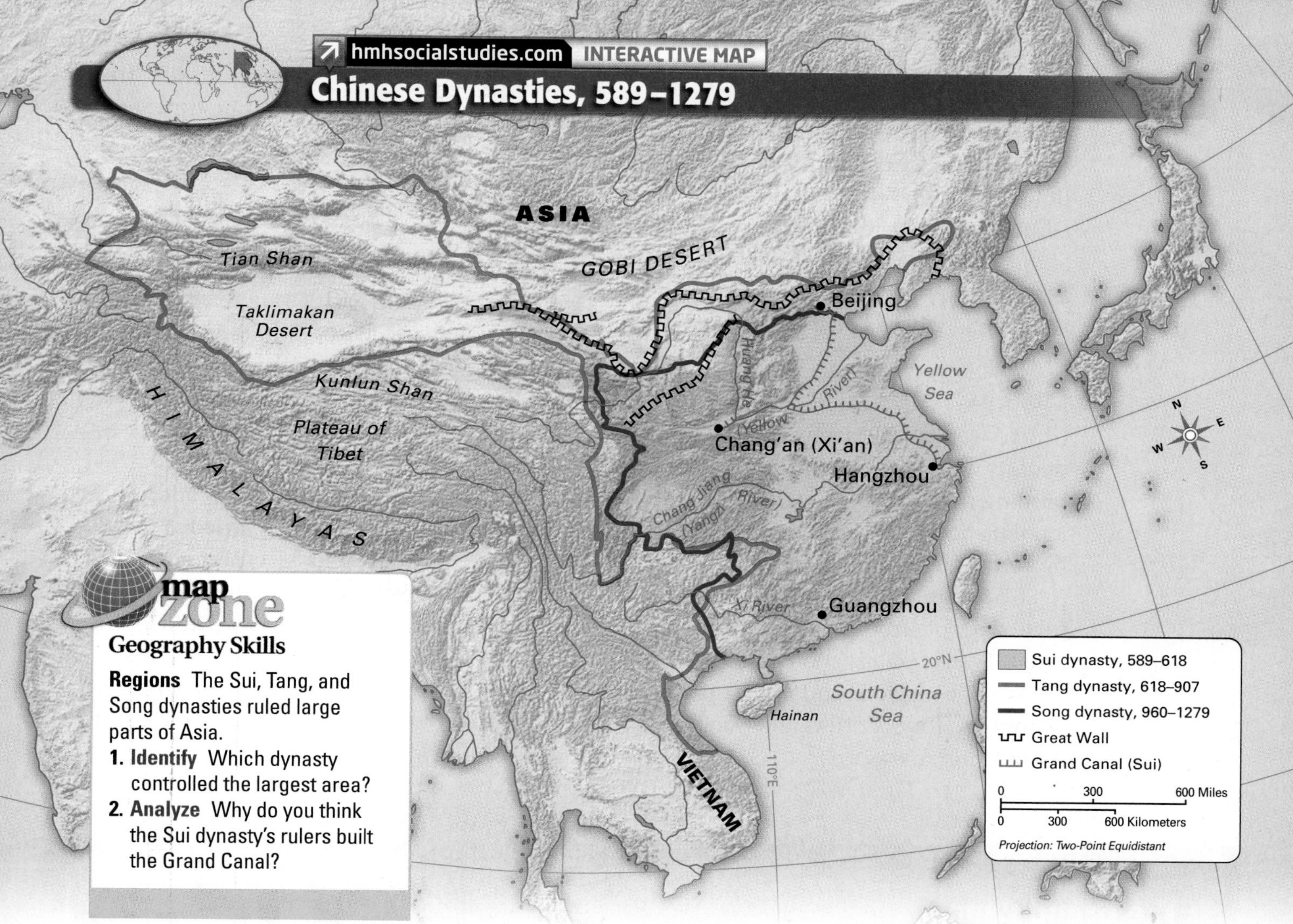

Geography Skills

Regions The Sui, Tang, and Song dynasties ruled large parts of Asia.

1. **Identify** Which dynasty controlled the largest area?
2. **Analyze** Why do you think the Sui dynasty's rulers built the Grand Canal?

Tang Dynasty

The Sui dynasty was followed by the Tang, which would rule for nearly 300 years. As you can see on the map, China grew under the Tang dynasty to include much of eastern and central Asia.

Historians view the Tang dynasty as a golden age. Tang rulers conquered many lands, reformed the military, and created law codes. The Tang period also saw great advances in art. Some of China's finest poets, for example, lived during this time.

The Tang dynasty also included the only woman to rule China—Empress Wu. Her methods were sometimes vicious, but she was intelligent and talented.

Song Dynasty

After the Tang dynasty fell, China entered another brief period of chaos and disorder, with separate kingdoms competing for power. As a result, this period in China's history is called the Five Dynasties and Ten Kingdoms. The disorder only lasted 53 years, though, from 907 to 960.

In 960, China was again reunified, this time by the Song dynasty. Like the Tang, the Song ruled for about 300 years, until 1279. Also like the Tang, the Song dynasty was a time of great achievements.

READING CHECK **Finding Main Ideas** What dynasties restored order to China?

FOCUS ON READING
What dynasty followed the Tang?

Cities and Trade

Throughout the Tang and Song dynasties, much of the food grown on China's farms flowed into the growing cities and towns. China's cities were crowded, busy places. Shopkeepers, government officials, doctors, artisans, entertainers, religious leaders, and artists made them lively places as well.

City Life

China's capital and largest city of the Tang dynasty was Chang'an (chahng-AHN), a huge, bustling trade center now called Xi'an. With a population of more than a million, it was by far the largest city in the world.

Chang'an, like other trading cities, had a mix of people from many cultures—China, Korea, Persia, Arabia, and Europe. It was also known as a religious and philosophical center, not just for Buddhists and Daoists but for Asian Christians as well.

Cities continued to grow under the Song. Several cities, including the Song capital, **Kaifeng** (KY-fuhng), had about a million people. A dozen more cities had populations of close to half a million.

Trade in China and Beyond

Trade grew along with Chinese cities. This trade, combined with China's agricultural base, made China richer than ever before.

Much trade took place within China itself. Traders used the country's rivers to ship goods on barges and ships.

The Grand Canal, a series of waterways that linked major cities, carried a huge amount of trade goods, especially farm products. Construction on the canal had begun during the Sui dynasty. During the Tang dynasty, it was improved and expanded. The Grand Canal allowed the Chinese to move goods and crops from distant agricultural areas into cities.

The Chinese also carried on trade with other lands and peoples. During the Tang dynasty, most foreign trade was over land routes leading to India and Southwest Asia, though Chinese traders also went to Korea and Japan in the east. The Chinese exported many goods, including tea, rice, spices, and jade. However, one export was especially important—silk. So valuable was silk that the Chinese kept the method of making it secret. In exchange for their exports, the Chinese imported different foods, plants, wool, glass, and precious metals like gold and silver.

During the Song dynasty, sea trade became more important. China opened its Pacific ports to foreign traders. The sea-trade routes connected China to many other countries. During this time, the Chinese also developed another valuable product—a thin, beautiful type of pottery called **porcelain**.

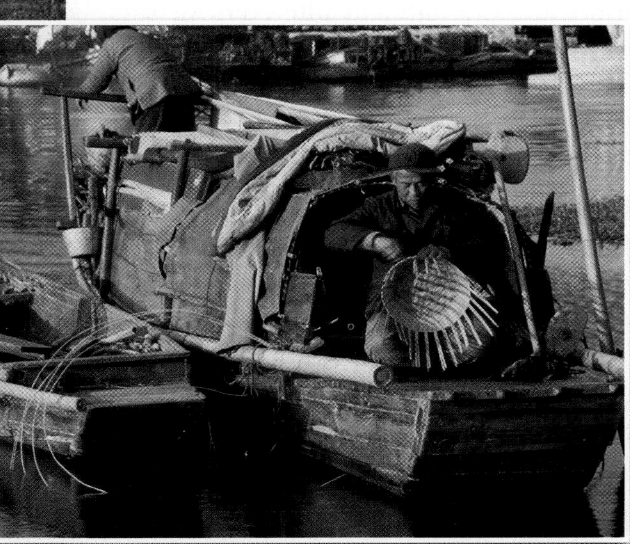

China's Grand Canal is the world's longest human-made waterway. It was built largely to transport rice and other foods from the south to feed China's cities and armies in the north. Barges like the ones at left crowd the Grand Canal, which is still an important transportation link in China. Some people even live on the canal in small houseboats like the one above.

All of this trade helped create a strong economy. As a result, merchants became important members of Chinese society during the Song dynasty. Also as a result of the growth of trade and wealth, the Song invented the world's first system of paper money in the 900s.

READING CHECK **Summarizing** How far did China's trade routes extend?

Arts and Inventions

While China grew rich economically, its cultural riches also increased. In literature, art, and science, China made huge advances.

Artists and Poets

The artists and writers of the Tang dynasty were some of China's greatest. Wu Daozi (DOW-tzee) painted murals that celebrated Buddhism and nature. Li Bo and Du Fu wrote poems that readers still enjoy for their beauty. This poem by Li Bo expresses the homesickness that one feels late at night:

> "Before my bed
> there is bright moonlight
> So that it seems
> like frost on the ground:
> Lifting my head
> I watch the bright moon,
> Lowering my head
> I dream that I'm home."
>
> –Li Bo, *Quiet Night Thoughts*

THE IMPACT TODAY

Porcelain became so popular in the West that it became known as chinaware, or just china.

Also noted for its literature, the Song period produced Li Qingzhao (ching-ZHOW), perhaps China's greatest female poet. She once said that the purpose of her poetry was to capture a single moment in time.

Artists of both the Tang and Song dynasties made exquisite objects in clay. Tang figurines of horses clearly show the animals' strength. Song artists made porcelain items covered in a pale green glaze called celadon (SEL-uh-duhn).

Chinese Inventions

Paper
Invented during the Han dynasty around 105, paper was one of the greatest of all Chinese inventions. It gave the Chinese a cheap and easy way of keeping records and made printing possible.

Porcelain
Porcelain was first made during the Tang dynasty, but it wasn't perfected for many centuries. Chinese artists were famous for their work with this fragile material.

Woodblock printing
The Chinese invented printing during the Tang dynasty, centuries before it was known in Europe. Printers could copy drawings or texts quickly, much faster than they could be copied by hand.

Gunpowder
Invented during the late Tang or early Song dynasty, gunpowder was used to make fireworks and signals. The Chinese did not generally use it as a weapon.

Movable type
Inventors of the Song dynasty created movable type, which made printing much faster. Carved letters could be rearranged and reused to print many different messages.

Magnetic compass
Invented no later than the Han period, the compass was greatly improved by the Tang. The new compass allowed sailors and merchants to travel vast distances.

Paper money
The world's first paper money was invented by the Song. Lighter and easier to handle than coins, paper money helped the Chinese manage their growing wealth.

Important Inventions

The Tang and Song dynasties produced some of the most remarkable—and most important—inventions in human history. Some of these inventions influenced events around the world.

According to legend, a man named Cai Lun invented paper in the year 105 during the Han dynasty. A later Tang invention built on this achievement—**woodblock printing**, a form of printing in which an entire page is carved into a block of wood. The printer applies ink to the block and presses paper against the block to create a printed page. The world's first known printed book was printed in this way in China in 868.

Another invention of the Tang dynasty was gunpowder. **Gunpowder** is a mixture of powders used in guns and explosives. It was originally used only in fireworks, but it was later used to make small bombs and rockets. Eventually, gunpowder was used to make explosives, firearms, and cannons. Gunpowder dramatically altered how wars were fought and, in doing so, changed the course of human history.

One of the most useful achievements of Tang China was the perfection of the magnetic **compass**. This instrument, which uses Earth's magnetic field to show direction, revolutionized travel. A compass made it possible to find direction more accurately than ever before. The perfection of the compass had far-reaching effects. Explorers the world over used the compass to travel vast distances. Both trading ships and warships also came to rely on the compass for their navigation. Thus, the compass has been a key factor in some of the most important sailing voyages in history.

The Song dynasty also produced many important inventions. Under the Song, the Chinese invented movable type. Movable type is a set of letters or characters that are

CONNECTING TO Economics

The Paper Trail

The dollar bill in your pocket may be crisp and new, but paper money has been around a long time. Paper money was printed for the first time in China in the AD 900s and was in use for about 700 years, through the Ming dynasty, when the bill shown here was printed. However, so much money was printed that it lost value. The Chinese stopped using paper money for centuries. Its use caught on in Europe, though, and eventually became common. Most countries now issue paper money.

Drawing Conclusions How would life be different today without paper money?

used to print books. Unlike the blocks used in block printing, movable type can be rearranged and reused to create new lines of text and different pages.

The Song dynasty also introduced the concept of paper money. People were used to buying goods and services with bulky coins made of metals such as bronze, gold, and silver. Paper money was far lighter and easier to use. As trade increased and many people in China grew rich, paper money became more popular.

READING CHECK **Finding Main Ideas** What were some important inventions of the Tang and Song dynasties?

SUMMARY AND PREVIEW The Tang and Song dynasties were periods of great advancement. Many great artists and writers lived during these periods. Tang and Song inventions also had dramatic effects on world history. Next, you will learn about major changes in China's government during the Song dynasty.

Section 3 Assessment

hmhsocialstudies.com
ONLINE QUIZ

Reviewing Ideas, Terms, and People

1. **a. Recall** What was the Period of Disunion? What dynasty brought an end to that period?
   b. Explain How did China change during the Tang dynasty?
2. **a. Describe** What were the capital cities of Tang and Song China like?
   b. Draw Conclusions How did geography affect trade in China?
3. **a. Identify** Who was Li Bo?
   b. Draw Conclusions How may the inventions of paper money and **woodblock printing** have been linked?
   c. Rank Which Tang or Song invention do you think was most important? Defend your answer.

Critical Thinking

4. **Categorizing** Copy the chart at right. Use it to organize your notes on the Tang and Song into categories.

	Tang dynasty	Song dynasty
Cities		
Trade		
Art		
Inventions		

FOCUS ON WRITING

5. **Identifying Achievements** Which achievements and inventions of the Tang and Song dynasties seem most important or most interesting? Make a list for later use.

SECTION 4

Confucianism and Government

What You Will Learn...

Main Ideas

1. Confucianism, based on Confucius's teachings about proper behavior, dramatically influenced the Song system of government.
2. Scholar-officials ran China's government during the Song dynasty.

The Big Idea

Confucian thought influenced the Song government.

Key Terms

bureaucracy, *p. 70*
civil service, *p. 70*
scholar-official, *p. 70*

Use the graphic organizer online to note details about Confucianism and the Song government.

If YOU lived there...

You are a student in China in 1184. Night has fallen, but you cannot sleep. Tomorrow you have a test. You know it will be the most important test of your entire life. You have studied for it, not for days or weeks or even months—but for *years*. As you toss and turn, you think about how your entire life will be determined by how well you do on this one test.

How could a single test be so important?

BUILDING BACKGROUND The Song dynasty ruled China from 960 to 1279. This was a time of improvements in agriculture, growing cities, extensive trade, and the development of art and inventions. It was also a time of major changes in Chinese government.

Confucianism

The dominant philosophy in China, Confucianism is based on the teachings of Confucius. He lived more than 1,000 years before the Song dynasty. His ideas, though, had a dramatic effect on the Song system of government.

Confucian Ideas

Confucius's teachings focused on ethics, or proper behavior, for individuals and governments. He said that people should conduct their lives according to two basic principles. These principles were *ren*, or concern for others, and *li*, or appropriate behavior. Confucius argued that society would **function** best if everyone followed *ren* and *li*.

Confucius thought that everyone had a proper role to play in society. Order was maintained when people knew their place and behaved appropriately. For example, Confucius said that young people should obey their elders and that subjects should obey their rulers.

Influence of Confucianism

After his death, Confucius's ideas were spread by his followers, but they were not widely accepted. In fact, the Qin dynasty officially suppressed Confucian ideas and teachings. By the time of the Han dynasty, Confucianism had again come into favor, and Confucianism became the official state philosophy.

During the Period of Disunion, which followed the Han dynasty, Confucianism was overshadowed by Buddhism as the major tradition in China. Many Chinese people had turned to Buddhism for peace and comfort during those troubled times. In doing so, they largely turned away from Confucian ideas and outlooks.

Later, during the Sui and early Tang dynasties, Buddhism was very influential. Unlike Confucianism, which focused on ethical behavior, Buddhism stressed a more spiritual outlook that promised escape from suffering. As Buddhism became more popular in China, Confucianism lost some of its influence.

ACADEMIC VOCABULARY

function work or perform

In addition to ethics, Confucianism stressed the importance of a good education. This painting, created in the Song period, shows Confucian scholars during the Period of Disunion sorting scrolls containing classic Confucian texts.

Civil Service Exams

This painting from the 1600s shows civil servants writing essays for China's emperor. Difficult exams were designed to make sure that government officials were chosen by ability—not by wealth or family connections.

Difficult Exams

- Students had to memorize entire Confucian texts.
- To pass the most difficult tests, students might study for more than 20 years!
- Some exams lasted up to 72 hours, and students were locked in private rooms while taking them.
- Some dishonest students cheated by copying Confucius's works on the inside of their clothes, paying bribes to the test graders, or paying someone else to take the test for them.
- To prevent cheating, exam halls were often locked and guarded.

Neo-Confucianism

Late in the Tang dynasty, many Chinese historians and scholars again became interested in the teachings of Confucius. Their interest was sparked by their desire to improve Chinese government and society.

During and after the Song dynasty, a new philosophy called Neo-Confucianism developed. The term *neo* means "new." Based on Confucianism, Neo-Confucianism was similar to the older philosophy in that it taught proper behavior. However, it also emphasized spiritual matters. For example, Neo-Confucian scholars discussed such issues as what made human beings do bad things even if their basic nature was good.

Neo-Confucianism became much more influential under the Song. Its influence grew even more later. In fact, the ideas of Neo-Confucianism became official government teachings after the Song dynasty.

ACADEMIC VOCABULARY
incentive something that leads people to follow a certain course of action

READING CHECK **Contrasting** How did Neo-Confucianism differ from Confucianism?

Scholar-Officials

The Song dynasty took another major step that affected China for centuries. They improved the system by which people went to work for the government. These workers formed a large **bureaucracy,** or a body of unelected government officials. They joined the bureaucracy by passing civil service examinations. **Civil service** means service as a government official.

To become a civil servant, a person had to pass a series of written examinations. The examinations tested students' grasp of Confucianism and related ideas.

Because the tests were so difficult, students spent years preparing for them. Only a very small fraction of the people who took the tests would reach the top level and be appointed to a position in the government. However, candidates for the civil service examinations had a strong **incentive** for studying hard. Passing the tests meant life as a **scholar-official**—an educated member of the government.

Scholar-Officials

First rising to prominence under the Song, scholar-officials remained important in China for centuries. These scholar-officials, for example, lived during the Qing dynasty, which ruled from the mid-1600s to the early 1900s. Their typical responsibilities might include running government offices; maintaining roads, irrigation systems, and other public works; updating and keeping official records; or collecting taxes.

Scholar-officials were elite members of society. They performed many important jobs in the government and were widely admired for their knowledge and ethics. Their benefits included considerable respect and reduced penalties for breaking the law. Many also became wealthy from gifts given by people seeking their aid.

The civil service examination system helped ensure that talented, intelligent people became scholar-officials. The civil service system was a major factor in the stability of the Song government.

READING CHECK **Analyzing** How did the Song dynasty change China's government?

SUMMARY AND PREVIEW During the Song period, Confucian ideas helped shape China's government. In the next section, you will read about the two dynasties that followed the Song—the Yuan and the Ming.

Section 4 Assessment

Reviewing Ideas, Terms, and People

1. a. **Identify** What two principles did Confucius believe people should follow?
   b. **Explain** What was Neo-Confucianism?
   c. **Elaborate** Why do you think Neo-Confucianism appealed to many people?
2. a. **Define** What was a **scholar-official**?
   b. **Explain** Why would people want to become scholar-officials?
   c. **Evaluate** Do you think **civil service** examinations were a good way to choose government officials? Why or why not?

Critical Thinking

3. **Sequencing** Review your notes to see how Confucianism led to Neo-Confucianism and Neo-Confucianism led to government bureaucracy. Use a graphic organizer like the one here.

Focus on Writing

4. **Gathering Ideas about Confucianism and Government** Think about what you might say about Confucianism in your article. Also, decide whether to include any of the Song dynasty's achievements in government.

SECTION 5

The Yuan and Ming Dynasties

What You Will Learn...

Main Ideas

1. The Mongol Empire included China, and the Mongols ruled China as the Yuan dynasty.
2. The Ming dynasty was a time of stability and prosperity.
3. The Ming brought great changes in government and relations with other countries.

The Big Idea

The Chinese were ruled by foreigners during the Yuan dynasty, but they threw off Mongol rule and prospered during the Ming dynasty.

Key Terms and Places

Use the graphic organizer online to keep track of important details about the Yuan and Ming dynasties.

If YOU lived there...

You are a farmer in northern China in 1212. As you pull weeds from a wheat field, you hear a sound like thunder. Looking toward the sound, you see hundreds—no, *thousands*—of warriors on horses on the horizon, riding straight toward you. You are frozen with fear. Only one thought fills your mind—the Mongols are coming.

What can you do to save yourself?

BUILDING BACKGROUND Throughout its history, northern China had been attacked over and over by nomadic peoples. During the Song dynasty these attacks became more frequent and threatening.

The Mongol Empire

Among the nomadic peoples who attacked the Chinese were the Mongols. For centuries, the Mongols had lived as tribes in the vast plains north of China. Then in 1206, a strong leader, or khan, united them. His name was Temüjin. When he became leader, though, he was given a new title: "Universal Ruler," or Genghis Khan (JENG-guhs KAHN).

The Mongol Conquest

Genghis Khan organized the Mongols into a powerful army and led them on bloody expeditions of conquest. The brutality of the Mongol attacks terrorized people throughout much of Asia and Eastern Europe. Genghis Khan and his army killed all of the men, women, and children in countless cities and villages. Within 20 years, he ruled a large part of Asia.

Genghis Khan then turned his attention to China. He first led his armies into northern China in 1211. They fought their way south, wrecking whole towns and ruining farmland. By the time of Genghis Khan's death in 1227, all of northern China was under Mongol control.

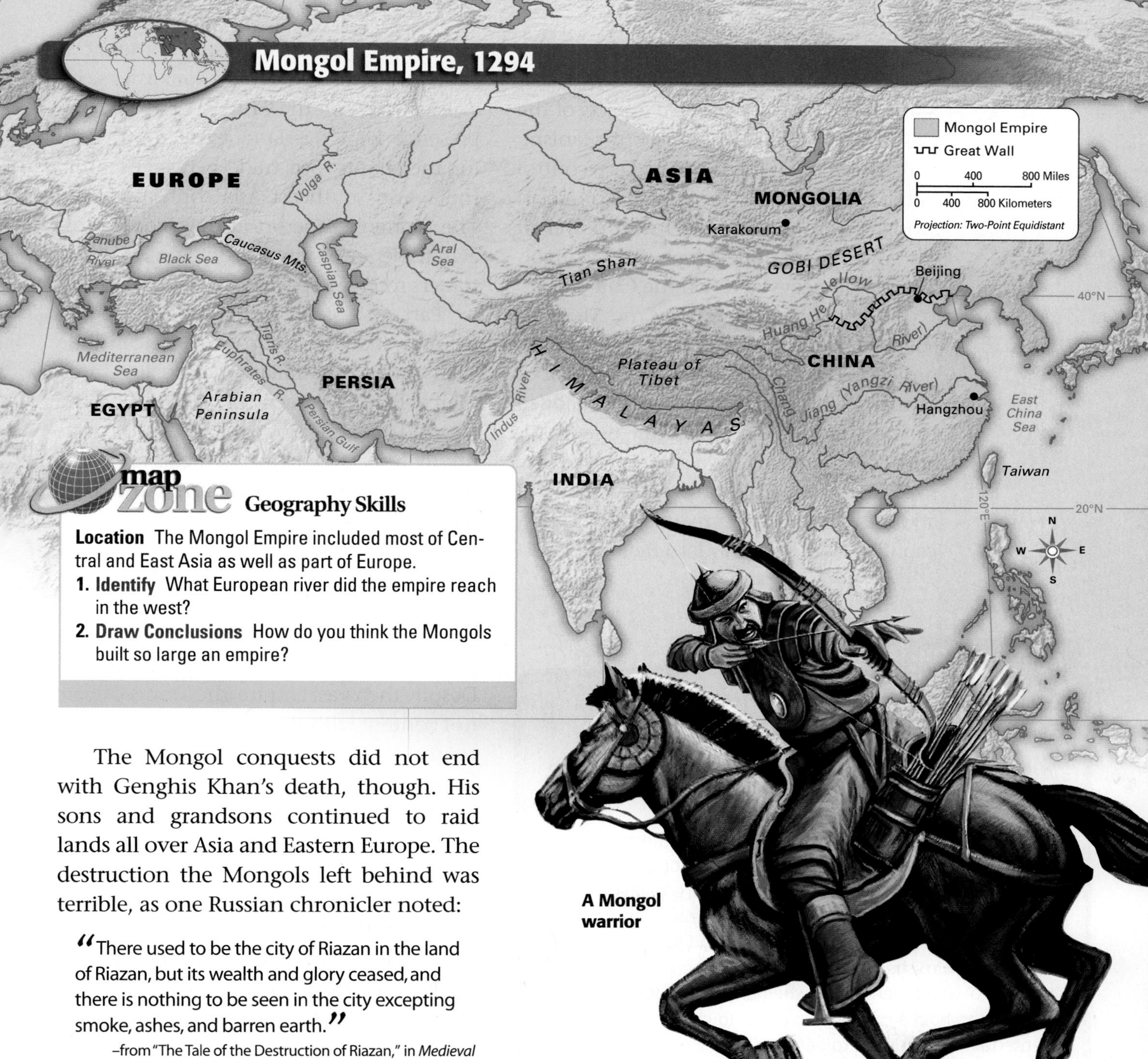

map zone Geography Skills

Location The Mongol Empire included most of Central and East Asia as well as part of Europe.

1. **Identify** What European river did the empire reach in the west?
2. **Draw Conclusions** How do you think the Mongols built so large an empire?

A Mongol warrior

The Mongol conquests did not end with Genghis Khan's death, though. His sons and grandsons continued to raid lands all over Asia and Eastern Europe. The destruction the Mongols left behind was terrible, as one Russian chronicler noted:

> "There used to be the city of Riazan in the land of Riazan, but its wealth and glory ceased, and there is nothing to be seen in the city excepting smoke, ashes, and barren earth."
>
> –from "The Tale of the Destruction of Riazan," in *Medieval Russia's Epics, Chronicles, and Tales*, edited by Serge Zenkovsky

In 1260 Genghis Khan's grandson Kublai Khan (KOO-bluh KAHN) became ruler of the Mongol Empire. He completed the conquest of China and in 1279 declared himself emperor of China. This began the Yuan dynasty, a period that some people also call the Mongol Ascendancy. For the first time in its long history, foreigners ruled all of China.

Life in Yuan China

Kublai Khan and the Mongol rulers he led belonged to a different ethnic group than the Chinese did. They spoke a different language, worshipped different gods, wore different clothing, and had different customs. The Chinese resented being ruled by these foreigners, whom they saw as rude and uncivilized.

However, Kublai Khan did not force the Chinese to accept Mongol ways of life. Some Mongols even adopted aspects of the Chinese culture, such as Confucianism. Still, the Mongols made sure to keep control of the Chinese. They prohibited Confucian scholars from gaining too much power in the government, for example. The Mongols also placed heavy taxes on the Chinese.

Much of the tax money the Mongols collected went to pay for vast public-works projects. These projects required the labor of many Chinese people. The Yuan added to the Grand Canal and built new roads and palaces. Workers also improved the roads used by China's postal system. In addition, the Yuan emperors built a new capital, Dadu, near modern **Beijing**.

Mongol soldiers were sent throughout China to keep the peace as well as to keep a close watch on the Chinese. The soldiers' presence kept overland trade routes safe for merchants. Sea trade between China, India, and Southeast Asia continued, too. The Mongol emperors also welcomed foreign traders at Chinese ports. Some of these traders received special privileges.

Part of what we know about life in the Yuan dynasty comes from one such trader, an Italian merchant named Marco Polo. Between 1271 and 1295 he traveled in and around China. Polo was highly respected by the Mongols and even served in Kublai Khan's court. When Polo returned to Europe, he wrote of his travels. Polo's descriptions of China fascinated many Europeans. His book sparked much European interest in China.

Primary Source

BOOK

A Chinese City

In this passage Marco Polo describes his visit to Hangzhou (HAHNG-JOH), a city in southeastern China.

"Inside the city there is a Lake . . . and all round it are erected [built] beautiful palaces and mansions, of the richest and most exquisite [finest] structure that you can imagine . . . In the middle of the Lake are two Islands, on each of which stands a rich, beautiful and spacious edifice [building], furnished in such style as to seem fit for the palace of an Emperor. And when any one of the citizens desired to hold a marriage feast, or to give any other entertainment, it used to be done at one of these palaces. And everything would be found there ready to order, such as silver plate, trenchers [platters], and dishes, napkins and table-cloths, and whatever else was needful. The King made this provision for the gratification [enjoyment] of his people, and the place was open to every one who desired to give an entertainment."

–Marco Polo, from *Description of the World*

ANALYSIS SKILL **ANALYZING PRIMARY SOURCES**

From this description, what impression might Europeans have of Hangzhou?

The End of the Yuan Dynasty

Despite their vast empire, the Mongols were not content with their lands. They decided to invade Japan. A Mongol army sailed to Japan in 1274 and 1281. The campaigns, however, were disastrous. Violent storms and fierce defenders destroyed most of the Mongol force.

The failed campaigns against Japan weakened the Mongol military. The huge, expensive public-works projects had already weakened the economy. These weaknesses, combined with Chinese resentment, made China ripe for rebellion.

In the 1300s many Chinese groups rebelled against the Yuan dynasty. In 1368 a former monk named Zhu Yuanzhang (JOO yoo-ahn-JAHNG) took charge of a rebel army. He led this army in a final victory over the Mongols. China was once again ruled by the Chinese.

READING CHECK **Finding Main Ideas** How did the Mongols come to rule China?

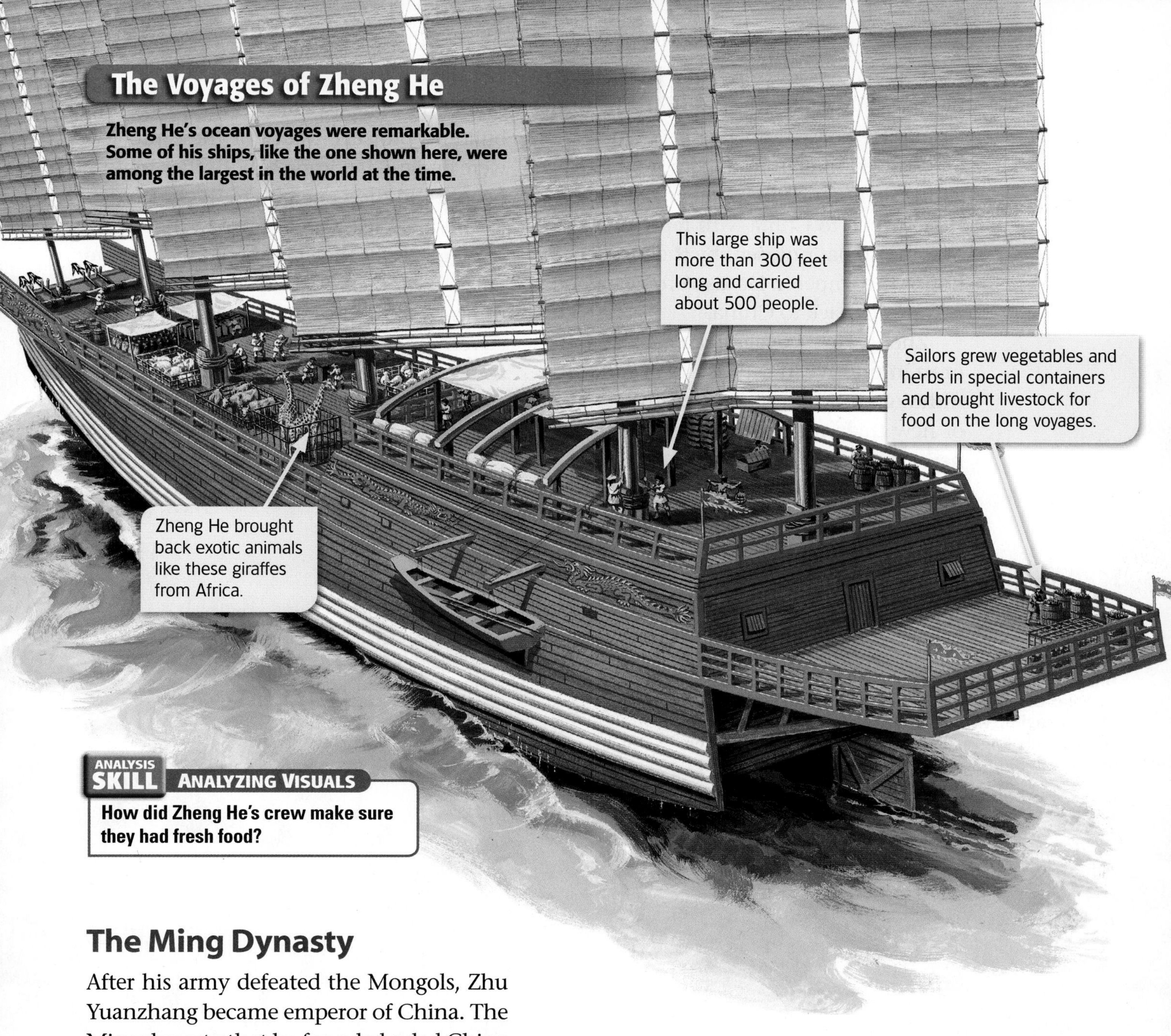

The Voyages of Zheng He
Zheng He's ocean voyages were remarkable. Some of his ships, like the one shown here, were among the largest in the world at the time.
This large ship was more than 300 feet long and carried about 500 people.
Sailors grew vegetables and herbs in special containers and brought livestock for food on the long voyages.
Zheng He brought back exotic animals like these giraffes from Africa.
ANALYSIS SKILL ANALYZING VISUALS
How did Zheng He's crew make sure they had fresh food?

The Ming Dynasty

After his army defeated the Mongols, Zhu Yuanzhang became emperor of China. The Ming dynasty that he founded ruled China from 1368 to 1644—nearly 300 years. Ming China proved to be one of the most stable and prosperous times in Chinese history. The Ming expanded China's fame overseas and sponsored incredible building projects across China.

Great Sea Voyages

During the Ming dynasty, the Chinese improved their ships and their sailing skills. The greatest sailor of the period was Zheng He (juhng HUH). Between 1405 and 1433, he led seven grand voyages to places around Asia. Zheng He's fleets were huge. One included more than 60 ships and 25,000 sailors. Some of the ships were gigantic too, perhaps more than 300 feet long. That is longer than a football field!

In the course of his voyages Zheng He sailed his fleet throughout the Indian Ocean. He sailed as far west as the Persian Gulf and the easternmost coast of Africa.

Everywhere his ships landed, Zheng He presented leaders with beautiful gifts from China. He boasted about his country and encouraged foreign leaders to send gifts to China's emperor. From one voyage, Zheng He returned to China with representatives of some 30 nations, sent by their leaders to honor the emperor. He also brought goods and stories back to China.

Zheng He's voyages rank among the most impressive in the history of seafaring. Although they did not lead to the creation of new trade routes or the exploration of new lands, they served as a clear sign of China's power.

Great Building Projects

The Ming were also known for their grand building projects. Many of these projects were designed to impress both the Chinese people and their enemies to the north.

In Beijing, for example, the Ming emperors built the **Forbidden City**, a huge palace complex that included hundreds of imperial residences, temples, and other government buildings. Within them were some 9,000 rooms. The name Forbidden City came from the fact that the common people were not even allowed to enter the complex. For centuries, this city within a city was a symbol of China's glory.

Close-up

The Forbidden City

The Forbidden City is not actually a city. It's a huge complex of almost 1,000 buildings in the heart of China's capital. The Forbidden City was built for the emperor, his family, his court, and his servants, and ordinary people were forbidden from entering.

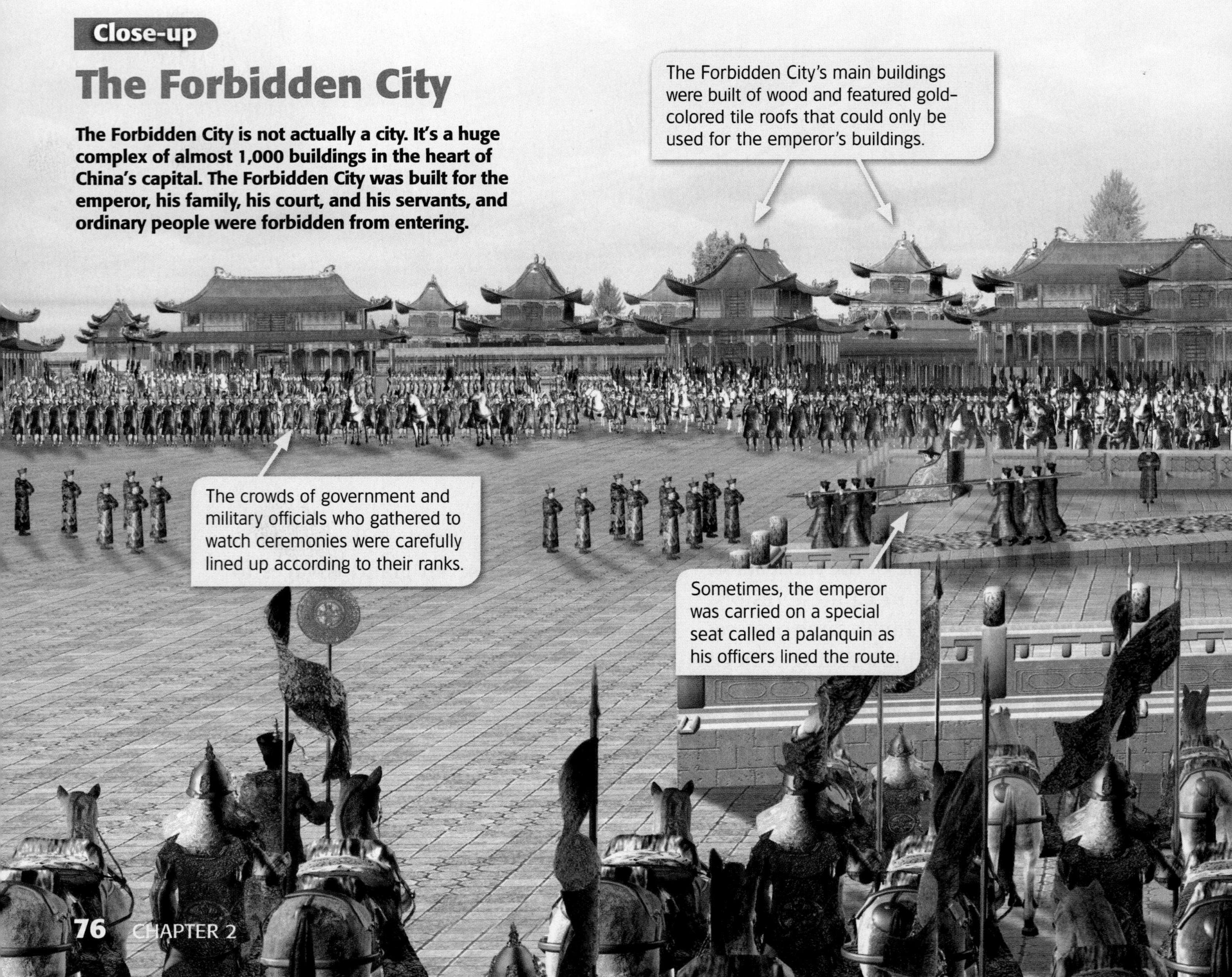

The Forbidden City's main buildings were built of wood and featured gold-colored tile roofs that could only be used for the emperor's buildings.
The crowds of government and military officials who gathered to watch ceremonies were carefully lined up according to their ranks.
Sometimes, the emperor was carried on a special seat called a palanquin as his officers lined the route.

Ming rulers also directed the restoration of the famous Great Wall of China. Large numbers of soldiers and peasants worked to rebuild fallen portions of walls, connect existing walls, and build new ones. The result was a construction feat unmatched in history. The wall was more than 2,000 miles long. It would reach from San Diego to New York! The wall was about 25 feet high and, at the top, 12 feet wide. Protected by the wall—and the soldiers who stood guard along it—the Chinese people felt safe from invasions by the northern tribes.

READING CHECK **Generalizing** In what ways did the Ming dynasty strengthen China?

China under the Ming

During the Ming dynasty, Chinese society began to change. This change was largely due to the efforts of the Ming emperors. Having expelled the Mongols, the Ming emperors worked to eliminate all foreign influences from Chinese society. As a result, China's government and relations with other countries changed dramatically.

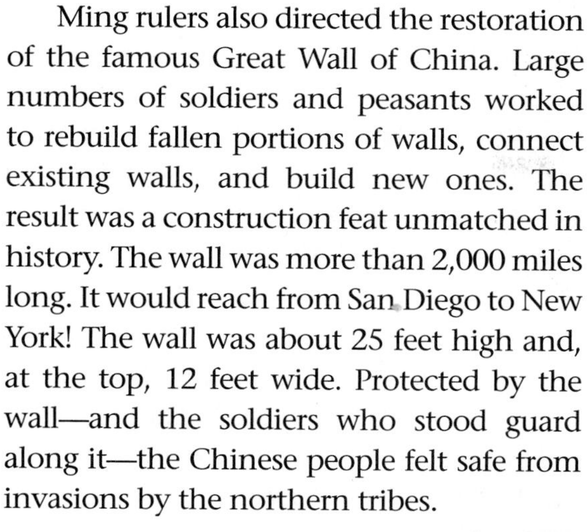

The Hall of Supreme Harmony is the largest building in the Forbidden City. Grand celebrations for important holidays, like the emperor's birthday and the New Year, were held there.

ANALYSIS SKILL **ANALYZING VISUALS**

How did the Forbidden City show the power and importance of the emperor?

Government

When the Ming took over China, they adopted many government programs that had been created by the Tang and the Song. However, the Ming emperors were much more powerful than the Tang and Song emperors had been. They abolished the offices of some powerful officials and took a larger role in running the government themselves. These emperors fiercely protected their power, and they punished anyone whom they saw as challenging their authority.

ACADEMIC VOCABULARY
consequences effects of a particular event or events

Despite their personal power, though, the Ming did not disband the civil service system. Because he personally oversaw the entire government, the emperor needed officials to keep his affairs organized.

The Ming also used examinations to appoint censors. These officials were sent all over China to investigate the behavior of local leaders and to judge the quality of schools and other institutions. Censors had existed for many years in China, but under the Ming emperors their power and influence grew.

Relations with Other Countries

In the 1430s a new Ming emperor made Zheng He return to China and dismantle his fleet. At the same time, he banned foreign trade. China entered a period of isolationism. **Isolationism** is a policy of avoiding contact with other countries.

In the end, this isolationism had great consequences for China. By the late 1800s the Western world had made huge leaps in technological progress. Westerners were able to take power in some parts of China. Partly due to its isolation and lack of progress, China was too weak to stop them. Gradually, China's glory faded.

READING CHECK **Identifying Cause and Effect** How did isolationism affect China?

SUMMARY AND PREVIEW In the last two chapters, you have learned about the long histories of India and China. Next, you will learn what the two countries are like today and how their pasts influence the present.

Section 5 Assessment

hmhsocialstudies.com
ONLINE QUIZ

Reviewing Ideas, Terms, and People

1. a. **Identify** Who was Genghis Khan?
   b. **Explain** How did the Mongols gain control of China?
   c. **Evaluate** Judge this statement: "The Mongols should never have tried to invade Japan."
2. a. **Identify** Who was Zheng He, and what did he do?
   b. **Analyze** What impression do you think the Forbidden City had on the residents of Beijing?
   c. **Develop** How may the Great Wall have both helped and hurt China?
3. a. **Define** What is **isolationism**?
   b. **Explain** How did the Ming change China?
   c. **Develop** How might a policy of isolationism have both advantages and disadvantages?

Critical Thinking

4. **Comparing and Contrasting** Draw a diagram like this one. Use your notes to see how the Yuan and Ming dynasties were alike and different.

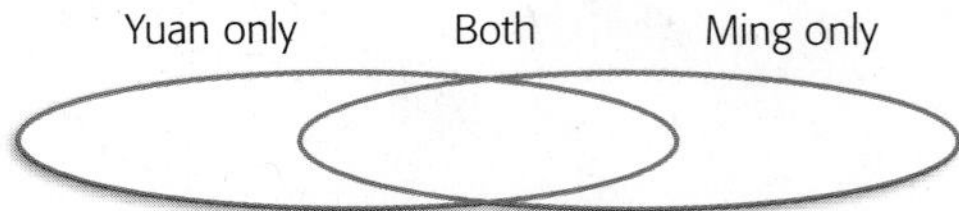

Focus on Writing

5. **Identifying Achievements of the Later Dynasties** Make a list of the achievements of the Yuan and Ming Dynasties. Then look back over all your notes and rate the achievements or inventions. Which four or five do you think are the most important?

BIOGRAPHY

Kublai Khan

How did a Mongol nomad settle down to rule a vast empire?

When did he live? 1215–1294

Where did he live? Kublai Khan came from Mongolia but spent much of his life in China. His capital, Dadu, was near the modern city of Beijing.

What did he do? Kublai Khan completed the conquest of China that Genghis Khan had begun. He ruled China as the emperor of the Yuan dynasty.

Why is he important? The lands Kublai Khan ruled made up one of the largest empires in world history. It stretched from the Pacific Ocean to Eastern Europe. As China's ruler, Kublai Khan welcomed foreign visitors, including the Italian merchant Marco Polo and the Arab historian Ibn Battutah. The stories these two men told helped create interest in China and its products among Westerners.

Generalizing How did Kublai Khan's actions help change people's views of China?

KEY FACTS

- Unified all of China under his rule
- Established peace, during which China's population grew
- Extended the Grand Canal so that food could be shipped from the Huang He (Yellow River) to his capital near modern Beijing
- Linked China to India and Persia with better roads
- Increased contact with the West

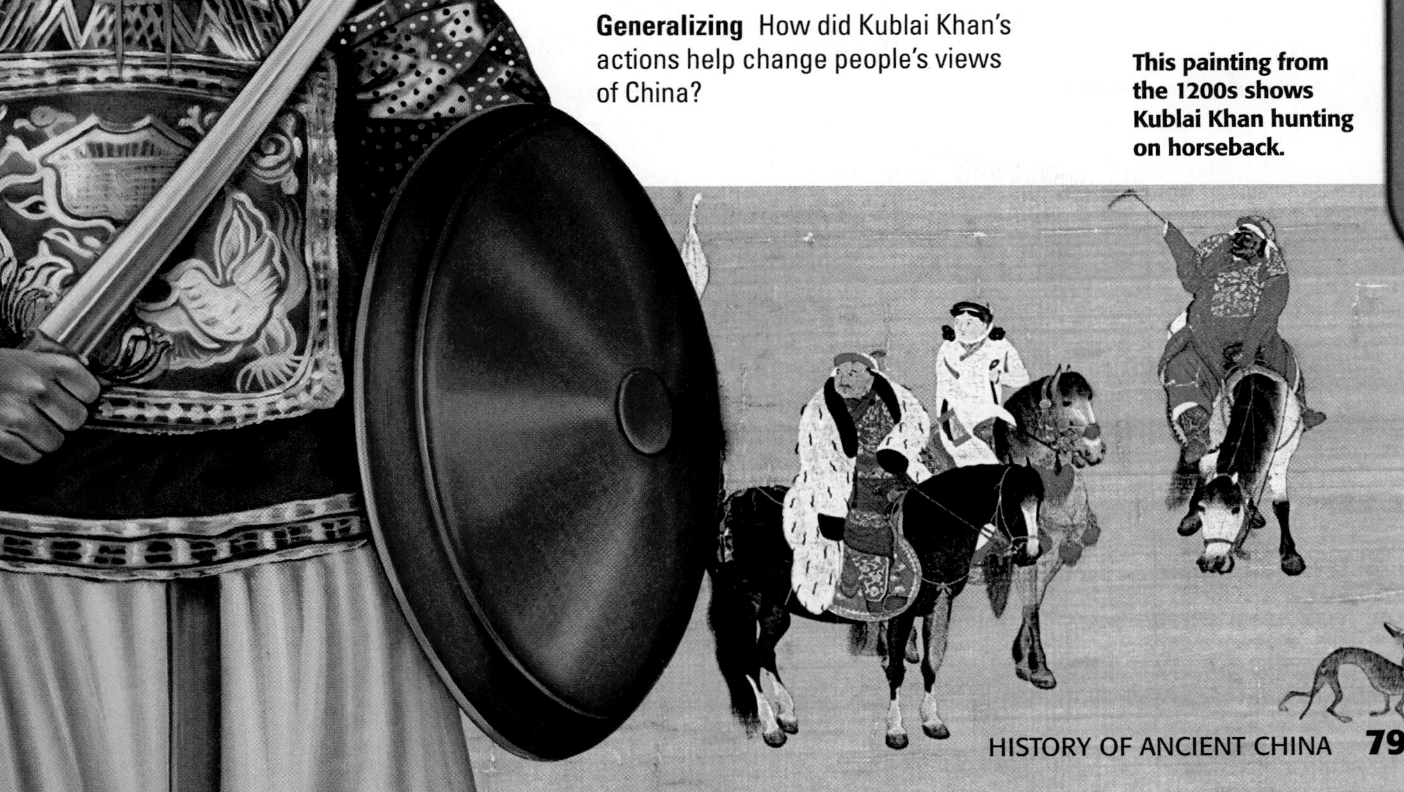

This painting from the 1200s shows Kublai Khan hunting on horseback.

Making Economic Choices

Learn

Economic choices are a part of geography. World leaders must make economic choices every day. For example, a country's president might face a choice about whether to spend government money on improving defense, education, or health care.

You also have to make economic choices in your own life. For example, you might have to decide whether to go to a movie with a friend or buy a CD. You cannot afford to do both, so you must make a choice.

Making economic choices involves sacrifices, or trade-offs. If you choose to spend your money on a movie, the trade-offs are the other things you want but cannot buy. By considering trade-offs, you can make better economic choices.

Practice

Imagine that you are in the school band. The band has enough money to make one major purchase this year. As the diagram below shows, the band can spend the money on new musical instruments, new uniforms, or a band trip. The band decides to buy new instruments.

1. Based on the diagram below, what are the trade-offs of the band's choice?
2. What would have been the trade-offs if the band had voted to spend the money on a trip instead?
3. How do you think creating a diagram like the one below might have helped the band make its economic choice?

Apply

1. Describe an example of an economic choice you might face that has three possible trade-offs.
2. For each possible economic choice, identify what the trade-offs are if you make that choice.
3. What final choice will you make? Why?
4. How did considering trade-offs help you make your choice?

CHAPTER 2

Chapter Review

Geography's Impact
video series
Review the video to answer the closing question:
Do you agree with Confucius's ideas concerning family? Why or why not?

Visual Summary

Use the visual summary below to help you review the main ideas of the chapter.

QUICK FACTS

The Shang, Qin, and Han dynasties ruled China and made many advances that were built on later.

Under the Tang and Song dynasties, Confucianism was an important element of Chinese government.

The Mongols invaded China and ruled it as the Yuan dynasty.

The powerful Ming dynasty strengthened China and expanded trade, but then China became isolated.

Reviewing Vocabulary, Terms, and Places

Match the words or names with their definitions or descriptions.

a. gunpowder
b. scholar-official
c. mandate of heaven
d. bureaucracy
e. seismograph
f. porcelain
g. Great Wall
h. isolationism
i. incentive

1. a device to measure the strength of earthquakes
2. something that leads people to follow a certain course of action
3. body of unelected government officials
4. thin, beautiful pottery
5. educated government worker
6. policy of avoiding contact with other countries
7. a barrier along China's northern border
8. a mixture of powders used in explosives
9. the idea that heaven chose who should rule

Comprehension and Critical Thinking

SECTION 1 *(Pages 50–53)*

10. a. Identify What was the first known dynasty to rule China? What did it achieve?

b. Analyze Why did the Qin dynasty not last long after Shi Huangdi's death?

c. Evaluate Do you think Shi Huangdi was a good ruler for China? Why or why not?

SECTION 2 *(Pages 54–59)*

11. a. Define What is Confucianism? How did it affect Han society?

b. Analyze What was life like for peasants in the Han period?

c. Elaborate What inventions show that the Han studied nature?

SECTION 3 *(Pages 62–67)*

12. a. Describe What did Wu Daozi, Li Bo, Du Fu, and Li Qingzhao contribute to Chinese culture?

b. Analyze How did the Tang rulers change China's government?

c. Evaluate Which Chinese invention has had a greater effect on world history—the magnetic compass or gunpowder? Why do you think so?

SECTION 4 *(Pages 68–71)*

13. a. Define How did Confucianism change in and after the Song dynasty?

b. Make Inferences Why do you think the civil service examination system was created?

c. Elaborate Why were China's civil service examinations so difficult?

SECTION 5 *(Pages 72–78)*

14. a. Describe How did the Mongols create their huge empire? What areas were included in it?

b. Draw Conclusions How did Marco Polo and Zheng He help shape ideas about China?

c. Elaborate Why do you think the Ming spent so much time and money on the Great Wall?

Using the Internet 

15. Activity: Creating a Mural The Tang and Song periods saw many agricultural, technological, and commercial developments. New irrigation techniques, movable type, and gunpowder were a few of them. Through the online book, learn more about such developments. Imagine that a city official has hired you to create a mural showing all of the great things the Chinese developed during the Tang and Song dynasties. Create a large mural that depicts as many advances as possible.

hmhsocialstudies.com

Social Studies Skills 

Making Economic Choices *You have enough money to buy one of the following items: shoes, a DVD, or a book.*

16. What are the trade-offs if you buy the DVD?

17. What are the trade-offs if you buy the book?

Map Activity 

18. Ancient China On a separate sheet of paper, match the letters on the map with their correct labels.

Chang'an	Beijing	Huang He
Kaifeng	Chang Jiang	

hmhsocialstudies.com INTERACTIVE MAP

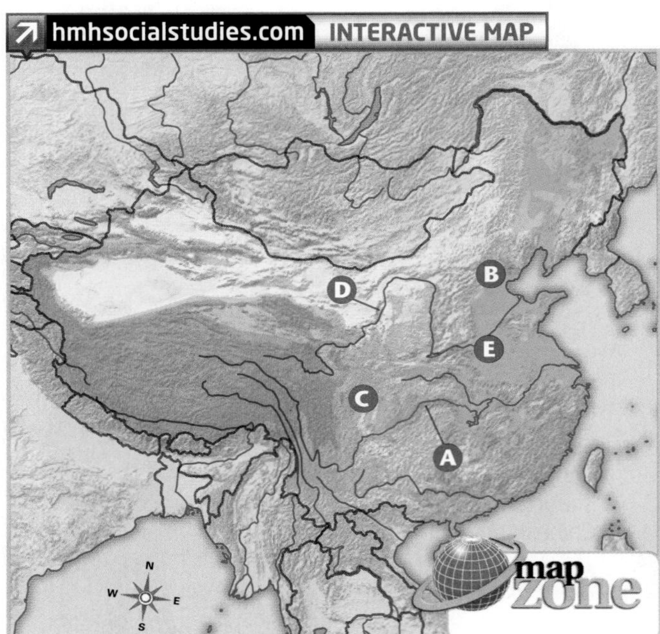

Focus on Reading and Writing

19. Understanding Chronological Order Arrange the following list of events in the order in which they happened. Then write a brief paragraph describing the events, using clue words such as *then* and *later* to show proper sequence.

- The Han dynasty rules China.
- The Shang dynasty takes power.
- Mongol armies invade China.
- The Ming dynasty takes control.

20. Writing Your Magazine Article Now that you have identified the achievements or inventions that you want to write about, begin your article. Open with a sentence that states your main idea. Include a paragraph of two or three sentences about each invention or achievement. Describe each achievement or invention and explain why it was so important. End your article with a sentence or two that summarizes China's importance to the world.

CHAPTER 2

Standardized Test Prep

DIRECTIONS: Read questions 1 through 7 and write the letter of the best response. Then read question 8 and write your own well-constructed response.

1 Who was the Chinese admiral who sailed all around Asia during the Ming dynasty?

A Li Bo
B Genghis Khan
C Zhu Yuanzhang
D Zheng He

2 Trade and other contact with peoples far from China stopped under which dynasty?

A Ming
B Yuan
C Song
D Sui

3 Which of the following was one way that Confucianism influenced China?

A emphasis on family and family values
B expansion of manufacturing and trade
C increase in taxes
D elimination of the government

4 Which of the following was an achievement of the Shang dynasty?

A invention of fireworks
B building of the Grand Canal
C creation of a writing system
D construction of the Forbidden City

5 This object displays Chinese expertise at working with

A woodblocks.
B gunpowder.
C cotton fibers.
D porcelain.

6 Emperor Shi Huangdi had laborers work on a structure that Ming rulers improved. What was that structure?

A the Great Wall
B the Great Tomb
C the Forbidden City
D the Temple of Buddha

7 The ruler who completed the Mongol conquest of China was named

A Shi Huangdi.
B Du Fu.
C Kublai Khan.
D Confucius.

8 Extended Response The ancient Chinese made advances in many fields. Some of their advances still affect life today. Choose one of these advances and write a short paragraph that explains how it still influences people's lives. Be sure to give examples to support your main idea.

CHAPTER 3

The Indian Subcontinent

Essential Question What are the unique geographic and cultural features of the Indian Subcontinent?

What You Will Learn...

In this chapter you will learn about the physical geography of the Indian Subcontinent. You will also discover the history and culture of the region. Finally, you will learn about the countries of the Indian Subcontinent today.

Focus on Reading and Viewing

Visualizing As you read, try to visualize the people, place or events that the text describes. Visualizing, or creating mental images, helps you to better understand and remember the information that is presented. Use your senses to imagine how things look, sound, smell, and feel. **See the lesson, Visualizing, on page 215.**

Presenting and Viewing a Travelogue You are journeying through the Indian Subcontinent, noting the sights and sounds of this beautiful and bustling region of the world. As you read this chapter you will gather details about this region. Then you will create an oral presentation of a travelogue, or traveler's journal. After you present your travelogue, you will watch and listen as your classmates present their travelogues.

IRAQ

IRAN

SAUDI ARABIA

OMAN

YEMEN

✪ National capital
● Major city
--- Disputed boundary
0 150 300 Miles
0 150 300 Kilometers
Projection: Albers Equal-Area

30°N
20°N
50°E
60°E

map zone

Geography Skills

Place The Indian Subcontinent is a large landmass in South Asia.

1. **Locate** What bodies of water border the Indian Subcontinent?
2. **Analyze** What separates the Indian Subcontinent from the rest of Asia?

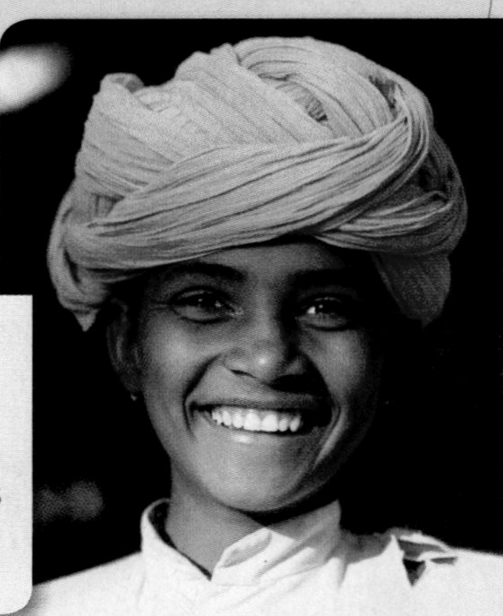

Culture The people of the subcontinent represent the many cultures and religions of the region.

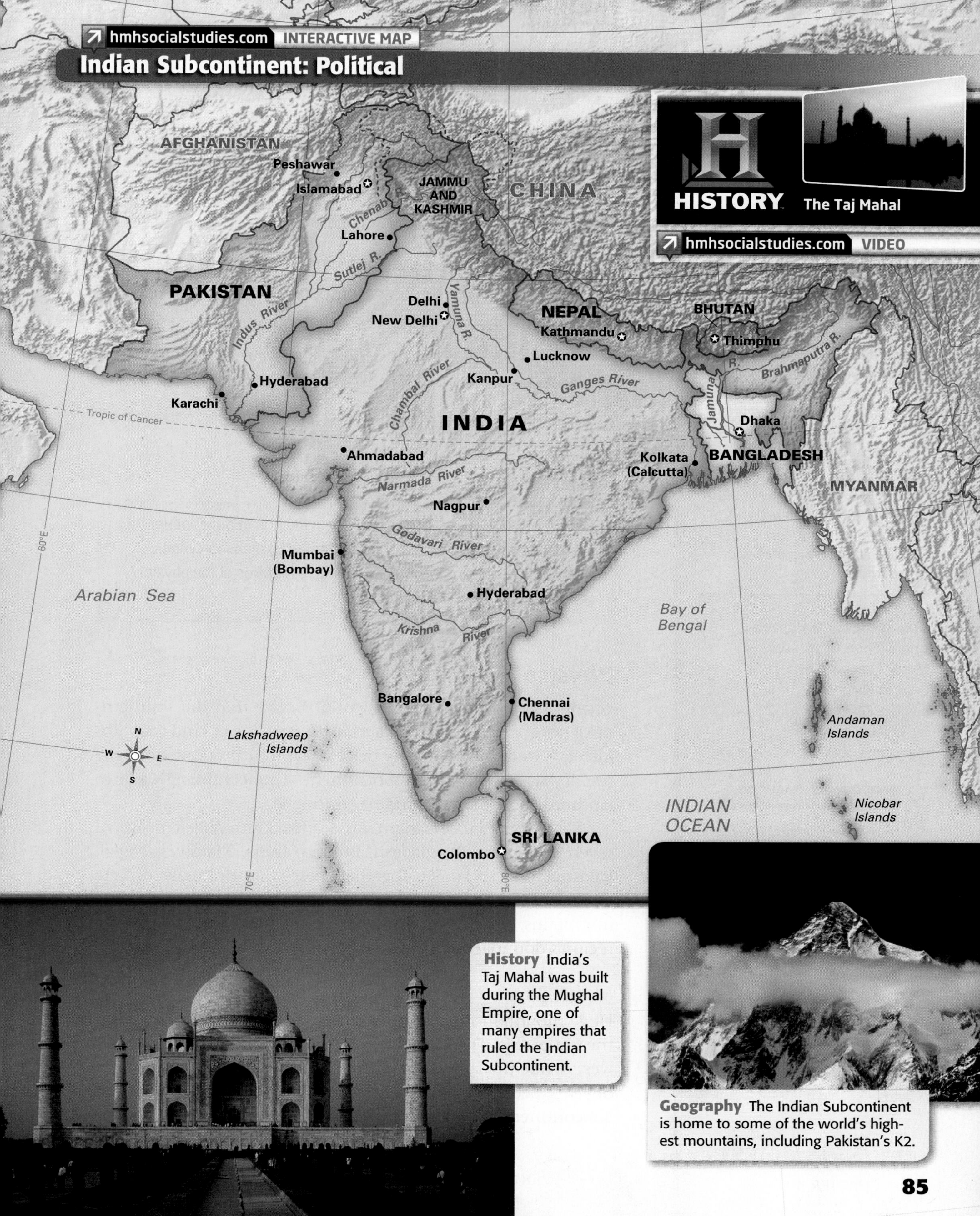

History India's Taj Mahal was built during the Mughal Empire, one of many empires that ruled the Indian Subcontinent.

Geography The Indian Subcontinent is home to some of the world's highest mountains, including Pakistan's K2.

SECTION 1

Physical Geography

What You Will Learn...

Main Ideas

1. Towering mountains, large rivers, and broad plains are the key physical features of the Indian Subcontinent.
2. The Indian Subcontinent has a great variety of climate regions and resources.

The Big Idea

The physical geography of the Indian Subcontinent features unique physical features and a variety of climates and resources.

Key Terms and Places

subcontinent, *p. 86*
Mount Everest, *p. 87*
Ganges River, *p. 87*
delta, *p. 87*
Indus River, *p. 88*
monsoons, *p. 89*

Use the graphic organizer online to take notes on the physical features, climates, and resources of the Indian Subcontinent.

If YOU lived there...

You live in a small farming village in central India. Every year your father talks about the summer monsoons, winds that can bring heavy rains to the region. You know that too much rain can cause floods that may threaten your house and family. Too little rain could cause your crops to fail.

How do you feel about the monsoons?

BUILDING BACKGROUND Weather in the Indian Subcontinent, a region in southern Asia, is greatly affected by monsoon winds. Monsoons are just one of the many unique features of the physical geography of the Indian Subcontinent.

Physical Features

Locate Asia on a map of the world. Notice that the southernmost portion of Asia creates a triangular wedge of land that dips into the Indian Ocean. The piece of land jutting out from the rest of Asia is the Indian Subcontinent. A **subcontinent** is a large landmass that is smaller than a continent.

The Indian Subcontinent, also called South Asia, consists of seven countries—Bangladesh, Bhutan, India, Maldives, Nepal, Pakistan, and Sri Lanka. Together these countries make up one of the most unique geographic regions in the world. Soaring mountains, powerful rivers, and fertile plains are some of the region's dominant features.

Mountains

Huge mountain ranges separate the Indian Subcontinent from the rest of Asia. The rugged Hindu Kush mountains in the northwest divide the subcontinent from Central Asia. For thousands of years, peoples from Asia and Europe have entered the Indian Subcontinent through mountain passes in the Hindu Kush.

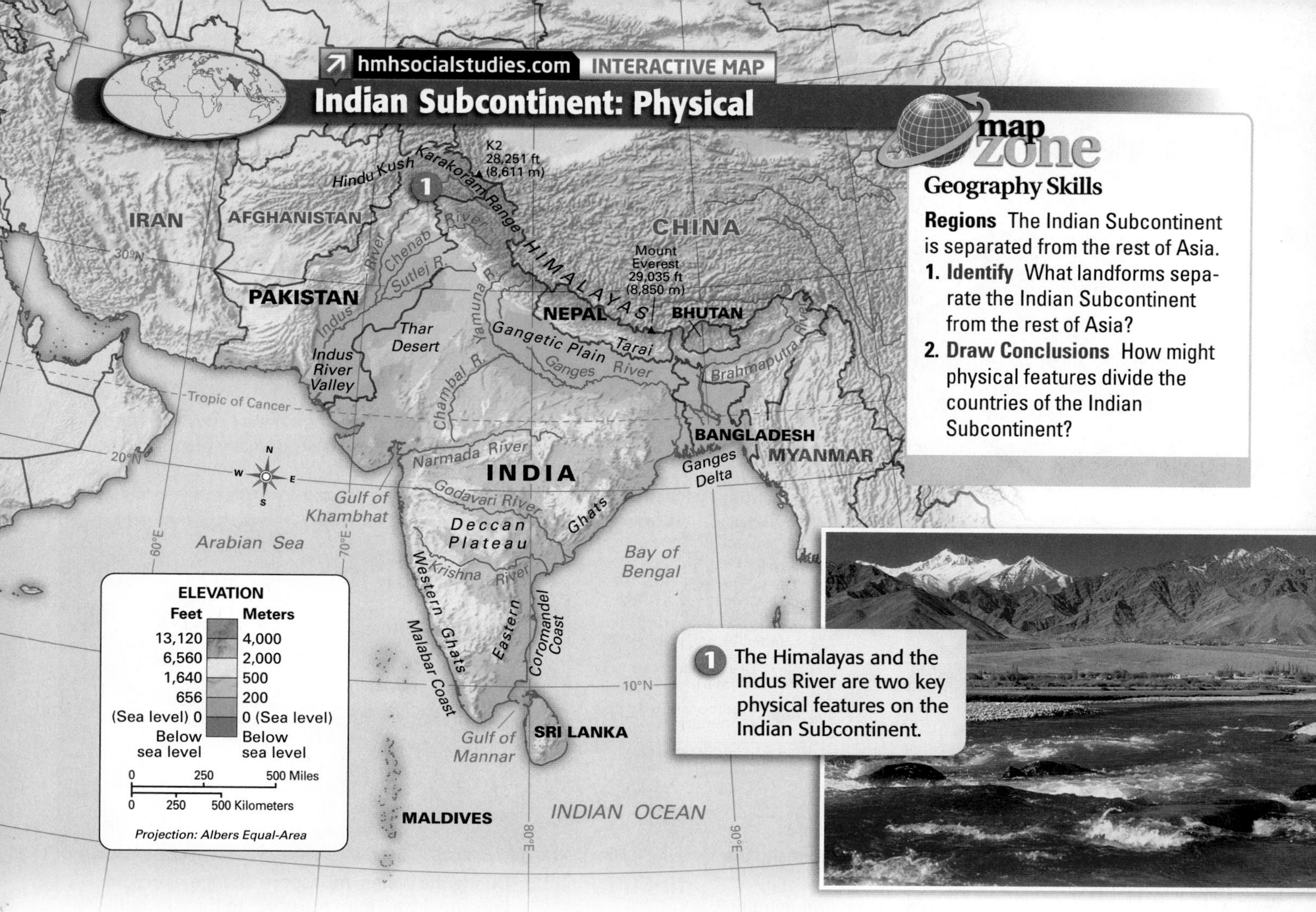

map zone

Geography Skills

Regions The Indian Subcontinent is separated from the rest of Asia.

1. **Identify** What landforms separate the Indian Subcontinent from the rest of Asia?
2. **Draw Conclusions** How might physical features divide the countries of the Indian Subcontinent?

1 The Himalayas and the Indus River are two key physical features on the Indian Subcontinent.

Two smaller mountain ranges stretch down India's coasts. The Eastern and Western Ghats (GAWTS) are low mountains that separate India's east and west coasts from the country's interior.

Perhaps the most impressive physical features in the subcontinent, however, are the Himalayas. These enormous mountains stretch about 1,500 miles (2,415 km) along the northern border of the Indian Subcontinent. Formed by the collision of two massive tectonic plates, the Himalayas are home to the world's highest mountains. On the border between Nepal and China is **Mount Everest**, the highest mountain on the planet. It measures some 29,035 feet (8,850 m). K2 in northern Pakistan is the world's second highest peak.

Rivers and Plains

Deep in the Himalayas are the sources of some of Asia's mightiest rivers. Two major river systems—the Ganges (GAN-jeez) and the Indus—originate in the Himalayas. Each carries massive amounts of water from the mountains' melting snow and glaciers. For thousands of years, these rivers have flooded the surrounding land, leaving rich soil deposits and fertile plains.

Focus on Reading

What words in this paragraph help you to visualize the information?

India's most important river is the Ganges. The **Ganges River** flows across northern India and into Bangladesh. There, the Ganges joins with other rivers and creates a huge delta. A **delta** is a landform at the mouth of a river created by sediment deposits. Along the length of the Ganges is a vast area of rich soil and fertile farmland.

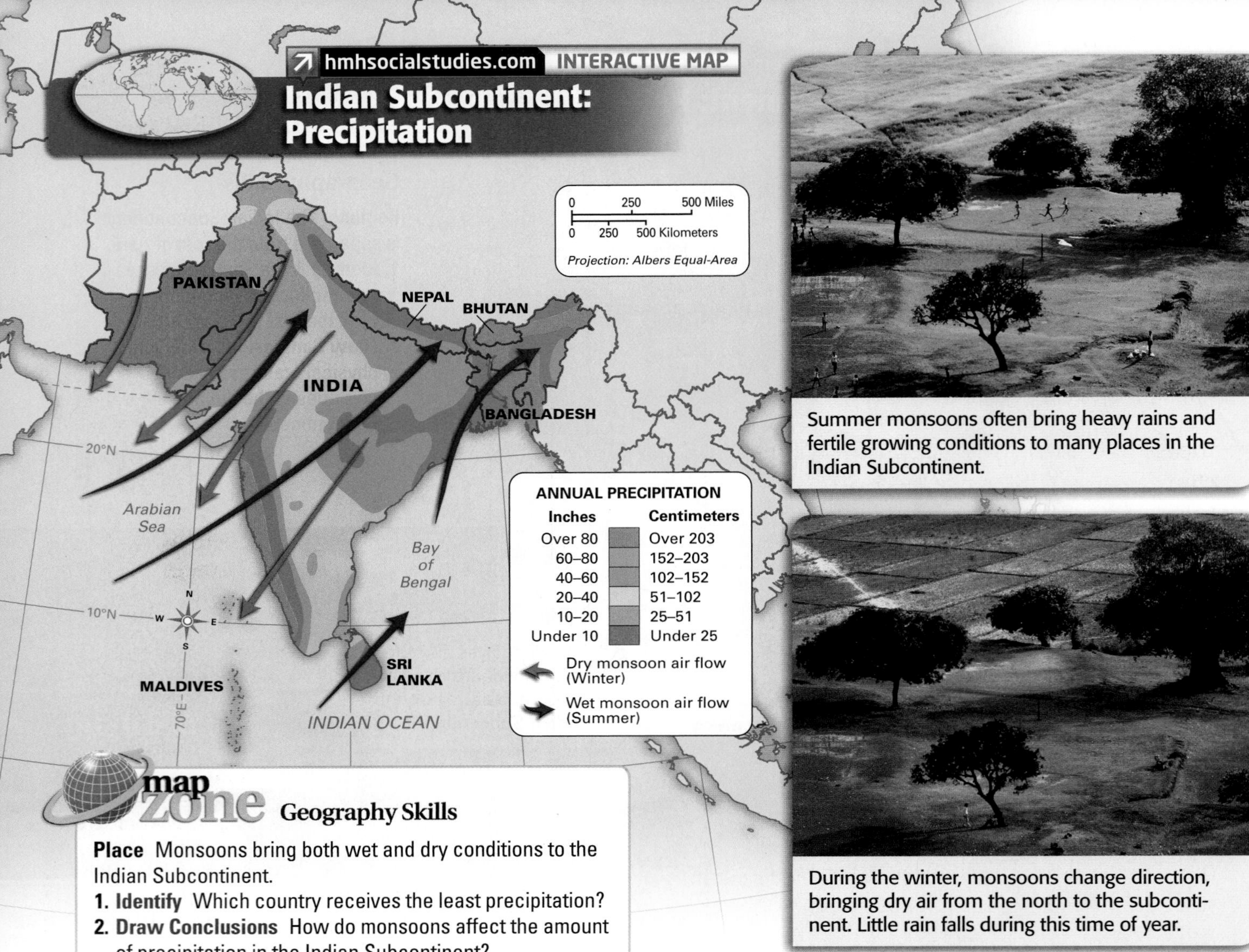

Summer monsoons often bring heavy rains and fertile growing conditions to many places in the Indian Subcontinent.

During the winter, monsoons change direction, bringing dry air from the north to the subcontinent. Little rain falls during this time of year.

map zone Geography Skills

Place Monsoons bring both wet and dry conditions to the Indian Subcontinent.

1. **Identify** Which country receives the least precipitation?
2. **Draw Conclusions** How do monsoons affect the amount of precipitation in the Indian Subcontinent?

Known as the Ganges Plain, this region is India's farming heartland.

Likewise, Pakistan's **Indus River** also creates a fertile plain known as the Indus River Valley. This valley was once home to the earliest Indian civilizations. Today, it is Pakistan's most densely populated region.

hmhsocialstudies.com
ANIMATED GEOGRAPHY
India's Resources: Ancient and Modern

Other Features

Other geographic features are scattered throughout the subcontinent. South of the Ganges Plain, for example, is a large, hilly plateau called the Deccan. East of the Indus Valley is the Thar (TAHR), or Great Indian Desert. Marked by rolling sand dunes, parts of this desert receive as little as 4 inches (100 mm) of rain per year. Still another geographic region is the Tarai (tuh-RY) in southern Nepal. It has fertile farmland and tropical jungles.

READING CHECK **Summarizing** What are the physical features of the Indian Subcontinent?

Climates and Resources

Just as the physical features of the Indian Subcontinent differ, so do its climates and resources. A variety of climates and natural resources exist throughout the region.

Climate Regions

From the Himalayas' snow-covered peaks to the dry Thar Desert, the climates of the Indian Subcontinent differ widely. In the Himalayas, a highland climate brings cool temperatures to much of Nepal and Bhutan. The plains south of the Himalayas have a humid subtropical climate. Hot, humid summers with plenty of rainfall are common in this important farming region.

Tropical climates dominate much of the subcontinent. The tropical savanna climate in central India and Sri Lanka keeps temperatures there warm all year long. This region experiences wet and dry seasons during the year. A humid tropical climate brings warm temperatures and heavy rains to parts of southwest India, Sri Lanka, Maldives, and Bangladesh.

The remainder of the subcontinent has dry climates. Desert and steppe climates extend throughout southern and western India and most of Pakistan.

Monsoons have a huge influence on the weather and climates in the subcontinent. **Monsoons** are seasonal winds that bring either moist or dry air to an area. From June to October, summer monsoons bring moist air up from the Indian Ocean, causing heavy rains. Flooding often accompanies these summer monsoons. In 2005, for example, the city of Mumbai (Bombay), India received some 37 inches (94 cm) of rain in just 24 hours. However, in winter the monsoons change direction, bringing dry air from the north. Because of this, little rain falls from November to January.

Natural Resources

A wide variety of resources are found on the Indian Subcontinent. Agricultural and mineral resources are the most plentiful.

Perhaps the most important resource is the region's fertile soil. Farms produce many different crops, such as tea, rice, nuts, and jute, a plant used for making rope. Timber and livestock are also key resources in the subcontinent, particularly in Nepal and Bhutan.

The Indian Subcontinent also has an abundance of mineral resources. Large deposits of iron ore and coal are found in India. Pakistan has natural gas reserves, while Sri Lankans mine many gemstones.

READING CHECK **Summarizing** What climates and resources are located in this region?

hmhsocialstudies.com
ANIMATED GEOGRAPHY
Monsoons

SUMMARY AND PREVIEW In this section you learned about the wide variety of physical features, climates, and resources in the Indian Subcontinent. Next, you will learn about the rich history and culture of this unique region.

Section 1 Assessment

hmhsocialstudies.com
ONLINE QUIZ

Reviewing Ideas, Terms, and Places

1. a. **Define** What is a **subcontinent**?
   b. **Make Inferences** Why do you think the **Indus River** Valley is so heavily populated?
   c. **Rank** Which physical features in the Indian Subcontinent would you most want to visit? Why?
2. a. **Identify** What natural resources are found in the Indian Subcontinent?
   b. **Analyze** What are some of the benefits and drawbacks of **monsoons**?

Critical Thinking

3. **Drawing Inferences** Draw a chart like the one shown here. Using your notes, write a sentence explaining how each aspect affects life on the Indian Subcontinent.

	Effect on Life
Physical Features	
Climates	
Natural Resources	

FOCUS ON VIEWING

4. **Telling about Physical Geography** What information and images of the region's physical geography might you include in your travelogue? Jot down some ideas.

SECTION 2

History and Culture of India

What You Will Learn...

Main Ideas

1. Advanced civilizations and powerful empires shaped the early history of India.
2. Powerful empires controlled India for hundreds of years.
3. Independence from Great Britain led to the division of India into several countries.
4. Religion and the caste system are two important parts of Indian culture.

The Big Idea

Ancient civilizations and powerful empires have shaped the history and culture of India.

Key Terms and Places

Delhi, *p. 92*
colony, *p. 92*
partition, *p. 93*
Hinduism, *p. 94*
Buddhism, *p. 94*
caste system, *p. 94*

hmhsocialstudies.com
TAKING NOTES

Use the graphic organizer online to take notes on the history and culture of India.

If YOU lived there...

You live in New Delhi, India's capital city. Museums in your city display artifacts from some of India's oldest civilizations. People can visit beautiful buildings built by powerful empires. Statues and parades celebrate your country's independence.

How does your city celebrate India's history?

BUILDING BACKGROUND The Indian Subcontinent has a rich and interesting history. Ancient civilizations, powerful empires, rule by foreigners, and the struggle for independence have shaped not only the history, but also the culture of India and its neighbors.

Early Civilizations and Empires

India, the largest country on the Indian Subcontinent, is one of the world's oldest civilizations. Early civilizations and empires greatly influenced the history of the Indian Subcontinent.

India's History

Ancient Civilizations

- Around 2300 BC the Harappan civilization begins in the Indus River Valley.
- The Aryans, migrants from Central Asia, enter India around 1500 BC.
- Aryan culture helps shape the languages, religion, and caste system of India.

Harappan artifact

Early Empires

- By 233 BC the Mauryan Empire controls most of the Indian Subcontinent.
- Emperor Asoka helps spread Buddhism in India.
- Indian trade and culture flourish during the Gupta Empire.

Mauryan troops atop a war elephant

Ancient Civilizations

The first urban civilization in the Indian Subcontinent was centered around the Indus River Valley in present-day Pakistan. We call this ancient Indian civilization the Harappan (huh-RA-puhn) civilization after one of its main cities. Historians believe that the Harappan civilization flourished between 2300 and 1700 BC. By about 1700 BC, however, this civilization began to decline. No one is certain what led to its decline. Perhaps invaders or natural disasters destroyed the Harappan civilization.

Not long after the Harappan civilization ended, a new group rose to power. Around 1500 BC the Aryans (AIR-ee-uhnz), a group of people from Central Asia, entered the Indian Subcontinent. Powerful warriors, the Aryans eventually conquered and settled the fertile plains along the Indus and Ganges rivers.

The Aryans greatly **influenced** Indian culture. Their language, called Sanskrit, served as the basis for several languages in South Asia. For example, Hindi, the official language of India, is related to Sanskrit. As the Aryans settled in India, they mixed with Indian groups already living there. Their religious beliefs and customs mixed as well, forming the beginnings of India's social system and Hindu religion.

Early Empires

Over time, powerful kingdoms began to emerge in northern India. One kingdom, the Mauryan Empire, dominated the region by about 320 BC. Strong Mauryan rulers raised huge armies and conquered almost the entire subcontinent. Asoka (uh-SOH-kuh), one of the greatest Mauryan emperors, helped expand the empire and improve trade. Asoka also encouraged the acceptance of other religions. After his death, however, the empire slowly crumbled. Power struggles and invasions destroyed the Mauryan Empire.

After the fall of the Mauryan Empire, India split into many small kingdoms. Eventually, however, a strong new empire rose to power. In the AD 300s, the Gupta (GOOP-tuh) Empire united much of northern India. Under Gupta rulers, trade and culture thrived. Scholars made important advances in math, medicine, and astronomy. Indian mathematicians, for example, first introduced the concept of zero.

Gradually, the Gupta Empire also declined. Attacks by invaders from Asia weakened the empire. By about 550, India was once again divided.

ACADEMIC VOCABULARY
influence change, or have an effect on

READING CHECK **Summarizing** How did early civilizations and empires influence India?

The Mughal Empire

- Babur establishes the Mughal Empire in northern India in 1526.
- Indian trade, culture, and religion thrive under the rule of Akbar the Great.
- By 1700 the Mughal Empire rules almost all of the Indian Subcontinent.

The first Mughal emperor, Babur

The British Empire

- The British East India Company establishes trade in northern India in the early 1600s.
- Indian troops trigger a massive revolt against the East India Company.
- The British government takes direct control of India in 1858.
- India and Pakistan gain independence in 1947.

Indian troop in the British Army

BIOGRAPHY

Mohandas Gandhi

(1869–1948)

Considered by many to be the father of modern India, Mohandas Gandhi led the struggle for Indian independence. As a leading member of the Indian National Congress, Gandhi introduced a policy of nonviolent resistance to British rule. He led millions in fasts, peaceful protest marches, and boycotts of British goods. His devotion to nonviolence earned him the name *Mahatma*, or "Great Soul." Gandhi's efforts proved successful. In 1947 India won its independence from Britain.

Drawing Conclusions Why did people call Gandhi *Mahatma*?

VIDEO
Gandhi

hmhsocialstudies.com

Powerful Empires

Powerful empires controlled India for much of its history. First the Mughal Empire and then the British Empire ruled India for hundreds of years.

The Mughal Empire

In the late 600s Muslim armies began launching raids into India. Some Muslims tried to take over Indian kingdoms. Turkish Muslims, for example, established a powerful kingdom at **Delhi** in northern India. In the 1500s a new group of Muslim invaders swept into the subcontinent. Led by the great warrior Babur (BAH-boohr), they conquered much of India. In 1526 Babur established the Mughal (MOO-guhl) Empire.

Babur's grandson, Akbar, was one of India's greatest rulers. Under Akbar's rule, trade flourished. Demand for Indian goods like spices and tea grew. The Mughal Empire grew rich from trade.

Akbar and other Mughal rulers also promoted culture. Although the Mughals were Muslim, most Indians continued to practice Hinduism. Akbar's policy of religious tolerance, or acceptance, encouraged peace throughout his empire. Architecture also thrived in the Mughal Empire. One of India's most spectacular buildings, the Taj Mahal, was built during Mughal rule.

The British Empire

The Mughals were not the only powerful empire in India. As early as the 1500s Europeans had tried to control parts of India. One European country, England, rose to power as the Mughal Empire declined.

The English presence in India began in the 1600s. At the time, European demand for Indian goods, such as cotton and sugar, was very high. Mughal rulers granted the East India Company, a British trading company, valuable trading rights.

At first, the East India Company controlled small trading posts. However, the British presence in India gradually grew. The East India Company expanded its territory and its power. By the mid-1800s the company controlled more than half of the Indian Subcontinent. India had become a British **colony**, a territory inhabited and controlled by people from a foreign land.

British rule angered and frightened many Indians. The East India Company controlled India with the help of an army made up mostly of Indian troops commanded by British officers. In 1857 Indian troops revolted, triggering violence all across India. The British government crushed the rebellion and took control of India away from the East India Company. With that, the British government began to rule India directly.

READING CHECK **Analyzing** How did powerful empires affect Indian history?

Independence and Division

By the late 1800s many Indians had begun to question British rule. Upset by their position as second-class citizens, a group of Indians created the Indian National Congress. Their goal was to gain more rights and opportunities.

As more and more Indians became dissatisfied with British rule, they began to demand independence. Mohandas Gandhi was the most important leader of this Indian independence movement. During the 1920s and 1930s his strategy of nonviolent protest convinced millions of Indians to support independence.

Finally, Great Britain agreed to make India independent. However, tensions between the Hindu and Muslim communities caused a crisis. Fearing they would have little say in the new government, India's Muslims called for a separate nation.

To avoid a civil war, the British government agreed to the **partition**, or division, of India. In 1947 two independent countries were formed. India was mostly Hindu. Pakistan, which included the area that is now Bangladesh, was mostly Muslim. As a result, some 10 million people rushed to cross the border. Muslims and Hindus wanted to live in the country where their religion held a majority.

Soon after India and Pakistan won their independence, other countries in the region gradually did too. Sri Lanka and Maldives gained their independence from Great Britain. In 1971, after a bloody civil war that killed almost 1 million people, East Pakistan broke away to form the country of Bangladesh.

READING CHECK **Identifying Cause and Effect** What were the effects of Indian independence from Great Britain?

FOCUS ON READING

As you read this paragraph, visualize the events described. Draw a rough sketch to depict what you imagine.

The Partition of India

A massive wave of migration took place after the partition of India and Pakistan. Millions of Hindus and Muslims crowded onto trains that would take them to their new homelands in India and Pakistan.

Indian Culture

As you might imagine, the rich and unique history of the Indian Subcontinent has created an equally unique culture. Two aspects of that culture are religion and a strict social class system.

Religion

Religion has played a very important role in Indian history. In fact, India is the birthplace of several major religions, including Hinduism and Buddhism.

Hinduism One of the world's oldest religions is **Hinduism**, the dominant religion of India. According to Hindu beliefs, everything in the universe is part of a single spirit called Brahman. Hindus believe that their ultimate goal is to reunite their souls with that spirit. Hinduism teaches that souls are reincarnated, or reborn, many times before they join with Brahman.

Buddhism Another Indian religion is Buddhism, which began in northern India in the late 500s BC. **Buddhism** is a religion based on the teachings of Siddhartha Gautama—the Buddha. According to the Buddha's teachings, people can rise above their desire for material goods and reach nirvana. Nirvana is a state of perfect peace in which suffering and reincarnation end.

Caste System

Thousands of years ago, the Aryans organized Indian society into a unique social class system known as the caste system. The **caste system** divided Indian society into groups based on a person's birth or occupation.

The caste system features four main classes, or castes, originally based on occupations. Below these four castes are the Dalits, members of India's lowest class. Many rules guided interaction between the classes. For example, people from different castes were not allowed to eat together.

READING CHECK **Analyzing** How do religion and the caste system influence Indian culture?

SUMMARY AND PREVIEW In this section you learned about the rich history and culture of the Indian Subcontinent. Next, you will learn about important issues that affect India today.

Section 2 Assessment

hmhsocialstudies.com
ONLINE QUIZ

Reviewing Ideas, Terms, and Places

1. **a. Identify** What different peoples ruled India?
   b. Analyze How did these early civilizations and empires influence Indian culture?
2. **a. Describe** What were some accomplishments of the Mughal Empire?
   b. Predict How might Indian history have been different if the British had not ruled India?
3. **a. Recall** Who was the leader of India's independence movement?
   b. Explain What led to the **partition** of India?
4. **a. Define** What is the **caste system**?
   b. Elaborate Why do you think India is home to some of the world's oldest religions?

Critical Thinking

5. **Summarizing** Use your notes and a diagram like the one here to write a sentence summarizing each aspect of Indian history and culture.

Focus on Viewing

6. **Discussing History and Culture** Which details about India's history and culture will you use? How will you explain and illustrate them?

Analyzing a Line Graph

Learn

Line graphs are drawings that display information in a clear, visual form. People often use line graphs to track changes over time. For example, you may want to see how clothing prices change from year to year. Line graphs also provide an easy way to see patterns, like increases or decreases, that emerge over time. Use the following guidelines to analyze a line graph.

- Read the title. The title will tell you about the subject of the line graph.
- Examine the labels. Note the type of information in the graph, the time period, and the units of measure.
- Analyze the information. Be sure to look for patterns that emerge over time.

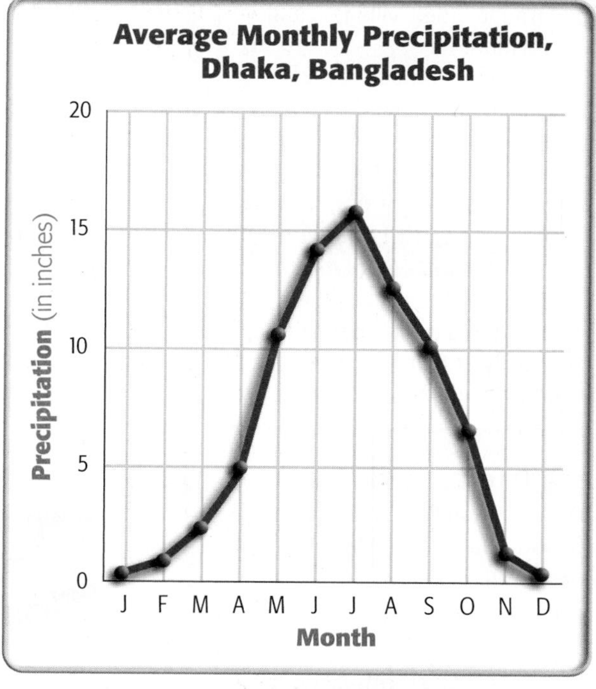

Source: *National Geographic Atlas of the World, Seventh Edition*

Practice

Examine the line graph carefully, then answer the questions below.

1. What is the subject of this line graph?
2. What units of measure are used? What period of time does the line graph reflect?
3. What pattern does the line graph indicate? How can you tell?

Apply

Create a line graph that tracks your grades in a particular class. Start by organizing your grades by the date of the assignment. Then plot your grades on a line graph. Be sure to use labels and a title to identify the subject and information presented in your line graph. Finally, identify any patterns that you see in the line graph.

SECTION 3

India Today

What You Will Learn...

Main Ideas

1. Daily life in India is centered around cities, villages, and religion.
2. Today India faces many challenges, including a growing population and economic development.

The Big Idea

India today features a blend of modern and traditional culture, a rapidly growing population, and a developing economy.

Key Terms and Places

Mumbai (Bombay), *p. 96*
Kolkata (Calcutta), *p. 96*
urbanization, *p. 98*
green revolution, *p. 99*

Use the graphic organizer online to take notes about daily life and challenges in India today.

If YOU lived there...

You live in Mumbai, India's largest city. A major port, Mumbai is home to many industries, such as textiles and electronics. Museums and theaters offer entertainment. Every year, thousands of people flock to Mumbai in search of jobs or to enroll in its universities. The streets are crowded, and pollution is often heavy.

Do you enjoy living in Mumbai? Why or why not?

BUILDING BACKGROUND India has undergone many changes since gaining its independence from Great Britain. Cities have grown dramatically, new businesses and industries have developed, and the population has exploded. India today faces many challenges.

Daily Life in India

Nearly 1.2 billion people live in India today. This huge population represents modern India's many different ethnic groups, religions, and lifestyles. Despite these many differences, city life, village life, and religion all help unite the people of India.

Cities

Millions of Indians live in large, bustling cities. In fact, India's three largest cities, **Mumbai (Bombay),** Delhi, and **Kolkata (Calcutta)**, are among the world's most populous cities. Many people in Indian cities work in factories and offices. Some cities, like Bangalore and Mumbai, are home to universities, research centers, and high-tech businesses. Most city-dwellers, however, struggle to earn a living. Many people live in shacks made of scraps of wood or metal. They often have no plumbing and little clean water.

Villages

Most Indians still live in rural areas. Hundreds of thousands of villages are home to more than 70 percent of India's population. Most villagers work as farmers and live with an extended family in simple homes. Only recently have paved roads and electricity reached many Indian villages.

Religion

In both cities and villages, religion plays a key role in Indian daily life. While most Indians practice Hinduism, many people follow several other religions such as Islam, Buddhism, and traditional religions. In addition, millions of Indians practice two native religions, Sikhism and Jainism.

Religious celebrations are an important part of Indian life today. One of India's most popular festivals is Diwali, the festival of lights. Diwali celebrates Hindu, Sikh, and Jain beliefs.

READING CHECK **Contrasting** How does life in Indian cities and villages differ?

Close-up

Diwali: The Festival of Lights

Diwali, or the festival of lights, is one of the most important celebrations in India. A variety of activities on each of the five days of Diwali celebrate Hindu, Sikh, and Jain beliefs.

Beautiful firework displays are common during Diwali.
Elaborate chalk designs, called rangolis, often decorate floors and walls.
Diwali is a time to spend with friends and family. Cards and small gifts, such as sweets and candles, are often exchanged.
Small oil lamps, or *diyas*, decorate homes inside and out.

ANALYSIS SKILL **ANALYZING VISUALS**

What elements of Indian daily life do you see in the illustration?

India's Challenges

India has undergone drastic changes since gaining independence. Today the country faces several challenges, such as dealing with a growing population and managing its economic development.

hmhsocialstudies.com
ANIMATED GEOGRAPHY
Population Density of India

Population

Its more than 1 billion people make India the world's second most populous country. Only China has a larger population. India's population has grown rapidly, doubling since 1947. This huge population growth places a strain on India's environment and many of its resources, including food, housing, and schools.

India's cities are particularly affected by the growing population. As the country's population has grown, urbanization has taken place. **Urbanization** is the increase in the percentage of people who live in cities. Many millions of people have moved to India's cities in search of jobs.

Government and Economy

Since India gained independence, its leaders have strengthened the government and economy. Today India is the world's

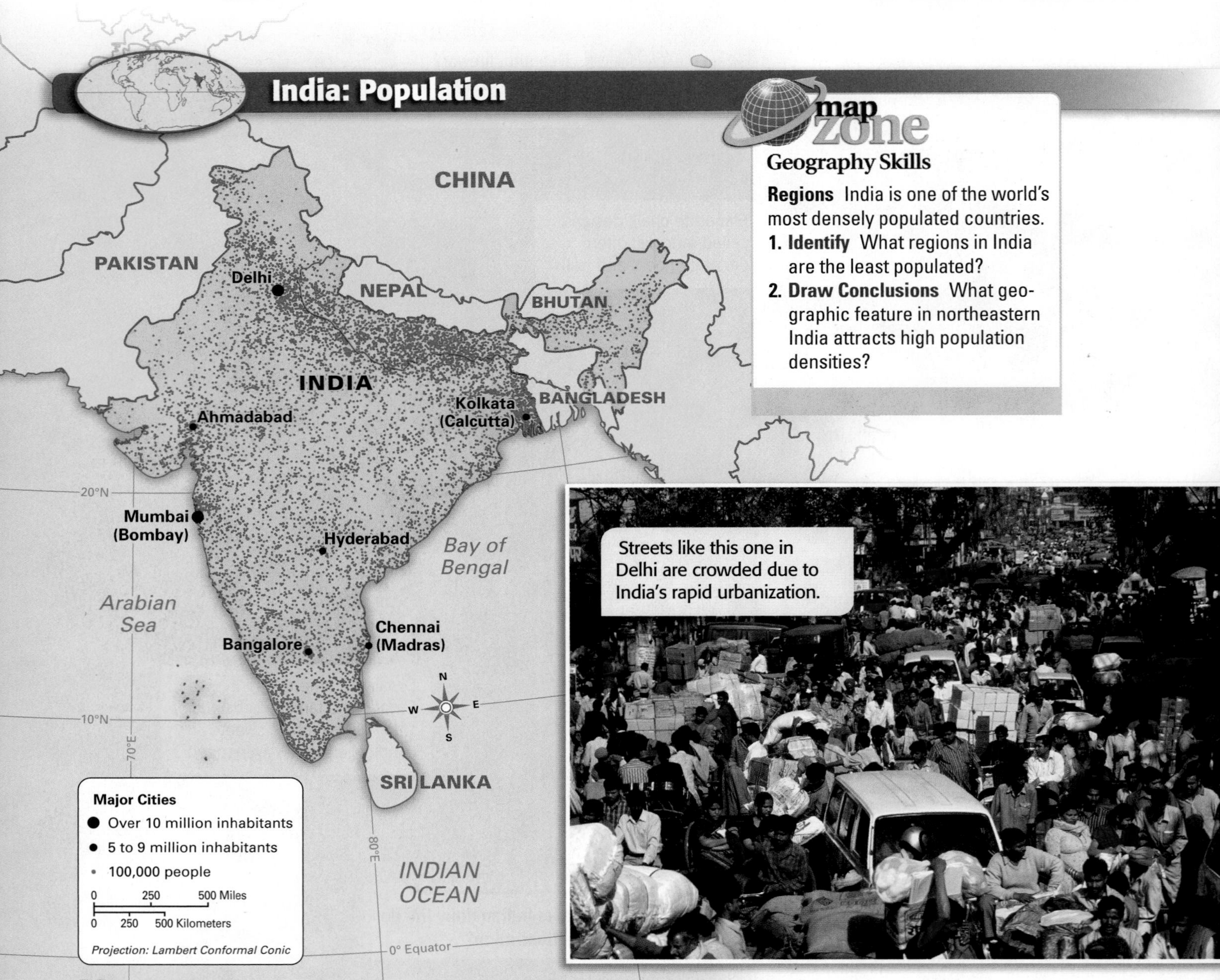

map zone
Geography Skills

Regions India is one of the world's most densely populated countries.

1. **Identify** What regions in India are the least populated?
2. **Draw Conclusions** What geographic feature in northeastern India attracts high population densities?

Streets like this one in Delhi are crowded due to India's rapid urbanization.

largest democracy and one of the strongest nations in Asia. The greatest challenges facing India's government are providing for a growing population and resolving conflicts with its neighbor, Pakistan. Both India and Pakistan have nuclear weapons.

India's gross domestic product (GDP) places it among the world's top 5 industrial countries. However, its per capita, or per person, GDP is only $2,900. As a result, millions of Indians live in poverty.

India's government has taken steps to reduce poverty. In the 1960s and 1970s the **green revolution**, a program that encouraged farmers to adopt modern agricultural methods, helped farmers produce more food. Recently, the government has succeeded in attracting many high-tech businesses to India.

READING CHECK **Finding Main Ideas** What are India's government and economy like?

SUMMARY AND PREVIEW India today faces many challenges as it continues to modernize. Next, you will learn about India's neighbors on the subcontinent.

CONNECTING TO Economics

Bollywood

One of India's largest industries is its moviemaking industry. Much of India's film industry is located in Mumbai (Bombay). Many people refer to the industry as Bollywood—a combination of Bombay and Hollywood. Bollywood produces more films every year than any other country. In fact, each year India produces almost twice the number of films produced in the United States. In recent years, Bollywood films have become increasingly popular outside of India—particularly in the United Kingdom and the United States.

Drawing Conclusions How might the film industry affect India's economy?

Section 3 Assessment

hmhsocialstudies.com
ONLINE QUIZ

Reviewing Ideas, Terms, and Places

1. a. **Identify** What different religions are practiced in India today?
   b. **Compare and Contrast** In what ways are Indian cities similar to cities in the United States? How are they different from U.S. cities?
   c. **Elaborate** Why do you think that a majority of Indians live in villages?
2. a. **Recall** What is **urbanization**? What is one cause of urbanization?
   b. **Make Inferences** How did the **green revolution** affect India's economy?
   c. **Predict** What effects might India's growing population have on its resources and environment in the future?

Critical Thinking

3. **Finding Main Ideas** Using your notes and the web diagram, write the main idea for each element of India today.

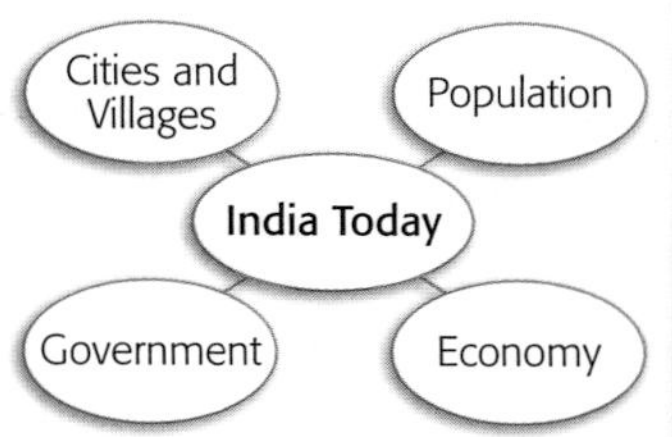

Focus on Viewing

4. **Telling about India Today** You will need some images, or pictures, for your travelogue. What images can you use to tell about India today?

SECTION 4

India's Neighbors

What You Will Learn...

Main Ideas

1. Many different ethnic groups and religions influence the culture of India's neighbors.
2. Rapid population growth, ethnic conflicts, and environmental threats are major challenges to the region today.

The Big Idea

Despite cultural differences, the countries that border India share similar challenges.

Key Terms and Places

Use the graphic organizer online to take notes on the culture and issues in the countries that border India.

If YOU lived there...

You live in the mountainous country of Bhutan. For many years Bhutan's leaders kept the country isolated from outsiders. Recently, they have begun to allow more tourists to enter the country. Some of your neighbors believe that tourism will greatly benefit the country. Others think it could harm the environment.

How do you feel about tourism in Bhutan?

BUILDING BACKGROUND After years of isolation or control by Great Britain, the 1900s brought great changes to the countries on the Indian Subcontinent. Today these countries face rapid population growth and economic and environmental concerns.

Culture

Five countries—Pakistan, Bangladesh, Nepal, Bhutan, and Sri Lanka—share the subcontinent with India. Though they are neighbors, these countries have significantly different cultures.

People The cultures of the countries that border India reflect the customs of many ethnic groups. For example, the **Sherpas**, an ethnic group from the mountains of Nepal, often serve as guides through the Himalayas. Members of Bhutan's largest ethnic group originally came from Tibet, a region in southern China. Many of Sri Lanka's Tamil (TA-muhl) people came from India to work the country's huge plantations.

Religion As you can see on the map on the next page, a variety of religions exist on the Indian Subcontinent. Most countries, like India, have one major religion. In Pakistan and Bangladesh, for example, most people practice Islam and small portions of the population follow Hinduism, Christianity, and tribal religions. In Nepal, the dominant religion is Hinduism, although Buddhism is practiced in some parts of the country. Buddhism dominates both Bhutan and Sri Lanka.

READING CHECK **Contrasting** In what ways are the cultures of this region different?

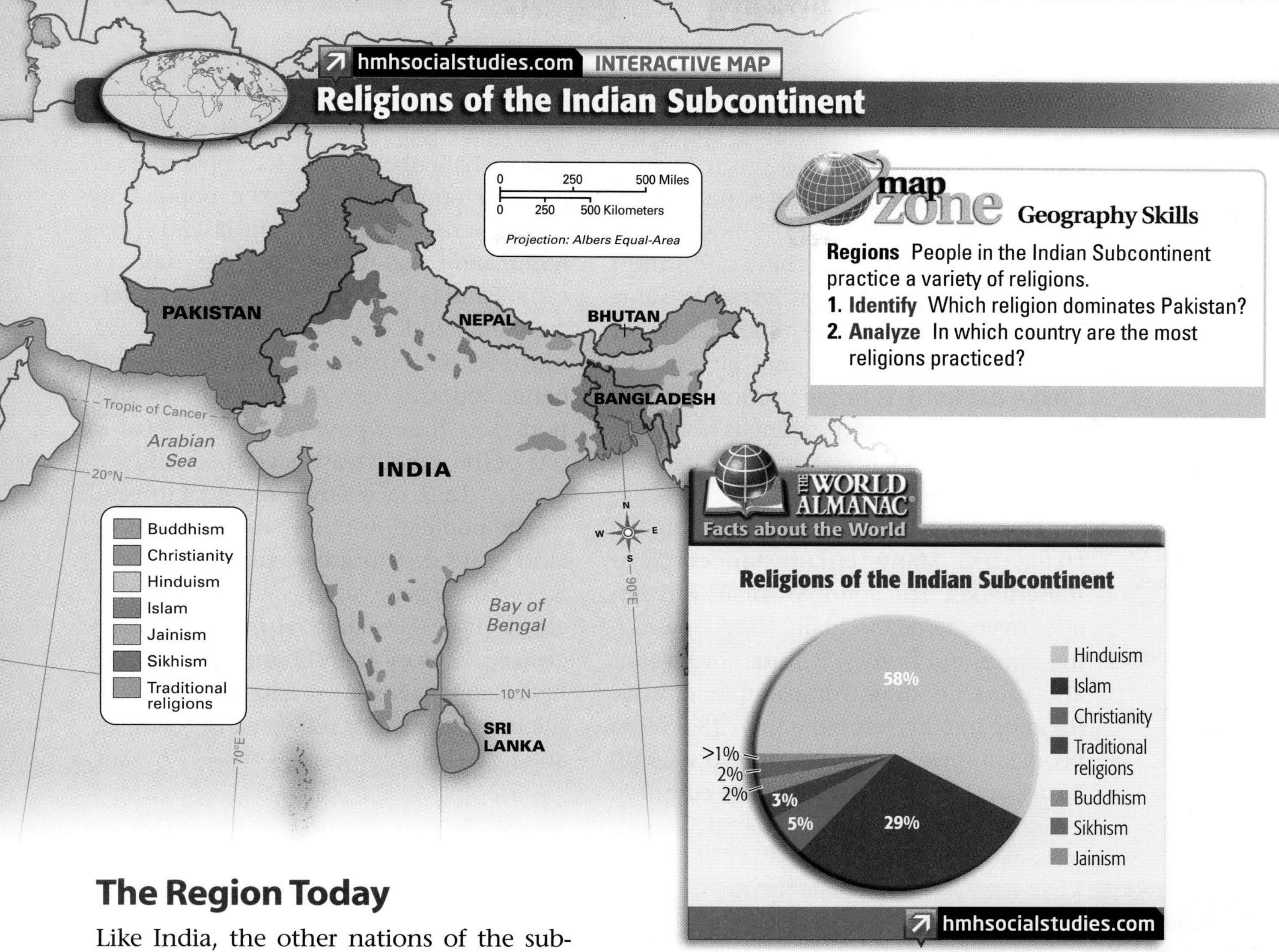

map zone Geography Skills

Regions People in the Indian Subcontinent practice a variety of religions.

1. **Identify** Which religion dominates Pakistan?
2. **Analyze** In which country are the most religions practiced?

THE WORLD ALMANAC® Facts about the World

Religions of the Indian Subcontinent

Religion	Percent
Hinduism	58%
Islam	29%
Christianity	5%
Traditional religions	3%
Buddhism	2%
Sikhism	2%
Jainism	>1%

hmhsocialstudies.com

The Region Today

Like India, the other nations of the subcontinent face a variety of challenges. Two of the greatest challenges are population growth and poverty.

Pakistan

One of the greatest challenges Pakistan faces is the lack of government stability. Since its creation in 1947, Pakistan has suffered from rebellions and assassinations of government leaders. In 2001, General Pervez Musharraf came to power in a military coup. Under pressure from protestors calling for democracy, Musharraf resigned in 2008. Pakistanis then elected Asif Ali Zardari as president.

Another challenge is Pakistan's rapid population growth. The country's government struggles to manage resources and to reduce poverty.

Relations with India are another important issue in Pakistan today. Since the partition in 1947, the two countries have clashed over the territory of **Kashmir**. Both India and Pakistan claim control of the region. Today Pakistan controls western Kashmir while India controls the east. Armed troops from both countries guard a "line of control" that divides Kashmir.

Since 2001 Pakistan has aided the United States in its war on terrorism. Pakistan's military has arrested hundreds of terrorists and provided information about suspected terrorists. Despite this crackdown, however, many people believe that there are still terrorists within Pakistan's borders.

FOCUS ON READING

Visualize the information described in this paragraph. Describe what mental images you see.

Bangladesh

Bangladesh is a small country about the same size as the state of Wisconsin. Despite its small size, Bangladesh's population is almost half the size of the U.S. population. As a result, it is one of the world's most densely populated countries with some 3,018 people per square mile (1,165 per square km). The capital and largest city, **Dhaka** (DA-kuh), is home to more than 13 million people. Overcrowding is not limited to urban areas, however. Rural areas are also densely populated.

ACADEMIC VOCABULARY
circumstances conditions that influence an event or activity

Flooding is one of Bangladesh's biggest challenges. Many **circumstances** cause these floods. The country's many streams and rivers flood annually, often damaging farms and homes. Summer monsoons also cause flooding. For example, massive flooding in 2004 left more than 25 million people homeless. It also destroyed schools, farms, and roads throughout the country.

Nepal

The small kingdom of Nepal also faces many challenges today. Its population is growing rapidly. In fact, the population has more than doubled in the last 30 years. **Kathmandu** (kat-man-DOO), the nation's capital and largest city, is troubled by overcrowding and poverty. Thousands have moved to Kathmandu in search of jobs and better opportunities. As a result of population growth and poor resources, Nepal is one of the world's least-developed nations.

Nepal also faces environmental threats. As the population grows, more and more land is needed to grow enough food. To meet this need, farmers clear forests to create more farmland. This deforestation causes soil erosion and harms the wildlife in the region. Nepal's many tourists add to the problem as they use valuable resources and leave behind trash.

Bhutan

Bhutan is a small mountain kingdom that lies in the Himalayas between India and China. Because of the rugged mountains, Bhutan has been isolated throughout much of its history. This isolation limited outside influences until the 1900s, when Bhutan's king established ties first with Great Britain and later with India. By the mid-1900s Bhutan had ended its long isolation. Efforts to modernize Bhutan resulted in the construction of new roads, schools, and hospitals.

Today Bhutan continues to develop economically. Most Bhutanese earn a living as farmers, growing rice, potatoes, and

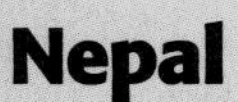

Nepal

Many of Nepal's people live in the rugged Himalayas and earn a living herding animals.

corn. Some raise livestock like yaks, pigs, and horses. Another important industry is tourism. The government, however, limits the number of visitors to Bhutan to protect Bhutan's environment and way of life.

Sri Lanka

Sri Lanka is a large island country located some 20 miles (32 km) off India's southeast coast. As a result of its close location, India has greatly influenced Sri Lanka. In fact, Sri Lanka's two largest ethnic groups—the Tamil and the Sinhalese (sin-huh-LEEZ)—are descended from Indian settlers.

Conflicts between the Sinhalese and the Tamil divide Sri Lanka today. The Tamil minority has fought for years to create a separate state. In 2009, government troops declared an end to the fighting after the Tamil leader was killed.

Parts of Sri Lanka were devastated by the 2004 tsunami in the Indian Ocean. Thousands of Sri Lankans were killed, and more than 500,000 people were left homeless. The tsunami also damaged Sri Lanka's fishing and agricultural industries, which are still struggling to rebuild.

READING CHECK **Summarizing** What key issues affect India's neighbors today?

Sri Lanka

These women are picking tea on one of Sri Lanka's many tea plantations.

SUMMARY AND PREVIEW You have learned about the important challenges that face India's neighbors on the subcontinent. In the next chapter, you will learn about the physical geography, history, and culture of China, Mongolia, and Taiwan.

Section 4 Assessment

hmhsocialstudies.com ONLINE QUIZ

Reviewing Ideas, Terms, and Places

1. a. **Identify** What are the major religions of the Indian Subcontinent?
   b. **Summarize** What cultural differences exist among India's neighbors?
   c. **Elaborate** Why do you think there are so many different religions in this region?
2. a. **Identify** What is the capital of Nepal?
   b. **Compare and Contrast** In what ways are the countries of this region similar and different?
   c. **Predict** How might conflict over **Kashmir** cause problems in the future?

Critical Thinking

3. **Solving Problems** Using your notes and a chart like the one here, identify one challenge facing each of India's neighbors. Then develop a solution for each challenge.

Challenges	Solutions

FOCUS ON VIEWING

4. **Telling about India's Neighbors** Your travels include voyages to India's neighbors. Include important or intriguing details and images in your travelogue.

Literature

from

Shabanu: Daughter of the Wind

by Suzanne Fisher Staples

A Pakistani bride on her wedding day

About the Reading *In* Shabanu, *writer Suzanne Fisher Staples writes about the life of Shabanu, a young girl who is part of a nomadic desert culture in Pakistan. In this passage, Shabanu and her family prepare for the wedding of her older sister.*

AS YOU READ **Look for details about the customs and traditions of Shabanu and her people.**

Two days before the wedding, Bibi Lal . . . heads a procession of women to our house for the *mahendi* celebration ❶ . . . Bibi Lal looks like a giant white lily among her cousins and nieces, who carry baskets of sweets atop their flower-colored *chadrs*. They sing and dance through the fields, across the canal, to our settlement at the edge of the desert.

Sakina carries a wooden box containing henna. The *mahendi* women, Hindus from a village deep in the desert who will paint our hands and feet, walk behind her. Musicians and a happy cacophony of horns, pipes, and cymbals drift around them.

Mama, the servant girl, and I have prepared a curry of chicken, dishes of spiced vegetables, sweet rice, and several kinds of bread to add to the food that the women of Murad's family bring . . . Sharma has washed and brushed my hair. I wear a new pink tunic. She lines my eyes and rubs the brilliant lapis powder into my lids. ❷

GUIDED READING

WORD HELP

chadrs cloths worn by women as a head cover

henna a reddish dye made from a shrub; often used to decorate the hands and feet

cacophony a combination of loud sounds

curry a dish prepared in a highly spiced sauce

lapis a stone with a rich, deep blue color

❶ At a *mahendi* celebration women gather to prepare the bride for her wedding day.

❷ To line the eyes means to darken the rims of the eyelids with black kohl, an eyeliner.

Connecting Literature to Geography

1. **Describing** How did the women prepare for the upcoming wedding? What was the *mahendi* celebration like?

2. **Interpreting** Women come to Shabanu's house from a distant village to paint the girls' hands and feet with henna. Why do you think this custom is important to the women and girls? What might it symbolize?

CHAPTER 3

Chapter Review

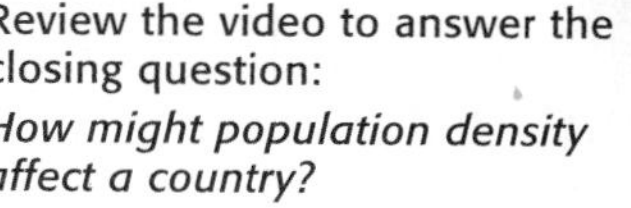

Geography's Impact
video series
Review the video to answer the closing question:
How might population density affect a country?

Visual Summary

Use the visual summary below to help you review the main ideas of the chapter.

QUICK FACTS

Towering mountains and powerful monsoons characterize the physical geography of the Indian Subcontinent.

India's Taj Mahal represents the subcontinent's rich history and culture.

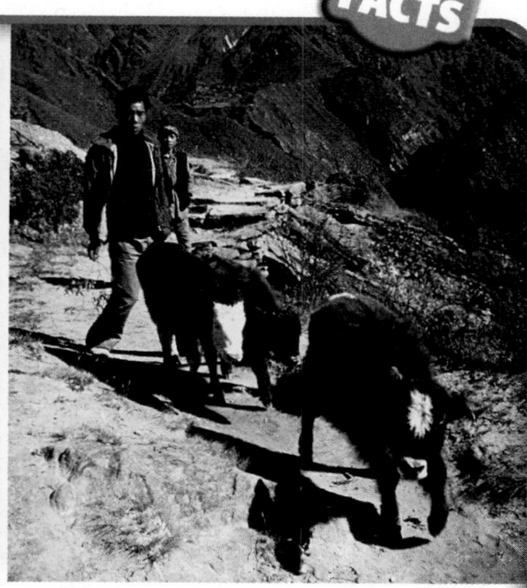

The nations that border India face many economic, political, and environmental challenges today.

Reviewing Vocabulary, Terms, and Places

Choose one word from each word pair to correctly complete each sentence below.

1. __________ often bring heavy rains to the Indian Subcontinent in summer. **(Monsoons/Ghats)**
2. The most popular religion in India today is __________. **(Buddhism/Hinduism/Islam)**
3. A __________ is a condition that influences an event or activity. **(feature/circumstance)**
4. __________ are an ethnic group from the mountains of Nepal. **(Tamil/Sherpas)**
5. The highest peak in the Indian Subcontinent and the world is __________. **(Mount Everest/K2)**
6. India's __________ system divides society based on a person's birth, wealth, and job. **(caste/colonial)**
7. Pakistan is located on the Indian __________, a large landmass. **(Peninsula/Subcontinent)**

Comprehension and Critical Thinking

SECTION 1 *(Pages 86–89)*

8. **a. Recall** What is a delta?
   b. Draw Conclusions Why are rivers important to the people of the Indian Subcontinent?
   c. Evaluate Do you think monsoons have a positive or negative effect on India? Why?

SECTION 2 *(Pages 90–94)*

9. **a. Describe** What was the partition of India? When and why did it take place?
   b. Compare and Contrast In what ways were Mughal and British rule of India similar and different?
   c. Evaluate In your opinion, was partitioning India a good decision? Why or why not?

SECTION 3 *(Pages 96–99)*

10. **a. Identify** What program introduced modern agricultural methods to India?

SECTION 3 *(continued)*

b. Analyze How has population growth affected India's economy?

c. Elaborate If you lived in India, would you prefer to live in a city or a village? Why?

SECTION 4 *(Pages 100–103)*

11. a. Identify What countries share the subcontinent with India?

b. Analyze How was Sri Lanka affected by the 2004 tsunami?

c. Predict How might conflict between India and Pakistan lead to problems in the future?

Social Studies Skills

Analyzing Line Graphs *Use the line graph to help you answer the questions that follow.*

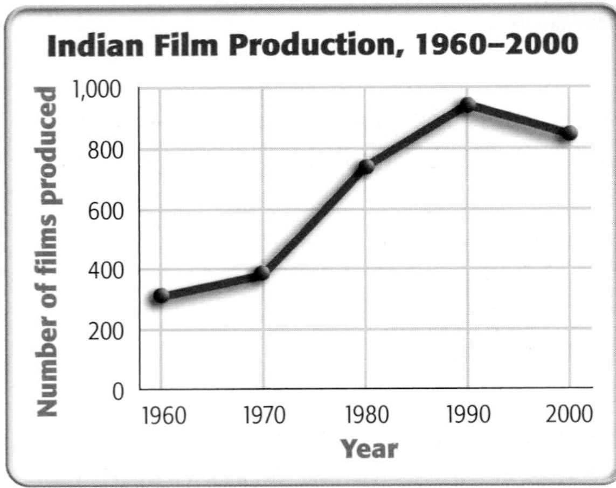

Source: *Bollywood, India's Film Industry*

12. What is the subject of the line graph?

13. What general pattern or trend does the line graph indicate?

Using the Internet 

14. Touring India Pack your bags and experience India! It's a country where you can climb towering mountains, journey across vast deserts, and even hike through rain forests. Through the online book, discover the regions of India. Then make an illustrated travel brochure that features some of the regions you have explored.

Map Activity 

15. The Indian Subcontinent On a separate sheet of paper, match the letters on the map with their correct labels.

Deccan	Mount Everest
Himalayas	Mumbai (Bombay)
Indus River	New Delhi
Kashmir	Sri Lanka

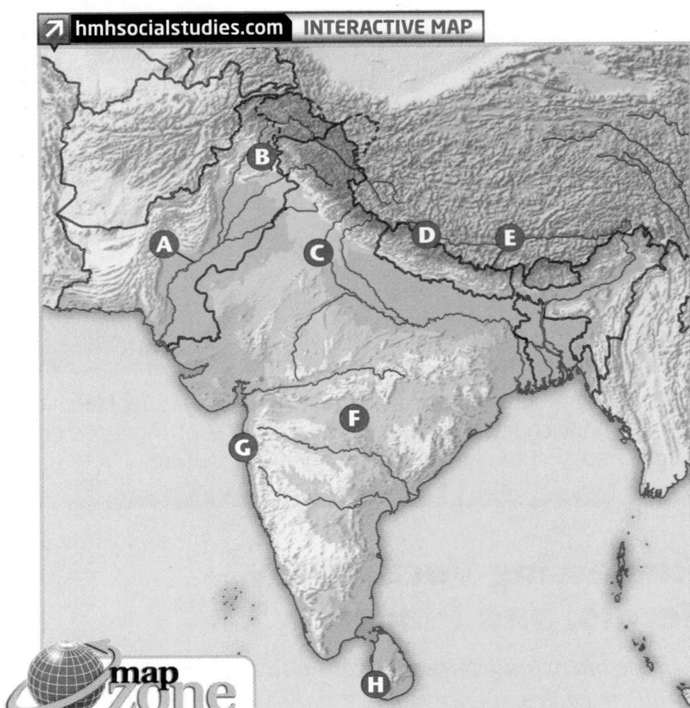

Focus on Reading and Viewing

16. Visualizing Read the literature selection *Shabanu: Daughter of the Wind*. As you read, visualize the scenes the author describes. Then make a list of words from the passage that help you create a mental image of the events. Lastly, draw a rough sketch of your mental image of the *mahendi* celebration.

17. Creating and Viewing a Travelogue Use your notes to create a one- to two-minute script describing your travels in the Indian Subcontinent. Identify and collect the images you need to illustrate your talk. Present your oral travelogue to the class, giving an exciting view of the region. Observe as others present their travelogues. How is each travelogue unique? How are they similar?

CHAPTER 3

Standardized Test Prep

DIRECTIONS: Read questions 1 through 7 and write the letter of the best response. Then read question 8 and write your own well-constructed response.

1 Which of the following is the *oldest* Indian civilization?

A Aryan
B Harappan
C Mughal
D Pakistani

2 Which of the following is a cause of India's rapid urbanization?

A People have moved away from cities to escape overcrowding and poverty.
B People have left villages to avoid rural warfare.
C People have left India in search of land.
D People have moved to cities in search of jobs.

3 Isolationism, Buddhism, and monarchy are all associated with which country?

A Bhutan
B India
C Nepal
D Sri Lanka

4 The majority of Indians today live

A in the Indus River Valley.
B on the coast.
C in cities.
D in villages.

5 The division of Indian society is known as

A the caste system.
B Diwali.
C Hinduism.
D the partition of India.

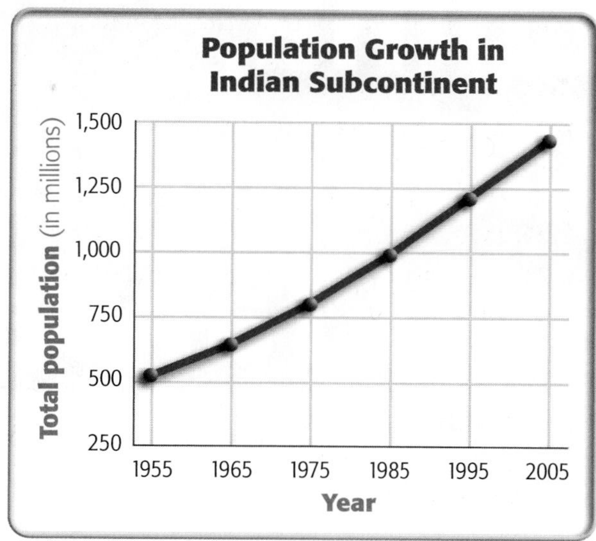

Source: United Nations Population Division

6 Based on the line graph above, what was the approximate population of South Asia in 1985?

A 500,000,000
B 760,000,000
C 1,000,000,000
D 1,400,000,000

7 These seasonal winds bring both wet and dry conditions to much of the Indian Subcontinent.

A hurricanes
B monsoons
C tsunamis
D typhoons

8 Extended Response Using information from the map in Section 3 titled India: Population, write a paragraph describing the settlement patterns in India today.

CHAPTER 4

China, Mongolia, and Taiwan

Essential Question How has the rise of communism shaped life in China and in the surrounding nations?

What You Will Learn...

In this chapter you will learn about the physical features, climate, and resources of China, Mongolia, and Taiwan. You will also study the histories of these countries and what life is like in these regions today.

The Big Idea Physical features, climate, and resources vary across China, Mongolia, and Taiwan.

The Big Idea Ruled by dynasties in its early history, China is a Communist country with an enormous population and ancient traditions.

The Big Idea China's economy and cities are growing rapidly, but the Chinese have little political freedom and many environmental problems.

The Big Idea Mongolia is a rugged land with a nomadic way of life and growing cities, while Taiwan is a densely settled and industrialized island.

Focus on Reading and Writing

Identifying Implied Main Ideas The main idea in a piece of writing is sometimes stated directly. Other times, you must figure out the main idea. As you read, look for key details or ideas to help you identify the implied main ideas. **See the lesson, Identifying Implied Main Ideas, on page 216.**

Writing a Legend Since ancient times, people have passed along legends. These stories often tell about supernatural people or events from the past. Read the chapter. Then write your own legend describing the creation of a physical feature in this region.

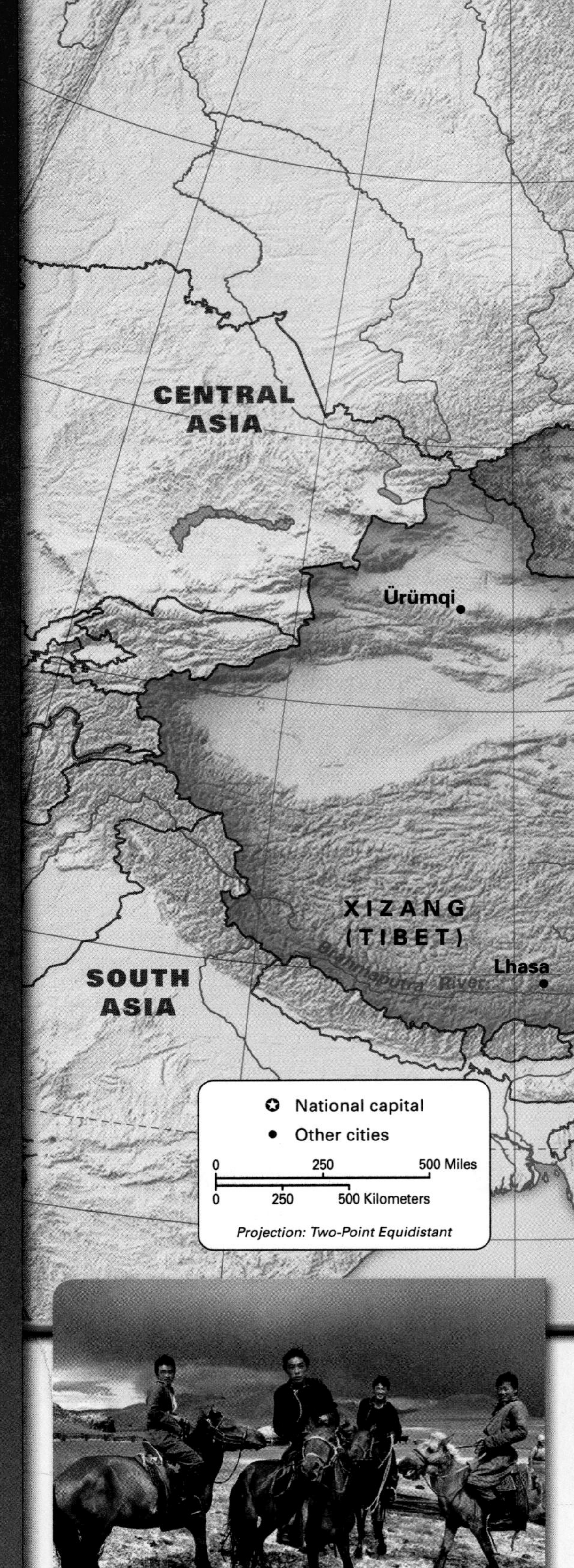

Geography Horses play an important role in Mongolian life and culture. Many Mongolians are nomads and use horses to travel across the country's large plains.

map zone Geography Skills

Regions China is the largest country in East Asia and is closely linked with Mongolia and Taiwan.

1. **Name** What are the capitals of China, Mongolia, and Taiwan?
2. **Contrast** Based on the map, how do the countries of Mongolia and Taiwan differ?

History The Great Wall of China stretches for many miles across China's northern lands.

Culture Chinese opera uses music and symbolism to tell stories. The actors wear bold and colorful makeup that has special meanings.

SECTION 1

Physical Geography

What You Will Learn...

Main Ideas

1. Physical features of China, Mongolia, and Taiwan include mountains, plateaus and basins, plains, and rivers.
2. China, Mongolia, and Taiwan have a range of climates and natural resources.

The Big Idea

Physical features, climate, and resources vary across China, Mongolia, and Taiwan.

Key Terms and Places

Himalayas, *p. 110*
Plateau of Tibet, *p. 111*
Gobi, *p. 111*
North China Plain, *p. 112*
Huang He, *p. 112*
loess, *p. 112*
Chang Jiang, *p. 112*

Use the graphic organizer online to take notes on the physical features, climate, and resources of China, Mongolia, and Taiwan.

If YOU lived there...

You are a young filmmaker who lives in Guangzhou, a port city in southern China. You are preparing to make a documentary film about the Huang He, one of China's great rivers. To make your film, you will follow the river across northern China. Your journey will take you from the Himalayas to the coast of the Yellow Sea.

What do you expect to see on your travels?

BUILDING BACKGROUND China, Mongolia, and Taiwan make up a large part of East Asia. They include a range of physical features and climates—dry plateaus, rugged mountains, fertile plains. This physical geography has greatly influenced life in each country.

Physical Features

Have you seen the view from the top of the world? At 29,035 feet (8,850 m), Mount Everest in the **Himalayas** is the world's highest mountain. From atop Everest, look east. Through misty clouds, icy peaks stretch out before you, fading to land far below. This is China. About the size of the United States, China has a range of physical features. They include not only the world's tallest peaks but also some of its driest deserts and longest rivers.

Two other areas are closely linked to China. To the north lies Mongolia (mahn-GOHL-yuh). This landlocked country is dry and rugged, with vast grasslands and desert. In contrast, Taiwan (TY-WAHN), off the coast of mainland China, is a green tropical island. Look at the map to see the whole region's landforms.

Mountains

Much of the large region, including Taiwan, is mountainous. In southwest China, the Himalayas run along the border. They are Earth's tallest mountain range. Locate on the map the region's other ranges. As a tip, the Chinese word *shan* means "mountain."

hmhsocialstudies.com INTERACTIVE MAP

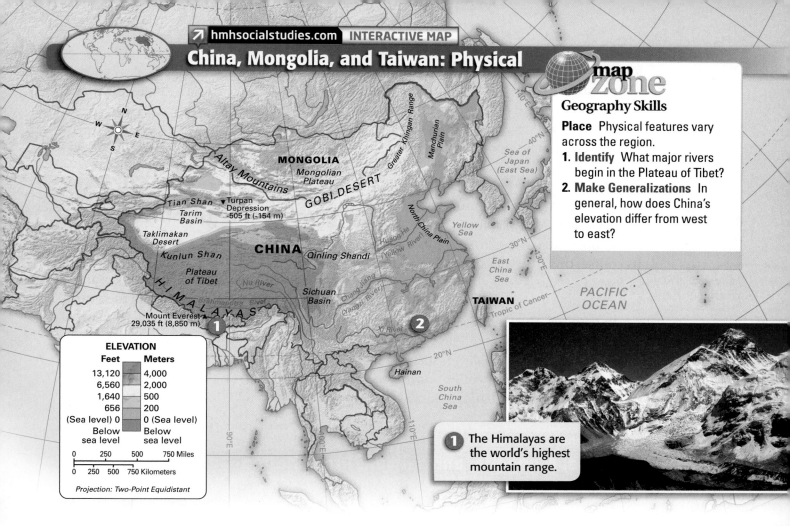

China, Mongolia, and Taiwan: Physical

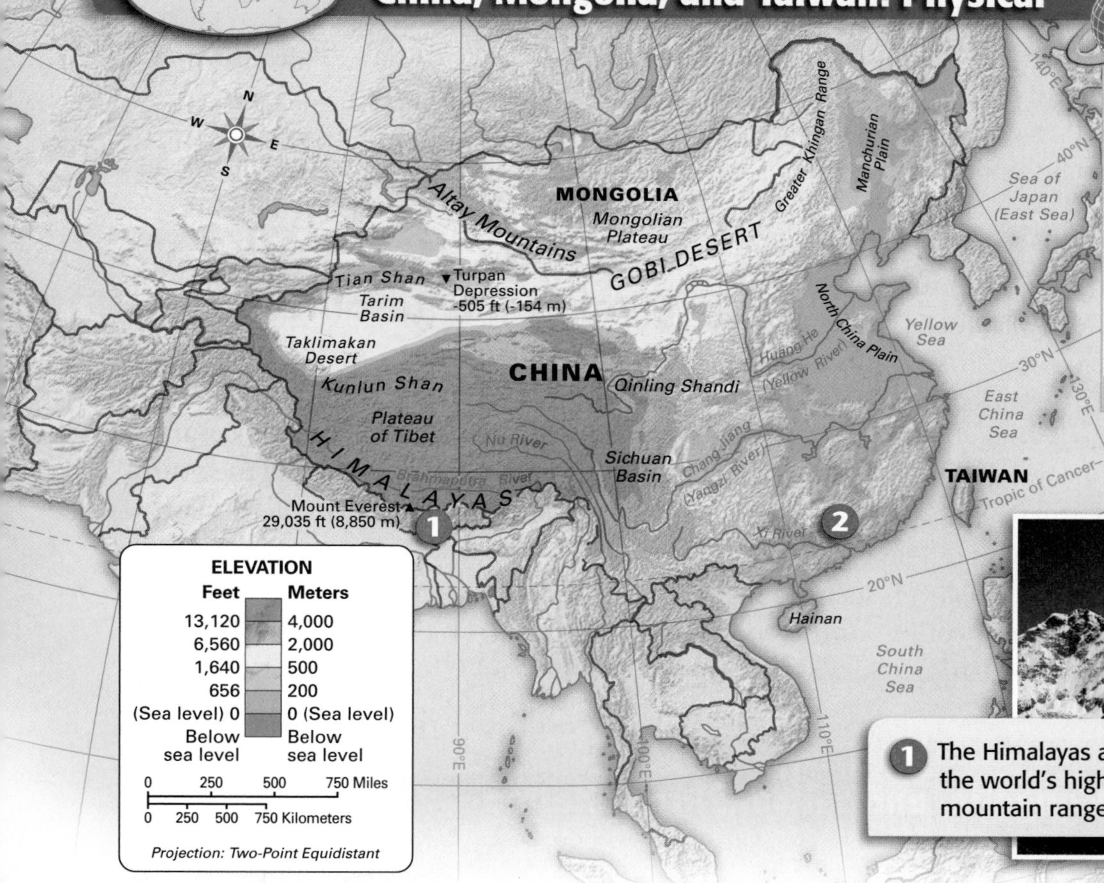

MONGOLIA
Mongolian Plateau
Altay Mountains
GOBI DESERT
Greater Khingan Range
Manchurian Plain
Sea of Japan (East Sea)
Tian Shan
Turpan Depression -505 ft (-154 m)
Tarim Basin
Taklimakan Desert
North China Plain
Huang He (Yellow River)
Yellow Sea
CHINA
Kunlun Shan
Qinling Shandi
Plateau of Tibet
Nu River
HIMALAYAS
Brahmaputra River
Sichuan Basin
Chang Jiang (Yangzi River)
East China Sea
TAIWAN
Tropic of Cancer
PACIFIC OCEAN
Mount Everest 29,035 ft (8,850 m)
Xi River
Hainan
South China Sea

ELEVATION

Feet	Meters
13,120	4,000
6,560	2,000
1,640	500
656	200
(Sea level) 0	0 (Sea level)
Below sea level	Below sea level

0 250 500 750 Miles
0 250 500 750 Kilometers
Projection: Two-Point Equidistant

map zone

Geography Skills

Place Physical features vary across the region.

1. **Identify** What major rivers begin in the Plateau of Tibet?
2. **Make Generalizations** In general, how does China's elevation differ from west to east?

1 The Himalayas are the world's highest mountain range.

Other Landforms

Many of the mountain ranges are separated by plateaus, basins, and deserts. In southwest China, the **Plateau of Tibet** lies north of the Himalayas. The world's highest plateau, it is called the Roof of the World.

Moving north, we find a low, dry area. A large part of this area is the Taklimakan (tah-kluh-muh-KAHN) Desert, a barren land of sand dunes and blinding sandstorms. In fact, sandstorms are so common that the desert's Turkish name, Taklimakan, has come to mean "Enter and you will not come out." To the northeast, the Turpan (toohr-PAHN) Depression is China's lowest point, at 505 feet (154 m) below sea level.

Continuing northeast, in Mongolia we find the **Gobi**. This harsh area of gravel and rock is the world's coldest desert. Temperatures can drop to below –40°F (–40°C).

hmhsocialstudies.com
ANIMATED GEOGRAPHY
Physical Geography of China

2 Hills that are called karst towers line the Li River in southeast China. These dramatic hills formed over time as rainwater eroded limestone.

In east China, the land levels out into low plains and river valleys. These fertile plains, such as the **North China Plain**, are China's main population centers and farmlands. On Taiwan, a plain on the west coast is the island's main population center.

Rivers

Focus on Reading

Which details help you identify the main idea of the paragraph to the right?

In China, two great rivers run west to east. The **Huang He** (HWAHNG HEE), or the Yellow River, flows across northern China. Along its course, this river picks up large amounts of **loess** (LES), or fertile, yellowish soil. The soil colors the river and gives it its name.

In summer, the Huang He often floods. The floods spread layers of loess, enriching the soil for farming. However, such floods have killed millions of people. For this reason, the river is called China's Sorrow.

The mighty **Chang** (CHAHNG) **Jiang**, or the Yangzi (YAHNG-zee) River, flows across central China. It is Asia's longest river and a major transportation route.

READING CHECK **Summarizing** What are the main physical features found in this region?

Climate and Resources

Climate varies widely across the region. The tropical southeast is warm to hot, and monsoons bring heavy rains in summer. In addition, typhoons can strike the southeast coast in summer and fall. Similar to hurricanes, these violent storms bring high winds and rain. As we move to the northeast, the climate is drier and colder. Winter temperatures can drop below 0°F (–18°C).

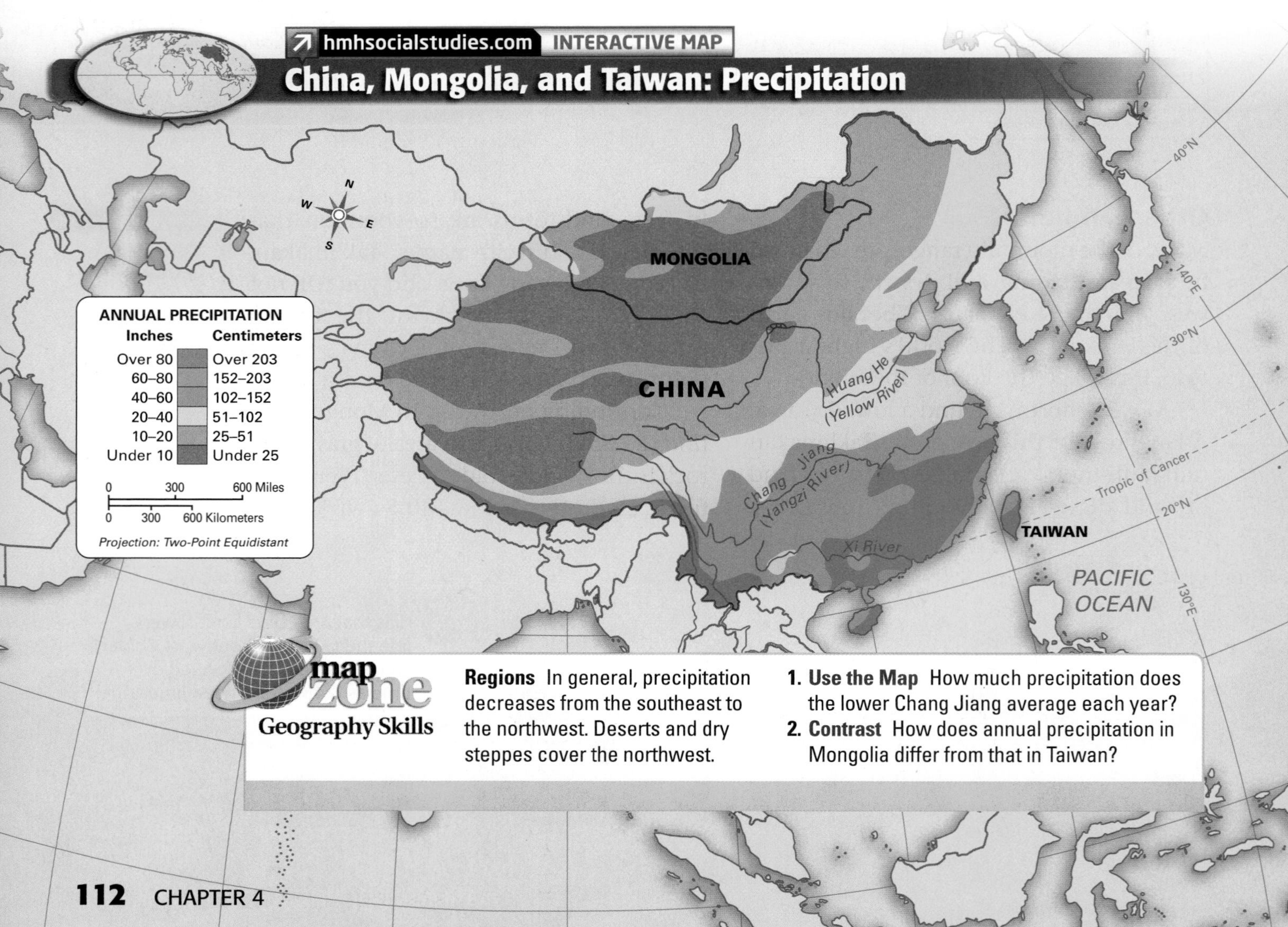

Regions In general, precipitation decreases from the southeast to the northwest. Deserts and dry steppes cover the northwest.

1. **Use the Map** How much precipitation does the lower Chang Jiang average each year?
2. **Contrast** How does annual precipitation in Mongolia differ from that in Taiwan?

Satellite View

Flooding in China

China's rivers and lakes often flood during the summer rainy season. The satellite images here show Lake Dongting Hu in southern China. The lake appears blue, and the land appears red. Soon after the Before image was taken, heavy rains led to flooding. The After image shows the results. Compare the two images to see the extent of the flood, which killed more than 3,000 people and destroyed some 5 million homes.

Before

After

For comparison, these arrows are pointing to the same place in each image.

Drawing Inferences Why might people continue to live in areas that often flood?

In the north and west, the climate is mainly dry. Temperatures vary across the area and can get both very hot and cold.

Like the climate, the region's natural resources cover a wide range. China has a wealth of natural resources. The country is rich in mineral resources and is a leading producer of coal, lead, tin, and tungsten. China produces many other minerals and metals as well. China's forestland and farmland are also valuable resources.

Mongolia's natural resources include minerals such as coal, iron, and tin as well as livestock. Taiwan's major natural resource is its farmland. Important crops include sugarcane, tea, and bananas.

READING CHECK **Contrasting** Which of these three countries has the most natural resources?

SUMMARY AND PREVIEW As you have read, China, Mongolia, and Taiwan have a range of physical features, climate, and resources. Next, you will read about the history and culture of China.

Section 1 Assessment

Reviewing Ideas, Terms, and Places

1. a. Identify What two major rivers run through China?
   b. Explain How does the **Huang He** both benefit and hurt China's people?
   c. Elaborate Why do you think many people in China live on the **North China Plain**?
2. a. Define What is a typhoon?
   b. Contrast What are some differences between the climates of southeast and northwest China?
   c. Rate Based on the different climates in this region, which part of the region would you prefer to live in? Why?

Critical Thinking

3. Categorizing Look back over your notes for this section. Then use a chart like the one shown here to organize, identify, and describe the main physical features of China, Mongolia, and Taiwan.

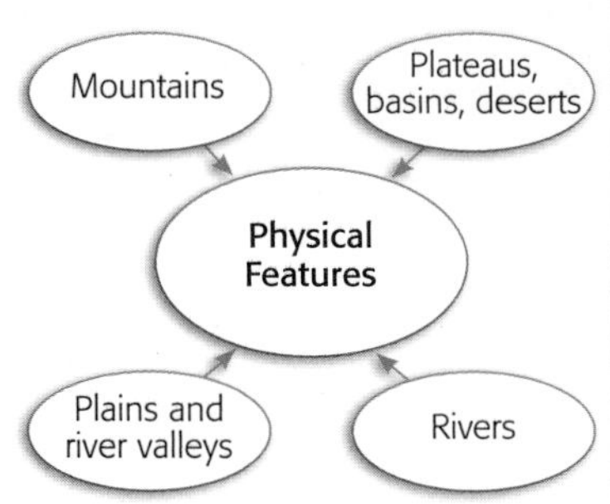

FOCUS ON WRITING

4. **Writing about Physical Geography** Note the main physical features of this region. Consider which feature you might want to explain in your legend. Features to consider include mountains, plateaus, and deserts.

SECTION 2

History and Culture of China

What You Will Learn...

Main Ideas

1. Family lines of emperors ruled China for most of its early history.
2. In China's modern history, revolution and civil war led to a Communist government.
3. China has the world's most people and a rich culture shaped by ancient traditions.

The Big Idea

Ruled by dynasties in its early history, China is a Communist country with an enormous population and ancient traditions.

Key Terms

Use the graphic organizer online to take notes on China's history, people, and culture.

If YOU lived there...

Your parents own a small farm in the Chinese countryside in the mid-1950s. China's new leaders are making changes, however. They are taking people's farms and combining them to create large government-run farms. Your family and neighbors will now work a large farm together. China's leaders will tell you what to grow and pay you based on how much the farm produces.

How do you feel about these changes?

BUILDING BACKGROUND In 1949 China established a strong central government. This new government changed many familiar patterns of life. For much of its history, though, China had been ruled by family lines of emperors. During this period, China developed one of the world's most advanced civilizations.

China's Early Dynasties

Dynasties ruled China for some 3,500 years. The major achievements of the early dynasties are shown here.

Shang, c. 1500–1050 BC

- First recorded Chinese dynasty
- Strongest in the Huang He valley
- Developed China's first writing system, a calendar, and chopsticks
- Skilled at bronze casting

Shang bronze tigress container

Zhou, c. 1050–400 BC

- Longest-lasting Chinese dynasty
- Expanded China but declined into a period of disorder
- Influenced by the new teachings of Confucianism, Daoism, and Legalism
- Began using iron tools and plows

Confucius, a Zhou thinker

China's Early History

When we enjoy the colorful fireworks on the Fourth of July, we can thank the early Chinese people. They invented fireworks. China's early civilization was one of the most advanced in the world. Its many achievements include the magnetic compass, gunpowder, paper, printing, and silk.

Today China can boast a civilization some 4,000 years old, older than any other. Understanding this long history is central to understanding China and its people.

China's Dynasties

For much of its history, China was ruled by dynasties. A **dynasty** is a series of rulers from the same family line. The rulers of China's dynasties were called emperors. Over time, many dynasties rose and fell in China. Between some dynasties, periods of chaos occurred as kingdoms or warlords fought for power. At other times, invaders came in and took control. Through it all, Chinese culture endured and evolved.

One of the most important dynasties is the Qin (CHIN), or Ch'in. It was the first dynasty to unite China under one empire. The greatest Qin ruler was Shi Huangdi (SHEE hwahng-dee). He ordered the building of much of the Great Wall of China. Made to keep out invaders, the wall linked many older walls in northern China. In addition, Shi Huangdi had thousands of terra-cotta, or clay, warriors made to guard his tomb. These life-size warriors, each of which is unique, are skillful works of art.

The last dynasty in China was the Qing (CHING). Invaders called the Manchu ruled this dynasty starting in 1644. In time, outside influences would help lead to its end.

Outside Influences in China

Throughout history, China often limited contact with the outside world. The Chinese saw their culture as superior and had little use for foreigners. The tall mountains, deserts, and seas around China further limited contact and isolated the region.

Yet, other people increasingly wanted Chinese goods such as silk and tea. To gain access to the goods, some European powers forced China to open up trade in the 1800s. Europeans took control of parts of the country as well. These actions angered many Chinese, some of whom blamed the emperor. At the same time, increased contact with the West exposed the Chinese to new ideas.

READING CHECK **Drawing Conclusions** How did geography affect China's early history?

Qin, c. 221–206 BC

- First unified Chinese empire
- Strong central government with strict laws
- Created standardized money and writing systems
- Built a network of roads and canals and much of the Great Wall

Qin life-size terra-cotta warrior

Han, c. 206 BC–AD 220

- Based government on Confucianism
- Began trading over Silk Road
- Spread of Buddhism from India
- Invented paper, sundial, and acupuncture

Han bronze oil lamp

China's Modern History

As foreign influences increased, China's people grew unhappy with imperial rule. This unhappiness sparked a revolution.

Revolution and Civil War

In 1911, rebels forced out China's last emperor. They then formed a republic, a political system in which voters elect their leaders. Power struggles continued, however. In time, two rival groups emerged—the Nationalists, led by Chiang Kai-shek (chang ky-SHEK), and the Communists, led by Mao Zedong (MOW ZUH-DOOHNG).

The two groups fought a violent civil war. That war ended in October 1949 with the Communists as victors. They founded a new government, the People's Republic of China. The Nationalists fled to Taiwan, where they founded the Republic of China.

FOCUS ON READING

What is the main idea of the second paragraph under Population and Settlement on the next page?

Communist China under Mao

Mao, the Communists' leader, became the head of China's new government. In a Communist system, the government owns most businesses and land and controls all areas of life. China's new Communist government began by taking over control of the economy. The government seized all private farms and organized them into large, state-run farms. It also took over all businesses and factories.

While some changes improved life, others did not. On one hand, women gained more rights and were able to work. On the other hand, the government limited freedoms and imprisoned people who criticized it. In addition, many economic programs were unsuccessful, and some were outright disasters. In the early 1960s, for example, poor planning and drought led to a famine that killed millions.

China: Population

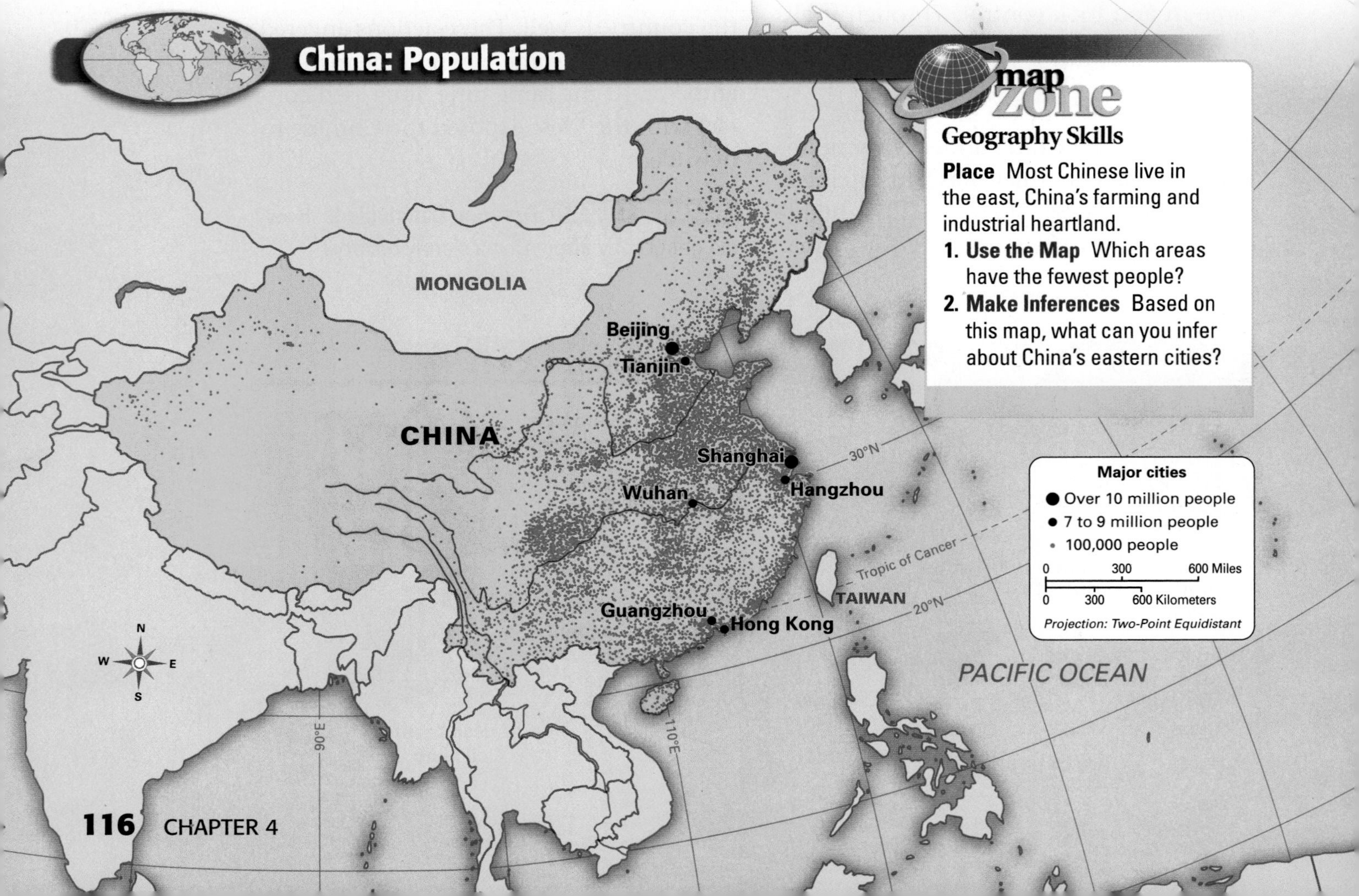

MONGOLIA
CHINA
Beijing
Tianjin
Shanghai
Hangzhou
Wuhan
Guangzhou
Hong Kong
TAIWAN
PACIFIC OCEAN
Tropic of Cancer
30°N
20°N
90°E
110°E
N
S
E
W

map zone

Geography Skills

Place Most Chinese live in the east, China's farming and industrial heartland.

1. **Use the Map** Which areas have the fewest people?
2. **Make Inferences** Based on this map, what can you infer about China's eastern cities?

Major cities

- Over 10 million people
- 7 to 9 million people
- 100,000 people

0 300 600 Miles
0 300 600 Kilometers
Projection: Two-Point Equidistant

Communist China Since Mao

Mao died in 1976, and Deng Xiaoping (DUHNG SHOW-PING) soon rose to power. Deng admitted the government had made mistakes. He then worked to modernize and improve China's economy. He allowed some private businesses and encouraged countries to invest in China. As a result, the economy began growing rapidly. Leaders after Deng continued economic reforms.

READING CHECK **Summarizing** How did communism change life in China?

China's People and Culture

One of China's best known features is its people—all 1.3 billion of them. China has the world's largest population. More people live there than in all of Europe, Russia, and the United States combined.

Population and Settlement

As the map shows, this huge population is not evenly spread out. Only 10 percent of the people live in the west, while the rest are jam-packed into the east. In fact, more people live in the Manchurian and North China Plains than in the United States!

Meanwhile, China's population continues to grow—by about 7 million each year. China's officials have worked to slow this growth. Officials have urged people to delay having children and have tried to limit each couple to one child. These actions have succeeded in slowing China's population growth.

Ethnic Groups and Language

Of China's millions of people, 92 percent identify their ancestry as Han Chinese. These people share the same culture and traditions. Many Han speak Mandarin, China's official language. Others speak a **dialect**, a regional version of a language.

Ethnic Groups

The majority of Chinese are Han. However, China includes 55 other ethnic groups. Most of these people live in western and southern China.

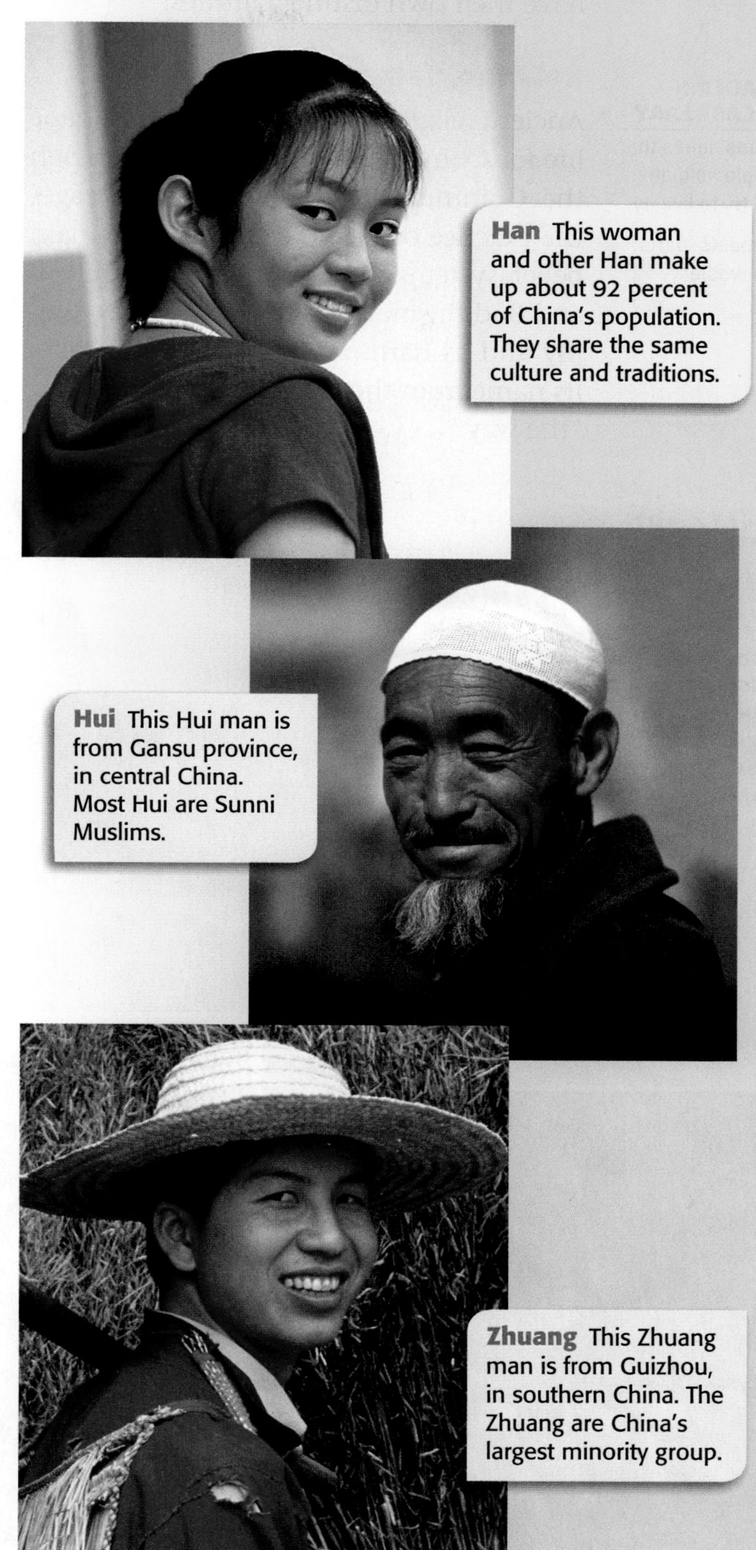

Han This woman and other Han make up about 92 percent of China's population. They share the same culture and traditions.

Hui This Hui man is from Gansu province, in central China. Most Hui are Sunni Muslims.

Zhuang This Zhuang man is from Guizhou, in southern China. The Zhuang are China's largest minority group.

Some 55 other ethnic groups make up the remaining 8 percent of China's population. Most of these minority groups live in western and southern China, where they have their own distinct cultures.

Religion, Values, and Beliefs

Academic Vocabulary

values ideas that people hold dear and try to live by

elements parts of a whole

Ancient religions, **values**, and beliefs shape life for China's many people, even though the Communist government discourages the practice of religion. China's two main belief systems are Daoism (DOW-i-zuhm) and Buddhism. **Daoism** stresses living simply and in harmony with nature. It takes its name from the word *Dao,* which means "the way."

Buddhism came to China from India about AD 100. This religion is based on the teachings of Siddhartha Gautama—the Buddha, who lived from 563 to 483 BC. Buddhists believe moral behavior, kindness, and meditation can lead to peace.

Many Chinese blend **elements** of Daoism and Buddhism with **Confucianism**, a philosophy based on the ideas and teachings of Confucius. This philosophy stresses the importance of family, moral values, and respect for one's elders.

Other major religions in China include Christianity and Islam. Ancestor worship and fortune-telling are popular among the Chinese as well.

Close-up

Beijing's National Day

China celebrates National Day on October 1 with huge parades in Tiananmen Square. This square is one of the world's largest public gathering places. The space is needed because parades can include more than 500,000 participants.

Beijing
CHINA
PACIFIC OCEAN
国万岁
The Gate of Heavenly Peace displays Mao Zedong's portrait above the entrance.
The parades include couples married on National Day, a popular time to wed.
A military parade of soldiers, tanks, and other equipment shows China's power.

The Arts and Popular Culture

China has a rich artistic tradition. Chinese crafts include items made of bronze, jade, ivory, silk, or wood. Chinese porcelain, which the ancient Chinese developed, is highly prized for its quality and beauty.

Traditional Chinese painting is done on silk or fine paper and reflects a focus on balance and harmony with nature. Popular subjects are landscapes, such as scenes of rugged mountains, trees, and lakes.

Chinese art often includes calligraphy, or decorative writing. Chinese writing uses symbols, or characters, instead of letters. This writing makes beautiful art, and some paintings feature just Chinese calligraphy.

In literature, the Chinese are known for their beautiful poetry. The Chinese highly value poetry, and poems appear on paintings and in novels and plays.

In theater, traditional Chinese opera is popular. These operas tell stories through spoken words, music, and dance. Actors wear elaborate costumes and makeup that have special meanings.

Traditional Chinese architecture features wooden buildings on stone bases. Large tiled roofs curve upward at the edge. Also common are **pagodas**, Buddhist temples that have multi-storied towers with an upward curving roof at each floor. Many cities are a mix of traditional and modern.

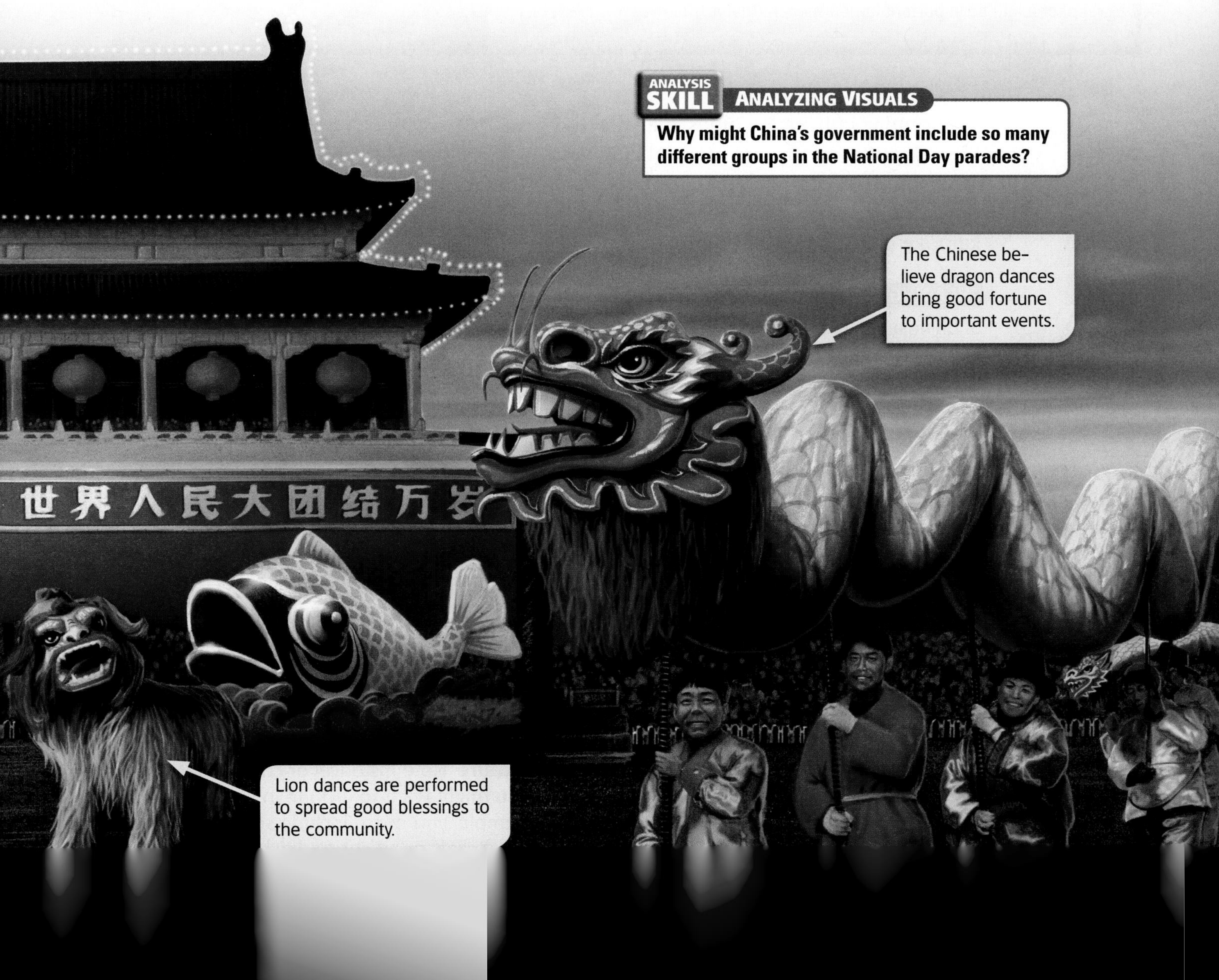

世界人民大团结万岁
ANALYSIS SKILL ANALYZING VISUALS
Why might China's government include so many different groups in the National Day parades?
The Chinese believe dragon dances bring good fortune to important events.
Lion dances are performed to spread good blessings to the community.

Focus on Culture

Chinese Martial Arts

Can you imagine getting up each day at 5 AM and exercising for 12 hours or more? Chinese teenagers who attend martial arts schools do just that. Many of the schools' instructors are Buddhist monks trained in the Chinese martial art of kung fu. These instructors teach their students self-defense techniques as well as the importance of hard work, discipline, and respect for one's elders. These values are important in Chinese culture and religion.

Starting as early as age 6, students memorize up to several hundred martial arts movements. These movements include different kicks, jumps, and punches. Some students dream of one day using their martial arts skills to star in a Chinese or American action movie.

Drawing Conclusions Why do you think discipline, hard work, and respect might be important for learning martial arts?

Popular culture includes many activities. Popular sports are martial arts and table tennis. A popular game is mah-jongg, played with small tiles. People also enjoy karaoke clubs, where they sing to music.

Reading Check **Evaluating** Which aspect of Chinese culture most interests you? Why?

Summary and Preview After centuries of imperial rule under dynasties, China became a Communist country. China has a rich and ancient culture and is the world's most populous country. In the next section you will read about China's economy, government, and cities.

Section 2 Assessment

hmhsocialstudies.com ONLINE QUIZ

Reviewing Ideas, Terms, and Places

1. a. **Define** What is a **dynasty**?
   b. **Summarize** How did outside influences affect China's early history?
2. a. **Recall** Which two groups fought for power during China's civil war, and which group won?
   b. **Contrast** How did China's economy under Mao differ from China's economy since his death?
3. a. **Recall** What are some popular pastimes in China today?
   b. **Explain** What are China's population problems, and how is China addressing them?
   c. **Elaborate** How are Buddhism, **Confucianism**, and **Daoism** important in Chinese culture?

Critical Thinking

4. **Sequencing** Look back over your notes and then create a chart like this one. List the main events in China's history in the order in which they occurred. Add or remove boxes as necessary.

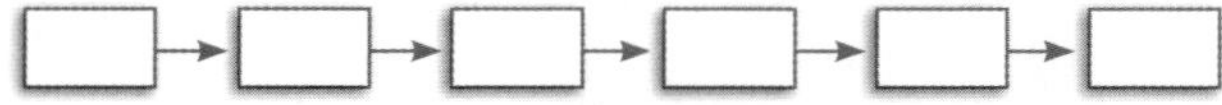

Focus on Writing

5. **Collecting Information about China's History and Culture** Note historical or cultural details that you might want to include in your legend. For example, you might include some aspect of Chinese beliefs or artistic traditions in your legend.

China Today

SECTION 3

If YOU lived there...

For many years your parents have been farmers, growing tea plants. Since the government began allowing private businesses, your parents have been selling tea in the market as well. With the money they have made, they are considering opening a tea shop.

What do you think your parents should do?

BUILDING BACKGROUND When a Communist government took over China in 1949, it began strictly controlling all areas of life. Over time, China's government has loosened control of the economy. Control over politics and other areas of life remains strict, however.

What You Will Learn...

Main Ideas

1. China's booming economy is based on agriculture, but industry is growing rapidly.
2. China's government controls many aspects of life and limits political freedom.
3. China is mainly rural, but urban areas are growing.
4. China's environment faces a number of serious problems.

The Big Idea

China's economy and cities are growing rapidly, but the Chinese have little political freedom and many environmental problems.

Key Terms and Places

command economy, *p. 121*
Beijing, *p. 122*
Tibet, *p. 123*
Shanghai, *p. 124*
Hong Kong, *p. 124*

Use the graphic organizer online to take notes on China today.

China's Economy

Think ahead to the day you start working. Would you rather choose your career or have the government choose it for you? The first situation describes a market economy, which we have in the United States. In this type of economy, people can choose their careers, decide what to make or sell, and keep the profits they earn. The second situation describes a **command economy**, an economic system in which the government owns all the businesses and makes all decisions, such as where people work. Communist China used to have a command economy. Then in the 1970s, China began allowing aspects of a market economy.

Farmers near Yunnan, in southern China, use traditional methods to work rice paddies.

China developed a mixed economy because it had major economic problems. For example, the production of goods had fallen. In response, the government closed many state-run factories and began allowing privately owned businesses. In addition, the government created special economic zones where foreign businesspeople could own companies. A mixed economic approach has helped China's economy boom. Today China has the world's second largest economy.

Agriculture and Industry

More Chinese work in farming than in any other economic activity. The country is a leading producer of several crops, such as rice, wheat, corn, and potatoes. China's main farmlands are in the eastern plains and river valleys. To the north, wheat is the main crop. To the south, rice is.

Only about 15 percent of China's land is good for farming. So how does China produce so much food? More than half of all Chinese workers are farmers. This large labor force can work the land at high levels. In addition, farmers cut terraces into hillsides to make the most use of the land.

Although China is mainly agricultural, industry is growing rapidly. Today China produces everything from satellites and chemicals to clothing and toys. Moreover, industry and manufacturing are now the most profitable part of China's economy.

Results of Economic Growth

Economic growth has improved wages and living standards in China. Almost all homes now have electricity, even in rural areas. More and more Chinese can afford goods such as TVs, computers, and even cars. At the same time, many rural Chinese remain poor, and unemployment is high.

READING CHECK **Summarizing** How has China changed its economy in recent times?

China's Government

More economic freedom in China has not led to more political freedom. The Communist government tightly controls most areas of life. For example, the government controls newspapers and Internet access, which helps to restrict the flow of information and ideas.

In addition, China harshly punishes people who oppose the government. In 1989 more than 100,000 pro-democracy protestors gathered in Tiananmen Square in **Beijing**, China's capital. The protestors were demanding more political rights and freedoms. The Chinese government tried to get the protestors to leave the square. When they refused, the government used troops and tanks to make them leave. Hundreds of protestors were killed, and many more were injured or imprisoned.

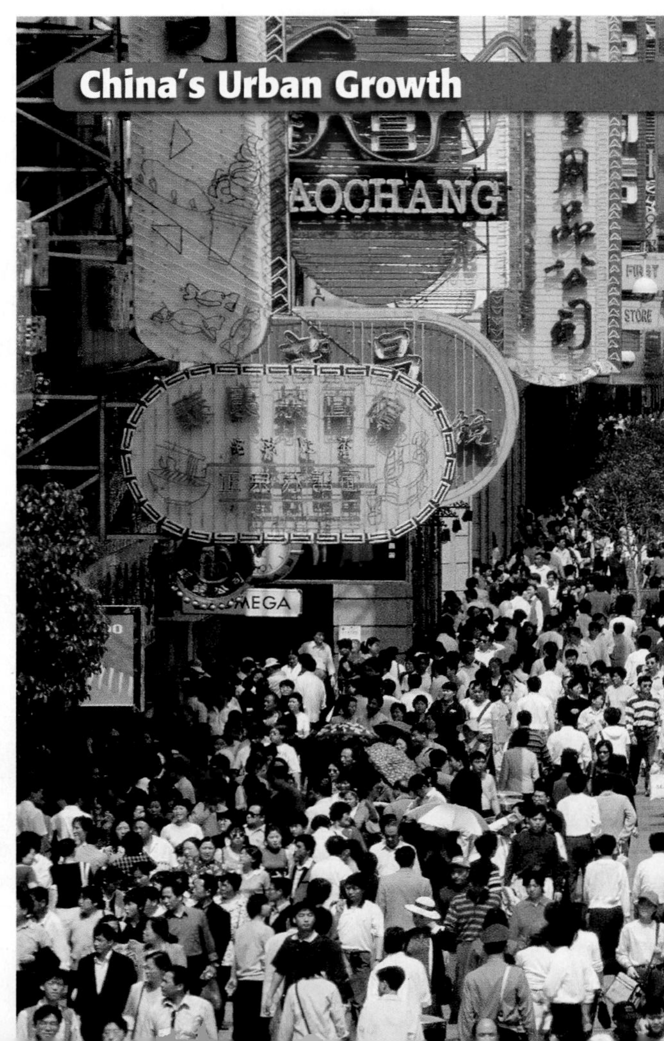

China has taken harsh actions against ethnic rebellions as well. As an example, since 1950 China has controlled the Buddhist region of **Tibet**, in southwest China. When the Tibetans rebelled in 1959, the Chinese quickly crushed the revolt. The Dalai Lama (dah-ly LAH-muh), Tibet's Buddhist leader, had to flee to India. China then cracked down on Tibetans' rights.

Because of actions such as these, many other countries have accused China of not respecting human rights. Some of these countries have considered limiting or stopping trade with China. For example, some U.S. politicians want our government to limit trade with China until it shows more respect for human rights.

READING CHECK **Analyzing** What adjectives might you use to describe China's government?

Rural and Urban China

hmhsocialstudies.com
ANIMATED GEOGRAPHY
Present-Day China

China is a land in the midst of change. Although its countryside remains set in the past, China's cities are growing rapidly and rushing headlong toward the future.

Rural China

Most of China's people live in small, rural villages. Farmers work the fields using the same methods they have used for decades. In small shops and along the streets, sellers cook food and offer goods. Although some villagers' standards of living are improving, the modern world often seems far away.

FOCUS ON READING
What is the implied main idea of the text under Rural China?

Urban China

Many people are leaving China's villages for its booming cities, however. The graph below shows how China's urban population is expected to rise in the future.

Many of China's rapidly growing cities are severely crowded, as can be seen in this Shanghai shopping area. Overcrowding is expected to worsen as China's cities continue to grow.

INTERPRETING GRAPHS About when is China's urban population expected to be larger than its rural population?

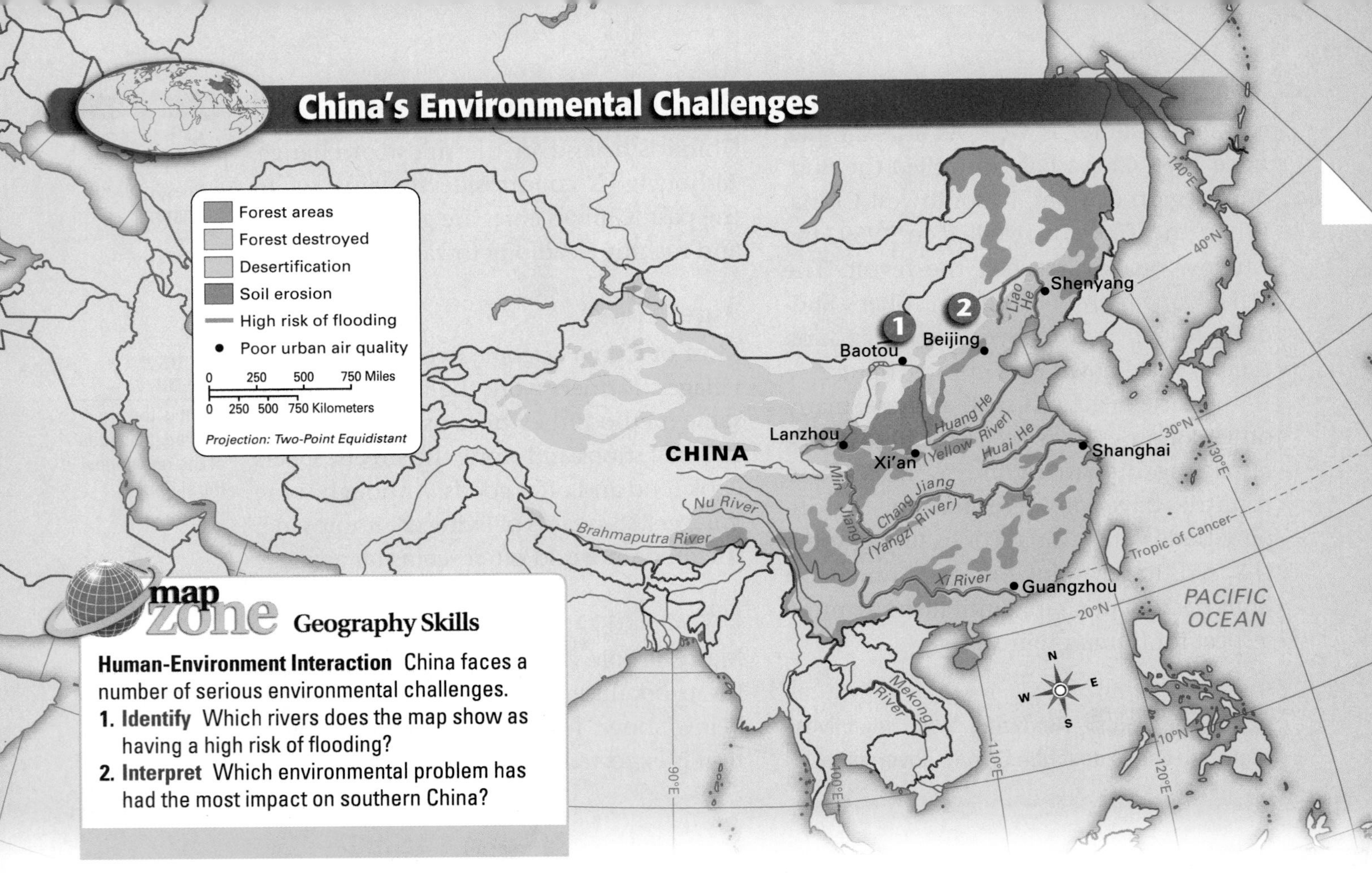

map zone Geography Skills

Human-Environment Interaction China faces a number of serious environmental challenges.

1. **Identify** Which rivers does the map show as having a high risk of flooding?
2. **Interpret** Which environmental problem has had the most impact on southern China?

China's growing economy has led to its rapid city growth. Look at the population map in Section 2 and find the cities with more than 7 million people. Most are on the coast or along major rivers. These areas have benefited from growing industry and trade. Places that were rice fields not long ago are now bustling urban centers with skyscrapers, factories, and highways.

China's largest city is **Shanghai**, with some 15 million people. Located where the Chang Jiang meets the East China Sea, it is China's leading seaport and an industrial and commercial center. The city is also known for its European feel and nightlife.

China's second-largest city is its capital, Beijing. Also known as Peking, this historic city has many beautiful palaces and temples. A mix of the old and new, Beijing is China's political and cultural center.

In central Beijing, large walls hide the golden-roofed palaces of the Forbidden City, former home of China's emperors. Once off-limits to all but the emperor's household, the city is now a museum open to the public. Nearby, Tiananmen Square is the site of many parades and other public events. Government buildings and museums line this immense square.

In southern China, **Hong Kong** and Macao (muh-KOW) are major port cities and centers of trade and tourism. Both cities were European colonies until recently. The United Kingdom returned Hong Kong to China in 1997, and Portugal returned Macao in 1999. The two modern, crowded cities provide a mix of cultures.

READING CHECK **Contrasting** In what ways might rural life differ from city life in China?

1 Residents of Baotou, in north-central China, wear masks to keep from inhaling harmful particles in the city's polluted air.

2 These children are planting trees to help create new forestland north of Beijing.

China's Environment

China's economic and urban growth has created serious environmental problems. A major problem is pollution. The country's rising number of cars and factories pollute the air and water. At the same time, China burns coal for much of its electricity, which further pollutes the air.

Another serious problem is the loss of forestland and farmland. For centuries the Chinese cut down trees without replanting more. In addition, many of China's expanding cities are in its best farmlands.

The Chinese are working to address such problems. For example, China hopes to lessen pollution by using more hydro-electric power, electricity produced from dams. China has built the Three Gorges Dam on the Chang Jiang. It is the world's largest dam and generates as much power as 15 coal-burning power plants. However, the water of the dam's reservoir now covers hundreds of towns and huge amounts of farmland. Millions of people have had to move, and plant and animal habitats have been harmed.

hmhsocialstudies.com
ANIMATED GEOGRAPHY
Three Gorges Dam

READING CHECK **Finding Main Ideas** What are some of China's environmental problems?

SUMMARY AND PREVIEW China's economy and cities are growing rapidly, but its government restricts political freedom and faces environmental problems. In the next section you will learn about Mongolia and Taiwan.

Section 3 Assessment

Reviewing Ideas, Terms, and Places

1. a. **Define** What is a **command economy**?
   b. **Identify Cause and Effect** What changes have helped lead to China's rapid economic growth?
2. a. **Describe** In what ways does China's government restrict freedom?
   b. **Evaluate** What is your opinion of China's handling of the 1989 demonstration at Tiananmen Square?
3. a. **Identify** What is China's largest city and leading port?
   b. **Compare** How are **Hong Kong** and Macao similar?
4. a. **Recall** What are China's environmental problems?
   b. **Evaluate** Do you think China should build the Three Gorges Dam? Why or why not?

Critical Thinking

5. **Categorizing** Create a table like the one shown to organize the challenges that China faces today.

Challenges Facing China		
Economic	Political	Environmental

FOCUS ON WRITING

6. **Collecting Information about China Today** Note any details about China's current economy, government, cities, or environment that you might include in your legend.

SECTION 4

Mongolia and Taiwan

What You Will Learn...

Main Ideas

1. Mongolia is a sparsely populated country where many people live as nomads.
2. Taiwan is a small island with a dense population and a highly industrialized economy.

The Big Idea

Mongolia is a rugged land with a nomadic way of life and growing cities, while Taiwan is a densely settled and industrialized island.

Key Terms and Places

Use the graphic organizer online to take notes on the history and culture of Mongolia and Taiwan, as well as life in these countries today.

If YOU lived there...

Like many Mongolians, you have loved horses since you were a small child. You live in an apartment in the city of Ulaanbaatar, however. Some of your family are talking about leaving the city and becoming nomadic herders like your ancestors were. You think you might like being able to ride horses more. You're not sure you would like living in a tent, though, especially in winter.

Do you want to move back to the land?

BUILDING BACKGROUND While Mongolia is a rugged land where some people still live as nomads, Taiwan is a modern and highly industrialized island. The two regions do have a few things in common, however. Mongolia and Taiwan are both neighbors of China, both are becoming more urban, and both are democracies.

Mongolia

A wild and rugged land, Mongolia is home to the Mongol people. They have a proud and fascinating history. This history includes conquests and empires and a culture that prizes horses.

Mongolia's History

Today when people discuss the world's leading countries, they do not mention Mongolia. However, 700 years ago Mongolia was perhaps the greatest power in the world. Led by the ruler Genghis Khan, the Mongols conquered much of Asia, including China. Later Mongol leaders continued the conquests. They built the greatest empire the world had seen at the time.

The Mongol Empire reached its height in the late 1200s. During that time, the empire stretched from Europe's Danube River in the west to the Pacific Ocean in the east. As time passed, however, the Mongol Empire declined. In the late 1600s China conquered Mongolia and ruled it for more than 200 years.

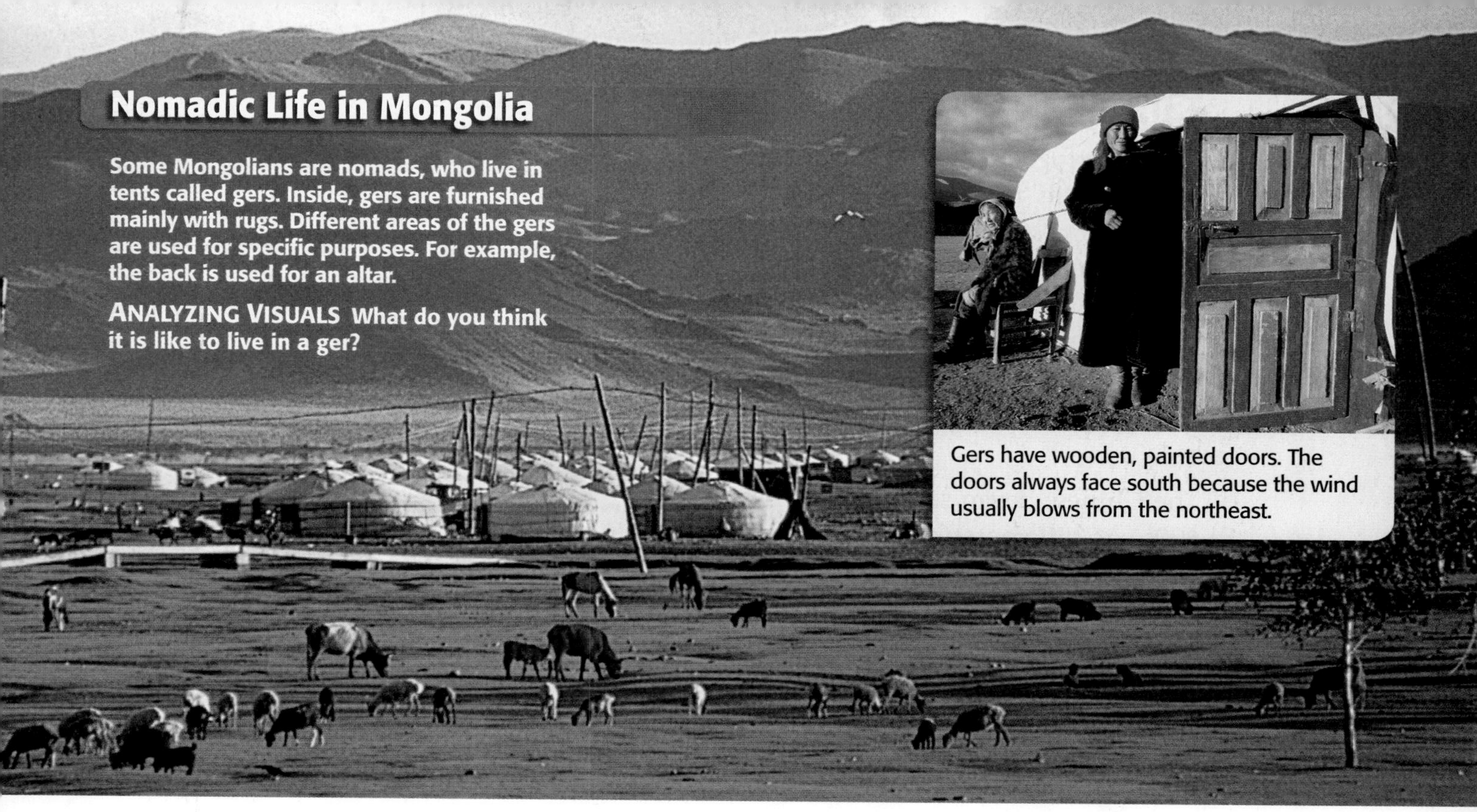

Nomadic Life in Mongolia
Some Mongolians are nomads, who live in tents called gers. Inside, gers are furnished mainly with rugs. Different areas of the gers are used for specific purposes. For example, the back is used for an altar.
ANALYZING VISUALS What do you think it is like to live in a ger?
Gers have wooden, painted doors. The doors always face south because the wind usually blows from the northeast.

With Russia's help, Mongolia declared independence from China in 1911. Soon Communists gained control and in 1924 formed the Mongolian People's Republic. Meanwhile, Russia had become part of the Soviet Union, a large Communist country north of Mongolia. The Soviet Union strongly influenced Mongolia and gave it large amounts of economic aid. This aid ended, however, after the Soviet Union collapsed in 1991. Since then, Mongolians have struggled to build a democratic government and a free-market economy.

Mongolia's Culture

In spite of years of Communist rule, the Mongolian way of life remains fairly traditional. Nearly half of Mongolia's people live as nomads. They herd livestock across Mongolia's vast grasslands and make their homes in **gers** (GUHRZ). These are large, circular, felt tents that are easy to put up, take down, and move.

Since many Mongols live as herders, horses play a major **role** in Mongolian life. As a result, Mongolian culture highly prizes horse skills, and Mongolian children often learn to ride when they are quite young.

ACADEMIC VOCABULARY
role part or function

Mongolia Today

Mongolia is sparsely populated. Slightly larger than Alaska, it has about 3 million people. More than a quarter of them live in **Ulaanbaatar** (oo-lahn-BAH-tawr), the capital and only large city. Mongolia's other cities are quite small. However, Mongolia's urban population is slowly growing.

The country's main industries include textiles, carpets, coal, copper, and oil. The city of Ulaanbaatar is the main industrial and commercial center. Mongolia produces little food other than from livestock, however, and faces food and water shortages.

FOCUS ON READING
Read the second paragraph under Mongolia Today. Determine the topic of each sentence. What is the implied main idea?

READING CHECK **Summarizing** What are some features of Mongolian culture?

Taiwan

When Portuguese sailors visited the island of Taiwan in the late 1500s, they called it *Ilha Formosa,* or "beautiful island." For many years, Westerners called Taiwan by the name Formosa. Today the loveliness of Taiwan's green mountains and waterfalls competes with its modern, crowded cities.

Taiwan's History

The Chinese began settling Taiwan in the 600s. At different times in history, both China and Japan have controlled Taiwan. In 1949, though, the Chinese Nationalists took over Taiwan. Led by Chiang Kai-shek, the Nationalists were fleeing the Communists, who had taken control of China's mainland. The Chinese Nationalist Party ruled Taiwan under martial law, or military rule, for 38 years. Today Taiwan's government is a multiparty democracy.

As the chart below explains, tensions remain between China and Taiwan. The Chinese government claims that Taiwan is a rebel part of China. In contrast, Taiwan's government claims to be the true government of China. For all practical purposes, though, Taiwan functions as an independent country.

Taiwan's Culture

Taiwan's history is reflected in its culture. Its population is about 85 percent native Taiwanese. These people are descendants of Chinese people who migrated to Taiwan largely in the 1700s and 1800s. As a result, Chinese ways dominate Taiwan's culture.

Other influences have shaped Taiwan's culture as well. Because Japan once ruled Taiwan, Japanese culture can be seen in some Taiwanese buildings and foods. More recently, European and American practices and customs are becoming noticeable in Taiwan, particularly in larger cities.

Taiwan Today

Taiwan is a modern country with a population of about 23 million. These people live on an island about the size of Delaware and Maryland combined. Because much of Taiwan is mountainous, most people live on the island's western coastal plain. This region is home to Taiwan's main cities.

The two largest cities are **Taipei** (TY-PAY) and **Kao-hsiung** (KOW-SHYOOHNG). Taipei, the capital, is Taiwan's main financial center. Because it has grown so quickly, it faces serious overcrowding and environmental problems. Kao-hsiung is a center of heavy industry and Taiwan's main seaport.

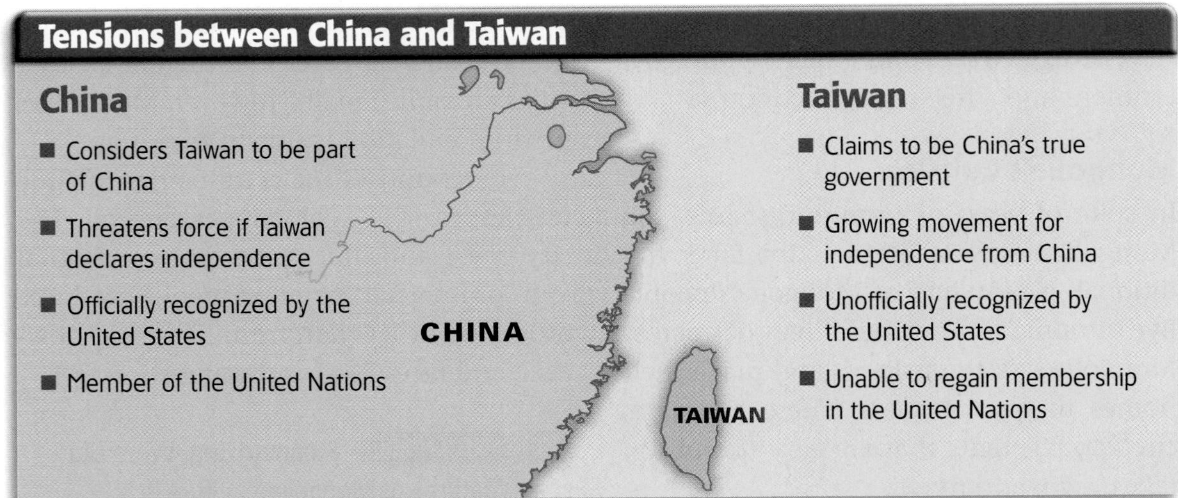

Tensions between China and Taiwan
China
Considers Taiwan to be part of China
Threatens force if Taiwan declares independence
Officially recognized by the United States
Member of the United Nations
CHINA
TAIWAN
Taiwan
Claims to be China's true government
Growing movement for independence from China
Unofficially recognized by the United States
Unable to regain membership in the United Nations

Taipei

Taipei, Taiwan's capital, is a bustling city of more than 2 million people. The tall tower in the photo is the Taipei 101, which is 101 stories tall.

Taiwan is one of Asia's richest and most industrialized countries. It is a leader in the production and export of computers and sports equipment. Taiwan's farmers grow many crops as well, such as sugarcane.

READING CHECK **Contrasting** How does Taiwan's economy differ from Mongolia's?

SUMMARY AND PREVIEW Mongolia and Taiwan are smaller countries bordering China. Mongolia is a wild land with a nomadic people who prize horses. In contrast, Taiwan is a modern and industrialized island. In the next chapter, you will learn about Japan and the Koreas.

Section 4 Assessment

hmhsocialstudies.com
ONLINE QUIZ

Reviewing Ideas, Terms, and Places

1. a. **Define** What are **gers**, and what are their roles in Mongolia's culture?
   b. **Make Inferences** Why might many Mongolians be proud of their country's history?
   c. **Elaborate** Why does Mongolia's culture prize horses?
2. a. **Recall** Why is **Taipei** an important Taiwanese city, and what problems does the city face?
   b. **Summarize** What is the significance of Chiang Kai-shek in Taiwan's history?
   c. **Evaluate** Would you rather live in Taiwan or Mongolia? Provide information about each place to explain your answer.

Critical Thinking

3. **Comparing and Contrasting** Create a Venn diagram like the one shown. Use your notes and compare and contrast the histories, cultures, and societies of Mongolia and Taiwan.

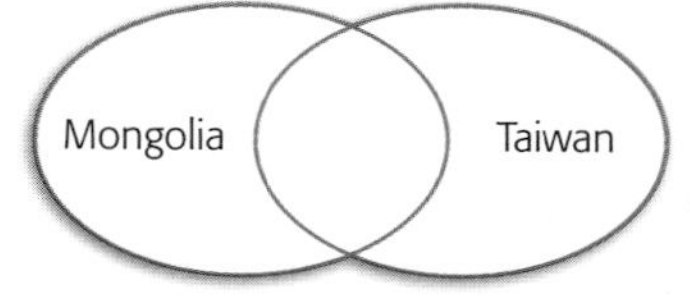

FOCUS ON WRITING

4. **Collecting Information about Mongolia and Taiwan** Consider Mongolia and Taiwan as settings for your legend. For example, your legend might explain the creation of the Gobi, a large desert located partly in Mongolia.

Social Studies Skills

Chart and Graph | **Critical Thinking** | Geography | Study

Analyzing Points of View

Learn

Geography involves issues, situations where people disagree. The way people look at an issue is their point of view. To analyze points of view, use these tips:

- Consider a person's background. Think about where the person lives, what the person does, and what his or her beliefs and attitudes are.
- Look for emotional language, such as name calling or biased terms. Emotional language often reveals a person's point of view.
- Look at the evidence, or facts and statistics, to see what point of view they support.
- Put it all together to identify the point of view.

Practice

Read the passage below about a law forbidding any part of China to declare independence. Then answer the questions that follow.

1. What is China's point of view about Taiwan?
2. What is Taiwan's point of view about China?

New Law Angers Taiwan

Taiwan's government has warned that China's new anti-secession [anti-independence] law . . . will have a "serious impact" on security in the region. . .

Taiwan officials were quick to call the measure a "war bill," coming as China boosts its military spending by 13 percent to $30 billion. . .

But Chinese Premier Wen Jiabao said the new legislation [law] was not a "war bill" and warned outsiders not to get involved . . . "It is not targeted at the people of Taiwan, nor is it a war bill," Wen said at a news conference.

Source: *CNN International,* March 14, 2005

Consider background—China considers Taiwan a rebel province. Taiwan has a growing movement for independence.

Look for emotional language—The phrase "war bill" appeals to the emotions. People have strong feelings about war.

Look at the evidence—The information about military spending is evidence supporting one point of view.

Put it all together to identify each point of view.

Apply

1. In the passage above, how does each side's background affect its point of view?
2. Which point of view does the evidence about China's military spending support?

CHAPTER 4

Chapter Review

Geography's Impact
video series
Review the video to answer the closing question:
If you were involved in the decision to build the Three Gorges Dam, would you support it or vote against it? Why?

Visual Summary

Use the visual summary below to help you review the main ideas of the chapter.

QUICK FACTS

China is a large Communist country with a rich culture. Both its economy and population are growing rapidly.

Mongolia lies to the north of China. It is a harsh, wild land. Many Mongolians are nomads who herd livestock.

Taiwan is an island off the southern coast of China. It is a modern and industrialized region.

Reviewing Vocabulary, Terms, and Places

Match the words or places below with their definitions or descriptions.

1. command economy
2. North China Plain
3. pagodas
4. gers
5. Tibet
6. dialect
7. Himalayas
8. Taipei

a. Buddhist region in southwest China
b. world's highest mountain range
c. regional version of a language
d. capital city of Taiwan
e. system in which the government owns most businesses and makes most economic decisions
f. fertile and highly populated region in eastern China
g. circular, felt tents in which Mongol nomads live
h. Buddhist temples with multiple stories

Comprehension and Critical Thinking

SECTION 1 *(Pages 110–113)*

9. a. Recall What physical features separate many of the mountain ranges in this region?

b. Explain What is the Huang He called in English, and how did the river get its name?

c. Elaborate What major physical features might a traveler see during a trip from the Himalayas, in southwestern China, to Beijing, in northeastern China?

SECTION 2 *(Pages 114–120)*

10. a. Identify Who is Mao Zedong, and why is he significant in China's history?

b. Summarize What are some of China's artistic traditions, and how have they contributed to world culture?

c. Predict What future challenges do you think China might face if its population continues to grow at its current rate?

SECTION 3 *(Pages 121–125)*

11. a. **Recall** What do more than half of China's workers do for a living?

 b. **Summarize** What elements of free enterprise does China's command economy now include?

 c. **Evaluate** What is your opinion about China's treatment of Tibet?

SECTION 4 *(Pages 126–129)*

12. a. **Identify** What is the capital of Mongolia?

 b. **Analyze** How is Taiwan's history reflected in the island's culture today?

 c. **Predict** Do you think China and Taiwan can resolve their disagreements? Why or why not?

Using the Internet

13. **Activity: Touring China's Great Wall** The construction of the Great Wall of China began more than 2,000 years ago. The wall was built over time to keep out invaders and to protect China's people. Through the online book, explore this wonder of the world. Take notes on the wall's history, myths and legends, and other interesting facts. Then make a brochure about your virtual visit to the Great Wall of China.

hmhsocialstudies.com

Social Studies Skills

Analyzing Points of View *Read the following passage from this chapter. Then answer the questions below.*

> "In 1989 more than 100,000 pro-democracy protestors gathered in Tiananmen Square in Beijing, China's capital. The protestors were demanding more political rights and freedoms. The Chinese government tried to get the protestors to leave the square. When they refused, the government used troops and tanks to make them leave. Hundreds of protestors were injured or killed."

14. What was the point of view of the protestors toward China's government?

15. What was the point of view of China's government toward the protestors?

Map Activity

16. **China, Mongolia, and Taiwan** On a separate sheet of paper, match the letters on the map with their correct labels below.

Beijing, China	Hong Kong, China
Chang Jiang	Huang He
Great Wall of China	Taipei, Taiwan
Himalayas	Ulaanbaatar, Mongolia

Focus on Reading and Writing

17. **Identifying Implied Main Ideas** Read the first paragraph under the heading Revolution and Civil War in Section 2. What is the implied main idea of this paragraph? What words and phrases help signal the implied main idea?

18. **Writing a Legend** Choose one physical feature and decide how you will explain its creation. Then review your notes and choose characters, events, and settings for your legend. Your legend should be two to three paragraphs. It should include (a) a beginning; (b) a middle that includes a climax, or high point of the story; and (c) a conclusion, or end. Remember, legends tell about extraordinary events, so you should use your imagination and creativity.

Standardized Test Prep

DIRECTIONS: Read questions 1 through 7 and write the letter of the best response. Then read question 8 and write your own well-constructed response.

1 What is the world's highest mountain range?

A Himalayas
B Kunlun Shan
C Tian Shan
D Qinling Shandi

2 Why is China's Qin dynasty significant?

A first recorded dynasty in China
B longest-lasting dynasty in China
C first dynasty to unify China
D first dynasty to practice Buddhism

3 In which area do most people in China live?

A west
B east
C south
D north

4 Which of these challenges faces China?

A slow population growth
B a weak economy
C lack of urban growth
D air and water pollution

5 Which phrase *best* describes Taiwan?

A a nomadic culture that prizes horses
B modern and industrialized cities
C strict government and few political freedoms
D mainly rural and agricultural

6 Who was a great ruler in Mongolian history?

A Genghis Khan
B Chiang Kai-shek
C Mao Zedong
D Shi Huangdi

China, Mongolia, and Taiwan: Precipitation

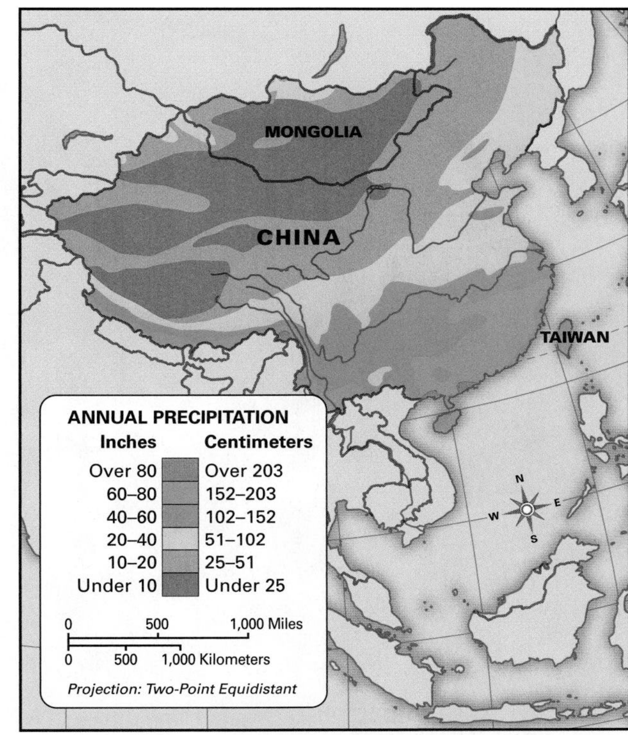

7 Based on the map, which statement best describes precipitation across this region?

A increases from east to west
B decreases from north to south
C decreases from the southeast to the northwest
D increases from the southeast to the northwest

8 Extended Response Look at the map titled China's Environmental Challenges in Section 3. Write two to three paragraphs explaining why the Chinese government should take action to address environmental problems. Make certain to include a description of the ways in which each problem affects China.

China and the Great Wall

Today, the Great Wall of China is an impressive symbol of the Asian giant's power, genius, and endurance. It wasn't always so. For much of its history, the Chinese people saw the Great Wall as a symbol of cruelty and oppression. This is just one way in which the wall differs from what we think we know. In contrast to popular notions, the wall that draws tourists to Beijing by the millions was not built 2,000 years ago. Nor is the Great Wall a single wall. Instead, it was patched together from walls built over many centuries. And for all its grandeur, the wall failed to keep China safe from invasion.

Explore facts and fictions about the Great Wall online. You can find more information, video clips, primary sources, activities, and more at hmhsocialstudies.com.

CLICK THROUGH

INTER/ACTIVITIES

hmhsocialstudies.com

The Great Wall of China

Watch the video to learn the history and significance of the magnificent, mysterious walls that snake across northern China.

A Land of Walls Within Walls

Watch the video to learn how the Great Wall fits within the ancient Chinese tradition of wall-building.

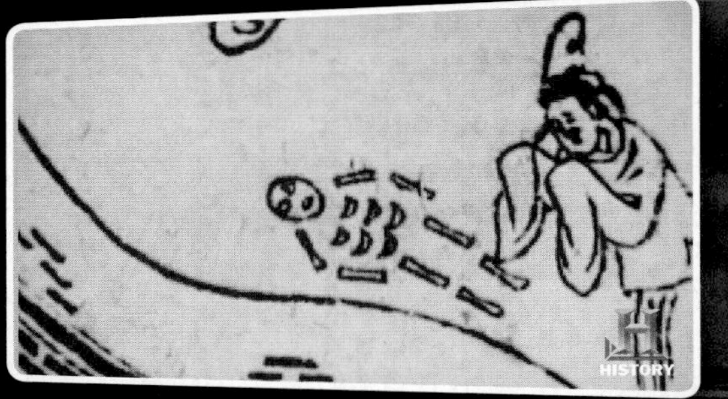

The Human Costs of Building

Watch the video to learn about the miseries that awaited the men who built the wall.

Twentieth-Century China

Watch the video to examine the role that the wall has played in modern Chinese history.

CHAPTER 5

Japan and the Koreas

Essential Question How does geography affect daily life in Japan and the Koreas?

What You Will Learn...

In this chapter you will learn about three countries—Japan, South Korea, and North Korea. Although the three share some physical features and have intertwined histories, they are all very different today.

Focus on Reading and Writing

Understanding Fact and Opinion A fact is a statement that can be proved true. An opinion is someone's belief about something. When you read a textbook, you need to recognize the difference between facts and opinions. **See the lesson, Understanding Fact and Opinion, on page 217.**

Composing a Five-Line Poem For centuries, Japanese poets have written five-line poems called tankas. Most tanka poems describe a single image or emotion in very few words. After you read this chapter, you will choose one image of Japan or the Koreas to use as the subject of your own five-line poem.

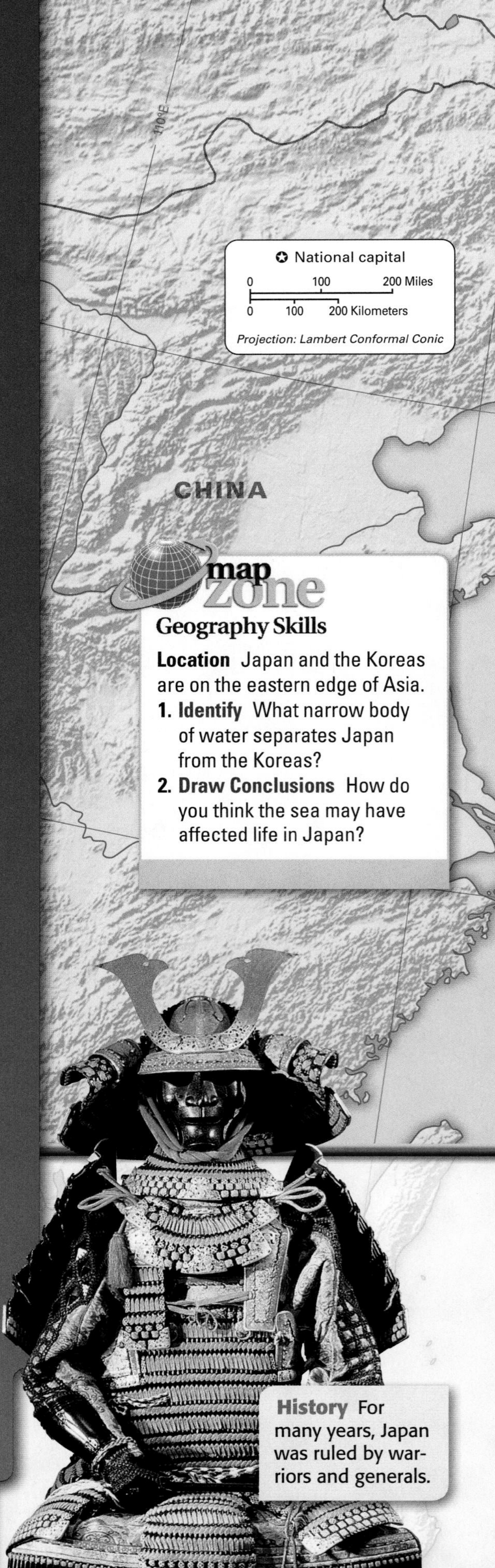

map zone

Geography Skills

Location Japan and the Koreas are on the eastern edge of Asia.

1. **Identify** What narrow body of water separates Japan from the Koreas?
2. **Draw Conclusions** How do you think the sea may have affected life in Japan?

History For many years, Japan was ruled by warriors and generals.

Geography Mount Fuji, a common symbol of Japan, is one of the thousands of mountains found in the region.

Culture Under Kim Il Sung, North Korea became a Communist country.

SECTION 1

Physical Geography

What You Will Learn...

Main Ideas

1. The main physical features of Japan and the Koreas are rugged mountains.
2. The climates and resources of Japan and the Koreas vary from north to south.

The Big Idea

Japan and Korea are both rugged, mountainous areas surrounded by water.

Key Terms and Places

Fuji, *p. 137*
Korean Peninsula, *p. 137*
tsunamis, *p. 138*
fishery, *p. 139*

hmhsocialstudies.com
TAKING NOTES

Use the graphic organizer online to take notes about the physical geography of Japan and the Korean Peninsula.

If YOU lived there...

You are a passenger on a very fast train zipping its way across the countryside. If you look out the window to your right, you can see the distant sparkle of sunlight on the ocean. If you look to the left, you see rocky, rugged mountains. Suddenly the train leaves the mountains, and you see hundreds of trees covered in delicate pink flowers. Rising above the trees is a single snowcapped volcano.

How does this scenery make you feel?

BUILDING BACKGROUND The train described above is one of the many that cross the islands of Japan every day. Japan's mountains, trees, and water features give the islands a unique character. Not far away, the Korean Peninsula also has a distinctive landscape.

Physical Features

Japan, North Korea, and South Korea are on the eastern edge of the Asian continent, just east of China. Separated from each other only by a narrow strait, Japan and the Koreas share many common landscape features.

Physical Features of Japan

Japan is an island country. It is made up of four large islands and more than 3,000 smaller islands. These islands are arranged in a long chain more than 1,500 miles (2,400 km) long. This is about the same length as the eastern coast of the United States, from southern Florida to northern Maine. All together, however, Japan's land area is slightly smaller than the state of California.

About 95 percent of Japan's land area is made up of four large islands. From north to south, these major islands are Hokkaido (hoh-KY-doh), Honshu (HAWN-shoo), Shikoku (shee-KOH-koo), and Kyushu (KYOO-shoo). Together they are called the home islands. Most of Japan's people live there.

Rugged, tree-covered mountains are a common sight in Japan. In fact, mountains cover some 75 percent of the country. For the most part, Japan's mountains are very steep and rocky. As a result, the country's largest mountain range, the Japanese Alps, is popular with climbers and skiers.

Japan's highest mountain, **Fuji**, is not part of the Alps. In fact, it is not part of any mountain range. A volcano, Mount Fuji rises high above a relatively flat area in eastern Honshu. The mountain's cone-shaped peak has become a symbol of Japan. In addition, many Japanese consider Fuji a sacred place. As a result, many shrines have been built at its foot and summit.

Physical Features of Korea

Jutting south from the Asian mainland, the **Korean Peninsula** includes both North Korea and South Korea. Like the islands of Japan, much of the peninsula is covered with rugged mountains. These mountains form long ranges that run along Korea's eastern coast. The peninsula's highest mountains are in the north.

Unlike Japan, Korea also has some large plains. These plains are found mainly along the peninsula's western coast and in river valleys. Korea also has more rivers than Japan does. Most of these rivers flow westward across the peninsula and pour into the Yellow Sea.

Focus on Reading

Are these sentences facts or opinions? How can you tell?

hmhsocialstudies.com

ANIMATED GEOGRAPHY

Physical Geography of Japan and the Koreas

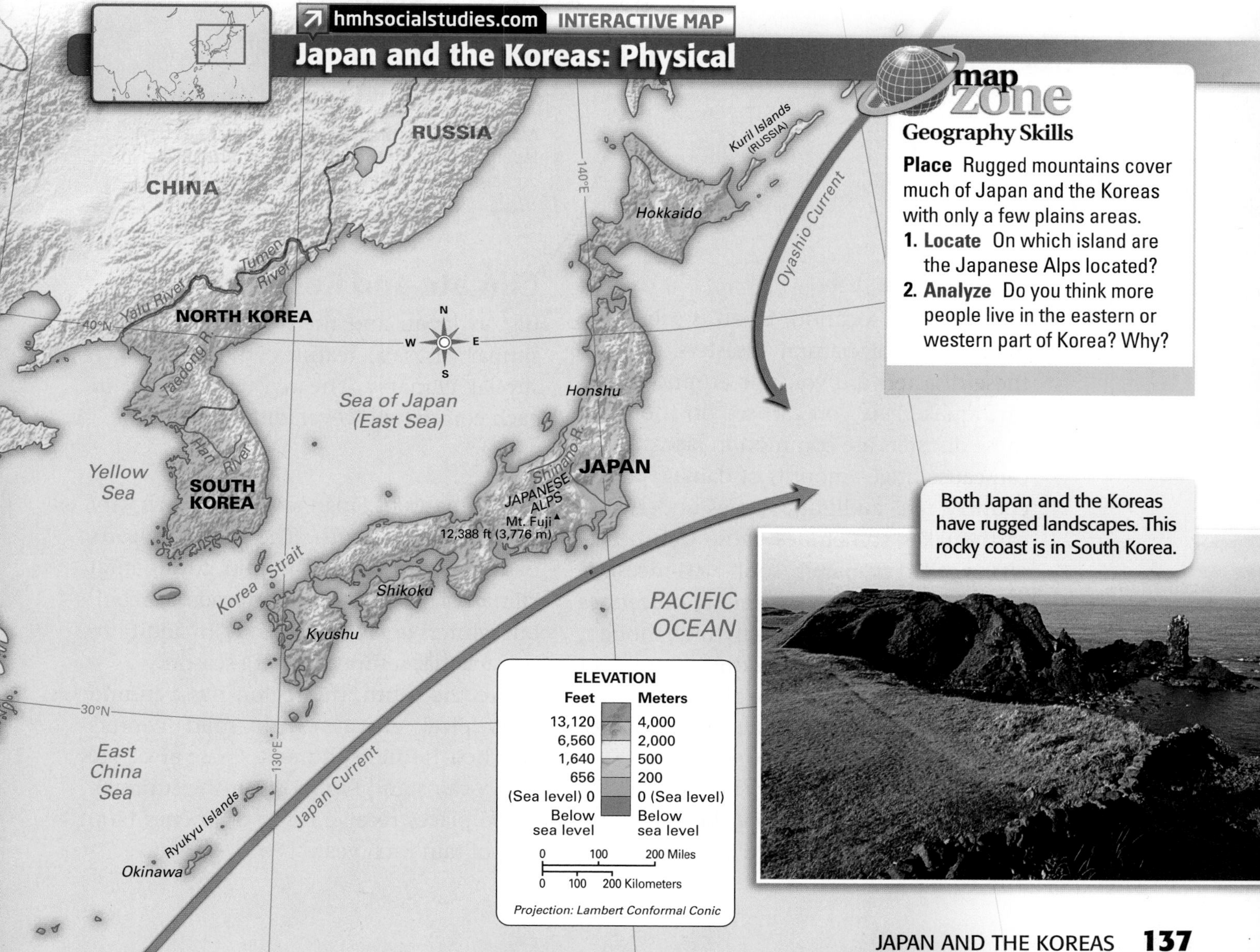

Geography Skills

Place Rugged mountains cover much of Japan and the Koreas with only a few plains areas.

1. **Locate** On which island are the Japanese Alps located?
2. **Analyze** Do you think more people live in the eastern or western part of Korea? Why?

Both Japan and the Koreas have rugged landscapes. This rocky coast is in South Korea.

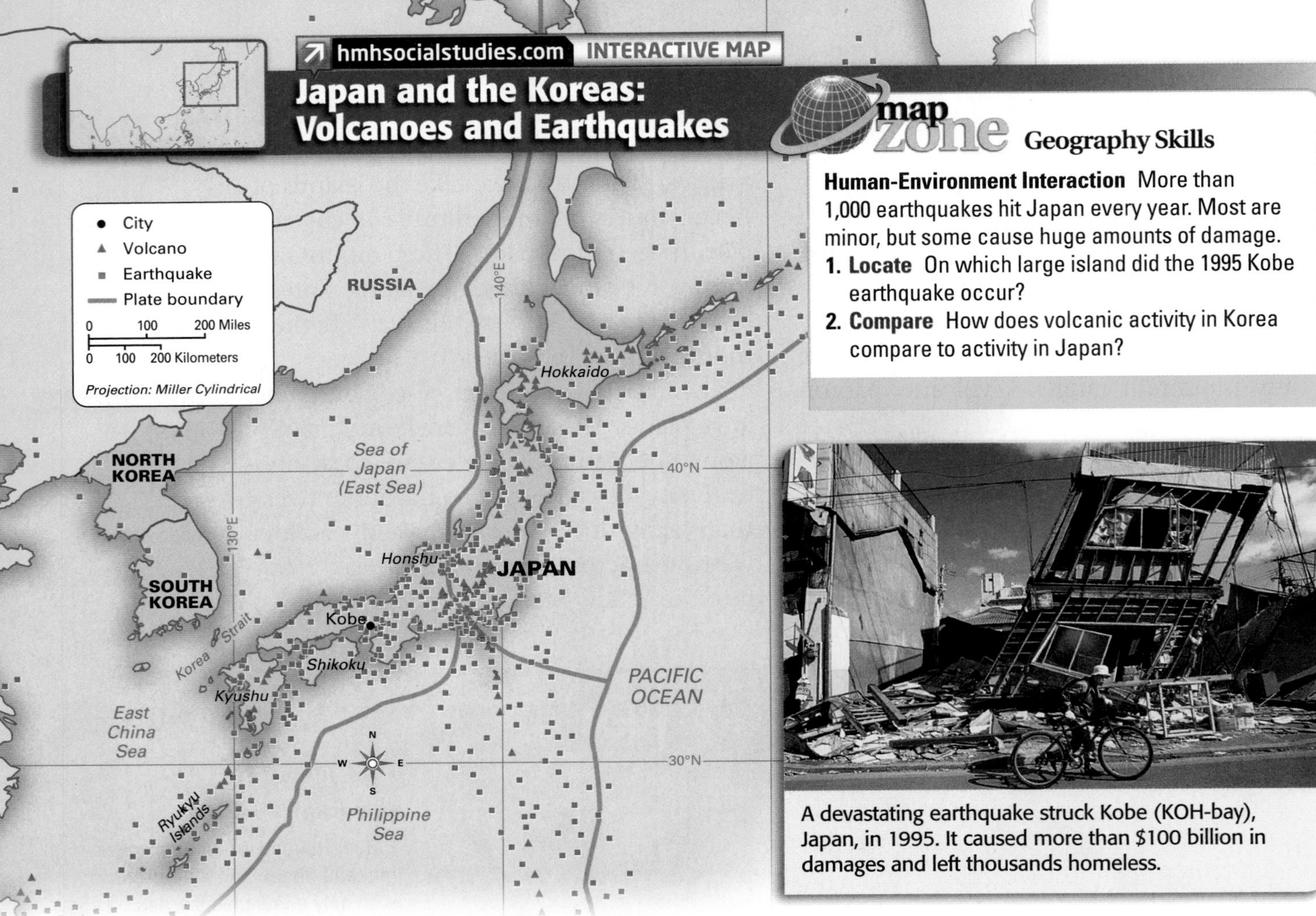

Geography Skills

Human-Environment Interaction More than 1,000 earthquakes hit Japan every year. Most are minor, but some cause huge amounts of damage.

1. **Locate** On which large island did the 1995 Kobe earthquake occur?
2. **Compare** How does volcanic activity in Korea compare to activity in Japan?

A devastating earthquake struck Kobe (KOH-bay), Japan, in 1995. It caused more than $100 billion in damages and left thousands homeless.

Natural Disasters

Because of its location, Japan is subject to many sorts of natural disasters. Among these disasters are volcanic eruptions and earthquakes. As you can see on the map, these disasters are common in Japan. They can cause huge amounts of damage in the country. In addition, large underwater earthquakes sometimes cause destructive waves called **tsunamis** (sooh-NAH-mees).

Korea does not have many volcanoes or earthquakes. From time to time, though, huge storms called typhoons sweep over the peninsula from the Pacific. These storms cause great damage in both the Korean Peninsula and Japan.

READING CHECK **Contrasting** How are the physical features of Japan and Korea different?

Climate and Resources

Just as Japan and the Koreas have many similar physical features, they also have similar climates. The resources found in each country, however, differ greatly.

Climate

The climates of Japan and the Koreas vary from north to south. The northern parts of the region have a humid continental climate. This means that summers are cool, but winters are long and cold. In addition, the area has a short growing season.

To the south, the region has a humid subtropical climate with mild winters and hot, humid summers. These areas see heavy rains and typhoons in the summer. Some places receive up to 80 inches (200 cm) of rain each year.

Resources

Resources are not evenly distributed among Japan and the Koreas. Neither Japan nor South Korea, for example, is very rich in mineral resources. North Korea, on the other hand, has large deposits of coal, iron, and other minerals.

Although most of the region does not have many mineral resources, it does have other resources. For example, the people of the Koreas have used their land's features to generate electricity. The peninsula's rocky terrain and rapidly flowing rivers make it an excellent location for creating hydroelectric power.

In addition, Japan has one of the world's strongest fishing economies. The islands lie near one of the world's most productive fisheries. A **fishery** is a place where lots of fish and other seafood can be caught. Swift ocean currents near Japan carry countless fish to the islands. Fishers then use huge nets to catch the fish and bring them to Japan's many bustling fish markets. These fish markets are among the busiest in the world.

READING CHECK **Analyzing** What are some resources found in Japan and the Koreas?

This fish market in Tokyo, Japan, is the busiest in the world. People gather here every morning to buy freshly caught fish.

SUMMARY AND PREVIEW The islands of Japan and the Korean Peninsula share many common features. In the next section, you will see how the people of Japan and Korea also share some similar customs and how their histories have been intertwined for centuries.

Section 1 Assessment

hmhsocialstudies.com ONLINE QUIZ

Reviewing Ideas, Terms, and Places

1. a. **Identify** What types of landforms cover Japan and the **Korean Peninsula**?
   b. **Compare and Contrast** How are the physical features of Japan and Korea similar? How are they different?
   c. **Predict** How do you think natural disasters affect life in Japan and Korea?
2. a. **Describe** What kind of climate is found in the northern parts of the region? What kind of climate is found in the southern parts?
   b. **Draw Conclusions** Why are **fisheries** important to Japan's economy?

Critical Thinking

3. **Categorizing** Draw a chart like this one. In each row, describe the region's landforms, climate, and resources.

	Japan	Korean Peninsula
Landforms		
Climate		
Resources		

FOCUS ON WRITING

4. **Thinking about Nature** Many Japanese poems deal with nature—the beauty of a flower, for example. What could you write about the region's physical environment in your poem?

Using a Topographic Map

Learn

Topographic maps show elevation, or the height of land above sea level. They do so with contour lines, lines that connect points on the map that have equal elevation. Every point on a contour line has the same elevation. In most cases, everything inside that line has a higher elevation. Everything outside the line is lower. Each contour line is labeled to show the elevation it indicates.

An area that has lots of contour lines is more rugged than an area with few contour lines. The distance between contour lines shows how steep an area is. If the lines are very close together, then the area has a steep slope. If the lines are farther apart, then the area has a much gentler incline. Other symbols on the map show features such as rivers and roads.

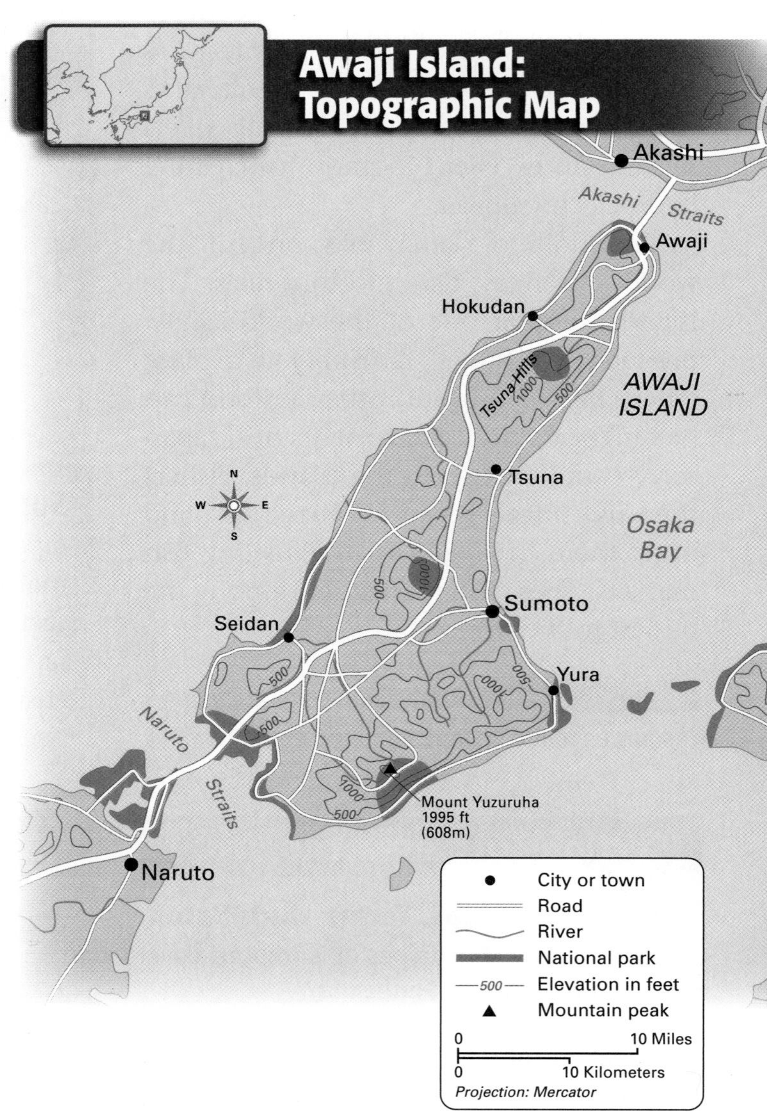

Practice

Use the topographic map on this page to answer the following questions.

1. Is Awaji Island more rugged in the south or the north? How can you tell?
2. Does the land get higher or lower as you travel west from Yura?

Apply

Search the Internet or look in a local library to find a topographic map of your area. Study the map to find three major landmarks and write down their elevations. Then write two statements about the information you can see on the map.

History and Culture

SECTION 2

If YOU lived there...

You live in Kyoto, one of the most beautiful cities in Japan. Your class is visiting a museum to see an amazing demonstration by a sword maker. You all stare in amazement as he hammers red-hot metal into a curved sword, then plunges it into cold water. He tells you that his family has been making swords for 300 years.

What kind of craft would you like to know?

BUILDING BACKGROUND Even though Japan is an industrial nation, the Japanese still respect and admire traditional arts and crafts and the people who make them, such as this sword maker. In fact, traditions continue to shape life in Japan and the Koreas today.

What You Will Learn...

Main Ideas

1. The early histories of Japan and Korea were closely linked, but the countries developed very differently.
2. Japanese culture blends traditional customs with modern innovations.
3. Though they share a common culture, life is very different in North and South Korea.

The Big Idea

History and tradition are very important to the people of Japan and the Koreas.

Key Terms and Places

Kyoto, *p. 142*
shoguns, *p. 142*
samurai, *p. 142*
kimonos, *p. 144*
kimchi, *p. 145*

hmhsocialstudies.com
TAKING NOTES

Use the graphic organizer online to take notes about the history and culture of Japan and the Koreas.

History

Both Japan and the Koreas have very long histories. Early in these histories, their cultures were intertwined. As time passed, though, Japan and the Koreas developed very differently.

Early History

Early in their histories, both Japan and the Koreas were influenced by China. Since the Korean Peninsula borders China, and Japan lies just across the sea, elements of Chinese culture seeped into both places.

Among the elements of Chinese culture that influenced Japan and Korea was Buddhism. Scholars and missionaries first brought Buddhism into Korea. From there, visitors carried it to Japan. Before long, Buddhism was the main religion in both countries.

Japanese Buddha statue

Emperors, Shoguns, and Samurai

Focus on Reading
Where could you look to find out whether these facts are true?

The first central government in Japan was based on China's government. For many centuries, emperors ruled in Japan just as they did in China. The imperial capital at Heian, now called **Kyoto**, was a center of art, literature, and learning. At times, some of Japan's emperors were more concerned with art than with running the country. Eventually, their power slipped away.

As the emperors' power faded, Japan fell under the control of military leaders called **shoguns**. Powerful generals, the shoguns ruled Japan in the emperor's name. Only one shogun could hold power at a time.

Serving under the shogun were armies of **samurai**, or highly trained warriors. They were fierce in battle and devoted to their leaders. As a result, the samurai were very respected in Japanese society. With their support, the shoguns continued to rule Japan well into the 1800s.

BIOGRAPHY

Hirohito
(1901–1989)

Hirohito was Japan's emperor for most of the 1900s. As such, he led the country through periods of great crisis and change. He was emperor when Japan launched wars against China and Russia in the 1930s. He was also in power in 1945 when the United States bombed Hiroshima and Nagasaki. After World War II ended, Hirohito led Japan through changes in its government and economy. Many of these changes affected Hirohito personally. For example, he gave up much of the power he had once held as emperor in favor of a democratic government.

Drawing Conclusions Why might a ruler give up much of his power?

Later Japan

Not everyone was happy with the rule of the shoguns. In 1868 a group of samurai overthrew the shogun and gave power back to the emperor.

When World War II began, Japan allied itself with Germany and Italy. It wanted to build an empire in Southeast Asia and the Pacific. The Japanese drew the United States into the war in 1941 when they bombed the naval base at Pearl Harbor, Hawaii. After many years of fighting, the Americans took drastic measures to end the war. They dropped devastating atomic bombs on two Japanese cities, Hiroshima and Nagasaki. Shocked by these terrible weapons, the Japanese surrendered.

Korea

Like Japan, the Korean Peninsula has long been influenced by China. Although Korea remained independent, it was considered part of China's empire. Later, the Japanese invaded the Korean Peninsula. They were harsh rulers, and the Korean people grew to resent the Japanese.

After World War II, Korea was taken away from Japan and once again made independent. Rather than forming one country, though, the Koreans formed two. Aided by the Soviet Union, North Korea created a Communist government. In South Korea, the United States helped build a democratic government.

In 1950 North Korea invaded South Korea, starting the Korean War. The North Koreans wanted to unify all of Korea under a Communist government. With the aid of many other countries, including the United States, the South Koreans drove the invaders back. The Korean War was costly, and its effects linger in the Koreas today.

Reading Check **Analyzing** How did the Koreas change after the Korean War?

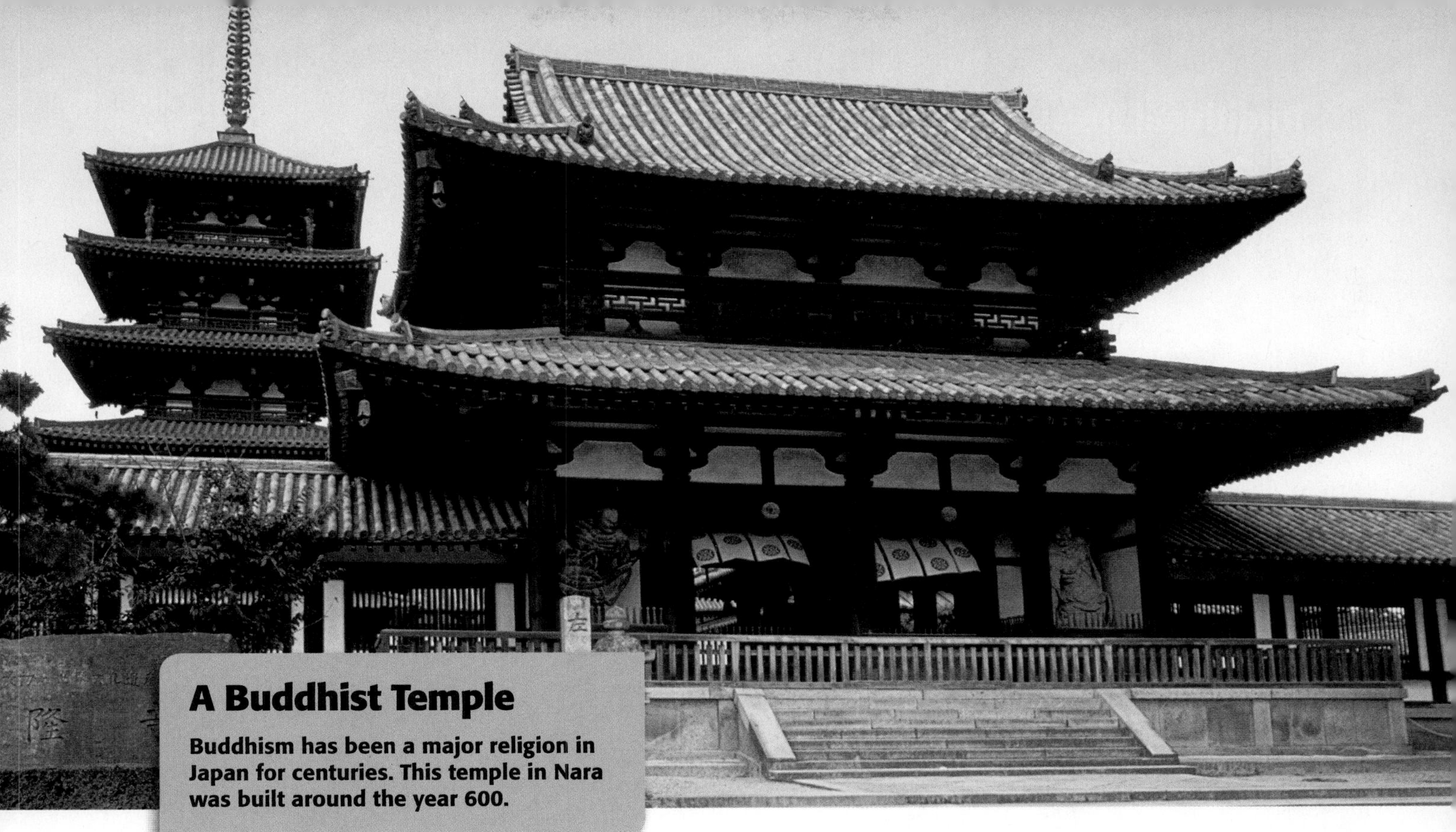

A Buddhist Temple

Buddhism has been a major religion in Japan for centuries. This temple in Nara was built around the year 600.

Japanese Culture

Japan's culture reflects the country's long and varied history. For example, some elements of the culture reflect the influence of the Chinese, while others are native to Japan. Since World War II, Western ideas and innovations have also helped shape Japanese life.

Language

Nearly everyone in Japan speaks Japanese. The Japanese language is complicated and can be difficult for other people to learn. This difficulty stems in large part from the Japanese writing system. Japanese writing uses two different types of characters. Some characters, called kanji, represent whole words. There are about 2,000 kanji characters in common use today. Other characters, called kana, stand for parts of words. Most texts written in Japanese use both kanji and kana characters.

Religion

Religion can also be complicated in Japan. Most people who live there blend elements of two religions—Shinto and Buddhism.

Unlike Buddhism, which was brought to Japan from Korea, Shinto is native to the islands. According to Shinto teachings, nature spirits called *kami* (KAH-mee) live in the world. Shintoists believe everything in nature—the sun, the moon, trees, rocks, waterfalls, and animals—has *kami*. They also believe that some *kami* help people live and keep them from harm. As a result, they build shrines to the *kami* and perform ceremonies to ask for their blessings.

Buddhists have also built shrines and temples all over Japan. Some temples, like the one pictured above, are very old. They date back to the earliest days of Buddhism in Japan. People visit these temples to seek peace and enlightenment. The search for enlightenment is Buddhists' main goal.

These Korean dancers are wearing traditional costumes to perform a fan dance. Most of the time, people in both South Korea and North Korea wear Western-style clothes.

Customs and Traditions

Japan's history lives on in its customs and traditions. For example, many Japanese wear traditional robes called **kimonos** on special occasions, just as samurai did long ago. Most of the time, though, people in Japan wear Western-style clothing.

Traditional forms of art are also still popular in Japan. Among these art forms are two types of drama, Noh and Kabuki. Noh plays use music and dance to tell a story. Actors do not move much and wear masks, using their gestures to convey their tale. Kabuki actors, on the other hand, are much more active. Kabuki plays tell stories, but they often teach lessons about duty and other abstract ideas as well.

ACADEMIC VOCABULARY
abstract expressing a quality or idea without reference to an actual thing

READING CHECK **Summarizing** How did Japan's history affect its culture today?

Korean Culture

Like Japan's, Korea's culture reflects the peninsula's long history. Traditional ways of life influence how people act and think.

Language and Religion

People in both North Korea and South Korea speak Korean. Unlike Japanese, Korean is written with an alphabet. People combine letters to form words, rather than using symbols to represent entire words or syllables as in Japanese.

In the past, most people in Korea were Buddhists and Confucianists. Recently, though, Christianity has also become widespread. About one-fourth of South Korea's people are Christian. North Korea, like many Communist countries, discourages people from practicing any religion.

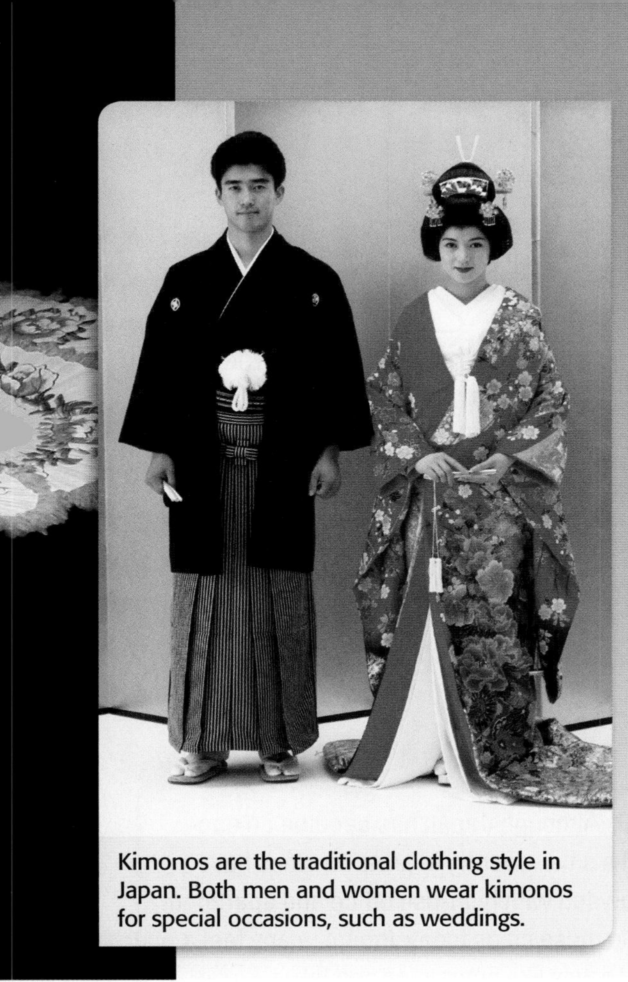
Kimonos are the traditional clothing style in Japan. Both men and women wear kimonos for special occasions, such as weddings.

Customs and Traditions

Like the Japanese, the people of Korea have kept many ancient traditions alive. Many Korean foods, for example, have been part of the Korean diet for centuries.

One example of a long-lasting Korean food is **kimchi**, a dish made from pickled cabbage and various spices. First created in the 1100s, kimchi is still served at many Korean meals. In fact, many people think of it as Korea's national dish.

Traditional art forms have also remained popular in parts of the Koreas. This is true especially in North Korea. Since World War II, the Communist government of North Korea has encouraged people to retain many of their old customs and traditions. The Communists think that Korean culture is the best in the world and do everything they can to preserve it.

In South Korea, urbanization and the spread of modern lifestyles have led to a decline in some traditional customs. Rural areas are still very traditional, but people in urban areas have adopted new ways of life. Many of these ways are combinations of old and new ideas. For example, Korean art today combines traditional themes such as nature with modern forms, like film.

READING CHECK **Contrasting** How are North and South Korea's cultures different?

SUMMARY AND PREVIEW In this section, you learned that the cultures of Japan and the Koreas have been shaped by the countries' histories. In the next section you will see how traditional cultures continue to influnce life in Japan today.

Section 2 Assessment

hmhsocialstudies.com
ONLINE QUIZ

Reviewing Ideas, Terms, and Places

1. **a. Define** Who were **shoguns**?
   b. Elaborate How did World War II affect life in Japan?
2. **a. Identify** What is one traditional style of clothing in Japan? What do people wear most of the time?
   b. Elaborate How does Japan's religion reflect its history?
3. **a. Recall** What is **kimchi**? Why is it important in Korea?
   b. Explain What has led to many of the differences between modern culture in North and South Korea?

Critical Thinking

4. **Analyzing** Draw a diagram like this one. Using your notes, list two features of Japanese culture in the left box and of Korean culture in the right box. Below each box, write a sentence about how each country's culture reflects its history.

Japanese Culture	Korean Culture

FOCUS ON WRITING

5. **Analyzing Cultures** Traditions and customs are central to life in Japan and the Koreas. How can you reflect this importance in your poem?

SECTION 3

Japan Today

What You Will Learn...

Main Ideas

1. Since World War II, Japan has developed a democratic government and one of the world's strongest economies.
2. A shortage of open space shapes daily life in Japan.
3. Crowding, competition, and pollution are among Japan's main issues and challenges.

The Big Idea

Japan has overcome many challenges to become one of the most highly developed countries in Asia.

Key Terms and Places

Diet, *p. 146*
Tokyo, *p. 146*
work ethic, *p. 147*
trade surplus, *p. 147*
tariff, *p. 147*
Osaka, *p. 150*

Use the graphic organizer online to take notes about Japan's government, economy, and daily life.

If YOU lived there...

You and your family live in a small apartment in the crowded city of Tokyo. Every day you and your friends crowd into jammed subway trains to travel to school. Since your work in school is very hard and demanding, you really look forward to weekends. You especially like to visit mountain parks where there are flowering trees, quiet gardens, and ancient shrines.

Do you like your life in Tokyo? Why or why not?

BUILDING BACKGROUND Although Japan has become an economic powerhouse, it is still a small country in area. Its cities have become more and more crowded with high-rise office and apartment buildings. Most people live in these cities today, though many feel a special fondness for natural areas like mountains and lakes.

Government and Economy

Do you own any products made by Sony? Have you seen ads for vehicles made by Honda, Toyota, or Mitsubishi? Chances are good that you have. These companies are some of the most successful in the world, and all of them are Japanese.

Since World War II, Japan's government and economy have changed dramatically. Japan was once an imperial state that was shut off from the rest of the world. Today Japan is a democracy with one of the world's strongest economies.

Government

Since the end of World War II, Japan's government has been a constitutional monarchy headed by an emperor. Although the emperor is officially the head of state, he has little power. His main role is to act as a symbol of Japan and of the Japanese people. In his place, power rests in an elected legislature called the **Diet** and in an elected prime minister. From the capital city of **Tokyo**, the Diet and the prime minister make the laws that govern life in Japan today.

Economy

Today Japan is an economic powerhouse. However, this was not always the case. Until the 1950s, Japan's economy was not that strong. Within a few decades, though, the economy grew tremendously.

The most successful area of Japan's economy is manufacturing. Japanese companies are known for making high-quality products, especially cars and electronics. Japanese companies are among the world's leading manufacturers of televisions, DVD players, CD players, and other electronic items. The methods that companies use to make these products are also celebrated. Many Japanese companies are leaders in new technology and ideas.

Reasons for Success Many factors have contributed to Japan's economic success. One factor is the government. It works closely with business leaders to control production and plan for the future.

Japan's workforce also contributed to its success. Japan has well-educated, highly trained workers. As a result, its companies tend to be both efficient and productive. Most workers in Japan also have a strong work ethic. A **work ethic** is the belief that work in itself is worthwhile. Because of their work ethic, most Japanese work hard and are loyal to their companies. As a result, the companies are successful.

Trade Japan's economy depends on trade. In fact, many products manufactured in the country are intended to be sold outside of Japan. Many of these goods are sent to China and the United States. The United States is Japan's major trading partner.

Japan's trade has been so successful that it has built up a huge trade surplus. A **trade surplus** exists when a country exports more goods than it imports. Because of this surplus, many Japanese companies have become very wealthy.

CONNECTING TO **Technology**

Building Small

The Japanese are known as masters of technology. Companies use this technology in many ways to create new products and improve existing ones. One way many Japanese companies have sought to improve their products—especially personal electronics products—is by making them smaller.

Since Sony released the first personal stereo system in the late 1970s, making small products has been a major business in Japan. Now shoppers can buy tiny radios, video games, cell phones, and cameras. Some of these products are smaller than the palm of your hand.

Generalizing Why might people want to buy small versions of products?

Japan is able to export more than it imports in part because of high tariffs. A **tariff** is a fee that a country charges on imports or exports. For many years, Japan's government has placed high tariffs on goods brought into the country. This makes imported goods more expensive, and so people buy Japanese goods rather than imported ones.

hmhsocialstudies.com
ANIMATED GEOGRAPHY
Present-Day Japan

Resources Although its economy is based on manufacturing, Japan has few natural resources. As a result, the country must import raw materials. In addition, Japan has little arable land. Farms cannot grow enough food for the country's growing population. Instead, the Japanese have to buy food from other countries, including China and the United States.

READING CHECK **Summarizing** What have the Japanese done to build their economy?

Daily Life

Japan is a densely populated country. Slightly smaller than California, it has nearly four times as many people! Most of these people live in crowded cities such as the capital, Tokyo.

Life in Tokyo

FOCUS ON READING

How can you tell that the statements in this paragraph are facts?

Besides serving as the national capital, Tokyo is the center of Japan's banking and communication industries. As a result, the city is busy, noisy, and very crowded. About 36 million people live in a relatively small area. Because Tokyo is so densely populated, land is scarce. As a result, Tokyo's real estate prices are among the highest in the world. Some people save up for years to buy homes in Tokyo. They earn money by putting money in savings accounts or by investing in stocks and bonds.

Because space is so limited in Tokyo, people have found creative ways to adapt. Buildings tend to be fairly tall and narrow so that they take less land area. People also use space under ground. For example, shops and restaurants can be found below the streets in subway stations. Another way the Japanese have found to save space is the capsule hotel. Guests in these hotels—mostly traveling businesspeople—crawl into tiny sleeping chambers rather than having rooms with beds.

Many people work in Tokyo but live outside the city. So many people commute to and from Tokyo that trains are very crowded. During peak travel times, commuters are crammed into train cars.

Tokyo is not all about work, though. During their leisure time, people can visit Tokyo's many parks, museums, and stores. They can also take short trips to local amusement parks, baseball stadiums, or other attractions. Among these attractions are a huge indoor beach and a ski resort filled with artificial snow.

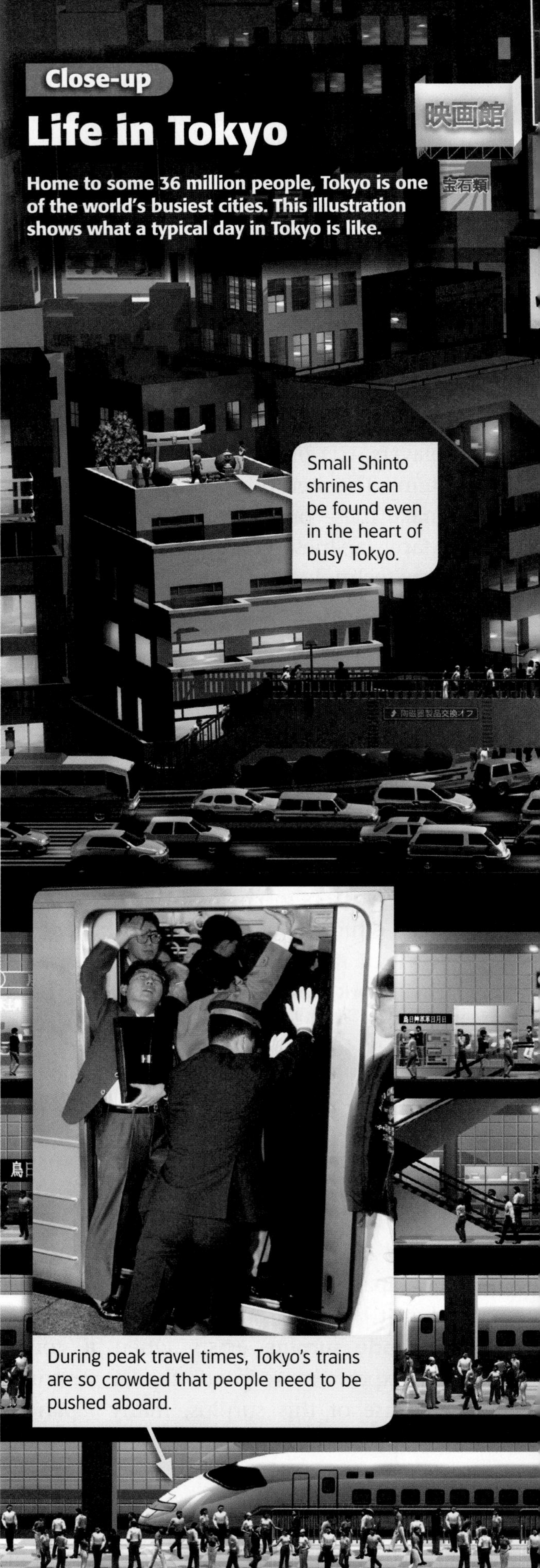
Close-up
Life in Tokyo
Home to some 36 million people, Tokyo is one of the world's busiest cities. This illustration shows what a typical day in Tokyo is like.
映画館
宝石類
Small Shinto shrines can be found even in the heart of busy Tokyo.
During peak travel times, Tokyo's trains are so crowded that people need to be pushed aboard.

電話
コンピュータ
ビデオゲーム
子供の衣類
催し物
人の衣類
バンク
旅行局
映画館
洋品店
貸自動車
劇場
割引屋
Gardens planted on the roofs of buildings help keep Tokyo's temperature down.
To save space, the Japanese build capsule hotels. Each guest sleeps in his or her own tiny chamber.
3056
3058
3060
3055
3057
3059
小さいレストラン
陶磁器製品
Bustling shopping centers can be found below many of Tokyo's streets.
ANALYSIS SKILL
ANALYZING VISUALS
Based on this image, how does life in Tokyo compare to daily life where you are?

Life in Other Cities

Most of Japan's other cities, like Tokyo, are crowded and busy. Many of them serve as centers of industry or transportation.

The second largest city in Japan, **Osaka**, is located in western Honshu. In Osaka—as in Tokyo and other cities—tall, modern skyscrapers stand next to tiny Shinto temples. Another major city is Kyoto. Once Japan's capital, Kyoto is full of historic buildings.

Transportation between Cities

To connect cities that lie far apart, the Japanese have built a network of rail lines. Some of these lines carry very fast trains called *Shinkansen*, or bullet trains. They can reach speeds of more than 160 miles per hour (250 kph). Japan's train system is very **efficient**. Trains nearly always leave on time and are almost never late.

ACADEMIC VOCABULARY
efficient productive and not wasteful

Rural Life

Not everyone in Japan lives in cities. Some people live in the country in small villages. The people in these villages own or work on farms.

Relatively little of Japan's land is arable, or suitable for farming. Much of the land is too rocky or steep to grow crops on. As a result, most farms are small. The average Japanese farm is only about 2.5 acres (1 hectare). In contrast, the average farm in the United States is 175 times that size.

Because their farms are so small and Japan imports so much of its food, many farmers cannot make a living from their crops. As a result, many people have left rural areas to find jobs in cities.

READING CHECK **Finding Main Ideas** What are Japanese cities like?

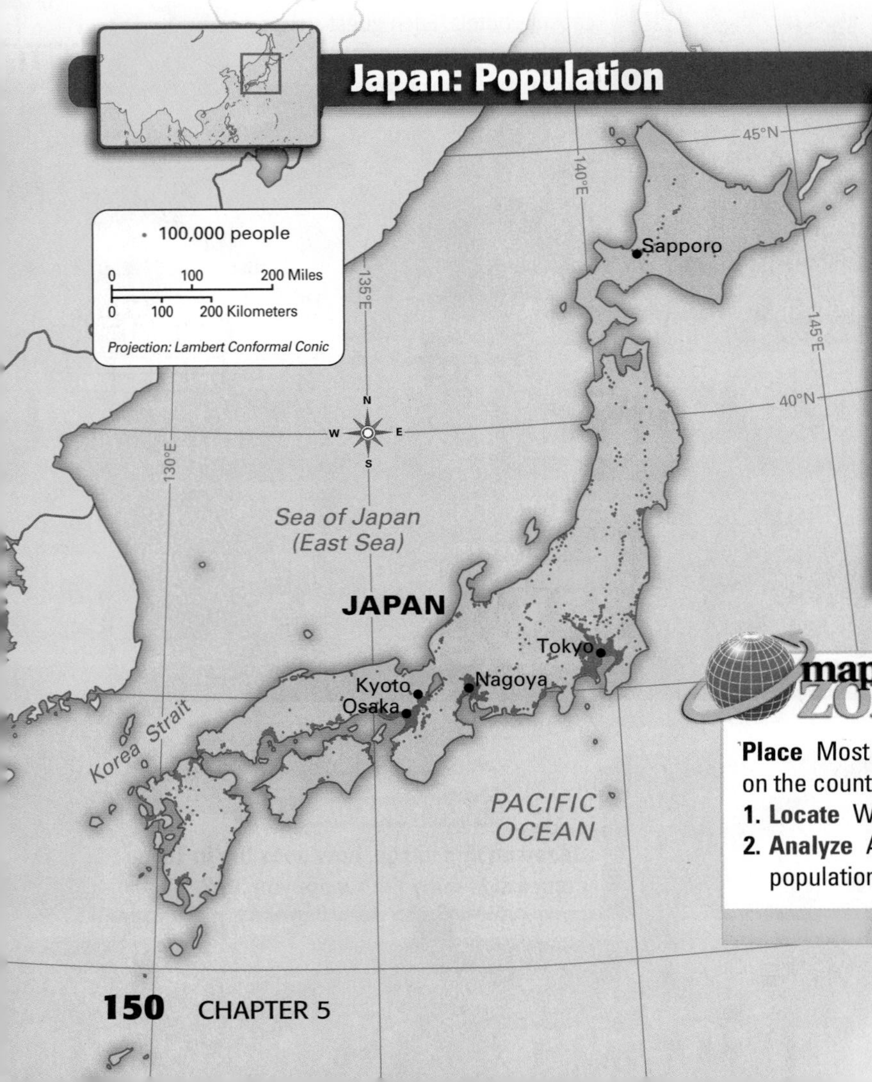

Japan: Population

THE WORLD ALMANAC® Facts about Countries

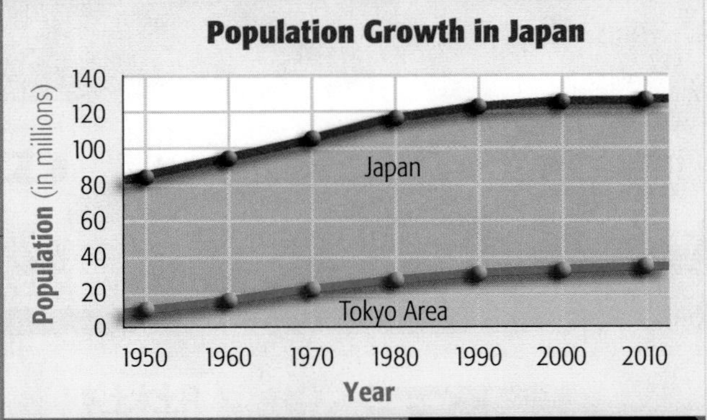

Population Growth in Japan

hmhsocialstudies.com

map zone Geography Skills

Place Most of Japan's people live in crowded cities on the country's few coastal plains.

1. **Locate** Where are Japan's most crowded cities?
2. **Analyze** According to the chart, what was Japan's population in 2000?

Issues and Challenges

Many people consider Japan one of the world's most successful countries. In recent years, however, a few issues have arisen that present challenges for Japan's future.

One of these issues is Japan's lack of space. As cities grow, crowding has become a serious issue. To make space, some people have begun to construct taller buildings. Such buildings have to be carefully planned, though, to withstand earthquakes.

Japan also faces economic challenges. For many years, it had the only strong economy in East Asia. Recently, however, other countries have challenged Japan's economic dominance. Competition from China and South Korea has begun taking business from some Japanese companies.

Pollution has also become a problem in Japan. In 1997 officials from more than 150 countries met in Japan to discuss the pollution problem. They signed the Kyoto Protocol, an agreement to cut down on pollution and improve air quality.

READING CHECK **Finding Main Ideas** What are three issues facing Japan?

Technology

Advanced technology has helped Japan keep its economic edge over other countries. In this photo, workers use robots to assemble a car.

SUMMARY AND PREVIEW Since World War II, Japan has created a democratic government and a strong, highly technological economy. In the next section, you will learn about changes that have occurred in South Korea and North Korea in the same time period.

Section 3 Assessment

hmhsocialstudies.com ONLINE QUIZ

Reviewing Ideas, Terms, and Places

1. a. **Identify** What are some goods made in Japan?
   b. **Explain** How has Japan's government changed since World War II?
   c. **Elaborate** Why do you think **work ethic** is so important to the Japanese economy?
2. a. **Describe** How have people tried to save space in Japanese cities?
   b. **Evaluate** Do you think you would like living in **Tokyo**? Why or why not?
3. a. **Identify** What is one issue that crowding has caused for Japan?
   b. **Analyze** How are other countries presenting challenges to Japan's economy?

Critical Thinking

4. **Analyzing** Draw a graphic organizer like the one shown here. In one circle, write two sentences about city life in Japan. In another, write two sentences about rural life. In the third, write two sentences about issues facing the Japanese.

FOCUS ON WRITING

5. **Thinking about Japan** What image, or picture, of life in Japan could you write about in your poem? List two or three ideas. Then decide which is the most promising idea for your poem.

SECTION 4

The Koreas Today

What You Will Learn...

Main Ideas

1. The people of South Korea today have freedom and economic opportunities.
2. The people of North Korea today have little freedom or economic opportunity.
3. Some people in both South and North Korea support the idea of Korean reunification.

The Big Idea

Though they share a common history and culture, the two Koreas have very different governments and economies.

Key Terms and Places

Seoul, *p. 153*
demilitarized zone, *p. 153*
Pyongyang, *p. 155*

Use the graphic organizer online to take notes about South Korea and North Korea.

If YOU lived there...

You live in Inchon, one of South Korea's largest cities. Sometimes your grandparents tell you about the other family members who still live in North Korea. You have never met them, of course, and your grandparents have not seen them since they were children, more than 50 years ago. After hearing stories about these family members, you are curious about their lives.

Would you like to visit North Korea?

BUILDING BACKGROUND A truce ended the Korean War in 1953, but it left the Korean Peninsula divided into two very different countries. The conflict separated families from their relatives on the other side of the zone that divides South Korea from North Korea. Since then, the countries have developed in very different ways.

South Korea Today

Japan's closest neighbor is both a major economic rival and a key trading partner. That neighbor is South Korea. Like Japan, South Korea is a democratic country with a strong economy. Unlike Japan, South Korea shares a border with a hostile neighbor—North Korea.

Government and Economy

The official name of South Korea is the Republic of Korea. As the name suggests, South Korea's government is a republic. It is headed by a president and an assembly elected by the people, much like the United States is. In fact, the United States helped create South Korea's government after World War II.

The United States also helped make South Korea's economy one of the strongest in East Asia. In addition, Korean business leaders and government officials have worked together to ensure that the economy stays strong. In recent years, South Korea has become a major manufacturing country, exporting goods to places all around the world.

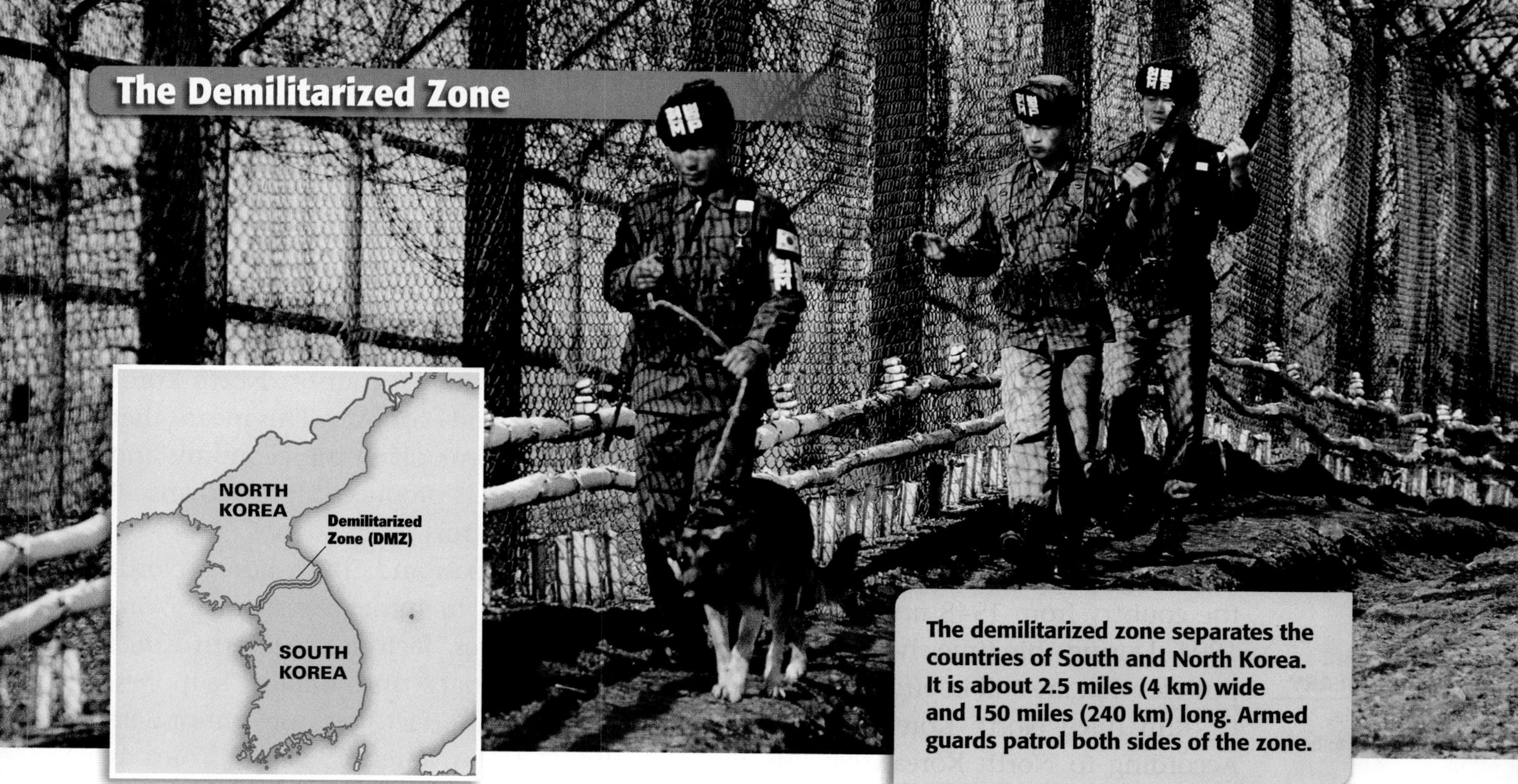

The demilitarized zone separates the countries of South and North Korea. It is about 2.5 miles (4 km) wide and 150 miles (240 km) long. Armed guards patrol both sides of the zone.

Daily Life

Like Japan, South Korea is very densely populated. The capital city, **Seoul** (SOHL), is one of the most densely populated cities in the world. It has more than 44,000 people per square mile (17,000/sq km).

Although parts of South Korea are densely populated, very few people live in the mountainous interior. Most people live near the coast. A coastal plain in western South Korea is the most crowded part of the country.

In South Korea's cities, most people live in small apartments. Because space is scarce, housing is expensive. Also, cities sometimes suffer from pollution from the many factories, cars, and coal-fired heating systems found there. In some cities, industrial waste has also polluted the water.

Outside the cities, many South Koreans still follow traditional ways of life. Most of them are farmers who grow rice, beans, and cabbage they can use to make kimchi. They usually live on small farms.

Issues and Challenges

Government policies and international politics have led to some challenges for South Korea. Although South Korea has a successful economy, some people feel that its government is corrupt. For many years, four families have controlled much of the country's industry. As a result, wealth and power became concentrated in the hands of big business. This led to corruption of government officials, but efforts are being made to reform business practices.

A bigger challenge to South Korea is its relationship with North Korea. Since the end of the Korean War in the 1950s, the two countries have been separated. Between them is a **demilitarized zone**, an empty buffer zone created to keep the two countries from fighting. Although troops are not allowed in the demilitarized zone, guards patrol both sides.

READING CHECK **Summarizing** What issues face South Korea today?

hmhsocialstudies.com
ANIMATED GEOGRAPHY
Present-Day Korean Peninsula

North Korea Today

The official name of North Korea is the Democratic People's Republic of Korea. Its name, however, is misleading. North Korea is neither a democracy nor a republic. It is a totalitarian state, and the Communist Party controls both the government and the economy.

Government and Economy

The Communist government of North Korea was created soon after World War II. Its first leader was Kim Il Sung. He ruled the country from 1948 until his death in 1994. During this time, he created many **policies** that are still in effect today.

ACADEMIC VOCABULARY
policy rule, course of action

Kim ruled North Korea as a dictator. According to North Korea's constitution, most power rests in an elected legislature. In truth, though, the legislature never had much power. Advised by members of the Communist Party, Kim ruled alone.

When Kim Il Sung died in 1994, his son Kim Jong Il took over. Like his father, the younger Kim rules as a dictator. He was elected by the North Korean legislature. The people had no say in his election.

As a Communist country, North Korea has a command economy. This means that the government plans the economy and decides what is produced. It also owns all land and controls access to jobs.

Unlike Japan and South Korea, North Korea is rich in mineral resources. With these resources, factories in North Korea make machinery and military supplies. However, most factories use out-of-date technology. As a result, North Korea is much poorer than Japan and South Korea.

Life in Korea

Because it is so rocky, very little of North Korea's land can be farmed. The farmland that does exist is owned by the government. It is farmed by cooperatives—large groups of farmers who work the land together. These cooperatives are not able to grow enough food for the country. As a result, the government has to import food. This can be a difficult task because North Korea's relations with most other countries are strained.

Daily Life

Like Japan and South Korea, North Korea is largely an urban society. Most people live in cities. The largest city is the capital, **Pyongyang** (PYUHNG-YAHNG), in the west. Pyongyang is a crowded urban area. More than 3 million people live in the city.

The differences between life in South Korea and North Korea can be seen in their capitals. Seoul, South Korea (shown to the left), is a busy, modern city and a major commercial center. In comparison, North Korea's capital, Pyongyang (shown above), has little traffic or commercial development.

ANALYZING VISUALS What do these photos suggest about life in Seoul and Pyongyang?

Life in Pyongyang is very different from life in Tokyo or Seoul. For example, few people in Pyongyang own private cars. The North Korean government allows only top Communist officials to own cars. Most residents have to use buses or the subway to get around. At night, many streets are dark because of electricity shortages.

The people of North Korea have fewer rights than the people of Japan or South Korea. For example, the government controls individual speech as well as the press. Because the government feels that religion conflicts with many Communist ideas, it also discourages people from practicing any religions.

Issues and Challenges

Why does North Korea, which is rich in resources, have shortages of electricity and food? These problems are due in part to choices the government has made. For years, North Korea had ties mostly with other Communist countries. Since the breakup of the Soviet Union, North Korea has been largely isolated from the rest of the world. It has closed its markets to foreign goods, which means that other countries cannot sell their goods there. At the same time, North Korea lacks the technology to take advantage of its resources. As a result, many people suffer and resources go unused.

In addition, many countries worry about North Korea's ability to make and use nuclear weapons. In 2002 North Korea announced that it had enough materials to build six nuclear bombs. Then in 2006 and again in 2009, it conducted nuclear weapons tests. These developments worried countries in Asia and around the world.

READING CHECK **Generalizing** What is North Korea's relationship with the world?

Young people at a political rally express support for reunification. The flag in the background shows a united Korea.

Korean Reunification

Focus on Reading
What opinion do many Koreans hold toward reunification?

For years, people from both South and North Korea have called for their countries to be reunited. Because the two Koreas share a common history and culture, these people believe they should be one country. As time has passed, more and more people have voiced support for reunification.

The governments of both South Korea and North Korea have also expressed their support for reunification. Leaders from the two countries met in 2000 for the first time since the Korean War. As part of their meeting, they discussed ways to improve relations and communication between the two countries. For example, they agreed to build a road through the demilitarized zone to connect the two Koreas.

The chief obstacle to the reunification of Korea is the question of government. South Koreans want a unified Korea to be a democracy. North Korean leaders, on the other hand, have insisted that Korea should be Communist. Until this issue is resolved, the countries will remain separate.

Reading Check **Summarizing** What issues stand in the way of Korean reunification?

Summary and Preview In this chapter you learned about the history, cultures, and people of Japan and the Koreas. In the next chapter, you will examine a region that lies farther south, a region called Southeast Asia.

Section 4 Assessment

hmhsocialstudies.com
ONLINE QUIZ

Reviewing Ideas, Terms, and Places

1. a. **Define** What is the **demilitarized zone**? Why does it exist?
   b. **Summarize** What factors have helped South Korea develop a strong economy?
2. a. **Identify** What is the capital of North Korea? What is life like there?
   b. **Contrast** How is North Korea's government different from South Korea's?
3. a. **Recall** Why do many Koreans support the idea of reunification?
   b. **Evaluate** If you lived in North or South Korea, do you think you would support the reunification of the countries? Why or why not?

Critical Thinking

4. **Analyze** Draw a diagram like the one below. In the left box, write three statements about South Korea. In the right box, write three statements about North Korea. In the oval, list one factor that supports reunification and one that hinders it.

South Korea   North Korea

Focus on Writing

5. **Considering Korea** As you read about the Koreas, did you think of an image, or picture, that would work in a poem? List your ideas.

CHAPTER 5

Chapter Review

Geography's Impact
video series
Review the video to answer the closing question:
How has Japan's location on the Ring of Fire made it so prone to natural hazards?

Visual Summary

Use the visual summary below to help you review the main ideas of the chapter.

QUICK FACTS

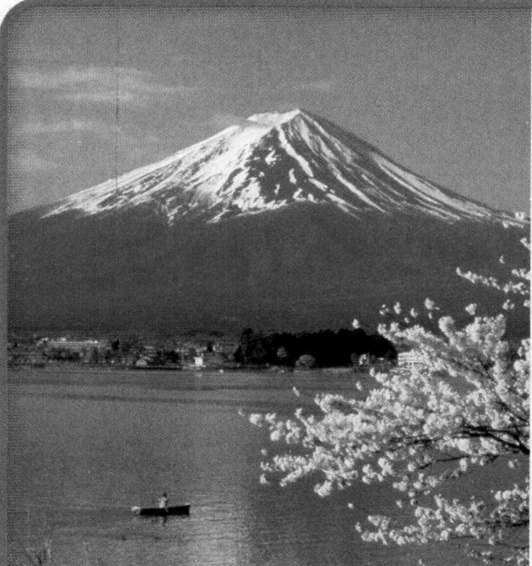

Japan and the Korean Peninsula have rugged landscapes that are largely covered by mountains.

Japan has one of the world's strongest economies, due in large part to its superior technology.

Since World War II, life in democratic South Korea has been very different from life in Communist North Korea.

Reviewing Vocabulary, Terms, and Places

Imagine these terms from the chapter are correct answers to items in a crossword puzzle. Write the clues for the answers.

1. Tokyo
2. abstract
3. trade surplus
4. tariff
5. kimono
6. efficient
7. work ethic
8. Seoul
9. fishery
10. Pyongyang
11. kimchi
12. policy

Comprehension and Critical Thinking

SECTION 1 *(Pages 136–139)*

13. a. Identify What physical feature covers most of Japan and the Korean Peninsula? What is one famous example of this landform?

b. Draw Conclusions Fish and seafood are very important in the Japanese diet. Why do you think this is so?

c. Predict How do you think earthquakes and typhoons would affect your life if you lived in Japan?

SECTION 2 *(Pages 141–145)*

14. a. Identify Who were the shoguns? What role did they play in Japanese history?

b. Explain What caused the Korean War? What happened as a result of the war?

c. Elaborate How have the histories of Japan and Korea affected their cultures?

SECTION 3 *(Pages 146–151)*

15. a. Recall What is the most important aspect of Japan's economy?

b. Make Inferences Why is Tokyo such a busy and crowded city?

c. Develop How might Japan try to address the problem of crowding in its cities?

SECTION 4 *(Pages 152–156)*

16. a. Recall What type of government does South Korea have? What type of government does North Korea have?

b. Contrast How is South Korea's economy different from North Korea's? Which has been more successful?

c. Predict Do you think the reunification of the Koreas will happen in the near future? Why or why not?

Social Studies Skills

Using a Topographic Map *Use the topographic map in this chapter's Social Studies Skills lesson to answer the following questions.*

17. What elevations do the contour lines on this map show?

18. Where are the highest points on Awaji Island located? How can you tell?

19. Is the city of Sumoto located more or less than 500 feet above sea level?

Using the Internet 

20. Activity: Comparing Schools Have you ever wondered what it would be like to live in Japan? How would your life be different if you lived there? What would you learn about in school? What would you eat for lunch? Learn about Japan and about Japanese culture by exploring the Web links provided through the online book. Look for ways that your life would be the same and different if you grew up in Japan. Then record what you learned in a chart or a graphic organizer.

Map Activity 

21. Japan and the Koreas On a separate sheet of paper, match the letters on the map with their correct labels.

North Korea
South Korea
Korea Strait
Tokyo, Japan
Hokkaido
Sea of Japan (East Sea)

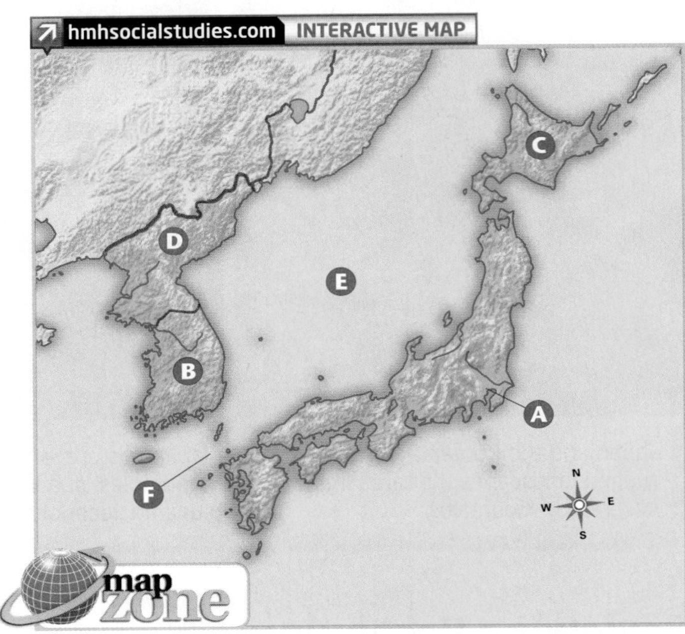

Focus on Reading and Writing

Understanding Fact and Opinion *Decide whether each of the following statements is a fact or an opinion.*

22. Japan would be a great place to live.

23. Japan is an island country.

24. North Korea should give up communism.

25. The Koreas should reunify.

Writing Your Five-Line Poem *Use your notes and the instructions below to create your poem.*

26. Review your notes and decide on a topic to write about. Remember that your poem should describe one image or picture—an object, a place, etc.—from Japanese or Korean culture.

The first three lines of your poem should describe the object or place you have chosen. The last two should express how it makes you feel. Try to use the traditional Tanka syllable count in your poem: five syllables in lines 1 and 3; seven in lines 2, 4, and 5. Remember that your poem does not have to rhyme.

CHAPTER 5

Standardized Test Prep

DIRECTIONS: Read questions 1 through 7 and write the letter of the best response. Then read question 8 and write your own well-constructed response.

1 Tokyo, Osaka, and Kyoto are all cities in what country?

A South Korea
B North Korea
C Japan
D Honshu

2 North Korea and South Korea are separated by the

A Korea Strait.
B demilitarized zone.
C Sea of Japan.
D Japanese Alps.

3 Kim Il Sung and Kim Jong Il are famous leaders from which country?

A South Korea
B North Korea
C Japan
D Honshu

4 The country that had the strongest influence on early Korea and Japan was

A Russia.
B India.
C China.
D the United States.

5 What is one reason that many people in Korea support reunification?

A They want a socialist government.
B They want to have the largest country in the world.
C They are afraid of an attack from Japan.
D They believe that all Koreans share a common history and culture.

Japan and the Koreas

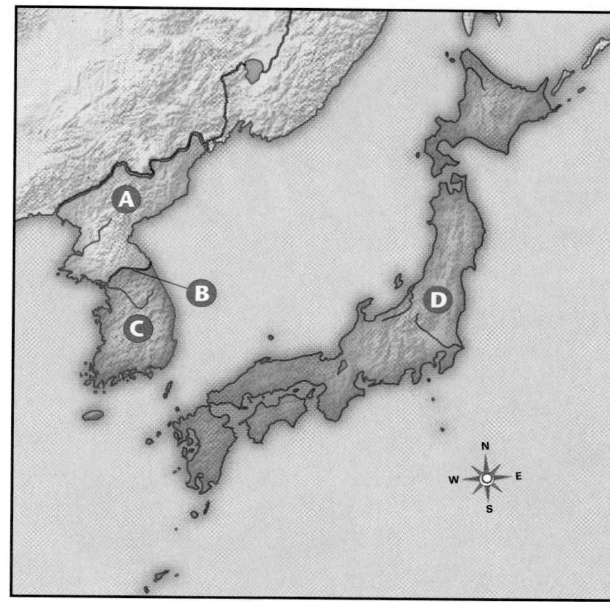

6 On the map above, which letter appears in an area led by a Communist government?

A A
B B
C C
D D

7 Which country has the strongest economy in the region?

A South Korea
B North Korea
C Japan
D Honshu

8 Extended Response Write a brief paragraph explaining why the coastal plains of Japan and Korea are so crowded. You may wish to refer to the map above as you prepare your answer.

Japan and the Samurai Warrior

For over a thousand years, the samurai—an elite warrior class—were a powerful force in Japanese society. The way of life of the samurai lords and warriors was, in many ways, like those of the medieval lords and knights of Europe. The great samurai warlords ruled large territories and relied on the fighting skills of their fierce samurai warriors to battle their enemies. But samurai warriors were more than just soldiers. Samurai were expected to embrace beauty and culture, and many were skilled artists. They also had a strict personal code that valued personal honor above all things—even life itself.

Explore the fascinating world of the samurai warrior online. You can find a wealth of information, video clips, primary sources, activities, and more at hmhsocialstudies.com.

Rise of the Samurai Class

Watch the video to learn how the samurai developed from armed tax collectors into warlords and armies that ruled Japan.

CLICK THROUGH

INTER/ACTIVITI

hmhsocialstudies.com

A New Way of Life in Japan

Watch the video to learn how peace and isolation took hold in Japan and changed the role of the samurai in society.

"*I have no eyes;*
I make the Flash of Lightning my Eyes.
I have no ears; I make Sensibility my Ears.
I have no limbs;
I make Promptitude my Limbs.
I have no laws;
I make Self-Protection my Laws."

A Code for Samurai Living

Read the document to learn about the strict but lyrical code of the samurai warrior.

Death of the Samurai Class

Watch the video to see how the end of Japan's isolation from the outside world signaled the beginning of the end of the samurai class.

CHAPTER 6

Southeast Asia

Essential Question What characteristics unite the diverse nations of Southeast Asia?

What You Will Learn...

In this chapter you will learn about the physical features, climate, and natural resources of Southeast Asia. You will also examine the histories and cultures of the countries in this region and explore what life is like there today.

The Big Idea Southeast Asia is a tropical region of peninsulas, islands, and waterways with diverse plants, animals, and resources.

The Big Idea People, ideas, and traditions from China, India, Europe, and elsewhere have shaped Southeast Asia's history and culture.

The Big Idea Many of the farming countries in Mainland Southeast Asia are poor but are working to improve their economies.

The Big Idea The countries of Island Southeast Asia range from wealthy and urban to poor and rural.

FOCUS ON READING AND SPEAKING

Using Context Clues–Definitions As you read, you may run across words you do not know. You can often figure out the meaning of an unknown word by using context clues. One type of context clue is a definition of a word, or a restatement of its meaning. To use these clues, look at the words and sentences around the unknown word—its context. **See the lesson, Using Context Clues–Definitions, on page 218.**

Presenting an Interview With a partner, you will role-play a journalist interviewing a regional expert on Southeast Asia. First, read about the region. Then, with your partner create a question-and-answer interview script about the region to present to your classmates.

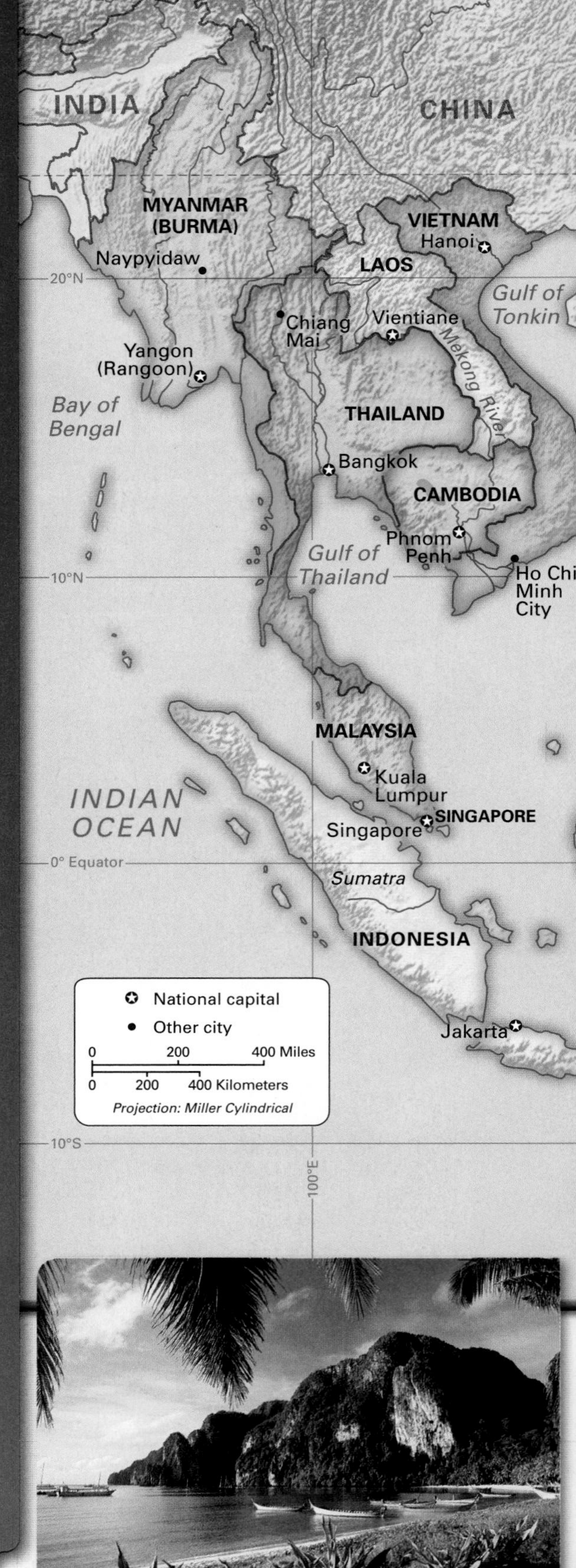

Geography Boats lie along the shore of Phi Phi Don Island in Thailand. The island's beauty makes it a popular vacation spot.

map zone Geography Skills

Regions The region of Southeast Asia includes 11 countries—some quite small.

1. **Name** What are the names of the 11 countries located in Southeast Asia?
2. **Make Inferences** The countries of Indonesia and the Philippines consist of many islands. How do you think this fact affects life there?

Culture Traditional dances remain an important part of the culture of Bali. *Barong* dancers use their hands, arms, and eyes to tell a traditional story.

History The golden Shwedagon Pagoda is a Buddhist shrine in Yangon, Myanmar. Pagodas have been on this site since the 500s BC.

SECTION 1

Physical Geography

What You Will Learn...

Main Ideas

1. Southeast Asia's physical features include peninsulas, islands, rivers, and many seas, straits, and gulfs.
2. The tropical climate of Southeast Asia supports a wide range of plants and animals.
3. Southeast Asia is rich in natural resources such as wood, rubber, and fossil fuels.

The Big Idea

Southeast Asia is a tropical region of peninsulas, islands, and waterways with diverse plants, animals, and resources.

Key Terms and Places

Indochina Peninsula, *p. 162*
Malay Peninsula, *p. 162*
Malay Archipelago, *p. 162*
archipelago, *p. 162*
New Guinea, *p. 163*
Borneo, *p. 163*
Mekong River, *p. 163*

Use the graphic organizer online to take notes on the physical geography of Southeast Asia.

If YOU lived there...

Your family lives on a houseboat on a branch of the great Mekong River in Cambodia. You catch fish in cages under the boat. Your home is part of a floating village of houseboats and houses built on stilts in the water. Boats loaded with fruits and vegetables travel from house to house. Even your school is on a nearby boat.

How does water shape life in your village?

BUILDING BACKGROUND Waterways, such as rivers, canals, seas, and oceans, are important to life in Southeast Asia. Waterways are both "highways" and sources of food. Where rivers empty into the sea, they form deltas, areas of rich soil good for farming.

Physical Features

Where can you find a flower that grows up to 3 feet across and smells like rotting garbage? How about a lizard that can grow up to 10 feet long and weigh up to 300 pounds? These amazing sights as well as some of the world's most beautiful tropical paradises are all in Southeast Asia.

The region of Southeast Asia is made up of two peninsulas and two large island groups. The **Indochina Peninsula** and the **Malay** (muh-LAY) **Peninsula** extend from the Asian mainland. We call this part of the region Mainland Southeast Asia. The two island groups are the Philippines and the **Malay Archipelago**. An **archipelago** (ahr-kuh-PE-luh-goh) is a large group of islands. We call this part of the region Island Southeast Asia.

Landforms

In Mainland Southeast Asia, rugged mountains fan out across the countries of Myanmar (MYAHN-mahr), Thailand (TY-land), Laos (LOWS), and Vietnam (vee-ET-NAHM). Between these mountains are low plateaus and river floodplains.

hmhsocialstudies.com INTERACTIVE MAP

Southeast Asia: Physical

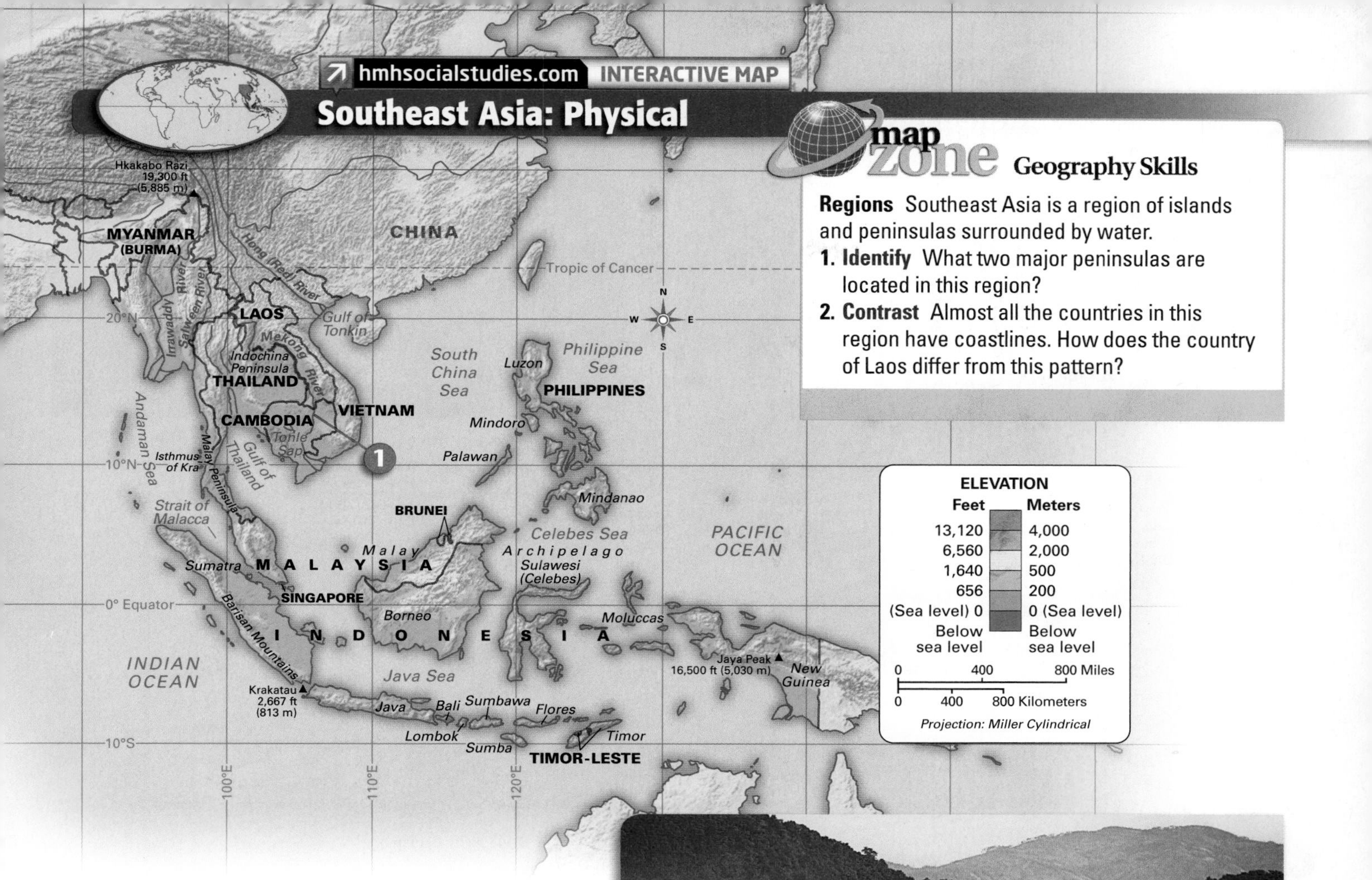

map zone Geography Skills

Regions Southeast Asia is a region of islands and peninsulas surrounded by water.

1. **Identify** What two major peninsulas are located in this region?
2. **Contrast** Almost all the countries in this region have coastlines. How does the country of Laos differ from this pattern?

Island Southeast Asia consists of more than 20,000 islands, some of them among the world's largest. **New Guinea** is Earth's second largest island, and **Borneo** its third largest. Many of the area's larger islands have high mountains. A few peaks are high enough to have snow and glaciers.

Island Southeast Asia is a part of the Ring of Fire as well. As a result, earthquakes and volcanic eruptions often rock the area. When such events occur underwater, they can cause tsunamis, or giant series of waves. In 2004 a tsunami in the Indian Ocean killed hundreds of thousands of people, many in Southeast Asia.

Bodies of Water

Water is a central part of Southeast Asia. Look at the map to identify the many seas, straits, and gulfs in this region.

1 Mist hovers over the Mekong River as it flows through the forested mountains of northern Thailand.

In addition, several major rivers drain the mainland's peninsulas. Of these rivers, the mighty **Mekong** (MAY-KAWNG) **River** is the most important. The mainland's fertile river valleys and deltas support farming and are home to many people.

READING CHECK **Finding Main Ideas** What are Southeast Asia's major physical features?

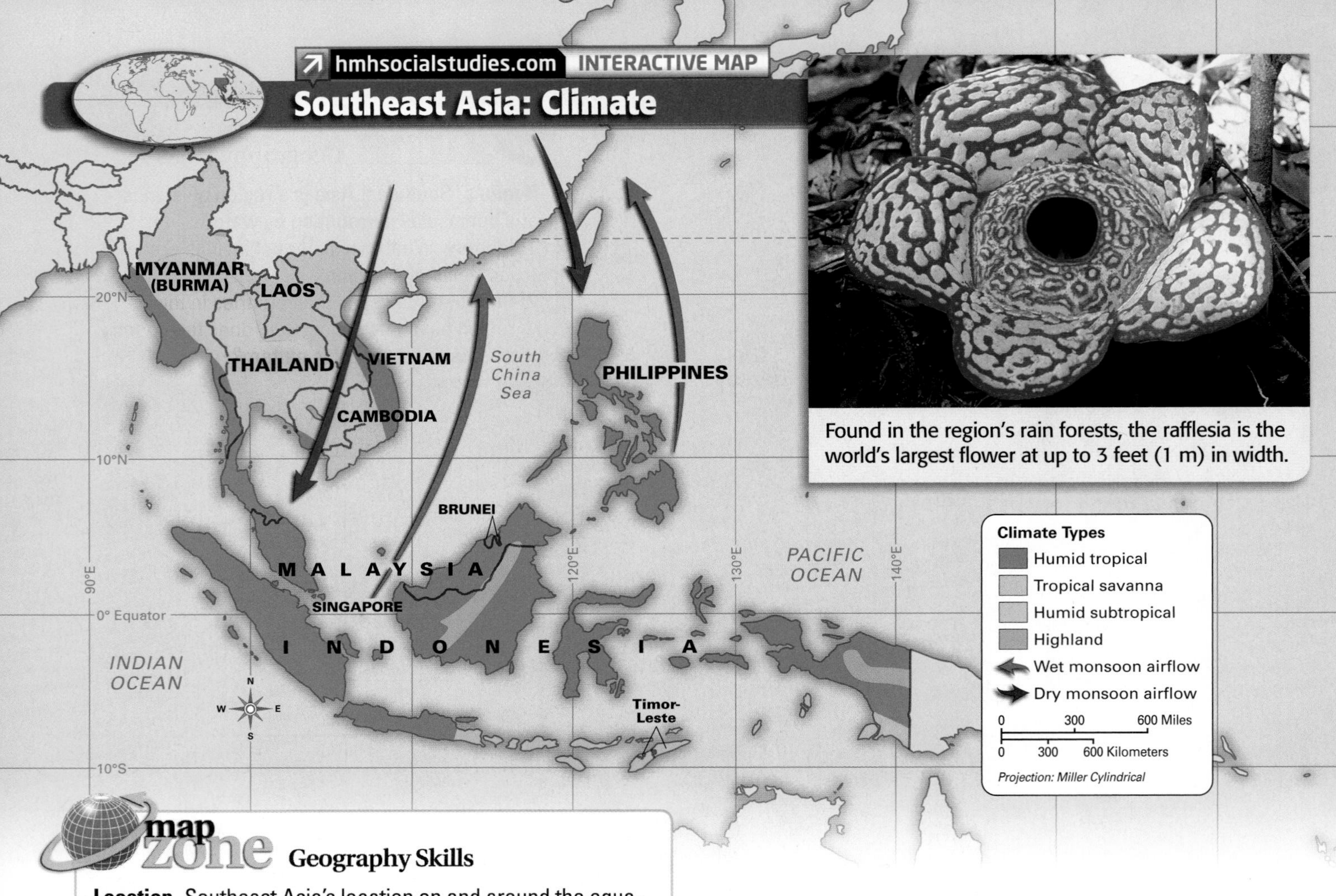

Found in the region's rain forests, the rafflesia is the world's largest flower at up to 3 feet (1 m) in width.

map zone Geography Skills

Location Southeast Asia's location on and around the equator affects the region's climate.

1. **Identify** What is the main climate found in Indonesia, Malaysia, and the Philippines?
2. **Interpret** Based on the map, how do monsoons affect the climate of this region?

Climate, Plants, and Animals

Southeast Asia lies in the tropics, the area on and around the equator. Temperatures are warm to hot year-round, but become cooler to the north and in the mountains.

Focus on Reading
What context clues help you figure out the definition of *monsoon?*

Much of the mainland has a tropical savanna climate. Seasonal monsoon winds from the oceans bring heavy rain in summer and drier weather in winter. Severe flooding is common during wet seasons. This climate supports savannas—areas of tall grasses and scattered trees and shrubs.

The islands and the Malay Peninsula mainly have a humid tropical climate. This climate is hot, muggy, and rainy all year. Showers or storms occur almost daily. In addition, huge storms called typhoons can bring heavy rains and powerful winds.

The humid tropical climate's heat and heavy rainfall support tropical rain forests. These lush forests are home to a huge number of different plants and animals. About 40,000 kinds of flowering plants grow in Indonesia alone. These plants include the rafflesia, the world's largest flower. Measuring up to 3 feet (1 m) across, this flower produces a horrible, rotting stink.

Rain forest animals include elephants, monkeys, tigers, and many types of birds. Some species are found nowhere else. They include orangutans and Komodo dragons, lizards that can grow 10 feet (3 m) long.

Orangutans live in the rain forests of Borneo and Sumatra. Deforestation has seriously reduced their habitat.

Many of these plants and animals are endangered because of loss of habitat. People are clearing the tropical rain forests for farming, wood, and mining. These actions threaten the area's future diversity.

READING CHECK **Analyzing** How does climate contribute to the region's diversity of life?

Natural Resources

Southeast Asia has a number of valuable natural resources. The region's hot, wet climate and rich soils make farming highly productive. Rice is a major crop, and others include coconuts, coffee, sugarcane, palm oil, and spices. Some countries, such as Indonesia and Malaysia (muh-LAY-zhuh), also have large rubber tree plantations.

The region's seas provide fisheries, and its tropical rain forests provide valuable hardwoods and medicines. The region also has many minerals and fossil fuels, including tin, iron ore, natural gas, and oil. For example, the island of Borneo sits atop an oil field.

READING CHECK **Summarizing** What are the region's major natural resources?

SUMMARY AND PREVIEW Southeast Asia is a tropical region of peninsulas, islands, and waterways with diverse life and rich resources. Next, you will read about the region's history and culture.

Section 1 Assessment

hmhsocialstudies.com ONLINE QUIZ

Reviewing Ideas, Terms, and Places

1. a. **Define** What is an **archipelago**?
b. **Compare and Contrast** How do the physical features of Mainland Southeast Asia compare and contrast to those of Island Southeast Asia?

2. a. **Recall** What type of forest occurs in the region?
b. **Summarize** What is the climate like across much of Southeast Asia?
c. **Predict** What do you think might happen to the region's wildlife if the tropical rain forests continue to be destroyed?

3. a. **Identify** Which countries in the region are major producers of rubber?
b. **Analyze** How does the region's climate contribute to its natural resources?

Critical Thinking

4. **Summarizing** Draw a chart like this one. Use your notes to provide information about the climate, plants, and animals in Southeast Asia. In the left-hand box, also note how climate shapes life in the region.

Focus on Speaking

5. **Writing Questions about the Region's Physical Geography** Note information about the region's physical features, climate, plants, animals, and natural resources. Write two questions and answers for your interview. For example, you might ask a question about the region's tropical rain forests.

Case Study

Tsunami!

Essential Elements

The World in Spatial Terms
Places and Regions
Physical Systems
Human Systems
Environment and Society
The Uses of Geography

Background "Huge Waves Hit Japan." This event is a tsunami (SOO-NAH-mee), a series of giant sea waves. Records of deadly tsunamis go back 3,000 years. Some places, such as Japan, have been hit time and again.

Tsunamis occur when an earthquake, volcanic eruption, or other event causes seawater to move in huge waves. The majority of tsunamis occur in the Pacific Ocean because of the region's many earthquakes.

Warning systems help alert people to tsunamis. The Pacific Tsunami Warning Center monitors tsunamis in the Pacific Ocean. Sensors on the ocean floor and buoys on the water's surface help detect earthquakes and measure waves. When a tsunami threatens, radio, TV, and sirens alert the public.

Indian Ocean Catastrophe

On December 26, 2004, a massive earthquake erupted below the Indian Ocean. The earthquake launched a monster tsunami. Within half an hour, walls of water up to 65 feet high came barreling ashore in Indonesia. The water swept away boats, buildings, and people. Meanwhile, the tsunami kept traveling in ever-widening rings across the ocean. The waves eventually wiped out coastal communities in a dozen countries. Some 200,000 people eventually died.

At the time, the Indian Ocean did not have a tsunami warning system. Tsunamis are rare in that part of the world. As a result, many countries there had been unwilling to invest in a warning system.

1 A 9.0 underwater earthquake caused the 2004 Indian Ocean tsunami. The event pushed up millions of tons of water.
2 The water surged up and outward in huge waves. The waves moved at speeds of about 500 mph.

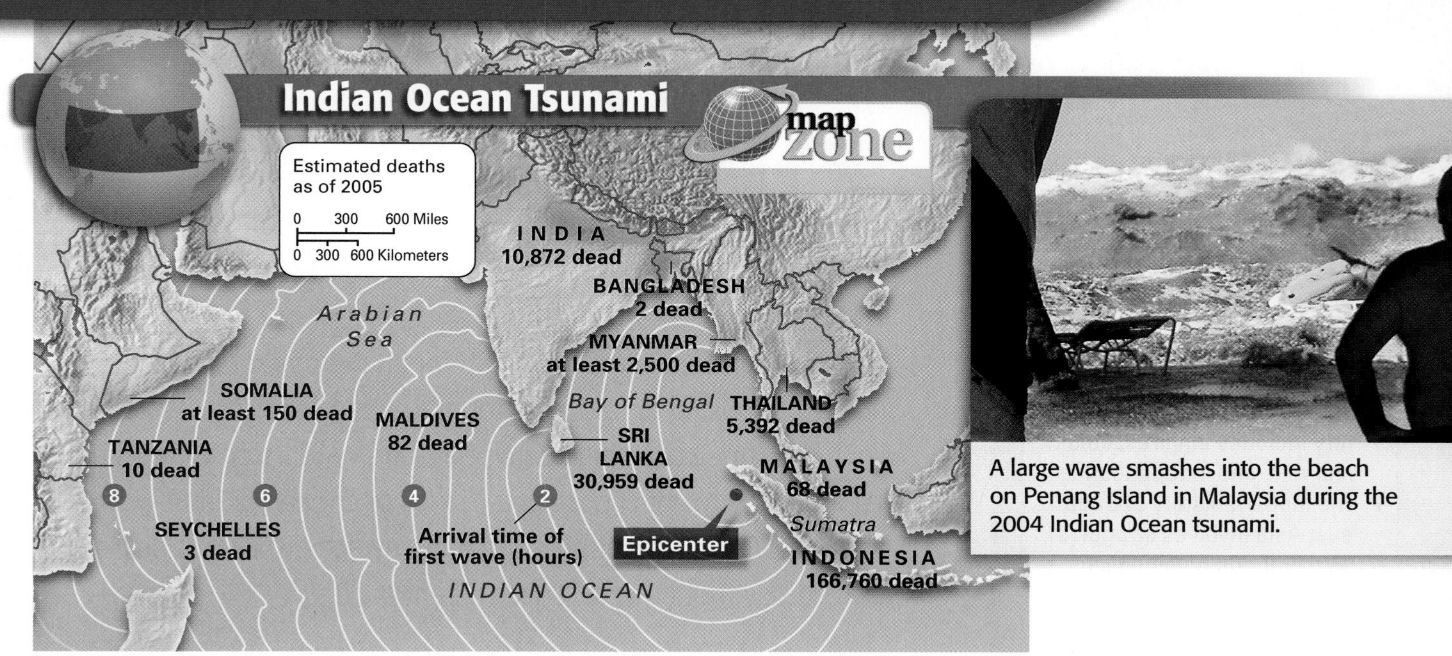

A large wave smashes into the beach on Penang Island in Malaysia during the 2004 Indian Ocean tsunami.

In 2004 these countries paid a terrible price for their decision. As the map shows, the 2004 tsunami hit countries from South Asia to East Africa. Most people had no warning of the tsunami. In addition, many people did not know how to protect themselves. Instead of heading to high ground, some people went to the beach for a closer look. Many died when later waves hit.

3 When they strike, tsunamis often look like a rapidly rising tide or swell of water. The water then rushes far inland and back out.

Tilly Smith, a 10-year-old on vacation in Thailand, was one of the few who understood the danger. Two weeks earlier, her geography teacher had discussed tsunamis. As the water began surging, Smith warned her family and other tourists to flee. Her geographic knowledge saved their lives.

What It Means No one can prevent tsunamis. Yet, by studying geography, we can prepare for these disasters and help protect lives and property. The United Nations is now working to create a global tsunami warning system. People are also trying to plant more mangroves along coastlines. These bushy swamp trees provide a natural barrier against high waves.

Geography for Life Activity

1. What steps are being taken to avoid another disaster such as the Indian Ocean tsunami in 2004?
2. About 75 percent of tsunami warnings since 1948 were false alarms. What might be the risks and benefits of early warnings to move people out of harm's way?
3. **Creating a Survival Guide** Create a tsunami survival guide. List the dos and don'ts for this emergency.

SECTION 2

History and Culture

What You Will Learn...

Main Ideas

1. Southeast Asia's early history includes empires, colonial rule, and independence.
2. The modern history of Southeast Asia involves struggles with war and communism.
3. Southeast Asia's culture reflects its Chinese, Indian, and European heritage.

The Big Idea

People, ideas, and traditions from China, India, Europe, and elsewhere have shaped Southeast Asia's history and culture.

Key Terms and Places

Timor, *p. 169*
domino theory, *p. 170*
wats, *p. 170*

Use the graphic organizer online to take notes on the history and culture of Southeast Asia.

If YOU lived there...

You and your friends are strolling through the market in Jakarta, Indonesia, looking for a snack. You have many choices—tents along the street, carts called gerobak, and vendors on bicycles all sell food. You might choose satay, strips of chicken or lamb grilled on a stick. Or you might pick one of many rice dishes. For dessert, you can buy fruit or order an ice cream cone.

What do you like about living in Jakarta?

BUILDING BACKGROUND Colonial rule helped shape Southeast Asia's history and culture—including foods. Throughout the region you can see not only a blend of different Asian influences but also a blend of American, Dutch, French, and Spanish influences.

Early History

Southeast Asia lies south of China and east of India, and both countries have played a strong role in the region's history. Over time, many people from China and India settled in Southeast Asia. As settlements grew, trade developed with China and India.

Early Civilization

The region's most advanced early civilization was the Khmer (kuh-MER). From the AD 800s to the mid-1200s the Khmer controlled a large empire in what is now Cambodia. The remains of Angkor Wat, a huge temple complex the Khmer built in the 1100s, reflect their advanced civilization and Hindu religion.

In the 1200s the Thai (TY) from southern China settled in the Khmer area. Around the same time, Buddhism, introduced earlier from India and Sri Lanka, began replacing Hinduism in the region.

Colonial Rule and Independence

As in many parts of the world, European powers started colonizing Southeast Asia during the 1500s. Led by Portugal, European powers came to the region in search of spices and other trade goods.

In 1521 explorer Ferdinand Magellan reached the Philippines and claimed the islands for Spain. The Spaniards who followed came to colonize, trade, and spread Roman Catholicism. This religion remains the main faith in the Philippines today.

In the 1600s and 1700s Dutch traders drove the Portuguese out of much of the region. Portugal kept only the small island of **Timor**. The Dutch gained control of the tea and spice trade on what became the Dutch East Indies, now Indonesia.

In the 1800s the British and French set up colonies with plantations, railroads, and mines. Many people from China and India came to work in the colonies. The British and French spread Christianity as well.

In 1898 the United States entered the region when it won the Philippines from Spain after the Spanish-American War. By the early 1900s, colonial powers ruled most of the region, as the map on the next page shows. Only Siam (sy-AM), now Thailand, was never colonized, although it lost land.

In World War II (1939–1945), Japan invaded and occupied most of Southeast Asia. After Japan lost the war, the United States gave the Philippines independence. Soon, other people in the region began to fight for their independence.

One of the bloodiest wars for independence was in French Indochina. In 1954 the French left. Indochina then split into the independent countries of Cambodia, Laos, and Vietnam. By 1970, most of Southeast Asia had thrown off colonial rule.

READING CHECK **Identifying Cause and Effect** What reasons led other countries to set up colonies across most of Southeast Asia?

Angkor Wat

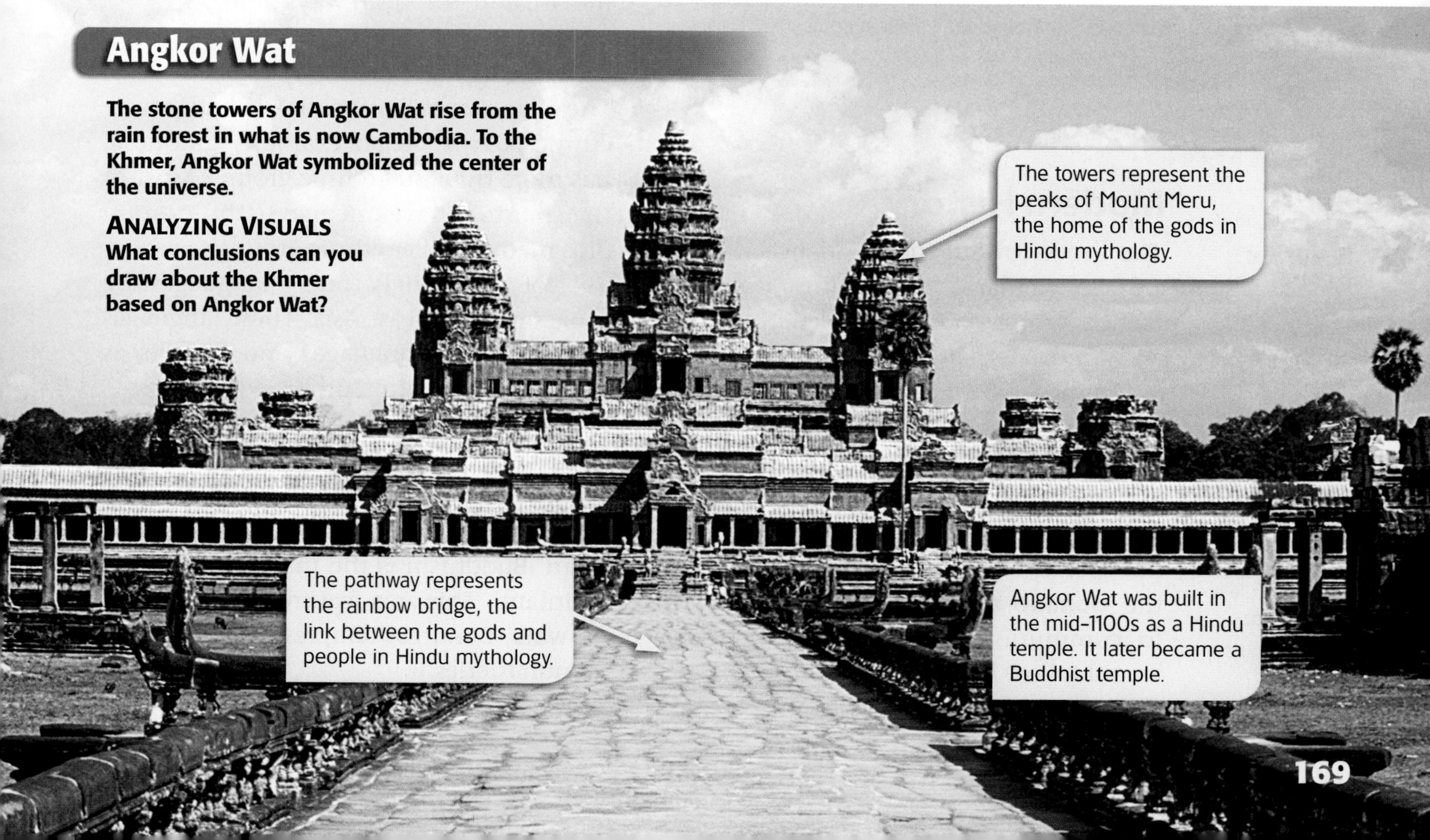

The towers represent the peaks of Mount Meru, the home of the gods in Hindu mythology.
The pathway represents the rainbow bridge, the link between the gods and people in Hindu mythology.
Angkor Wat was built in the mid-1100s as a Hindu temple. It later became a Buddhist temple.

The stone towers of Angkor Wat rise from the rain forest in what is now Cambodia. To the Khmer, Angkor Wat symbolized the center of the universe.

ANALYZING VISUALS
What conclusions can you draw about the Khmer based on Angkor Wat?

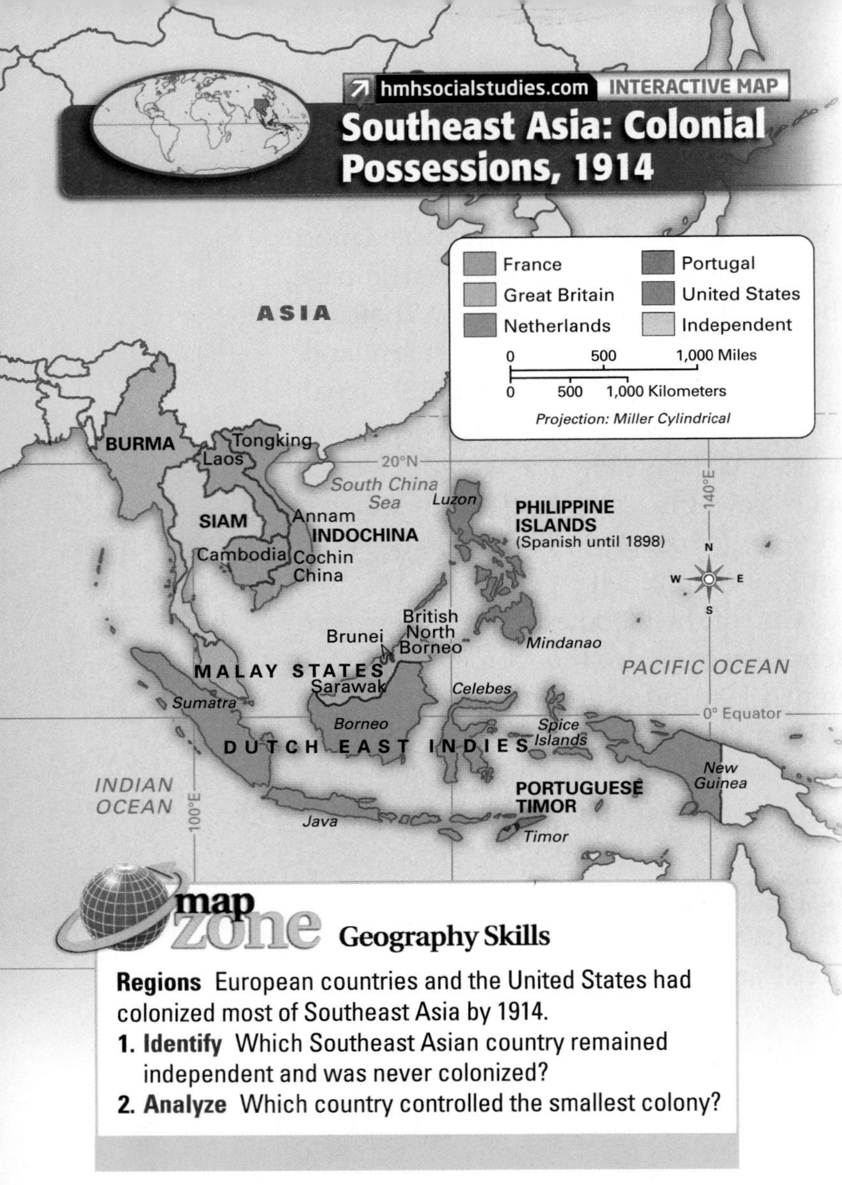

Geography Skills

Regions European countries and the United States had colonized most of Southeast Asia by 1914.

1. **Identify** Which Southeast Asian country remained independent and was never colonized?
2. **Analyze** Which country controlled the smallest colony?

Modern History

FOCUS ON READING

How does the context help explain the meaning of the term *oust* in the paragraph to the right?

The move toward independence was not easy. In Vietnam, the fighting to oust the French left the country divided into North and South Vietnam. A civil war then broke out in the South. To defend South Vietnam from Communist forces in that war, the United States sent in troops in the 1960s.

ACADEMIC VOCABULARY

criterion rule or standard for defining

The United States based its decision to send troops on one **criterion**—the potential spread of communism. According to the **domino theory**, if one country fell to communism, other countries nearby would follow like falling dominoes.

Years of war caused millions of deaths and terrible destruction. In the end, North and South Vietnam reunited as one Communist country. As the Communists took over, about 1 million refugees fled South Vietnam. Many went to the United States.

Civil wars also raged in Cambodia and Laos. In 1975 Communist forces took over both countries. The government in Cambodia was brutal, causing the deaths of more than 1 million people there. Then in 1978 Vietnam helped to overthrow Cambodia's government. This event sparked further fighting, which continued off and on until the mid-1990s. The United Nations then helped Cambodia achieve peace.

READING CHECK **Summarizing** What are some key events in the region's modern history?

Culture

The many groups that influenced Southeast Asia's history also shaped its culture. This diverse culture blends native, Chinese, Indian, and European ways of life.

People and Languages

The countries in Southeast Asia have many ethnic groups. As an example, Indonesia has more than 300 ethnic groups. Most of the countries have one main ethnic group plus many smaller ethnic groups.

Not surprisingly, many languages are spoken in Southeast Asia. These languages include native languages and dialects as well as Chinese and European languages.

Religions

The main religions in Southeast Asia are Buddhism, Christianity, Hinduism, and Islam. Buddhism is the main faith on the mainland. This area features many beautiful **wats**, Buddhist temples that also serve as monasteries.

Islam is the main religion in Malaysia, Brunei, and Indonesia. In fact, Indonesia has more Muslims than any other country. In the Philippines, most people are Roman Catholic. Hinduism is practiced in Indian communities and on the island of Bali.

Customs

Customs differ widely across the region, but some similarities exist. For example, religion often shapes life, and people celebrate many religious festivals. Some people continue to practice traditional customs, such as dances and music. These customs are especially popular in rural areas. In addition, many people wear traditional clothing, such as sarongs, strips of cloth worn wrapped around the body.

READING CHECK **Generalizing** How has Southeast Asia's history influenced its culture?

SUMMARY AND PREVIEW Southeast Asia has a long history that has helped shape its diverse culture. Next, you will read about Mainland Southeast Asia.

FOCUS ON CULTURE

Thai Teenage Buddhist Monks

Would you be willing to serve as a monk for a few months? In Thailand, many Buddhist boys and young men serve as monks for a short period. This period might last from one week to a few months. These temporary monks follow the lifestyle of actual Buddhist monks, shaving their heads, wearing robes, and maintaining a life of simplicity. During their stay, the teenage monks learn about Buddhism and practice meditation. Some Thai teens decide to become Buddhist monks permanently. This decision is considered a great honor for their families.

Summarizing What are some of the things that Thai boys and young men do while serving as Buddhist monks?

Section 2 Assessment

hmhsocialstudies.com ONLINE QUIZ

Reviewing Ideas, Terms, and Places

1. a. **Describe** What was the significance of the Khmer Empire?
   b. **Identify Cause and Effect** What was the result of the war for independence in French Indochina?
   c. **Elaborate** How did European colonization shape Southeast Asia's history?
2. a. **Define** What was the **domino theory**?
   b. **Summarize** What role has communism played in Southeast Asia's modern history?
3. a. **Define** What is a **wat**?
   b. **Contrast** How does religion in the mainland and island countries differ?
   c. **Elaborate** How has the history of Southeast Asia shaped the region's culture?

Critical Thinking

4. **Sequencing** Copy the time line shown below. Using your notes, identify on the time line the important people, periods, events, and years in Southeast Asia's history.

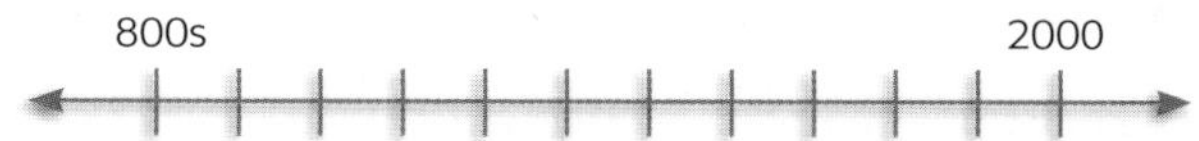

Focus on Speaking

5. **Writing Questions about History and Culture** What interesting questions could you ask about the history and culture of Southeast Asia? Write two questions and their answers to add to your notes.

21ST CENTURY

Analyzing Visuals

Learn

Geographers get information from many sources. These sources include not only text and data but also visuals, such as diagrams and photographs. Use these tips to analyze visuals:

- **Identify the subject.** Read the title and caption, if available. If not, look at the content of the image. What does it show? Where is it located?
- **Analyze the content.** What is the purpose of the image? What information is in the image? What conclusions can you draw from this information? Write your conclusions in your notes.
- **Summarize your analysis.** Write a summary of the information in the visual and of the conclusions you can draw from it.

Practice

Analyze the photograph at right. Then answer the following questions.

1. What is the title of the photograph?
2. Where is this scene, and what is happening?
3. What conclusions can you draw from the information in the photograph?

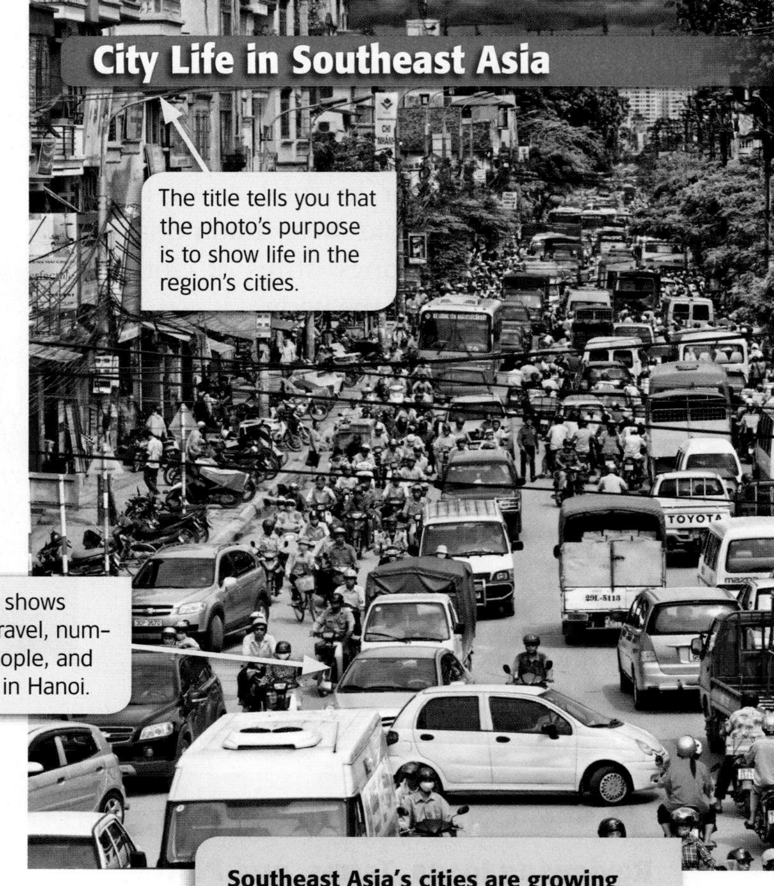
City Life in Southeast Asia
The title tells you that the photo's purpose is to show life in the region's cities.
The photo shows forms of travel, numbers of people, and air quality in Hanoi.
TOYOTA

Southeast Asia's cities are growing rapidly. In Hanoi, Vietnam, vehicles and people crowd the streets.

Apply

Analyze the images of the rubber tree plantation in Section 4. Then answer the following questions.

1. What is the purpose of the two photos?
2. What do the photos show about rubber tree farming?
3. Based on the information in the photos, what conclusions can you draw about rubber tree farming in particular and about agriculture in Island Southeast Asia in general?

Mainland Southeast Asia Today

SECTION 3

If YOU lived there...

You live in Vietnam, where your family works on a collective state-run farm. On the side, your family also sells vegetables. Now your older brother wants to start his own business—a bicycle repair shop. The Communist government allows this, but your parents think it is safer for him to keep working on the farm.

What do you think your brother should do?

BUILDING BACKGROUND After decades of war and hardship, most countries in Mainland Southeast Asia are moving forward. Even those countries with Communist governments, such as Vietnam and Laos, are working to develop freer and stronger economies.

What You Will Learn...

Main Ideas

1. The area today is largely rural and agricultural, but cities are growing rapidly.
2. Myanmar is poor with a harsh military government, while Thailand is a democracy with a strong economy.
3. The countries of Indochina are poor and struggling to rebuild after years of war.

The Big Idea

Many of the farming countries in Mainland Southeast Asia are poor but are working to improve their economies.

Key Terms and Places

Yangon, *p. 174*
human rights, *p. 174*
Bangkok, *p. 174*
klongs, *p. 174*
Phnom Penh, *p. 177*
Hanoi, *p. 177*

hmhsocialstudies.com
TAKING NOTES

Use the graphic organizer online to take notes on each country in Mainland Southeast Asia.

The Area Today

Look at the map at the start of the chapter and identify the countries of Mainland Southeast Asia. These countries include Myanmar, Thailand, Cambodia, Laos, and Vietnam.

War, harsh governments, and other problems have slowed progress in most of Mainland Southeast Asia. However, the area's countries have rich resources and are working to improve their futures. For example, as of 2010 all the countries of Southeast Asia except Timor-Leste had joined the Association of Southeast Asian Nations (ASEAN). This organization promotes political, economic, and social cooperation throughout the region.

Rural Life

Mainland Southeast Asia is largely rural. Most people are farmers who live in small villages and work long hours in the fields. Most farm work is done by hand or using traditional methods. Farmers grow rice, the region's main crop, on fertile slopes along rivers and on terraced shelves of land. The wet, tropical climate enables farmers to grow two or three crops each year.

hmhsocialstudies.com
ANIMATED GEOGRAPHY
Present-Day Southeast Asia

Most rural people live in the area's fertile river valleys and deltas, which have the best farmland. A delta is an area of fertile land around the mouth of a river. A few people live in remote villages in the rugged, forested mountains. These areas have poor soils that make farming difficult. Many of the people who live there belong to small ethnic groups known as hill peoples.

Urban Life

Although most people live in rural areas, Mainland Southeast Asia has several large cities. Most are growing rapidly as people move to them for work. Rapid growth has led to crowding and pollution. People, bicycles, scooters, cars, and buses clog city streets. Smog hangs in the still air. Growing cities also mix the old and new. Skyscrapers tower over huts, and cars zip past pedicabs, taxicabs that are pedaled like bikes.

FOCUS ON READING
What words in the paragraph to the right tell you the definition of *pedicabs?*

READING CHECK **Finding Main Ideas** Where do most people in Mainland Southeast Asia live?

BIOGRAPHY

Aung San Suu Kyi

(1945–)

Aung San Suu Kyi has dedicated herself to making life better in her native Myanmar. Suu Kyi is the best-known opponent of the country's harsh military government. Her party, the National League for Democracy (NLD), won control of the country's parliament in 1990. The military government refused to give up power, however. The government then placed Aung San Suu Kyi and other NLD members under house arrest. For her efforts to bring democracy to Myanmar, Suu Kyi received the Nobel Peace Prize in 1991. Even though she has been repeatedly placed under house arrest, Suu Kyi continues to fight for democratic reform and free elections. Her efforts have led the United States and some Asian countries to press Myanmar's government to change.

Identifying Points of View What does Aung San Suu Kyi hope to achieve through her efforts in Myanmar?

Myanmar and Thailand

Myanmar and Thailand form the northwestern part of Mainland Southeast Asia. While Myanmar is poor, Thailand boasts the area's strongest economy.

Myanmar

Myanmar lies south of China on the Bay of Bengal. Also known as Burma, the country gained independence from Great Britain in 1948. The capital is **Yangon**, or Rangoon, and the administrative capital is Naypyidaw.

Most of the people in Myanmar are Burmese. Many live in small farming villages in houses built on stilts. Buddhism is the main religion, and village life often centers around a local Buddhist monastery.

Life is difficult in Myanmar because a harsh military government rules the country. The government abuses **human rights**, rights that all people deserve such as rights to equality and justice. A Burmese woman, Aung San Suu Kyi (awng sahn soo chee), has led a movement for more democracy and rights. She and others have been jailed and harassed for their actions.

Myanmar's poor human-rights record has isolated the country and hurt its economy. Some countries, such as the United States, will no longer trade with Myanmar. Despite rich natural resources—such as oil, timber, metals, jade, and gems—Myanmar and most of its people remain poor.

Thailand

To the southwest of Malaysia is Thailand, once known as Siam. The capital and largest city is **Bangkok**. Modern and crowded, it lies near the mouth of the Chao Phraya (chow PRY-uh) River. Bangkok is known for its many spectacular palaces and Buddhist wats. The city is also famous for its **klongs**, or canals. Klongs are used for transportation and trade, and to drain floodwater.

Close-up

A Bangkok Canal

Sick of crowded roads? In Bangkok, you can use a network of canals, called klongs, to travel through parts of the city. Water taxis and boats transport people and goods. At floating markets, vendors sell fish, fruit, and other foods to locals and tourists.

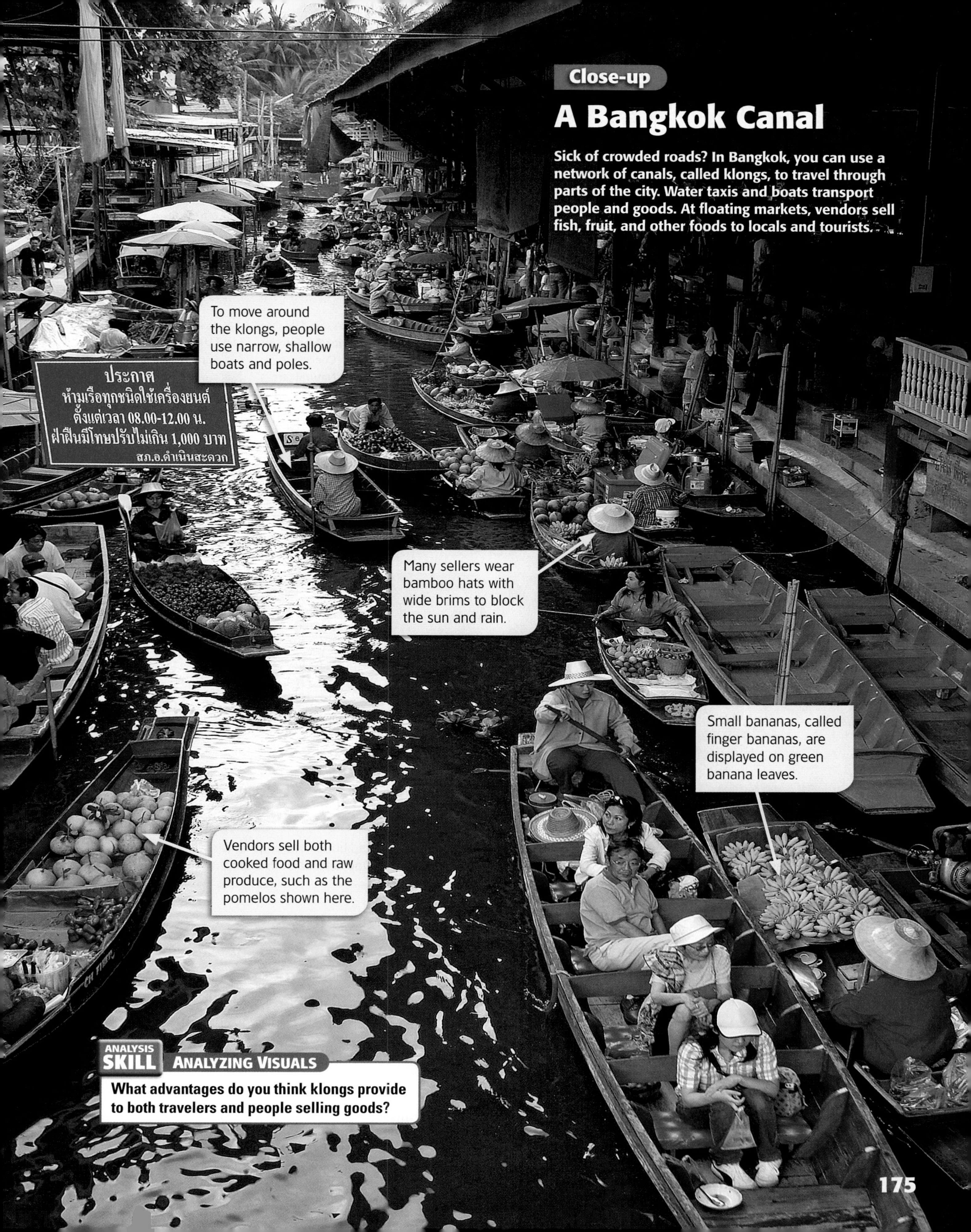

To move around the klongs, people use narrow, shallow boats and poles.
ประกาศ
ห้ามเรือทุกชนิดใช้เครื่องยนต์
ตั้งแต่เวลา 08.00-12.00 น.
ฝ่าฝืนมีโทษปรับไม่เกิน 1,000 บาท
สภ.อ.ดำเนินสะดวก
Many sellers wear bamboo hats with wide brims to block the sun and rain.
Small bananas, called finger bananas, are displayed on green banana leaves.
Vendors sell both cooked food and raw produce, such as the pomelos shown here.

ANALYSIS SKILL ANALYZING VISUALS

What advantages do you think klongs provide to both travelers and people selling goods?

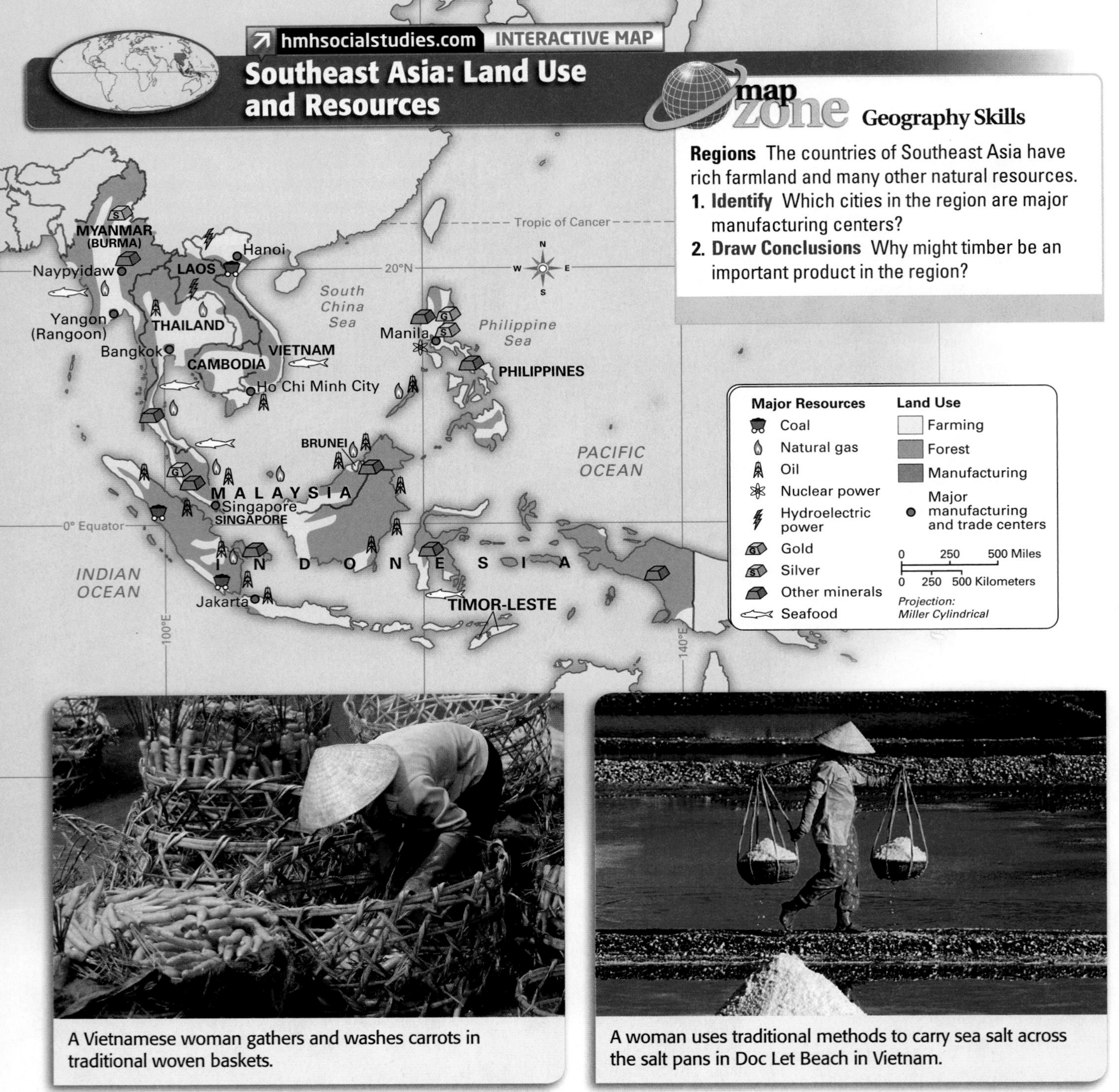

map zone Geography Skills

Regions The countries of Southeast Asia have rich farmland and many other natural resources.

1. **Identify** Which cities in the region are major manufacturing centers?
2. **Draw Conclusions** Why might timber be an important product in the region?

A Vietnamese woman gathers and washes carrots in traditional woven baskets.

A woman uses traditional methods to carry sea salt across the salt pans in Doc Let Beach in Vietnam.

Thailand is a constitutional monarchy. A monarch, or king, serves as a ceremonial head of state. A prime minister and elected legislature hold the real power, however.

A democratically elected government and rich resources have helped Thailand's economy to grow. Industry, farming, fishing, mining, and tourism fuel this growth. Farms produce rice, pineapples, and rubber. Factories produce computers, textiles, and electronics. Magnificent Buddhist wats and unspoiled beaches draw tourists.

READING CHECK **Comparing and Contrasting** What are some similarities and differences between Myanmar and Thailand?

The Countries of Indochina

The former countries of French Indochina lie to the east and south of Thailand. They are struggling to overcome decades of war.

Cambodia

Cambodia lies to the northeast of the Gulf of Thailand. **Phnom Penh** (puh-NAWM pen) is the capital and chief city. Located in the Mekong River valley, it is a center of trade.

Some 20 years of war, terror, and devastation in Cambodia finally ended in the early 1990s. Today the country has a stable, elected government similar to Thailand's. Years of conflict left their mark, however. Although farming has improved, the country has little industry. In addition, many land mines remain hidden in the land.

Laos

Laos is landlocked with rugged mountains. Poor and undeveloped, it has few roads, no railroads, and limited electricity.

The Communist government of Laos has been increasing economic freedom in hopes of improving the economy. Even so, Laos remains the area's poorest country.

The economy is based on farming, but good farmland is limited. Most people are subsistence farmers, meaning they grow just enough food for their families.

Vietnam

Like Laos, Vietnam is rugged and mountainous. The capital, **Hanoi**, is located in the north in the Hong (Red) River delta. The largest city, Ho Chi Minh City, is in the south in the Mekong delta.

Vietnam's Communist government has been allowing more economic freedom and private business. The changes have helped the economy grow. Most people still farm, but industry and services are expanding. Fishing and mining are also important.

READING CHECK **Evaluating** How would you rate the economies of these three countries?

SUMMARY AND PREVIEW The mainland countries are rural and agricultural with fast-growing cities. Most of the countries are poor despite rich resources. Next, you will read about Island Southeast Asia.

Section 3 Assessment

hmhsocialstudies.com ONLINE QUIZ

Reviewing Ideas, Terms, and Places

1. a. **Recall** In what areas do most people in Mainland Southeast Asia live?
   b. **Identify Cause and Effect** How has rapid growth affected the area's cities?
2. a. **Define** What are **klongs**, and in what ways are they used?
   b. **Contrast** How does Thailand's economy differ from Myanmar's economy?
   c. **Predict** How might Myanmar's economy change if the country had a government that respected **human rights**? Explain your answer.
3. a. **Identify** What is the area's poorest country?
   b. **Summarize** What issues and challenges face Cambodia, Laos, and Vietnam?

Critical Thinking

4. **Categorizing** Draw a chart like the one shown. Use your notes to provide information for each category in the chart.

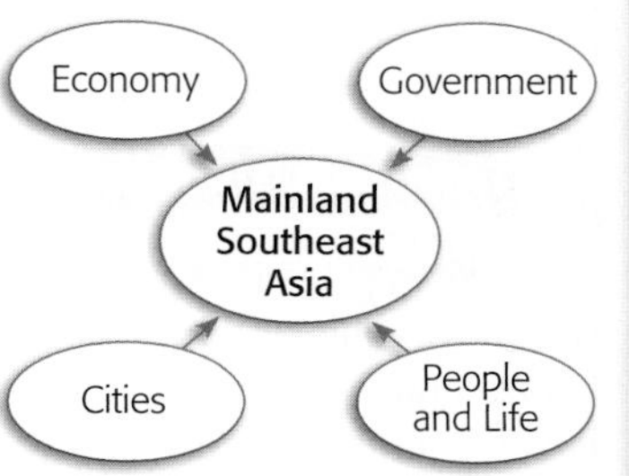

Focus on Speaking

5. **Writing Questions about Mainland Southeast Asia Today** Write one interview question about each country covered in this section. Your questions might highlight differences among the countries or focus on similarities across the area.

SECTION 4

Island Southeast Asia Today

What You Will Learn...

Main Ideas

1. The area today has rich resources and growing cities but faces challenges.
2. Malaysia and its neighbors have strong economies but differ in many ways.
3. Indonesia is big and diverse with a growing economy, and East Timor is small and poor.
4. The Philippines has less ethnic diversity, and its economy is improving.

The Big Idea

The countries of Island Southeast Asia range from wealthy and urban to poor and rural.

Key Terms and Places

kampong, *p. 179*
Jakarta, *p. 179*
Kuala Lumpur, *p. 179*
free ports, *p. 180*
sultan, *p. 181*
Java, *p. 181*
Manila, *p. 182*

Use the graphic organizer online to take notes on each country in Island Southeast Asia.

If YOU lived there...

You live in Canada but are visiting your cousins in Singapore. You start to cross the street in the middle of a block, but your cousin quickly stops you. "You have to pay a big fine if you do that!" he says. Singapore has many strict laws and strong punishments, he explains. These laws are meant to make the city safe.

What do you think about Singapore's laws?

BUILDING BACKGROUND Singapore and the other countries of Island Southeast Asia present many contrasts. You can quickly go from skyscrapers to rice paddies to tropical rain forests. Many ethnic groups may live in one country, which can lead to unrest.

The Area Today

Island Southeast Asia lies at a crossroads between major oceans and continents. The area's six countries are Malaysia, Singapore, Brunei (brooh-NY), Indonesia, Timor-Leste, and the Philippines.

The future for these countries could be bright. They have the potential for wealth and good standards of living, such as rich resources and a large, skilled labor force. In addition, all but one of the countries have growing economies and belong to ASEAN. This organization promotes cooperation in Southeast Asia.

Island Southeast Asia faces challenges, however. First, violent ethnic conflicts have hurt progress in some countries. Second, many people live in poverty, while a few leaders and businesspeople control much of the money. Third, the area has many environmental problems, such as pollution.

Rural and Urban Life

Many people in Island Southeast Asia live in rural areas, where they farm or fish. As on the mainland, rice is the main crop. Others include coffee, spices, sugarcane, tea, and tropical fruit.

Rubber is a major crop as well, and Indonesia and Malaysia are the world's largest producers of natural rubber. Seafood is the area's main source of protein.

As on the mainland, many people in Island Southeast Asia are leaving rural villages to move to cities for work. The largest cities, the major capitals, are modern and crowded. Common problems in these cities include smog and heavy traffic. Some cities also have large slums.

In Malaysia, Indonesia, and other parts of the area, many people live in kampongs. A **kampong** is a village or city district with traditional houses built on stilts. The stilts protect the houses from flooding, which is common in the area. The term *kampong* also refers to the slums around the area's cities such as **Jakarta**, Indonesia's capital.

READING CHECK **Summarizing** Why could the future be bright for Island Southeast Asia?

Malaysia and Its Neighbors

Malaysia and its much smaller neighbors, Singapore and Brunei, were all once British colonies. Today all three countries are independent and differ in many ways.

Malaysia

Malaysia consists of two parts. One is on the southern end of the Malay Peninsula. The other is on northern Borneo. Most of the country's people live on the peninsula. **Kuala Lumpur** (KWAH-luh LOOHM-poohr), Malaysia's capital, is there as well. The capital is a cultural and economic center.

Malaysia is ethnically diverse. The Malays are the main ethnic group, but many Chinese and other groups live in Malaysia as well. As a result, the country has many languages and religions. Bahasa Malay is the main language, and Islam and Buddhism are the main religions.

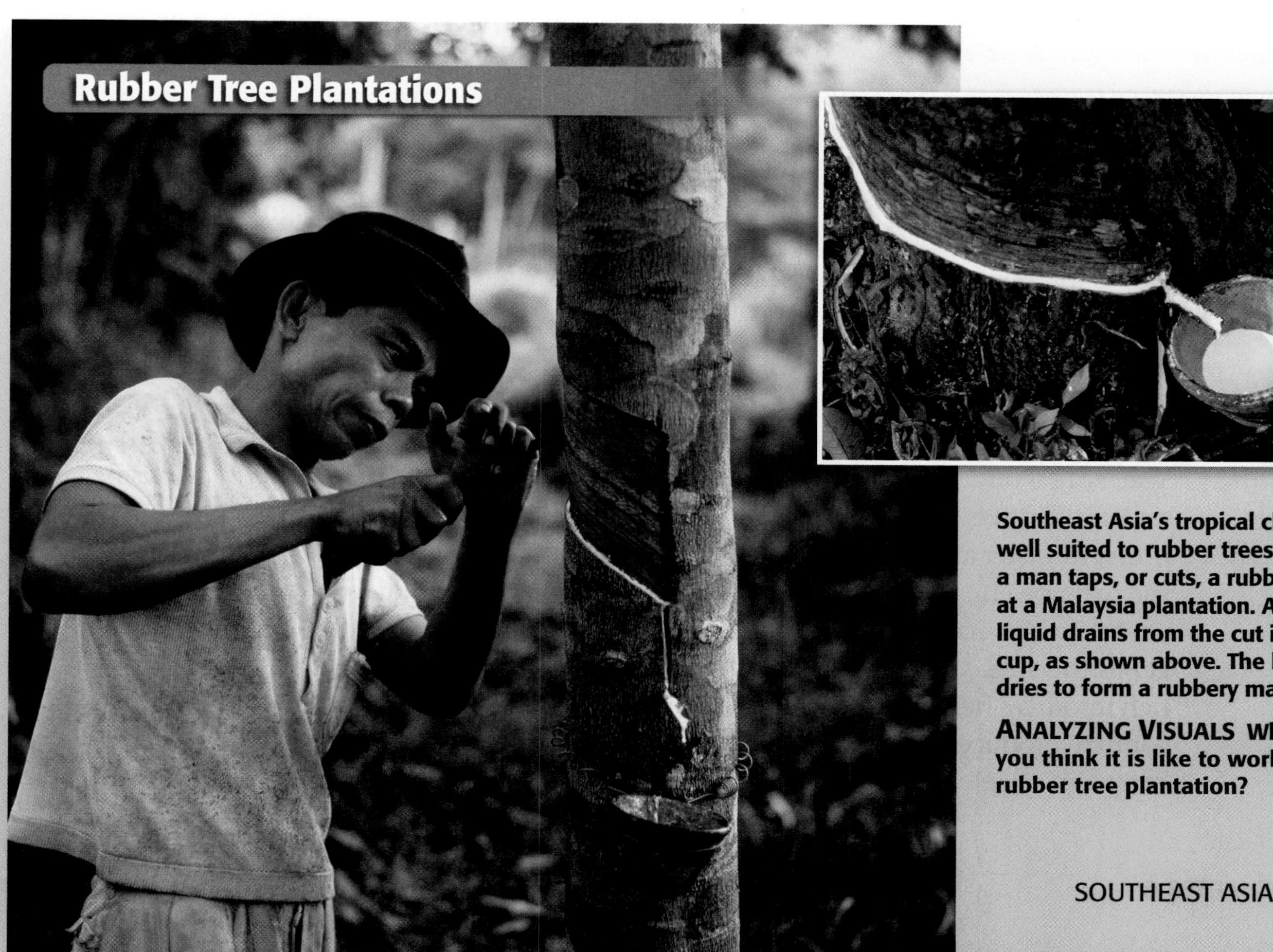

Rubber Tree Plantations

Southeast Asia's tropical climate is well suited to rubber trees. At left, a man taps, or cuts, a rubber tree at a Malaysia plantation. A milky liquid drains from the cut into a cup, as shown above. The liquid dries to form a rubbery material.

ANALYZING VISUALS What do you think it is like to work on a rubber tree plantation?

Primary Source

INTERVIEW

Lee Kuan Yew on Singapore

Lee Kuan Yew was Singapore's prime minister from 1959 to 1990. He remade the tiny country into an economic power. In a 1994 interview, Lee discussed Singapore's strict laws.

> "The expansion of the right of the individual to behave or misbehave as he pleases has come at the expense of orderly society. In the East the main object is to have a well-ordered society so that everybody can have maximum enjoyment of his freedoms. This freedom can exist only in an ordered state."
>
> —from "A Conversation with Lee Kuan Yew"

ANALYSIS SKILL ANALYZING PRIMARY SOURCES

Do you agree with Lee that freedom for all can exist only in a society with strict order? Why or why not?

Malaysia is a constitutional monarchy. The king's duties are largely ceremonial, and local rulers take turns being king. A prime minister and elected legislature hold the real power.

ACADEMIC VOCABULARY
concrete specific, real

Malaysia's economy is one of the stronger in the area. Well-educated workers and rich resources help drive this economy. The country produces and exports natural rubber, palm oil, electronics, oil, and timber.

Singapore

A populous country, Singapore is squeezed onto a tiny island at the tip of the Malay Peninsula. The island lies on a major shipping route. This location has helped make Singapore a rich country.

Today Singapore is one of the world's busiest **free ports**, ports that place few if any taxes on goods. It is also an industrial center, and many foreign banks and high-tech firms have located offices there.

Singapore sparkles as the gem of Southeast Asia. The country is modern, wealthy, orderly, and clean. Crime rates are low.

How has Singapore achieved such success? The government has worked hard to clean up slums and improve housing. In addition, laws are extremely strict. To provide concrete examples, fines for littering are stiff, and people caught with illegal drugs can be executed. Moreover, the government strictly controls politics and the media. Certain movies are banned, as are satellite dishes. Recently, however, Singapore has loosened up some restrictions.

Brunei

The tiny country of Brunei is on the island of Borneo, which it shares with Malaysia and Indonesia. A **sultan**, the supreme ruler of a Muslim country, governs Brunei.

The country has grown wealthy from large oil and gas deposits. Because of this wealth, Brunei's citizens do not pay income tax and receive free health care and other benefits. Brunei's oil will run out around 2020, however. As a result, the government is developing other areas of the economy.

READING CHECK **Contrasting** How do Malaysia, Singapore, and Brunei differ?

Indonesia and Timor-Leste

Indonesia is the largest of the island countries. Timor-Leste, once part of Indonesia, is one of the area's smallest countries.

Indonesia

Indonesia has several claims to fame. It is the world's largest archipelago, with some 13,500 islands. It has the fourth-largest population of any country as well as the largest Muslim population. Indonesia is extremely diverse as well, as you have read. It has more than 300 ethnic groups who speak more than 250 languages.

Indonesia's main island is **Java**. The capital, Jakarta, is there, as are more than half of Indonesia's people. For this reason, Java is extremely crowded. To reduce the crowding, the government has been moving people to less-populated islands. Many people on those islands dislike that policy.

Indonesia's rich resources have helped its economy to grow. The main resources include rubber, oil and gas, and timber. The country also has good farmland for rice and other crops. Factories turn out clothing and electronics. Islands such as Bali draw thousands of tourists each year.

At the same time, problems have hurt Indonesia's economy. Many of the people are poor, and unemployment is high. In some areas, ethnic and religious conflicts have led to fighting and terrorism.

FOCUS ON READING

How does the highlighted text help you understand the meaning of *sultan?*

Timor-Leste

Timor-Leste is located on the small island of Timor. In 1999 Timor-Leste declared independence from Indonesia. The island then plunged into violence. Timor-Leste only gained its independence after the United Nations sent in troops to restore peace. Years of fighting have left Timor-Leste one of the region's poorest countries. Most people farm, and coffee is the main export.

READING CHECK **Generalizing** How has violence affected Indonesia and Timor-Leste?

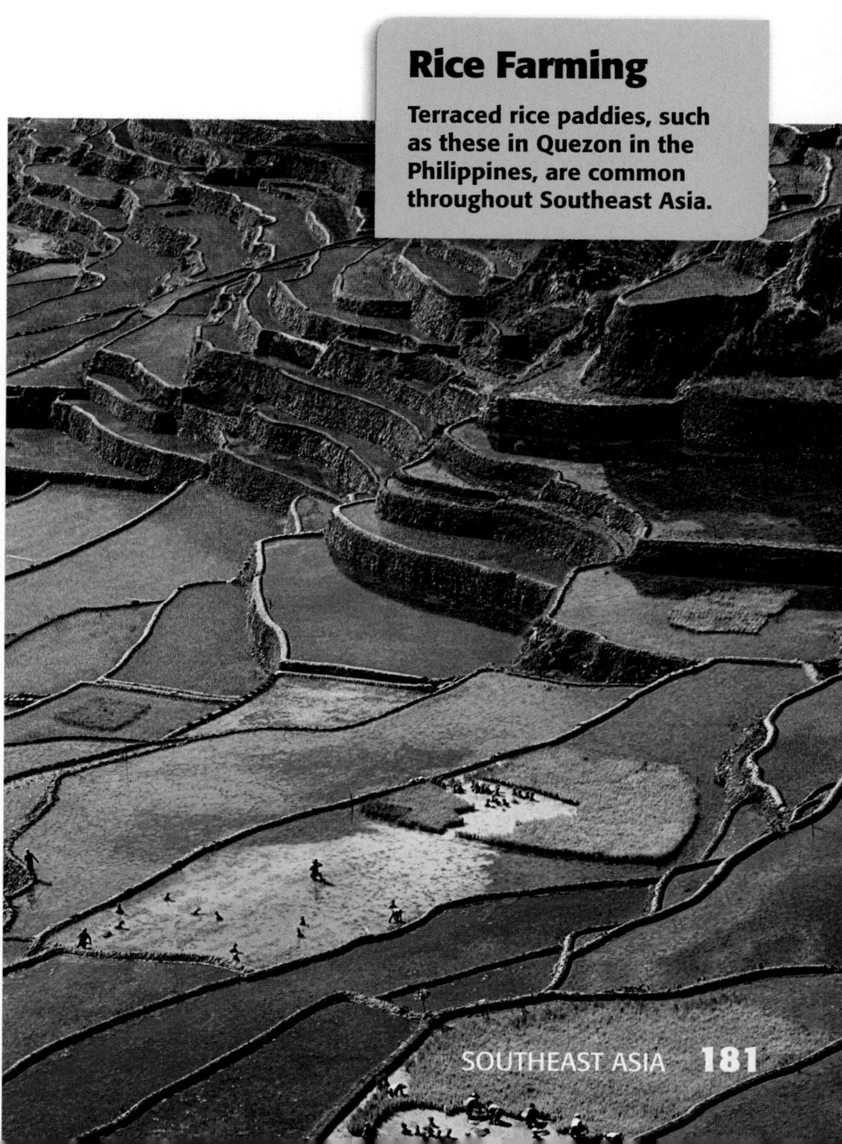

Rice Farming

Terraced rice paddies, such as these in Quezon in the Philippines, are common throughout Southeast Asia.

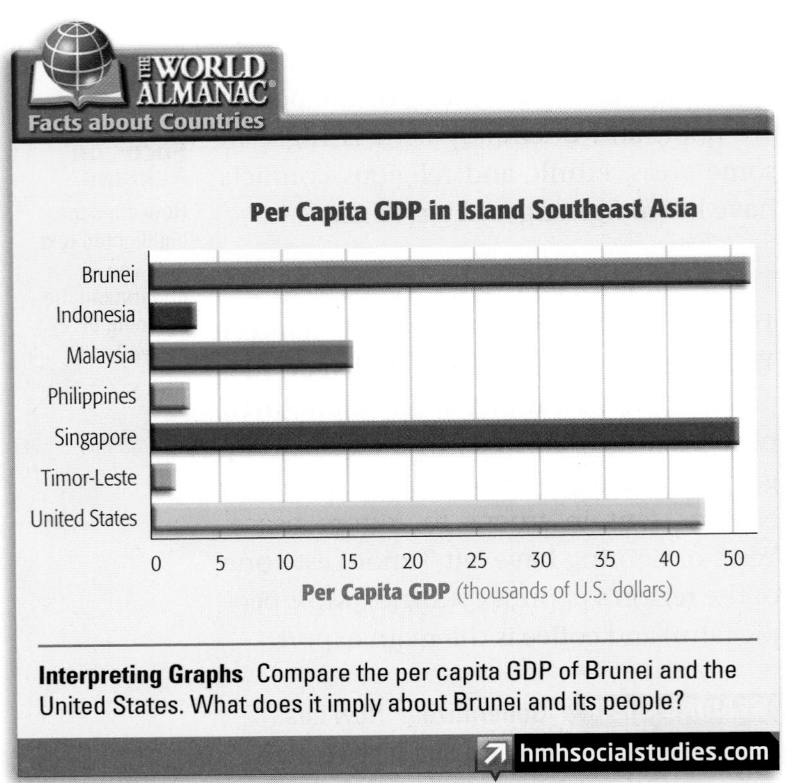

Interpreting Graphs Compare the per capita GDP of Brunei and the United States. What does it imply about Brunei and its people?

hmhsocialstudies.com

The Philippines

The Philippines includes more than 7,000 islands. The largest and most populated is Luzon, which includes the capital, **Manila**. The Philippines has less ethnic diversity than the other island countries. Almost all Filipinos are ethnic Malays.

The Philippines has many resources to fuel economic growth. Natural resources include copper and other metals, oil, and tropical wood. Farmers grow coconuts, sugarcane, rice, and corn. Factories produce and export clothing and electronics.

Although the economy of the Philippines has improved in recent years, a wide gap still exists between the rich and the poor. A few Filipinos are wealthy. Most, however, are poor farmers who do not own the land they work.

The Philippines has experienced religious conflict as well. Although the country is mainly Roman Catholic, some areas are largely Muslim and want independence.

READING CHECK **Contrasting** How does the Philippines differ from much of the area?

SUMMARY AND PREVIEW You have read that Island Southeast Asia has many contrasts. While some countries are wealthy, others are poor. While some countries are modern and urban, others are more traditional and rural. In the next chapter you will read about the Pacific World.

Section 4 Assessment

hmhsocialstudies.com
ONLINE QUIZ

Reviewing Ideas, Terms, and Places

1. a. **Identify** What problems does the area face?
   b. **Compare** How does urban life compare between the island and mainland countries?
2. a. **Define** What is a **sultan**?
   b. **Explain** How have Singapore and Brunei become rich countries?
3. a. **Recall** What island is **Jakarta** located on?
   b. **Sequence** What series of events led to Timor-Leste's independence?
4. a. **Identify** What are the capital city and the main island in the Philippines?
   b. **Analyze** Why is the Philippines' economic improvement not benefiting many of its people?

Critical Thinking

5. **Categorizing** Draw a chart like the one shown. Use your notes to provide information for each category in the chart.

Economy | Government | Island Southeast Asia | Cities | People and life

Focus on Speaking

6. **Writing Questions about Island Southeast Asia Today** Write one interview question about each country covered in this section. Your questions might highlight differences among the countries or focus on similarities across the area.

CHAPTER 6

Chapter Review

Geography's Impact
video series
Review the video to answer the closing question:
Why do you think it is important to preserve the environment of the Malay Archipelago?

Visual Summary

Use the visual summary below to help you review the main ideas of the chapter.

QUICK FACTS

Southeast Asia is a tropical region of peninsulas, islands, and water. Its history includes empires and colonization.

Mainland Southeast Asia is rural with growing cities. Many of the countries are poor but have rich resources.

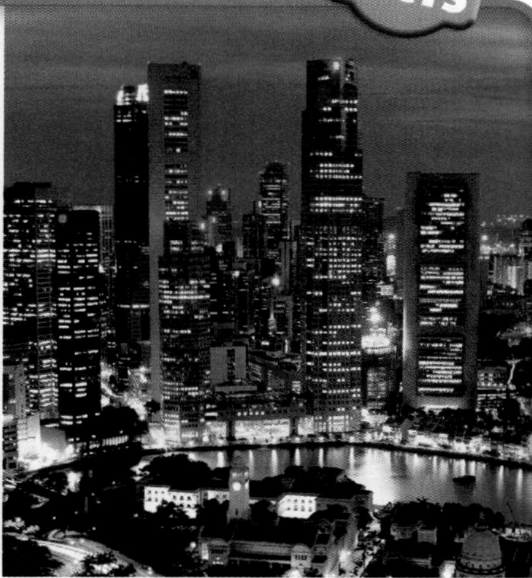

Island Southeast Asia is more urban, and some countries are wealthy. Many of the area's people are poor, though.

Reviewing Vocabulary, Terms, and Places

For each group of terms below, write a sentence that shows how all the terms in the group are related.

1. archipelagos
Indonesia
Philippines
2. Aung San Suu Kyi
human rights
Myanmar
3. Bangkok
klongs
4. Indochina
domino theory
5. Jakarta
kampongs
6. Singapore
free port
7. Brunei
sultan

Comprehension and Critical Thinking

SECTION 1 *(Pages 162–165)*

8. a. **Identify** What are the two peninsulas and the two archipelagos that make up the region of Southeast Asia?

b. **Compare and Contrast** In what ways are the main climate of Mainland Southeast Asia and of Island Southeast Asia similar and different?

c. **Develop** What different needs should people weigh when considering how best to protect the region's tropical rain forests?

SECTION 2 *(Pages 168–171)*

9. a. **Recall** What theory led the U.S. military to become involved in Southeast Asia?

b. **Identify Cause and Effect** Why are so many languages spoken in Southeast Asia?

c. **Predict** How do you think Southeast Asia might be different today if Europeans had never explored and colonized the area?

SECTION 3 *(Pages 173–177)*

10. a. Describe Where do most people live and work in Mainland Southeast Asia?

b. Summarize What factors have slowed economic progress in Mainland Southeast Asia?

c. Develop What actions might Myanmar take to try to improve its economy?

SECTION 4 *(Pages 178–182)*

11. a. Identify Which two countries in Island Southeast Asia have wealthy economies?

b. Compare What are some ways in which Indonesia and the Philippines are similar?

c. Elaborate How has ethnic diversity affected the countries of Island Southeast Asia?

Using the Internet 

12. Activity: Writing a Report on Rain Forests The tropical rain forests of Indonesia are home to a rich diversity of life. Research these rain forests through the online book. Then write a short report that summarizes the threats they face.

hmhsocialstudies.com

Social Studies Skills 

Analyzing Visuals *Turn to Section 3 and analyze the large photograph of a Bangkok canal. Then answer the following questions about the photograph.*

13. What are the title and location of the photo?

14. How do the captions help you understand the information in the photograph?

15. What types of activities are taking place in the photograph?

16. Based on the information in the photo, what conclusions can you draw about the use of canals in the city of Bangkok?

Map Activity 

17. Southeast Asia On a separate sheet of paper, match the letters on the map with their correct labels below.

Bangkok, Thailand	Jakarta, Indonesia
Borneo	Malay Peninsula
Hanoi, Vietnam	Manila, Philippines
Indochina Peninsula	Singapore

hmhsocialstudies.com INTERACTIVE MAP

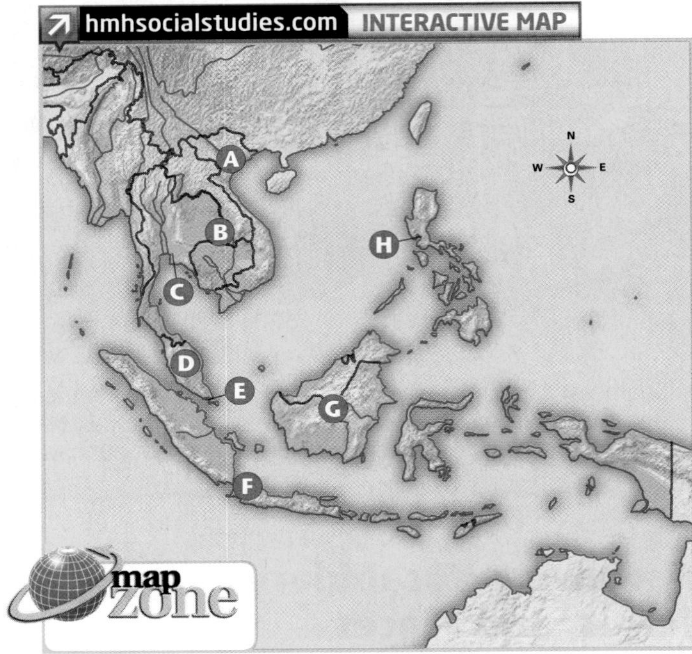

Focus on Reading and Speaking

Using Context Clues–Definitions *Add a phrase or sentence to provide a definition for the underlined word.*

18. In Thailand, many young men serve for short periods in Buddhist monasteries.

19. Much of the cultivated land in Southeast Asia is used to grow rice.

Presenting an Interview *Use your interview notes to complete the activity below.*

20. Working with your partner, choose the five best questions and answers for your interview. Write a brief introduction and conclusion for the journalist to present at the start and end of the interview. Decide who will play the journalist and who will play the expert. Practice the interview until it sounds natural and then present it to your class.

CHAPTER 6 Standardized Test Prep

DIRECTIONS: Read questions 1 through 7 and write the letter of the best response. Then read question 8 and write your own well-constructed response.

1 The two peninsulas in Southeast Asia are the Indochina Peninsula and the

A Burma Peninsula.
B Malay Peninsula.
C Philippine Peninsula.
D Thai Peninsula.

2 What is the largest island in this region?

A Bali
B Borneo
C Java
D New Guinea

3 Which early advanced society in Southeast Asia was located in what is now Cambodia?

A Burmese
B Khmer
C Malays
D Thais

4 Which country in Mainland Southeast Asia has a harsh military government?

A Cambodia
B Laos
C Myanmar
D Thailand

5 What interesting feature of Bangkok helps people get around the city?

A kampongs
B klongs
C sultans
D wats

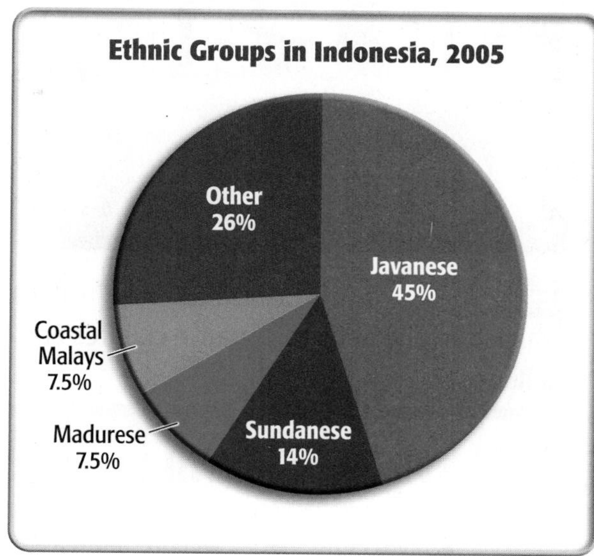

Source: Central Intelligence Agency, *The World Factbook 2005*

6 Based on the circle graph above, which of the following was the largest ethnic group in Indonesia in 2005?

A Coastal Malays
B Javanese
C Madurese
D Sundanese

7 Which small country in Island Southeast Asia has become wealthy from oil?

A Brunei
B Timor-Leste
C Indonesia
D Philippines

8 Extended Response Examine the Section 1 map titled Southeast Asia: Climate. Based on the information in the map and in the text, write two or three paragraphs explaining how climate affects life in Southeast Asia. Consider plant life, animal life, and how people live and work.

CHAPTER 7

The Pacific World

Essential Question How has the Pacific world been shaped by the mixture of native cultures and Western influence?

What You Will Learn...

In this chapter you will learn about the vast world located in the Pacific Ocean. You will study the geography, history, and culture of Australia and New Zealand. You will also discover one of the most unique places in the world—the Pacific Islands. Finally, you will examine the immense and isolated continent of Antarctica.

FOCUS ON READING AND WRITING

Drawing Conclusions When you read, you discover new information. However, to find out what that information means, you have to draw conclusions. Conclusions are judgments we make as we combine new information with what we already know. As you read about the Pacific world, draw conclusions about the information you come across. **See the lesson, Drawing Conclusions, on page 219.**

Creating a Brochure You work for an advertising agency, and your assignment is to create a brochure about the natural resources in the Pacific world. Your goal is to encourage people to invest money in developing the local economies. As you read this chapter, collect information to use in your brochure.

Geography From Uluru in the dry Australian Outback to freezing Antarctica, the Pacific world is a land of great geographic variety.

hmhsocialstudies.com INTERACTIVE MAP

The Pacific World: Political

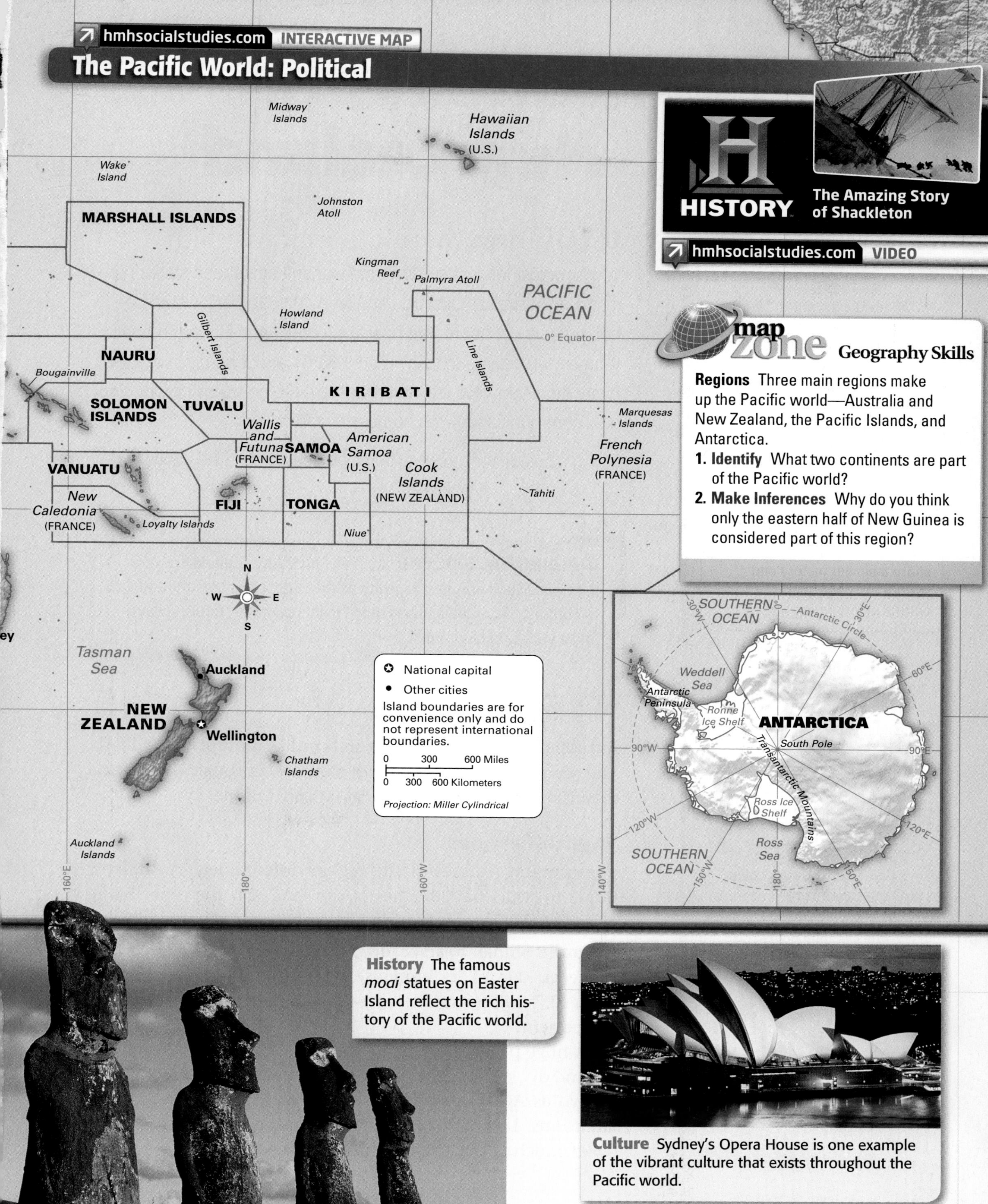

HISTORY

The Amazing Story of Shackleton

hmhsocialstudies.com VIDEO

map zone Geography Skills

Regions Three main regions make up the Pacific world—Australia and New Zealand, the Pacific Islands, and Antarctica.

1. **Identify** What two continents are part of the Pacific world?
2. **Make Inferences** Why do you think only the eastern half of New Guinea is considered part of this region?

History The famous *moai* statues on Easter Island reflect the rich history of the Pacific world.

Culture Sydney's Opera House is one example of the vibrant culture that exists throughout the Pacific world.

SECTION 1

Australia and New Zealand

What You Will Learn...

Main Ideas

1. The physical geography of Australia and New Zealand is diverse and unusual.
2. Native peoples and British settlers shaped the history of Australia and New Zealand.
3. Australia and New Zealand today are wealthy and culturally diverse countries.

The Big Idea

Australia and New Zealand share a similar history and culture but have unique natural environments.

Key Terms and Places

Great Barrier Reef, *p. 189*
coral reef, *p. 189*
Aborigines, *p. 191*
Maori, *p. 191*
Outback, *p. 192*

Use the graphic organizer online to take notes on Australia and New Zealand's physical geography, history, and situation today.

If YOU lived there...

You have just taken a summer job working at a sheep station, or ranch, in Australia's Outback. You knew the Outback would be hot, but you did not realize how hot it could get! During the day, temperatures climb to over 100°F (40°C), and it hardly ever rains. In addition, you have learned that there are no towns nearby. Your only communication with home is by radio.

How will you adapt to living in the Outback?

BUILDING BACKGROUND Australia and New Zealand are very different. Much of Australia, such as the Outback, is hot, dry, and flat. In contrast, New Zealand has much milder climates, fertile valleys, and a variety of landforms.

Physical Geography

Australia and New Zealand are quite unlike most places on Earth. The physical features, variety of climates, unusual wildlife, and plentiful resources make the region truly unique.

Physical Features

The physical features of the region differ widely. Australia is home to wide, flat stretches of dry land. On the other hand, New Zealand features beautiful green hills and tall mountains.

Australia Similar to an island, Australia is surrounded by water. However, due to its immense size—almost 3 million square miles (7.7 million square km)—geographers consider Australia a continent.

A huge plateau covers the western half of Australia. Mostly flat and dry, this plateau is home to Uluru, a rock formation also known as Ayers Rock. Uluru is one of Australia's best-known landforms. Low mountains, valleys, and a major river system cover much of Eastern Australia. Fertile plains lie along the

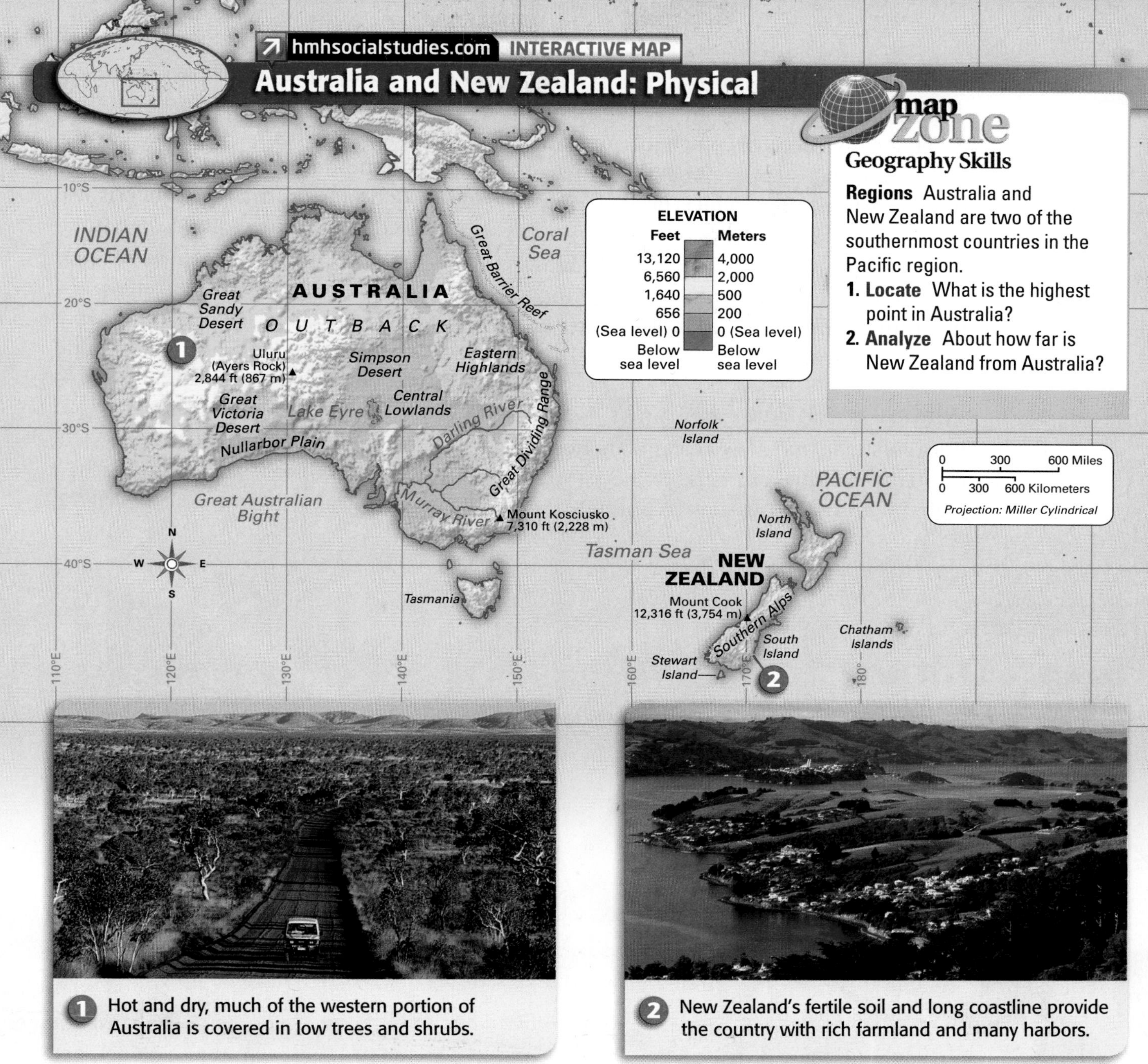

Geography Skills

Regions Australia and New Zealand are two of the southernmost countries in the Pacific region.

1. **Locate** What is the highest point in Australia?
2. **Analyze** About how far is New Zealand from Australia?

1. Hot and dry, much of the western portion of Australia is covered in low trees and shrubs.

2. New Zealand's fertile soil and long coastline provide the country with rich farmland and many harbors.

coasts. Off Australia's northeastern coast is the **Great Barrier Reef**, the world's largest coral reef. A **coral reef** is a collection of rocky material found in shallow, tropical waters. The Great Barrier Reef is home to an incredible variety of marine animals.

New Zealand New Zealand, located some 1,000 miles southeast of Australia, includes two main islands, North Island and South Island. North Island is covered by hills and coastal plains. It is also home to volcanoes, geysers, and hot springs. One of the key features on South Island is a large mountain range called the Southern Alps. Thick forests, deep lakes, and even glaciers are found in the Southern Alps. The rest of the island is covered by fertile hills and rich plains. Fjords, or narrow inlets of the sea, create many natural harbors along the coasts of both islands.

hmhsocialstudies.com
ANIMATED GEOGRAPHY
The Great Barrier Reef

Climates

The climates of Australia and New Zealand differ greatly. Because much of Australia has desert and steppe climates, temperatures are warm and rainfall is limited. However, along the coasts the climate is more temperate. Unlike Australia, New Zealand is mild and wet. A marine climate brings plentiful rainfall and mild temperatures to much of the country.

Wildlife and Resources

Both Australia and New Zealand are home to many unique animals. Some of the region's most famous native animals are Australia's kangaroo and koala and New Zealand's kiwi, a flightless bird.

Australia is rich in resources. It is the world's top producer of bauxite and lead as well as diamonds and opals. Australia is also home to energy resources like coal, natural gas, and oil. Despite poor soil, farms and ranches raise wheat, cotton, and sheep.

Unlike Australia, New Zealand has a great deal of fertile land but few mineral resources. New Zealand's main resources are wool, timber, and gold.

READING CHECK **Contrasting** How does the physical geography of the two countries differ?

Close-up

Maori Culture

The Maori, the descendants of New Zealand's earliest settlers, lived in small settlements throughout the islands. Their rich culture and traditions are still alive in New Zealand today.

Beautifully decorated storehouses served as a sign of a village's wealth and power. They often held weapons, tools, and foods.
The *moko*, or tattoos, of Maori warriors were symbols of a warrior's bravery. They also helped intimidate the enemy during battle.
The Maori used elaborately carved war canoes to launch attacks on their enemies.

History

Despite their many geographic differences, Australia and New Zealand share a similar history. Both countries were originally inhabited by settlers from other parts of the Pacific. Later, both Australia and New Zealand were colonized by the British.

Early Settlers

The first settlers in Australia likely migrated there from Southeast Asia at least 40,000 years ago. These settlers, the **Aborigines** (a-buh-RIJ-uh-nees), were the first humans to live in Australia. Early Aborigines were nomads who gathered various plants and hunted animals with boomerangs and spears. Nature played an important role in the religion of the early Aborigines, who believed that it was their duty to preserve the land.

New Zealand's first settlers came from other Pacific islands more recently, about 1,200 years ago. The descendants of these early settlers, the **Maori** (MOWR-ee), settled throughout New Zealand. Like Australia's Aborigines, the Maori were fishers and hunters. Unlike the Aborigines, however, the Maori also used farming to survive.

Maori life centered around a village meetinghouse, where important gatherings like weddings and funerals were held.

ANALYSIS SKILL **ANALYZING VISUALS**

Based on the illustration, what elements were important in Maori culture?

The Arrival of Europeans

European explorers first sighted Australia and New Zealand in the 1600s. It wasn't until later, however, that Europeans began to explore the region. In 1769 British explorer James Cook explored the main islands of New Zealand. The following year, Cook landed on the east coast of Australia and claimed the land for Britain.

Within 20 years of Cook's claim, the British began settling in Australia. Many of the first to arrive were British prisoners, but other settlers came, too. As the settlers built farms and ranches, they took over the Aborigines' lands. Many Aborigines died of diseases introduced by the Europeans.

FOCUS ON READING

What conclusions can you draw about why European settlers were attracted to Australia?

In New Zealand, large numbers of British settlers started to arrive in the early 1800s. After the British signed a treaty with the Maori in 1840, New Zealand became a part of the British Empire. However, tensions between the Maori and British settlers led to a series of wars over land.

Australia and New Zealand both gained their independence in the early 1900s. Today the two countries are members of the British Commonwealth of Nations and are close allies of the United Kingdom.

READING CHECK **Finding Main Ideas** How did early settlers influence the region?

FOCUS ON CULTURE

Australian Sports

Outdoor sports are tremendously popular in sunny Australia. Some of Australia's most popular activities include water sports, such as swimming, surfing, and water polo. In recent years, many Australians have dominated the swimming competition at the summer Olympic Games.

Australia's national sport is cricket, a game played with a bat and ball. Cricket was first introduced to Australia by British settlers. Other popular sports with British roots are rugby and Australian Rules football. These two sports allow players to kick, carry, or pass the ball with their hands or feet. Every year hundreds of thousands of Australians attend professional rugby matches like the one in the photo below.

Drawing Conclusions Why do you think outdoor sports are so popular in Australia?

hmhsocialstudies.com
ANIMATED GEOGRAPHY
Present-Day Australia and New Zealand

Australia and New Zealand Today

Despite their isolation from other nations, Australia and New Zealand today are rich and well-developed. Their governments, economies, and people make them among the world's most successful countries.

Government

As former British colonies, the British style of government has influenced both Australia and New Zealand. As a result, both countries have similar governments. For example, the British monarch is the head of state in both Australia and New Zealand. Both countries are parliamentary democracies, a type of government in which citizens elect members to represent them in a parliament. Each country has a prime minister. The prime minister, along with Parliament, runs the government.

The governments of Australia and New Zealand have many features in common with the U.S. government. For example, Australia has a federal system like that of the United States. In this system, a central government shares power with the states. Australia's Parliament, similar to the U.S. Congress, consists of two houses—a House of Representatives and a Senate. A Bill of Rights also protects the individual rights of New Zealand's citizens.

Economy

Australia and New Zealand are both rich, economically developed countries. Agriculture is a major part of their economies. The two countries are among the world's top producers of wool. In fact, Australia regularly supplies about one-quarter of the wool used in clothing. Both countries also export meat and dairy products.

Australia and New Zealand also have other important industries. Mining is one of Australia's main industries. Companies mine bauxite, gold, and uranium throughout the **Outback**, Australia's interior. Other industries include steel, heavy machines, and computers. New Zealand has also become more industrialized in recent years. Factories turn out processed food, clothing, and paper products. Banking, insurance, and tourism are also important industries.

People

Today Australia and New Zealand have diverse populations. Most Australians and New Zealanders are of British ancestry. In recent years, however, peoples from around the world have migrated to the region. For example, since the 1970s Asians and Pacific Islanders have settled in Australia and New Zealand in growing numbers.

Native Maori and Aborigines make up only a small percentage of New Zealand's and Australia's populations. One challenge facing both countries today is improving the economic and political status of the those populations. Many of the region's Maori and Aborigines trail the rest of the population in terms of education, land ownership, and employment.

Most Australians and New Zealanders live in urban areas. About 90 percent of Australia's population lives in large cities along the coasts. Sydney and Melbourne, Australia's two largest cities, are home to about 8 million people. Rural areas like the Outback, on the other hand, have less than 10 percent of the population. In New Zealand, a majority of the population lives on the North Island. There, large cities like Auckland are common.

READING CHECK **Summarizing** What are the economic strengths of these countries?

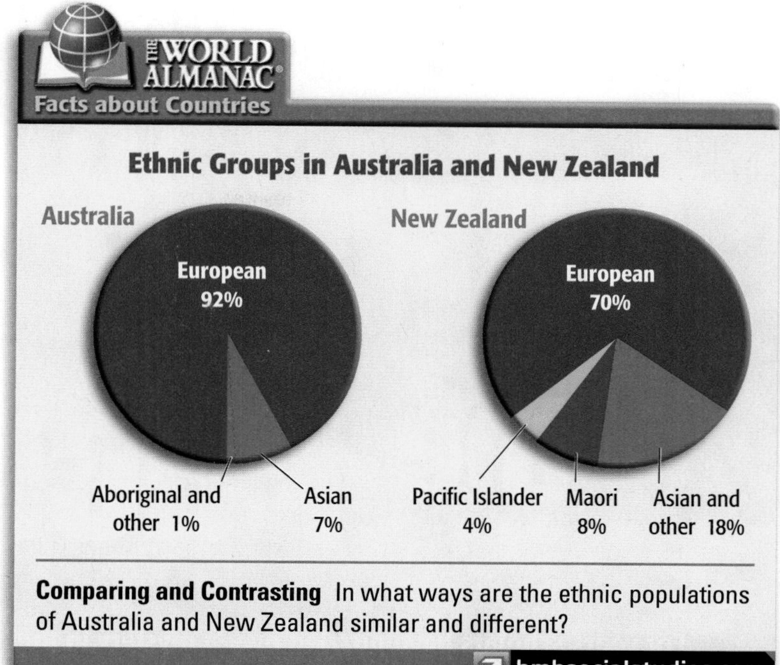

Comparing and Contrasting In what ways are the ethnic populations of Australia and New Zealand similar and different?

hmhsocialstudies.com

SUMMARY AND PREVIEW Despite their geographical differences, Australia and New Zealand have much in common. The two countries share a similar history, culture, and economy. In the next section you will learn about another region in the Pacific world—the Pacific Islands.

Section 1 Assessment

hmhsocialstudies.com ONLINE QUIZ

Reviewing Ideas, Terms, and Places

1. a. **Identify** What is the **Great Barrier Reef**? Where is it located?
   b. **Elaborate** Given its harsh climate, why do you think so many people have settled in Australia?
2. a. **Describe** Who are the **Maori**? From where did they originate?
   b. **Draw Conclusions** How might the **Aborigines'** relationship with nature have differed from that of other peoples?
3. a. **Recall** Where do most Australians and New Zealanders live?
   b. **Compare and Contrast** How are the governments of Australia and New Zealand similar to and different from that of the United States?

Critical Thinking

4. **Comparing and Contrasting** Use your notes and a diagram like the one here to compare and contrast the geography, history, and culture of Australia and New Zealand.

Australia	Both	New Zealand

Focus on Writing

5. **Describing Australia and New Zealand** What natural resources do these two countries produce? Make a list of the ones people might want to invest in. What illustrations could you include.

Geography and History

Settling the Pacific

For years scholars have puzzled over a mystery in the Pacific. How exactly did humans reach the thousands of islands scattered throughout the Pacific world? While we don't know all the details, evidence suggests that people from Southeast Asia originally settled the Pacific Islands. Over tens of thousands of years these people and their descendants slowly migrated throughout the Pacific. Thanks to expert canoe-building and navigational skills, these settlers reached islands many thousands of miles apart.

Many long-distance voyages were likely made on double canoes built with two hulls carved from huge logs.

Stick Charts Stick charts like this one from the Marshall Islands were probably used to navigate from island to island. The sticks show the direction of waves and ocean currents. Shells indicate the location of islands and other landmarks.

Settling the Pacific

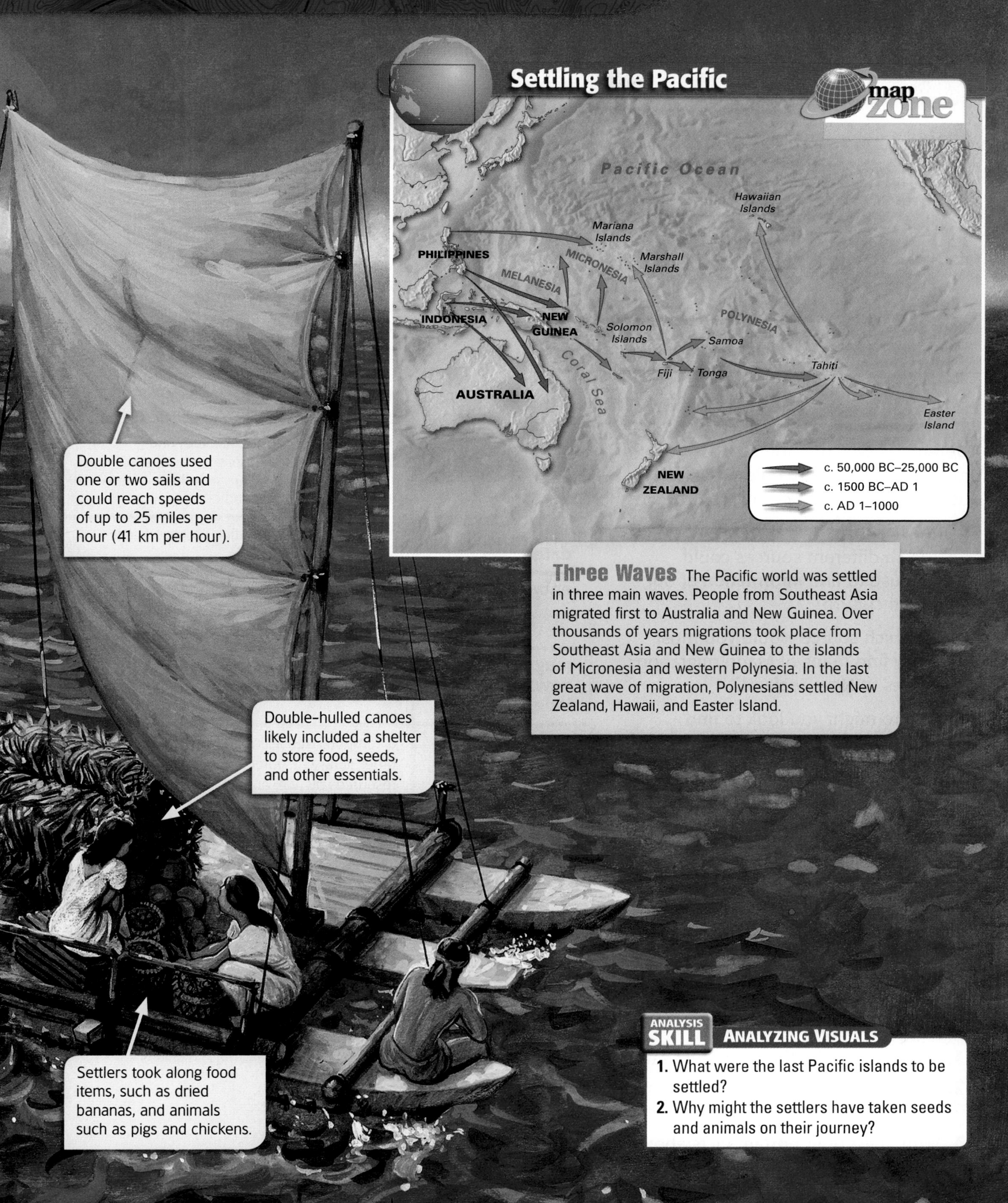

Three Waves The Pacific world was settled in three main waves. People from Southeast Asia migrated first to Australia and New Guinea. Over thousands of years migrations took place from Southeast Asia and New Guinea to the islands of Micronesia and western Polynesia. In the last great wave of migration, Polynesians settled New Zealand, Hawaii, and Easter Island.

ANALYSIS SKILL **ANALYZING VISUALS**

1. What were the last Pacific islands to be settled?
2. Why might the settlers have taken seeds and animals on their journey?

Social Studies Skills

Chart and Graph	Critical Thinking	Geography	Study

Locating Information

Learn

Your teacher has asked you to find information about New Zealand's Maori. Where should you go? What should you do? The best place to start your search for information is in the library. The chart at right includes some library resources you may find helpful.

Practice

Determine which of the sources described here you would most likely use to locate the information in the questions that follow.

1. Which different sources could you use to find information about Maori culture?
2. In which source would you most likely find maps of Maori migration routes to New Zealand?
3. Where might you look to find videos about Maori art and music?
4. Which resource would be best for locating information about the current population of Maori in New Zealand?

Library Resources

almanac	a collection of current statistics and general information usually published annually
atlas	a collection of maps and charts
electronic database	a collection of information you can access and search by computer
encyclopedias	books or computer software with short articles on a variety of subjects, usually arranged in alphabetical order
magazine and newspaper indexes	listings of recent and past articles from newspapers and magazines
online catalog	a computerized listing of books, videos, and other library resources; you search for resources by title, author, keyword, or subject
World Wide Web	a collection of information on the Internet; if you use a Web site, be sure to carefully examine its reliability, or trustworthiness

Apply

Use resources from a local library to answer the questions below.

1. About when did the Maori first settle in New Zealand?
2. What different subtopics can you find on the Maori in the library catalog?
3. Write a list of important facts about the Maori.

The Pacific Islands

SECTION 2

If YOU lived there...

You live on a small island in the South Pacific. For many years, the people on your island have made their living by fishing. Now, however, a European company has expressed interest in building an airport and a luxury hotel on your island. It hopes that tourists will be drawn by the island's dazzling beaches and tropical climate. The company's leaders want your permission before they build.

Will you give them permission? Why or why not?

BUILDING BACKGROUND Thousands of islands are scattered across the Pacific Ocean. Many of these islands are tiny and have few mineral resources. Among the resources they do have are pleasant climates and scenic landscapes. As a result, many Pacific islands have become popular tourist destinations.

Physical Geography

The Pacific Ocean covers more than one-third of Earth's surface. Scattered throughout this ocean are thousands of islands with similar physical features, climates, and resources.

Island Regions

We divide the Pacific Islands into three regions—Micronesia, Melanesia, and Polynesia—based on their culture and geography. **Micronesia**, which means "tiny islands," is located just east of the Philippines. Some 2,000 small islands make up this region. South of Micronesia is **Melanesia**, which stretches from New Guinea in the west to Fiji in the east. Melanesia is the most heavily populated Pacific Island region. The largest region is **Polynesia**, which means "many islands." Among Polynesia's many islands are Tonga, Samoa, and the Hawaiian Islands.

Physical Features

The Pacific Islands differ greatly. Some islands, like New Guinea (GI-nee), cover thousands of square miles. Other islands are tiny. For example, Nauru covers only 8 square miles (21 square km).

What You Will Learn...

Main Ideas

1. Unique physical features, tropical climates, and limited resources shape the physical geography of the Pacific Islands.
2. Native customs and contact with the western world have influenced the history and culture of the Pacific Islands.
3. Pacific Islanders today are working to improve their economies and protect the environment.

The Big Idea

The Pacific islands have tropical climates, rich cultures, and unique challenges.

Key Terms and Places

Micronesia, *p. 197*
Melanesia, *p. 197*
Polynesia, *p. 197*
atoll, *p. 198*
territory, *p. 199*

Use the graphic organizer online to take notes on the Pacific Islands.

Geographers classify the islands of the Pacific as either high islands or low islands. High islands tend to be mountainous and rocky. Most high islands are volcanic islands. They were formed when volcanic mountains grew from the ocean floor and reached the surface. The islands of Tahiti and Hawaii in Polynesia are examples of high islands. Other high islands, such as New Guinea, are formed from continental rock rather than volcanoes. For example, the country of Papua (PA-pyooh-wuh) New Guinea, located on the eastern half of the island of New Guinea, has rocky mountains that rise above 13,000 feet (3,960 m).

Low islands are typically much smaller than high islands. Most barely rise above sea level. Many low islands are atolls. An **atoll** is a small, ring-shaped coral island that surrounds a lagoon. Wake Island, west of the Hawaiian Islands, is an example of an atoll. Wake Island rises only 21 feet (6.4 m) above sea level and covers only 2.5 square miles (6.5 square km).

High and Low Islands

Many high islands, like the island of Hawaii, often have mountainous terrain, rich soils, and dense rain forests. Many low islands, like this small island in the Society Islands chain, are formed from coral reefs. Because most low islands have poor soils, agriculture is limited.

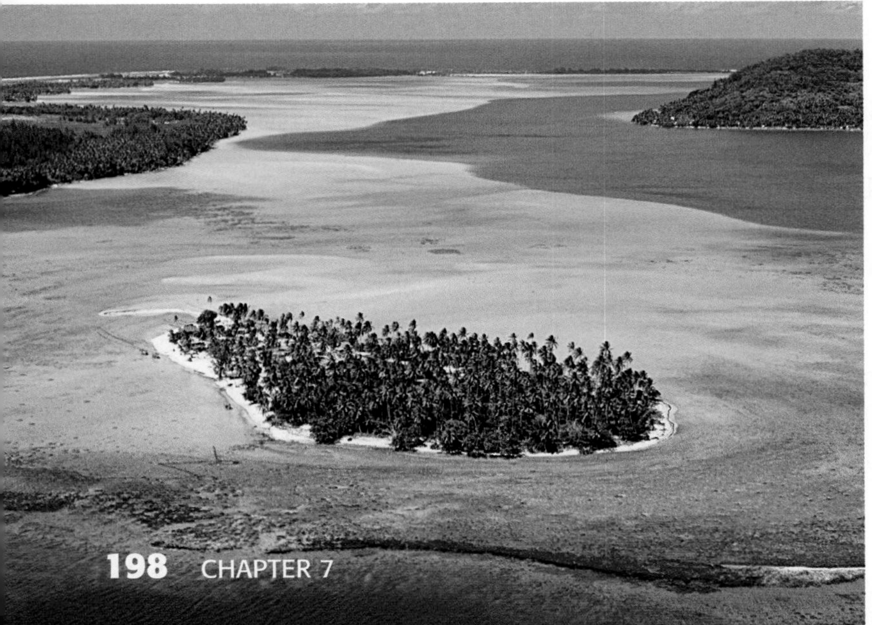

Climate and Resources

All but two of the Pacific Island countries lie in the tropics. As a result, most islands have a humid tropical climate. Rain falls all year and temperatures are warm. Tropical savanna climates with rainy and dry seasons exist in a few places, such as New Caledonia. The mountains of New Guinea are home to a cool highland climate.

Resources in the Pacific Islands vary widely. Most low islands have thin soils and little vegetation. They have few trees other than the coconut palm. In addition, low islands have few mineral or energy resources. Partly because of these conditions, low islands have small populations.

In contrast to low islands, the Pacific's high islands have many natural resources. Volcanic soils provide fertile farmland and dense forests. Farms produce crops such as coffee, cocoa, bananas, and sugarcane. Some high islands also have many mineral resources. Papua New Guinea, for example, exports gold, copper, and oil.

READING CHECK **Contrasting** How do the Pacific's low islands differ from high islands?

CONNECTING TO **Science**

The Formation of an Atoll

The Pacific Islands are home to many atolls, or small coral islands that surround shallow lagoons. Coral reefs are formed from the skeletons of many tiny sea animals. When a coral reef forms on the edges of a volcanic island, it often forms a barrier reef around the island.

As the volcanic island sinks, the coral remains. Sand and other debris gradually collects on the reef's surface, raising the land above sea level. Eventually, all that remains is an atoll.

Sequencing Describe the process in which atolls form.

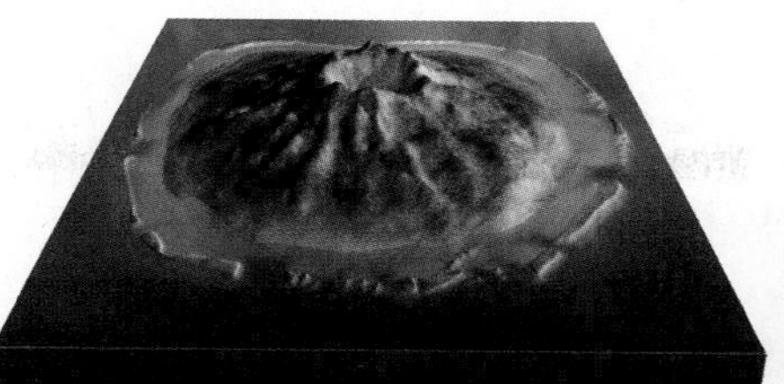

Coral reefs will sometimes form along the edges of a volcanic island, creating a ring around the island.

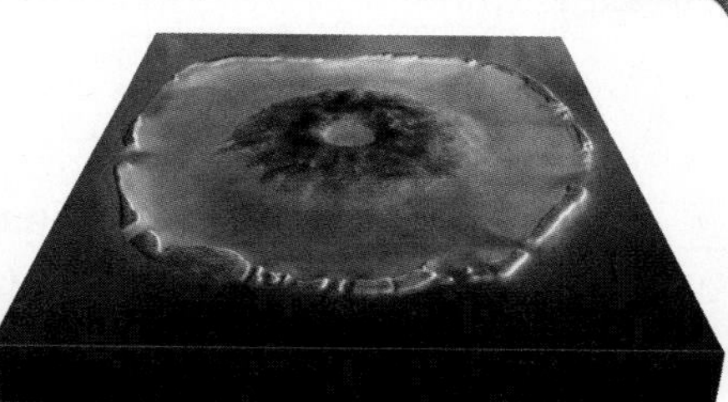

As the island sinks into the ocean floor, the coral reef grows upward and forms an offshore barrier reef.

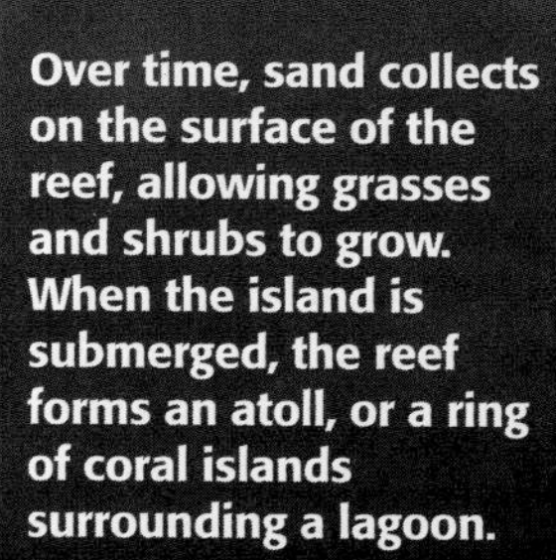

Over time, sand collects on the surface of the reef, allowing grasses and shrubs to grow. When the island is submerged, the reef forms an atoll, or a ring of coral islands surrounding a lagoon.

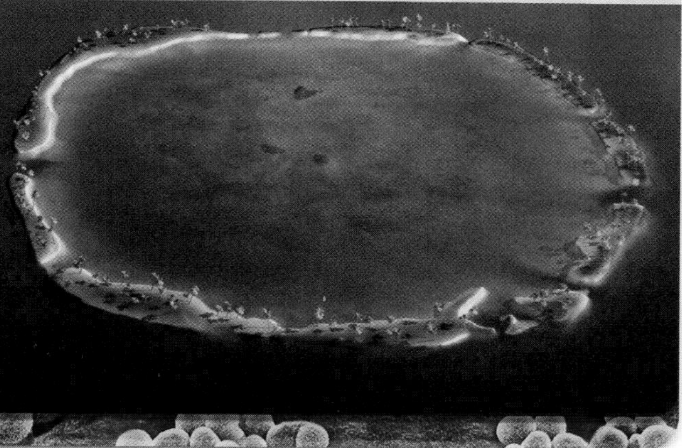

History and Culture

The Pacific Islands were one of the last places settled by humans. Because of their isolation from other civilizations, the islands have a unique history and culture.

Early History

Scholars believe that people began settling the Pacific Islands at least 35,000 years ago. The large islands of Melanesia were the first to be settled. Over time, people spread to the islands of Micronesia and Polynesia.

Europeans first encountered the Pacific Islands in the 1500s. Two centuries later, British captain James Cook explored all the main Pacific Island regions. By the late 1800s European powers such as Spain, Great Britain, and France controlled most of the Pacific Islands.

Modern History

By the early 1900s, other countries were entering the Pacific as well. In 1898 the United States defeated Spain in the Spanish-American War. As a result, Guam became a U.S. territory. A **territory** is an area that is under the authority of another government. Japan also expanded its empire into the Pacific Ocean in the early 1900s. In World War II, the Pacific Islands were the scene of many tough battles between Allied and Japanese forces. After Japan's defeat in 1945, the United Nations placed some islands under the control of the United States and other Allies.

In the last half of the 1900s many Pacific Islands gained their independence. However, several countries—including the United States, France, and New Zealand—still have territories in the Pacific Islands.

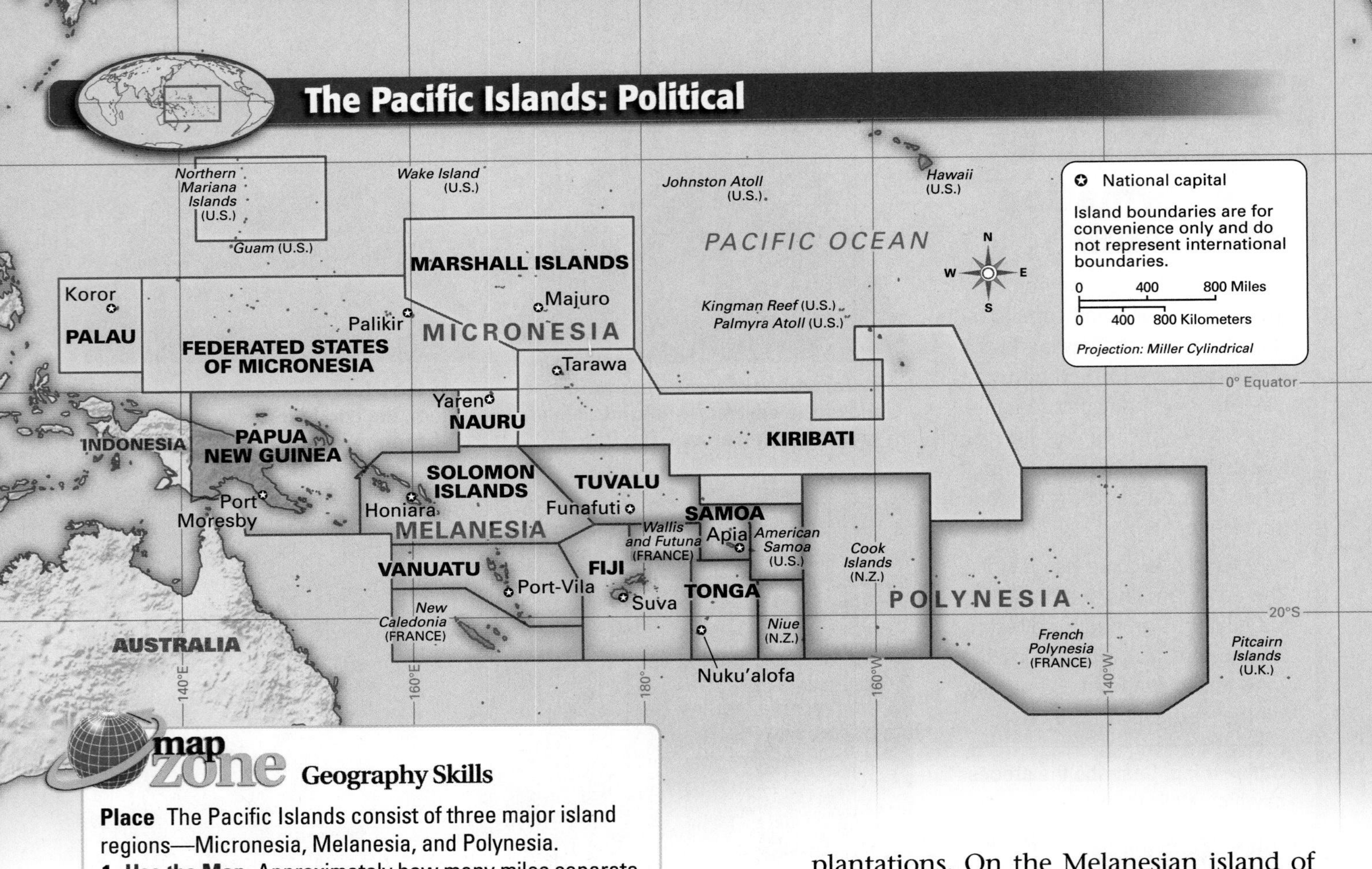

map zone Geography Skills

Place The Pacific Islands consist of three major island regions—Micronesia, Melanesia, and Polynesia.

1. **Use the Map** Approximately how many miles separate the islands of Palau and French Polynesia?
2. **Contrast** Based on the map, how do the Melanesian islands differ from those of French Polynesia?

Culture

A variety of cultures thrive throughout the Pacific Islands. Some culture traits, such as fishing, are common throughout the entire region. Others are only found on a specific island or island chain.

Focus on Reading
What can you conclude about the influence other cultures have had on the Pacific Islands?

People Close to 9 million people live in the Pacific Islands today. Most Pacific Islanders are descendants of the region's original settlers. However, the population of the Pacific Islands also includes large numbers of ethnic Europeans and Asians, particularly Indians and Chinese. Many ethnic Asians are descended from people brought to the islands to work on colonial plantations. On the Melanesian island of Fiji, for example, Indians make up nearly half of the population.

Before the arrival of Europeans, the people of the Pacific Islands practiced hundreds of different religions. Today most Pacific Islanders are Christian. In Melanesia, however, some people continue to practice traditional local religions.

Traditions Although modern culture exists throughout the Pacific Islands, many people continue to practice traditional customs. In parts of Polynesia, for example, people still construct their homes from bamboo and palm leaves. Many Pacific Islanders today continue to live in ancient villages, practice customary art styles, and hold ceremonies that feature traditional costumes and dances.

Reading Check **Making Inferences** In what ways have the Pacific Islands been influenced by contact with westerners?

The Pacific Islands Today

Many people imagine sunny beaches and tourists when they think of the Pacific Islands today. Despite the region's healthy tourism industry, however, Pacific Island countries face important challenges.

The countries of the Pacific Islands have developing economies. Fishing, tourism, and agriculture are key industries. Some countries, particularly Papua New Guinea, export minerals and timber. The region's isolation from other countries, however, hinders its ability to trade.

The environment is an important concern in the Pacific Islands. The Pacific Islands were used for nuclear testing grounds from the 1940s to the 1990s. Many people fear that one **effect** of these tests may be health problems for people in the region. Global warming also concerns Pacific Islanders. Some researchers believe that rising temperatures may cause polar ice to melt. The rise in ocean levels would threaten low-lying Pacific Islands.

READING CHECK **Summarizing** What are some challenges Pacific Islanders face today?

Villagers on Tanna Island in Vanuatu perform a traditional dance.

SUMMARY AND PREVIEW The Pacific Islands are one of the most isolated regions in the world. As a result, unique cultures and challenges exist in the region. In the next section you will learn about another isolated part of the globe—Antarctica.

ACADEMIC VOCABULARY

effect the results of an action or decision

Section 2 Assessment

hmhsocialstudies.com ONLINE QUIZ

Reviewing Ideas, Terms, and Places

1. a. **Describe** Into what regions are the Pacific Islands divided?
   b. **Draw Conclusions** Why might high islands have larger populations than low islands?
2. a. **Define** What is a **territory**?
   b. **Make Inferences** Why did other countries seek to control the Pacific Islands?
   c. **Elaborate** Why do you think that many Pacific Islanders continue to practice traditional customs?
3. a. **Recall** What economic resources are available to the Pacific Islands?
   b. **Predict** How might the Pacific Islands be affected by global warming in the future?

Critical Thinking

4. **Finding Main Ideas** Draw a chart like the one shown. Using your notes, identify the main idea of each topic and write a sentence for each.

Physical Geography	History	Culture	Issues Today

FOCUS ON WRITING

5. **Telling about the Resources of the Pacific** Add to your list by noting the natural resources of the Pacific Islands. Which resources will you describe in your brochure? How might you describe them.

SECTION 3

Antarctica

What You Will Learn...

Main Ideas

1. Freezing temperatures, ice, and snow dominate Antarctica's physical geography.
2. Explorations in the 1800s and 1900s led to Antarctica's use for scientific research.
3. Research and protecting the environment are key issues in Antarctica today.

The Big Idea

Antarctica's unique environment has made it an important site for research.

Key Terms and Places

ice shelf, *p. 203*
icebergs, *p. 203*
Antarctic Peninsula, *p. 203*
polar desert, *p. 203*
ozone layer, *p. 204*

Use the graphic organizer online to take notes on Antarctica's physical geography, early exploration, and issues today.

If YOU lived there...

You are a scientist working at a research laboratory in Antarctica. One day you receive an e-mail message from a friend. She wants to open a company that will lead public tours through Antarctica so people can see its spectacular icy landscapes and wildlife. Some of your fellow scientists think that tours are a good idea, while others think that they could ruin the local environment.

What will you tell your friend?

BUILDING BACKGROUND Antarctica, the continent surrounding the South Pole, has no permanent residents. The only people there are scientists who research the frozen land. For many years, people around the world have debated the best way to use this frozen land.

Physical Geography

In the southernmost part of the world is the continent of Antarctica. This frozen land is very different from any other place on Earth.

The Land

Ice covers about 98 percent of Antarctica's 5.4 million square miles (14 million square km). This ice sheet contains more than 90 percent of the world's ice. On average the ice sheet is more than 1 mile (1.6 km) thick.

Penguins live in the icy waters around Antarctica, a continent almost completely covered in ice.

The weight of Antarctica's ice sheet causes ice to flow slowly off the continent. As the ice reaches the coast, it forms a ledge over the surrounding seas. This ledge of ice that extends over the water is called an **ice shelf**. Antarctica's ice shelves are huge. In fact, the Ross Ice Shelf, Antarctica's largest, is about the size of France.

Sometimes parts of the ice shelf break off into the surrounding water. Floating masses of ice that have broken off a glacier are **icebergs**. When one iceberg recently formed, it was approximately the size of the country of Luxembourg.

In western Antarctica, the **Antarctic Peninsula** extends north of the Antarctic Circle. As a result, temperatures there are often warmer than in other parts of the continent.

Climate and Resources

Most of Antarctica's interior is dominated by a freezing ice-cap climate. Temperatures can drop below –120°F (–84°C), and very little precipitation falls. As a result, much of Antarctica is considered a **polar desert**, a high-latitude region that receives very little precipitation. The precipitation that does fall does not melt due to the cold temperatures. Instead, it remains as ice.

Because of Antarctica's high latitude, the continent is in almost total darkness during winter months. Seas clog with ice as a result of the extreme temperatures. In the summer, the sun shines around the clock and temperatures rise to near freezing.

Plant life only survives in the ice-free tundra areas. Insects are the frozen land's only land animals. Penguins, seals, and whales live in Antarctica's waters. Antarctica has many mineral resources, including iron ore, gold, copper, and coal.

READING CHECK **Summarizing** What are the physical features and resources of Antarctica?

Primary Source

BOOK

Crossing Antarctica

In 1989 a six-person team set off to cross Antarctica on foot. The 3,700-mile journey took seven months to complete. Team member Will Steger describes his first view of the continent.

> Now, flying over the iceberg-laden Weddell Sea, the biggest adventure of my life was about to begin . . .
>
> To the south I could barely pick out the peaks of mountains, mountains I knew jutted three thousand feet into the air. They lined the peninsula's coast for hundreds of miles. Leading up to them was a two-mile-wide sheet of snow and ice, preceded by the blue of the sea. It was a picture of purity, similar to many I had seen in the picture books . . .

—from *Crossing Antarctica*, by Will Steger and John Bowermaster

ANALYSIS SKILL **ANALYZING PRIMARY SOURCES**

What physical features does the author notice on his trip over Antarctica?

Antarctic Exploration

In the early 1900s several expeditions set out to find the South Pole. The first to reach the pole were members of a Norwegian expedition led by Roald Amundsen. In this photo a member of the Norwegian expedition poses with his team of dogs near the flag that marks the South Pole.

BIOGRAPHY

Sir Ernest Shackleton

(1874–1922)

Irish-born Ernest Shackleton was one of several early explorers of Antarctica. Shackleton led a British expedition in 1907–1909 that climbed Mt. Erebus, an active volcano, discovered the Beardmore Glacier, and came within 97 miles of the South Pole—the farthest south anyone had ever been.

HISTORY

VIDEO
The Amazing Story of Shackleton

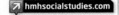

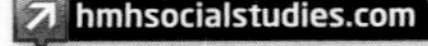

hmhsocialstudies.com

Early Explorations

The discovery of Antarctica is a fairly recent one. Although explorers long believed there was a southern continent, it was not until 1775 that James Cook first sighted the Antarctic Peninsula. In the 1800s explorers first investigated Antarctica. One **motive** of many explorers was to discover the South Pole and other new lands. In 1911 a team of Norwegian explorers became the first people to reach the South Pole.

ACADEMIC VOCABULARY
motive a reason for doing something

Since then, several countries—including the United States, Australia, and Chile—have claimed parts of Antarctica. In 1959 the international Antarctic Treaty was signed to preserve the continent "for science and peace." This treaty banned military activity in Antarctica and set aside the entire continent for research.

FOCUS ON READING
What conclusions can you draw about why some countries wanted to preserve Antarctica for research?

READING CHECK **Making Inferences** Why do you think Antarctica is set aside for research?

Antarctica Today

Today Antarctica is the only continent without a permanent human population. Scientists use the continent to conduct research and to monitor the environment.

Scientific Research

While they are conducting research in Antarctica, researchers live in bases, or stations. Several countries, including the United States, the United Kingdom, and Russia, have bases in Antarctica.

Antarctic research covers a wide range of topics. Some scientists concentrate on the continent's plant and animal life. Others examine weather conditions. One group of researchers is studying Earth's ozone layer. The **ozone layer** is a layer of Earth's atmosphere that protects living things from the harmful effects of the sun's ultraviolet rays. Scientists have found a thinning in the ozone layer above Antarctica.

Environmental Threats

Many people today are concerned about Antarctica's environment. Over the years, researchers and tourists have left behind trash and sewage, polluting the environment. Oil spills have damaged surrounding seas. In addition, companies have hoped to exploit Antarctica's valuable resources.

Some people fear that any mining of the resources in Antarctica will result in more environmental problems. To prevent this, a new international agreement was reached in 1991. This agreement forbids most activities that do not have a scientific purpose. It bans mining and drilling and limits tourism.

READING CHECK **Finding Main Ideas** What are some issues that affect Antarctica today?

SUMMARY In this section, you have learned about Antarctica's unusual physical geography and harsh climates. Despite the difficulty of living in such harsh conditions, Antarctica remains an important place for scientific research.

Satellite View

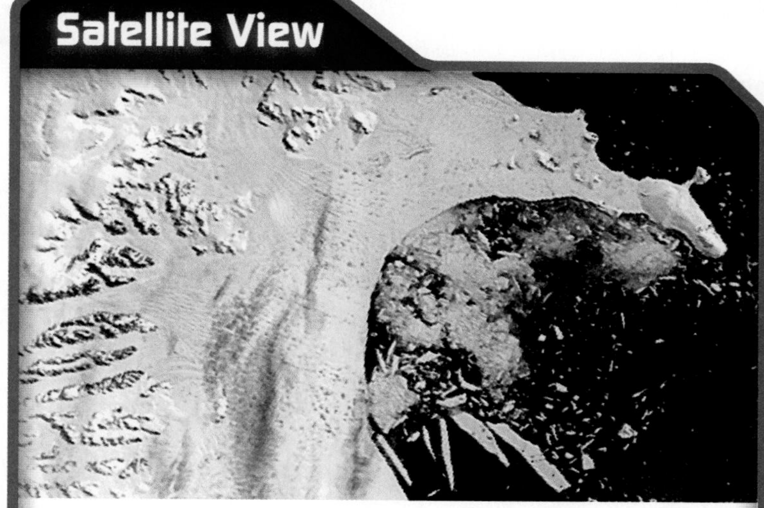

Antarctica's Ice Shelves

Antarctica is home to many large ice shelves. An ice shelf is a piece of a glacier that extends over the surrounding seas. In recent years, scientists have become concerned that rising temperatures on the planet are causing the rapid disintegration of some of Antarctica's ice shelves. This satellite image from 2002 shows the breakup of a huge portion of Antarctica's Larsen B Ice Shelf, located on the Antarctic Peninsula. The breakup of this ice shelf released some 720 billion tons of ice into the Weddell Sea.

Identifying Cause and Effect What do scientists believe has led to growing disintegration of Antarctica's ice shelves?

Section 3 Assessment

hmhsocialstudies.com ONLINE QUIZ

Reviewing Ideas, Terms, and Places

1. a. **Define** What are **ice shelves** and **icebergs**?
   b. **Contrast** How does Antarctica differ from most other continents?
   c. **Elaborate** What aspects of Antarctica's physical geography would you most like to see? Why?
2. a. **Identify** What was the Antarctic Treaty of 1959?
   b. **Predict** What might have happened if countries had not agreed to preserve Antarctica for research?
3. a. **Recall** What is Antarctica used for today?
   b. **Analyze** How has Antarctic research benefited science?
   c. **Elaborate** Do you agree with bans on tourism and mining in Antarctica? Why or why not?

Critical Thinking

4. **Summarizing** Draw a diagram like the one here. Use your notes to list three facts about each aspect of Antarctica's physical geography.

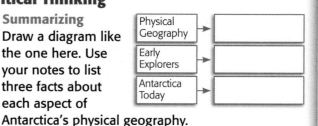

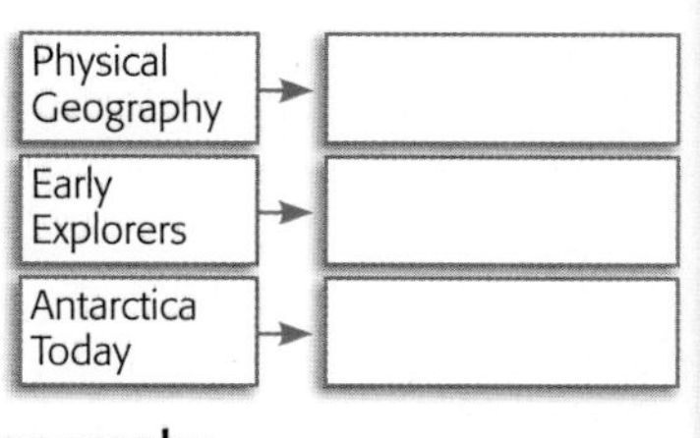

FOCUS ON WRITING

5. **Describing Antarctica** In your notebook, describe the natural resources of Antarctica. Decide which to include in your brochure. What illustrations might you include.

Adelie penguins jump off an iceberg near Antarctica.

GUIDED READING

WORD HELP

rampart an embankment made of earth used for protection

① The Weddell Sea is a part of the Southern Ocean, which borders the western part of Antarctica.

from

Antarctic Journal:

Four Months at the Bottom of the World

by Jennifer Owings Dewey

About the Reading *In her book,* Antarctic Journal: Four Months at the Bottom of the World, *writer and artist Jennifer Owings Dewey describes her four-month visit to Antarctica as a visiting researcher at Palmer research station.*

AS YOU READ **Identify what the icebergs mean to the author.**

Coming back we see icebergs drifting south out of the Weddell Sea. ① The bergs originate hundreds of miles away and ride ocean currents.

We sail close, but not too close, for beneath the waves is where the bulk of an iceberg is.

Seawater splashes up on iceberg shores shaped by years of wave action. Sunlight strikes gleaming ramparts that shine with rainbow colors. Erosion works at the ice, creating caves and hollows, coves and inlets.

Penguins and seals hitch rides on icebergs. Gulls and other seabirds rest on high points.

One iceberg collides in slow motion with another. The smaller one topples, rolls, and heaves like a dying rhinoceros, emerald seawater mixed with spray drenching its surfaces.

I yearn to ride an iceberg like a penguin or a gull, touching its frozen sides, drifting slowly on the waves. I draw them, but I can't capture their splendour.

Connecting Literature to Geography

1. **Describe** What details in the passage tell you that the icebergs are in motion?
2. **Compare and Contrast** The author was clearly moved by the beauty of the place she was observing. Think of a place you have seen in your community that made a lasting impression on your senses. Tell how the author's description of icebergs is like your own experience. Then explain how the two experiences are different.

CHAPTER 7

Chapter Review

Geography's Impact
video series
Review the video to answer the closing question:
What are some ways to help prevent or limit the spread of nonnative species?

Visual Summary

Use the visual summary below to help you review the main ideas of the chapter.

QUICK FACTS

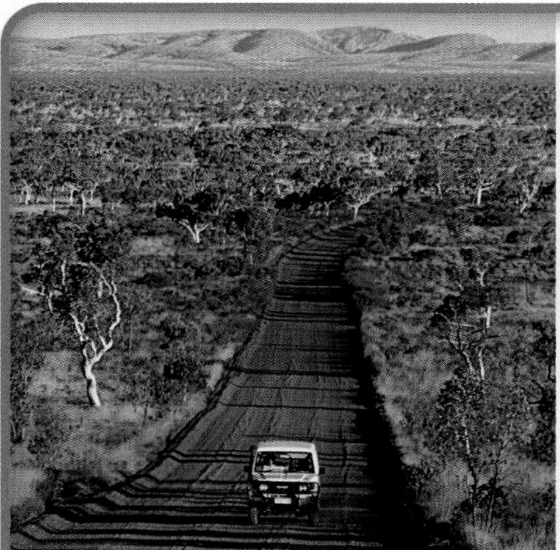

Australia and New Zealand
Despite different physical features, Australia and New Zealand have much in common.

The Pacific Islands
The Pacific Islands are home to tropical climates and beautiful beaches.

Antarctica
Antarctica's unique environment makes it an important site for scientific research.

Reviewing Vocabulary, Terms, and Places

Choose the letter of the answer that best completes each statement below.

1. The original inhabitants of Australia are the
- **a.** Aborigines
- **b.** Maori
- **c.** Papuans
- **d.** Polynesians

2. A floating mass of ice that has broken off a glacier is a(n)
- **a.** atoll
- **b.** coral reef
- **c.** iceberg
- **d.** polar desert

3. Located off the northeast coast of Australia, this is the world's largest coral reef
- **a.** Australian Reef
- **b.** Great Barrier Reef
- **c.** Kiwi Reef
- **d.** Reef of the Coral Sea

4. The result of an action or decision is a(n)
- **a.** agreement
- **b.** effect
- **c.** motive
- **d.** purpose

Comprehension and Critical Thinking

SECTION 1 *(Pages 188–193)*

5. a. Describe What is the physical geography of Australia like?

b. Compare and Contrast In what ways are the countries of Australia and New Zealand similar and different?

c. Elaborate Why do you think the economies of Australia and New Zealand are so strong?

SECTION 2 *(Pages 197–201)*

6. a. Identify What two types of islands are commonly found in the Pacific Ocean? How are they different?

b. Analyze How were the islands of the Pacific Ocean originally settled?

c. Elaborate Many Pacific Islands are very isolated from other societies. Would you want to live in these isolated communities? Why or why not?

SECTION 3 *(Pages 202–205)*

7. a. Describe What types of wildlife are found in and around Antarctica?

b. Draw Conclusions Why do you think many of the world's countries supported setting aside Antarctica for scientific research?

c. Predict What effects might the thinning of the ozone layer have on Antarctica?

Social Studies Skills 

Locating Information *Use your knowledge about locating information to answer the questions below.*

8. Where might you look to find information about recent weather statistics in Antarctica?

9. What types of sources might you use to find books about early explorations of Antarctica?

10. What sources could you use to find electronic resources about Antarctica?

Using the Internet 

11. Activity: Creating a Display The original people of Australia, the Aborigines, came from Southeast Asia at least 40,000 years ago. Today many Aborigines work to keep their languages, religion, and customs alive. Take notes about Aborigine culture as you view the Web sites through the online book. Then create a visual display or multimedia presentation featuring the interesting things you discover about their dreamtime, art, music, and more.

hmhsocialstudies.com

Map Activity 

12. The Pacific World On a separate sheet of paper, match the letters on the map with their correct labels.

Great Barrier Reef	Pacific Ocean
Melbourne	Papua New Guinea
North Island	Perth
Outback	Sydney

hmhsocialstudies.com INTERACTIVE MAP

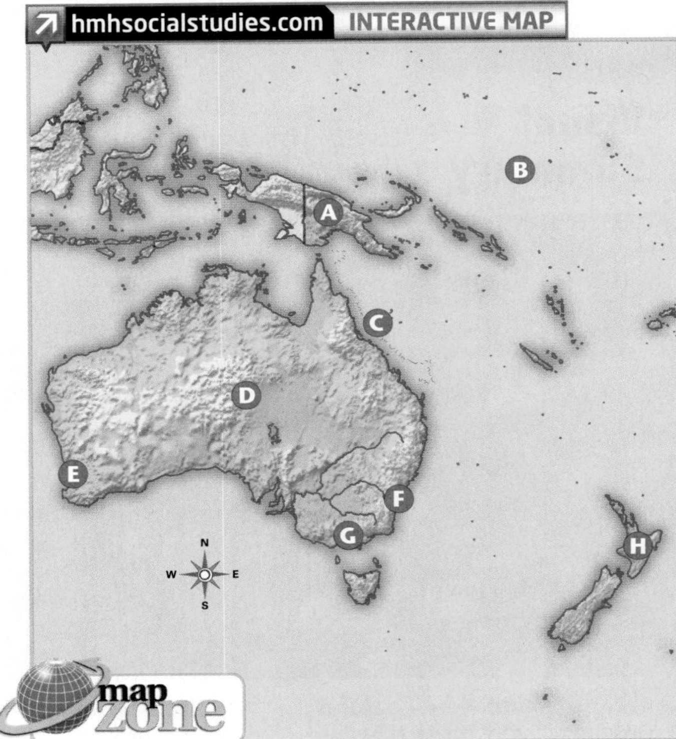

Focus on Reading and Writing

Drawing Conclusions *Read the paragraph below. Then answer the questions that follow.*

> Getting an education can be a challenge in the Outback, where students are spread across vast distances. Basic education comes from the School of the Air, which broadcasts classes via radio. Other lessons are conducted by video or mail. The internet, e-mail, and videoconferencing have also been used in recent years.

13. What did you know about education and Australia before you read this paragraph?

14. What conclusion(s) can you draw about education in Australia's Outback?

Writing a Brochure *Use your notes and the directions below to create a brochure.*

15. Divide your brochure into sections—one on Australia and New Zealand, one on the Pacific Islands, and one on Antarctica. In each section, identify the important resources and try to convince the reader to invest in them. Use illustrations to support the points you want to make. Finally, design a cover page for your brochure.

CHAPTER 7

Standardized Test Prep

DIRECTIONS: Read questions 1 through 7 and write the letter of the best response. Then read question 8 and write your own well-constructed response.

1 What is the world's only country that is also a continent?

A Australia
B Micronesia
C New Zealand
D Polynesia

2 What physical feature lies off Australia's northeastern coast?

A Nullarbor Plain
B Central Lowlands
C Great Barrier Reef
D Outback

3 The descendants of the first people to live in New Zealand are called the

A Aborigines.
B Maori.
C goa.
D kiwi.

4 A ring-shaped island surrounding a lagoon is called

A a high island.
B a low island.
C an atoll.
D a territory.

5 The only people who live in Antarctica are

A scientists.
B tourists.
C miners.
D government officials.

Australia and New Zealand: Climate

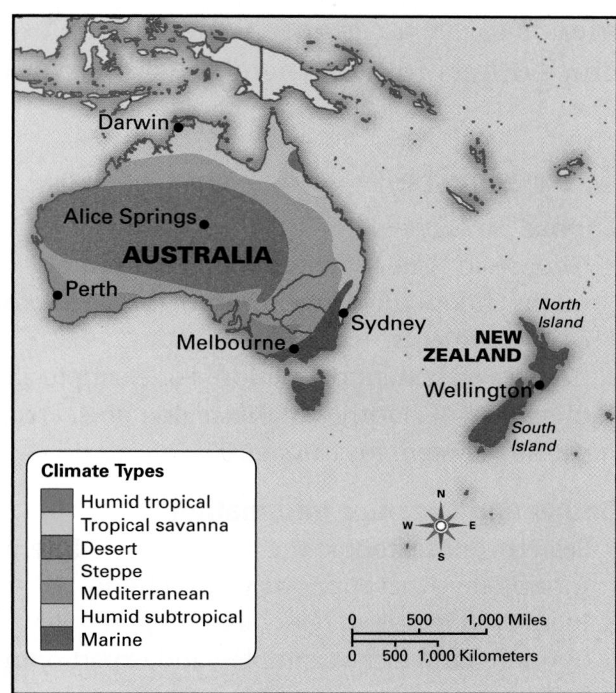

6 According to the map above, what city has a desert climate?

A Alice Springs
B Melbourne
C Perth
D Wellington

7 According to the map, New Zealand has what kind of climate?

A humid tropical
B steppe
C tropical savanna
D marine

8 Extended Response The vast majority of Australia's population lives along the coast, especially the east and southeast coasts. Study the map above. Then write a brief paragraph explaining why you think this is true.

Persuasion

Persuasion is about convincing others to act or believe in a certain way. Just as you use persuasion to convince your friends to see a certain movie, people use persuasion to convince others to help them solve the world's problems.

Assignment
Write a persuasive paper about an issue faced by the people of Asia and the Pacific. Choose an issue related to the natural environment or culture of the area.

1. Prewrite

Choose an Issue

- Choose an issue to write about. For example, you might choose the danger of tsunamis or the role of governments.
- Create a statement of opinion. For example, you might say, "Countries in this region must create a warning system for tsunamis."

Gather and Organize Information

- Search your textbook, the library, or the Internet for evidence that supports your opinion.
- Identify at least two reasons to support your opinion. Find facts, examples, and expert opinions to support each reason.

TIP **That's a Reason** Convince your readers by presenting reasons to support your opinion. For example, one reason to create a warning system for tsunamis is to save lives.

2. Write

Use a Writer's Framework

A Writer's Framework

Introduction

- Start with a fact or question related to the issue you will discuss.
- Clearly state your opinion in a sentence.

Body

- Write one paragraph for each reason. Begin with the least important reason and end with the most important.
- Include facts, examples and expert opinions as support.

Conclusion

- Restate your opinion and summarize your reasons.

3. Evaluate and Revise

Review and Improve Your Paper

- As you review your paper, use the questions below to evaluate it.
- Make changes to improve your paper.

Evaluation Questions for a Persuasive Essay

1. Do you begin with an interesting fact or question related to the issue?
2. Does your introduction clearly state your opinion and provide any necessary background information?
3. Do you discuss your reasons from least to most important?
4. Do you provide facts, examples, or expert opinions to support each of your reasons?
5. Does your conclusion restate your opinion and summarize your reasons?

4. Proofread and Publish

Give Your Paper the Finishing Touch

- Make sure you have correctly spelled and capitalized all names of people or places.
- Check for correct comma usage when presenting a list of reasons or evidence.
- Decide how to share your paper. For example, could you publish it in a school paper or in a classroom collection of essays?

5. Practice and Apply

Use the steps and strategies outlined in this workshop to write your persuasive essay. Share your opinion with others to see whether they find your opinion convincing.

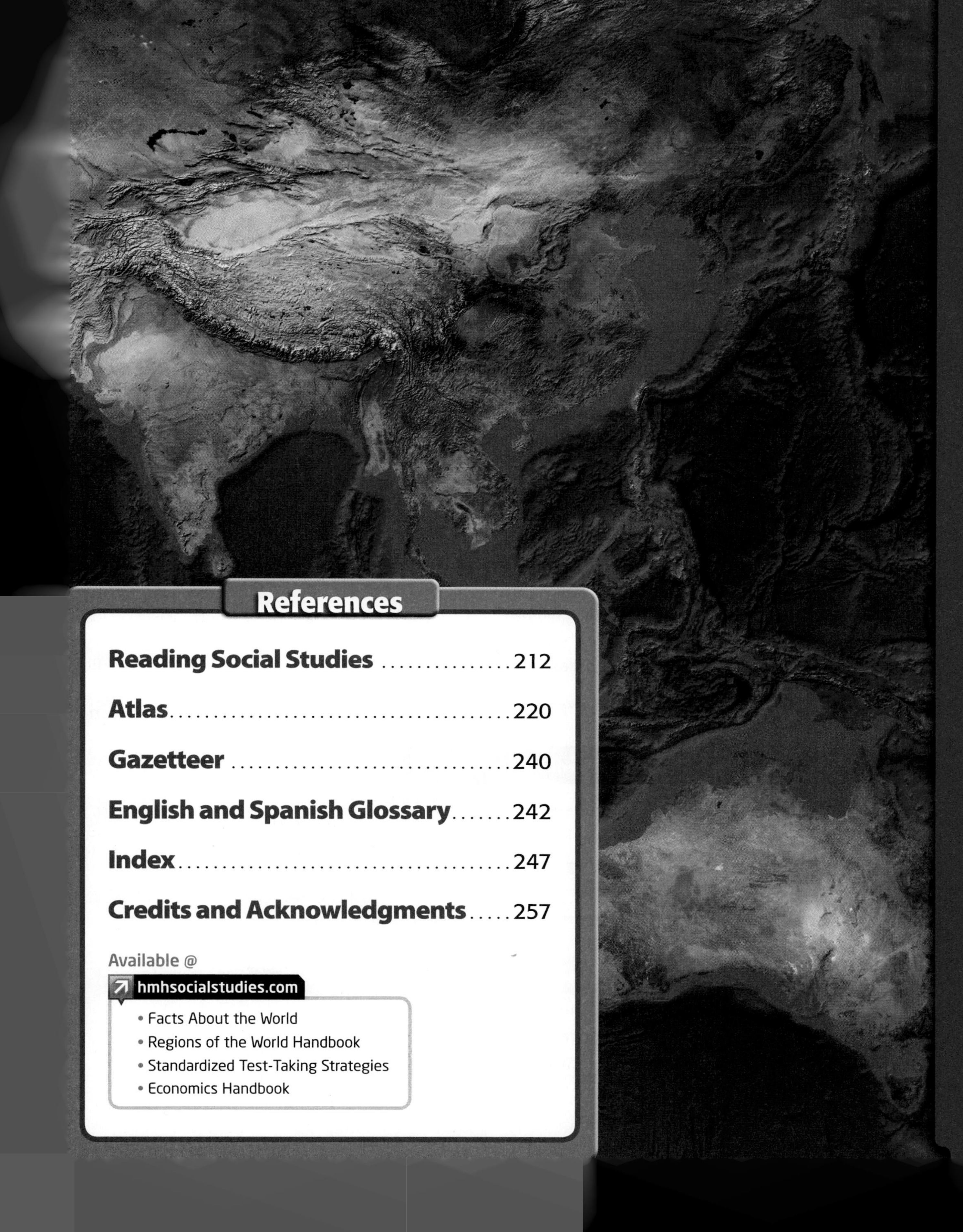

References

Available @

hmhsocialstudies.com

- Facts About the World
- Regions of the World Handbook
- Standardized Test-Taking Strategies
- Economics Handbook

Understanding Signal Words

Writers use patterns, or structures, to organize ideas or events. Recognizing these patterns will help you understand the ideas and information in a text. One way to spot these patterns is to look for the clues the writer provides for the reader. We call those clues signal words. Here are some signal words and groups of words that will give you clues to the basic organizational patterns writers use.

Chronological Pattern (Time Order)		
after	first	prior to
afterward	following	second
as	last	then
before	later	when
during	now	while
finally		

Comparison (Similarities)		
also	for example	likewise
as well as	in the same way	similarly
not only...but also	just as	too
equally		

Contrast (Differences)		
although	even though	on the other hand
but	however	regardless
by contrast	in contrast	still
conversely	in spite of	yet
despite	nevertheless	

Cause and Effect		
as a result	if...then	therefore
because	since	this led to
consequently	so that	thus

Sequencing

FOCUS ON READING

Have you ever used written instructions to put together an item you bought? If so, you know that the steps in the directions need to be followed in order. The instructions probably included words like *first, next,* and *then* to help you figure out what order you needed to do the steps in. The same kinds of words can help you when you read a history book. Words such as *first, then, later, next,* and *finally* can help you figure out the sequence, or order, in which events occurred. Read the passage below, noting the underlined clue words. Notice how they indicate the order of the events listed in the sequence chain at right.

> Not long after the Harappan civilization crumbled, a new group arrived in the Indus Valley. These people were called the Aryans. They were originally from the area around the Caspian Sea in Central Asia. Over time, however, they became the dominant group in India.
>
> *From Section 1, Early Indian Civilizations*

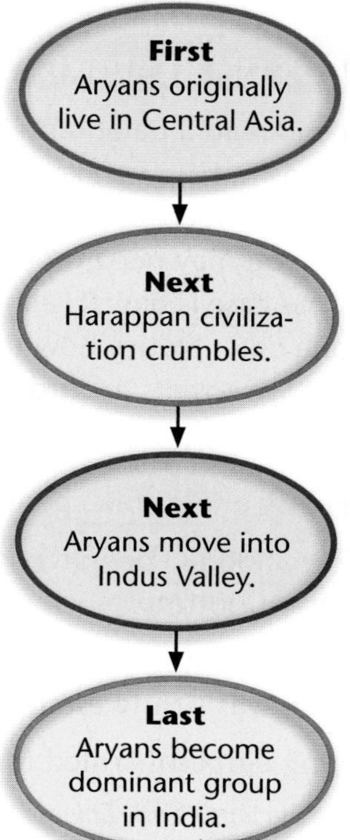

First
Aryans originally live in Central Asia.
Next
Harappan civilization crumbles.
Next
Aryans move into Indus Valley.
Last
Aryans become dominant group in India.

YOU TRY IT!

Read the following passage. Look for clue words to help you figure out the order of the events described in it. Then make a sequence chain like the one above to show that order.

> For many years, Asoka watched his armies fight bloody battles against other peoples. A few years into his rule, however, Asoka converted to Buddhism. When he did, he swore that he would not launch any more wars of conquest. After converting to Buddhism, Asoka had the time and resources to improve the lives of his people.
>
> *From Section 4, Indian Empires*

Understanding Chronological Order

Focus on Reading

When you read a paragraph in a history text, you can usually use clue words to help you keep track of the order of events. When you read a longer section of text that includes many paragraphs, though, you may need more clues. One of the best clues you can use in this case is dates. Each of the sentences below includes at least one date. Notice how those dates were used to create a time line that lists events in chronological, or time, order.

> As early as 7000 BC people had begun to farm in China.
>
> After 3000 BC people began to use potter's wheels to make many types of pottery.
>
> The first dynasty for which we have clear evidence is the Shang, which was firmly established by the 1500s BC.
>
> Shang emperors ruled in China until the 1100s BC.
>
> *From Section 1, Early China*

7000 BC People begin farming in China.

5000 BC

3000 BC People begin using potter's wheels.

1500s BC Shang dynasty rules China.

1100s BC Shang lose power.

1 BC

You Try It!

Read the following sentences. Use the dates in the sentences to create a time line listing events in chronological order.

> The Ming dynasty that he founded ruled China from 1368 to 1644.
>
> Genghis Khan led his armies into northern China in 1211.
>
> Between 1405 and 1433, Zheng He led seven grand voyages to places around Asia.
>
> In the 1300s many Chinese groups rebelled against the Yuan dynasty.
>
> *From Section 5, The Yuan and Ming Dynasties*

Visualizing

Focus on Reading

Maybe you have heard the saying "a picture is worth a thousand words." That means a picture can show in a small space what might take many words to describe. Visualizing, or creating mental pictures, can help you see and remember what you read. When you read, try to imagine what a snapshot of the images in the passage might look like. First, form the background or setting in your mind. Then keep adding specific details that can help you picture the rest of the information.

Form the background picture: I see the shape of the Indian subcontinent.

Add more specific details: I see two large crowds of people moving toward the diagonal line and the number 10,000,000.

To avoid a civil war, the British agreed to the partition, or division, of India. In 1947 two independent countries were formed. India was mostly Hindu. Pakistan, which included the area that is now Bangladesh, was mostly Muslim. As a result, some 10 million people rushed to cross the border. Muslims and Hindus wanted to live in the country where their religion held a majority.

From Section 2, History and Culture of India

Add specific details: I see a huge diagonal line near the top left dividing the country into India and Pakistan.

Add more specific details: I see two large arrows. The arrow pointing left says, "This way to Pakistan for Muslims." The arrow pointing right says, "This way to India for Hindus."

You Try It!

Read the following sentences. Then, using the process explained above, describe the images you see.

Flooding is one of Bangladesh's biggest challenges. Many circumstances cause these floods. The country's many streams and rivers flood annually, often damaging farms and homes. Summer monsoons also cause flooding. For example, massive flooding in 2004 left more than 25 million people homeless. It also destroyed schools, farms, and roads throughout the country.

From Section 4, India's Neighbors

Identifying Implied Main Ideas

FOCUS ON READING

Main ideas are often stated in a paragraph's topic sentence. When the main idea is not stated directly, however, you can find it by looking at the details in the paragraph. First, read the text carefully and think about the topic. Next, look at the facts and details and ask yourself what details are repeated. What points do those details make? Then create a statement that sums up the main idea. Examine how this process works for the paragraph below.

> Yet, other people increasingly wanted Chinese goods such as silk and tea. To gain access to the goods, some European powers forced China to open up trade in the 1800s. Europeans took over parts of the country as well. These actions angered many Chinese, some of whom blamed the emperor. At the same time, increased contact with the West exposed the Chinese to new ideas.
>
> *From Section 2, History and Culture of China*

1. What is the topic?
China's contact with Europe

2. What are the facts and details?
- Europe forced China to trade.
- Europeans took over some parts of China.
- Some Chinese blamed the emperor.
- The Chinese heard new ideas.

3. What details are repeated?
Increased contact with Europe

4. What is the main idea?
Increased contact with Europe had both positive and negative effects on China.

YOU TRY IT!

Read the following sentences. Then use the steps listed to the right to develop a statement that expresses the main idea of the paragraph.

> Only about 15 percent of China's land is good for farming. So how does China produce so much food? More than half of all Chinese workers are farmers. This large labor force can work the land at high levels. In addition, farmers cut terraces into hillsides to make the most use of the land.
>
> *From Section 3, China Today*

Understanding Fact and Opinion

Focus on Reading

When you read, it is important to distinguish facts from opinions. A fact is a statement that can be proved or disproved. An opinion is a personal belief or attitude, so it cannot be proved true or false. When you are reading a social studies text, you want to read only facts, not the author's opinions. To determine whether a sentence is a fact or an opinion, ask if it can be proved using outside sources. If it can, the sentence is a fact. The following pairs of statements show the difference between facts and opinions.

Fact: Hirohito was Japan's emperor for most of the 1900s. *(This fact can be proved through research.)*

Opinion: I believe Hirohito was Japan's best emperor. *(The word* best *signifies that this is the writer's judgment, or opinion.)*

Fact: One example of a long-lasting Korean food is kimchi, a dish made from pickled cabbage and various spices. *(The ingredients in kimchi can be checked for accuracy.)*

Opinion: Kimchi is a delicious dish made from pickled cabbage and various spices. *(No one can prove kimchi is delicious, because it is a matter of personal taste.)*

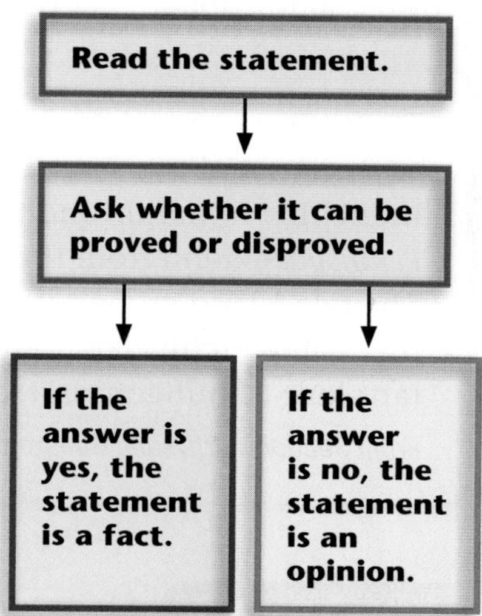

Read the statement.
Ask whether it can be proved or disproved.
If the answer is yes, the statement is a fact.
If the answer is no, the statement is an opinion.

You Try It!

Read the following sentences and identify each as a fact or an opinion.

1. The second largest city in Japan, Osaka, is located in western Honshu.
2. In Osaka—as in Tokyo and other cities—tall modern skyscrapers stand next to tiny Shinto temples.
3. Osaka is more beautiful than Tokyo.
4. Another major city is Kyoto, which all tourists should visit.
5. Once Japan's capital, Kyoto is full of historic buildings.
6. Tokyo has the country's best restaurants.

Using Context Clues—Definitions

FOCUS ON READING

One way to figure out the meaning of an unfamiliar word or term is by finding clues in its context, the words or sentences surrounding the word or term. A common context clue is a restatement. Restatements are simply a definition of the new word using ordinary words you already know. Notice how the following passage uses a restatement to define archipelago. Some context clues are not as complete or obvious. Notice how the following passage provides a description that is a partial definition of peninsula.

The region of Southeast Asia is made up of two *peninsulas* and two large island groups. The Indochina *Peninsula* and the Malay (muh-LAY) *Peninsula* extend from the Asian mainland. . . The two island groups are the Philippines and the Malay Archipelago. An *archipelago* (ahr-kuh-PE-luh-goh) is a large group of islands.

From Section 1, Physical Geography

Peninsula: land that extends from a mainland out into water

Archipelago: large group of islands

YOU TRY IT!

Read the following passages and identify the meaning of the italicized words by using definitions, or restatements, in context.

The many groups that influenced Southeast Asia's history also shaped its culture. This *diverse* culture blends native, Chinese, Indian, and European ways of life.

From Section 2, History and Culture

The economy is based on farming, but good farmland is limited. Most people are *subsistence farmers,* meaning they grow just enough food for their families.

From Section 3, Mainland Southeast Asia Today

Drawing Conclusions

Focus on Reading

You have probably heard the phrase, "Put two and two together." When people say that, they don't mean "2 + 2 = 4." They mean, "put the information together." When you put together information you already know with information you have read, you can draw a conclusion. To make a conclusion, read the passage carefully. Then think about what you already know about the topic. Put the two together to draw a conclusion.

> Off Australia's northeastern coast is the Great Barrier Reef, the world's largest coral reef. A coral reef is a collection of rocky material found in shallow, tropical waters. The Great Barrier Reef is home to an incredible variety of marine animals.
>
> *From Section 1, Australia and New Zealand*

Information gathered from the passage: Australia has the world's largest coral reef.

+

What you already know: I know many people like to snorkel or scuba dive at coral reefs.

=

Add the information up to reach your conclusion: Australia probably has many tourists who come to visit the Great Barrier Reef.

You Try It!

Read the following paragraphs. Think about what you know about living in a very cold climate. Then use the process described above to draw a conclusion about the following passage.

> Because of Antarctica's high latitude, the continent is in almost total darkness during winter months. Seas clog with ice as a result of the extreme temperatures. In the summer, the sun shines around the clock and temperatures rise to near freezing.
>
> Plant life only survives in the ice-free tundra areas. Insects are the frozen land's only land animals. Penguins, seals, and whales live in Antarctica's waters.
>
> *From Section 3, Antarctica*

ATLAS

United States: Physical

Strait of Juan de Fuca
Puget Sound
Mount Rainier 14,410 ft (4,392 m)
CASCADE RANGE
COAST RANGES
Columbia River
Franklin D. Roosevelt Lake
Pend Oreille
Clark Fork
Flathead River
Lewis Range
Flathead Lake
Bitterroot Range
Salmon River
Salmon River Mts.
Sawtooth Mts.
Columbia Plateau
Snake River
Willamette River
Klamath River
Goose Lake
Cape Mendocino
Shasta Lake
Sacramento River
Central Valley
SIERRA NEVADA
Pyramid Lake
Lake Tahoe
San Francisco Bay
San Joaquin River
Monterey Bay
Coast Ranges
Mount Whitney 14,494 ft (4,419 m)
Death Valley
Mojave Desert
GREAT BASIN
Great Salt Lake
Utah Lake
Wasatch Range
Uinta Mts.
ROCKY MOUNTAINS
CONTINENTAL DIVIDE
Milk River
Missouri River
Fort Peck Lake
Yellowstone River
Yellowstone Lake
Grand Tetons
Gannett Peak 13,804 ft (4,207 m)
Wind River Range
Wind River
Bighorn Mts.
Bighorn River
Powder River
Green River
Colorado River
Mount Elbert 14,433 ft (4,400 m)
Pikes Peak 14,110 ft (4,301 m)
Front Range
COLORADO PLATEAU
Lake Powell
San Juan River
San Luis Valley
Sangre De Cristo Mts.
Grand Canyon
Lake Mead
Painted Desert
Rio Grande
Gila River
Sonoran Desert
Salton Sea
Imperial Valley
Gulf of California
PACIFIC OCEAN
Channel Islands
GREAT PLAINS
INTERIOR
Lake Sakakawea
Lake Oahe
Black Hills
Cheyenne River
White River
James River
Niobrara River
North Platte River
Platte River
South Platte River
Republican River
Smoky Hill River
Canadian River
Pecos River
Colorado River
Amistad Reservoir
Nueces River
Padre Island
MEXICO
45°N
40°N
35°N
30°N
125°W
120°W

To understand the relative locations of Alaska and Hawaii, as well as the vast distances separating them from the rest of the United States, see the world map.

HAWAII
Kauai
Niihau
Oahu
Molokai
Maui
Lanai
Kahoolawe
Mauna Kea 13,796 ft (4,206 m)
Hawaii
PACIFIC OCEAN
22°N
19°N
155°W
160°W
0 75 150 Miles
0 75 150 Kilometers
Projection: Mercator

ARCTIC OCEAN
Bering Strait
Arctic Circle
RUSSIA
BROOKS RANGE
Yukon River
Tanana River
St. Lawrence Island
St. Matthew Island
Nunivak Island
Kuskokwim River
ALASKA RANGE
Mount McKinley 20,320 ft (6,194 m)
CANADA
Bering Sea
Attu Island
ALEUTIAN ISLANDS
Kodiak Island
Gulf of Alaska
Alexander Archipelago
PACIFIC OCEAN
0 250 500 Miles
0 250 500 Kilometers
Projection: Albers Equal Area
55°N
50°N
170°E
180°
170°W
160°W
150°W
140°W

ATLAS

CANADA

ATLANTIC OCEAN

Gulf of Mexico

BAHAMAS

Red River
Mesabi Range
Isle Royale
Lake Superior
Minnesota River
Mississippi River
Wisconsin River
Lake Michigan
Lake Huron
Lake Ontario
Lake Erie
St. Lawrence River
St. Lawrence Seaway
St. John River
Lake Champlain
Adirondack Mts.
Green Mts.
White Mts.
Longfellow Mts.
Penobscot River
Hudson R.
Connecticut River
Catskill Mts.
Cape Cod
Long Island Sound
Long Island
40°N
Allegheny R.
PLATEAU
Susquehanna River
Delaware River
MOUNTAINS
Missouri River
Des Moines River
Illinois River
Wabash River
Scioto River
Monongahela R.
Potomac River
Delaware Bay
Kansas R.
PLAINS
ALLEGHENY
APPALACHIAN
Ohio River
Kanawha River
James River
Chesapeake Bay
70°W
Lake of the Ozarks
OZARK PLATEAU
Lake Barkley
Cumberland River
Cumberland Plateau
BLUE RIDGE MOUNTAINS
Roanoke River
PIEDMONT
Pamlico Sound
Cape Hatteras
35°N
Keystone Lake
Kentucky Lake
White River
Arkansas River
Eufaula Lake
Great Smoky Mts.
Tennessee River
Ouachita Mts.
Lake Texoma
Tombigbee River
Coosa River
Oconee River
Savannah River
Chattahoochee River
Alabama R.
Altamaha River
Sea Islands
Trinity River
Saline River
Red River
Mississippi River
Pearl River
Toledo Bend Reservoir
Brazos River
GULF COASTAL PLAIN
Okefenokee Swamp
Chandeleur Islands
Mississippi Delta
FLORIDA PENINSULA
Cape Canaveral
80°W
Lake Okeechobee
The Everglades
Cape Sable
Florida Keys
Straits of Florida
25°N
75°W
95°W
90°W
85°W

N
E
S
W

ELEVATION

Feet	Meters
13,120	4,000
6,560	2,000
1,640	500
656	200
(Sea level) 0	0 (Sea level)
Below sea level	Below sea level

0 100 200 Miles
0 100 200 Kilometers

Projection: Albers Equal Area

United States: Political

To understand the relative locations of Alaska and Hawaii, as well as the vast distances separating them from the rest of the United States, see the world map.

CANADA

MINNESOTA
Grand Forks
Fargo
Duluth
Minneapolis
St. Paul
Red River
Minnesota River

WISCONSIN
Superior
Green Bay
Madison
Milwaukee

MICHIGAN
Marquette
Sault Ste. Marie
Grand Rapids
Lansing
Saginaw
Detroit
Ann Arbor

Lake Superior
Lake Michigan
Lake Huron
Lake Ontario
Lake Erie
Lake Champlain

IOWA
Sioux Falls
Sioux City
Cedar Rapids
Davenport
Des Moines
Omaha
Lincoln

ILLINOIS
Rockford
Chicago
Peoria
Springfield
East St. Louis
Illinois River
Mississippi River
Missouri River

INDIANA
Gary
South Bend
Fort Wayne
Indianapolis
Evansville

OHIO
Toledo
Cleveland
Youngstown
Akron
Columbus
Dayton
Cincinnati

PENNSYLVANIA
Erie
Pittsburgh
Harrisburg
Allentown
Philadelphia
Susquehanna River

NEW YORK
Buffalo
Rochester
Syracuse
Albany
Yonkers
New York City
Hudson R.
St. Lawrence River

VT
Burlington
Montpelier

NH
Concord
Manchester

MAINE
Augusta
Portland

MA
Boston
Worcester
Springfield
Cape Cod

CT
Hartford
Bridgeport
New Haven
Connecticut R.

RI
Providence

Long Island Sound
Long Island

NJ
Jersey City
Newark
Trenton
Camden
Atlantic City

DE
Dover

MD
Baltimore
Annapolis
Washington, D.C.

Delaware Bay
Chesapeake Bay

WEST VIRGINIA
Charleston

VIRGINIA
Richmond
Newport News
Norfolk
Virginia Beach

ATLANTIC OCEAN

KENTUCKY
Louisville
Frankfort
Lexington
Ohio River
Lake Barkley

MISSOURI
Kansas City
Kansas City
Topeka
St. Louis
Jefferson City
Wichita
Lake of the Ozarks
Springfield

Keystone Lake
Tulsa
Eufaula Lake
Lake Texoma

TENNESSEE
Nashville
Knoxville
Chattanooga
Memphis
Kentucky Lake

NORTH CAROLINA
Winston-Salem
Greensboro
Durham
Raleigh
Asheville
Charlotte
Cape Hatteras

ARKANSAS
Fayetteville
Little Rock
Pine Bluff

SOUTH CAROLINA
Greenville
Columbia
Charleston
Savannah River

MISSISSIPPI
Vicksburg
Jackson
Meridian
Biloxi

ALABAMA
Huntsville
Birmingham
Montgomery
Mobile

GEORGIA
Atlanta
Macon
Columbus
Savannah
Sea Islands
Chattahoochee R.

LOUISIANA
Shreveport
Baton Rouge
New Orleans
Red River
Toledo Bend Reservoir
Chandeleur Islands

Dallas
Waco
Beaumont
Houston
Galveston

FLORIDA
Pensacola
Tallahassee
Jacksonville
Gainesville
Orlando
Cape Canaveral
Tampa
St. Petersburg
Lake Okeechobee
Fort Myers
Fort Lauderdale
Miami
Cape Sable
Florida Keys
Straits of Florida

Gulf of Mexico

BAHAMAS

40°N
35°N
30°N
25°N
70°W
75°W
80°W
85°W
90°W
95°W

N
S
E
W

National capital
State capitals
Other cities

0 100 200 Miles
0 100 200 Kilometers

Projection: Albers Equal Area

World: Physical

ELEVATION

Feet	Meters
13,120	4,000
6,560	2,000
1,640	500
656	200
(Sea level) 0	0 (Sea level)
Below sea level	Below sea level

Ice cap

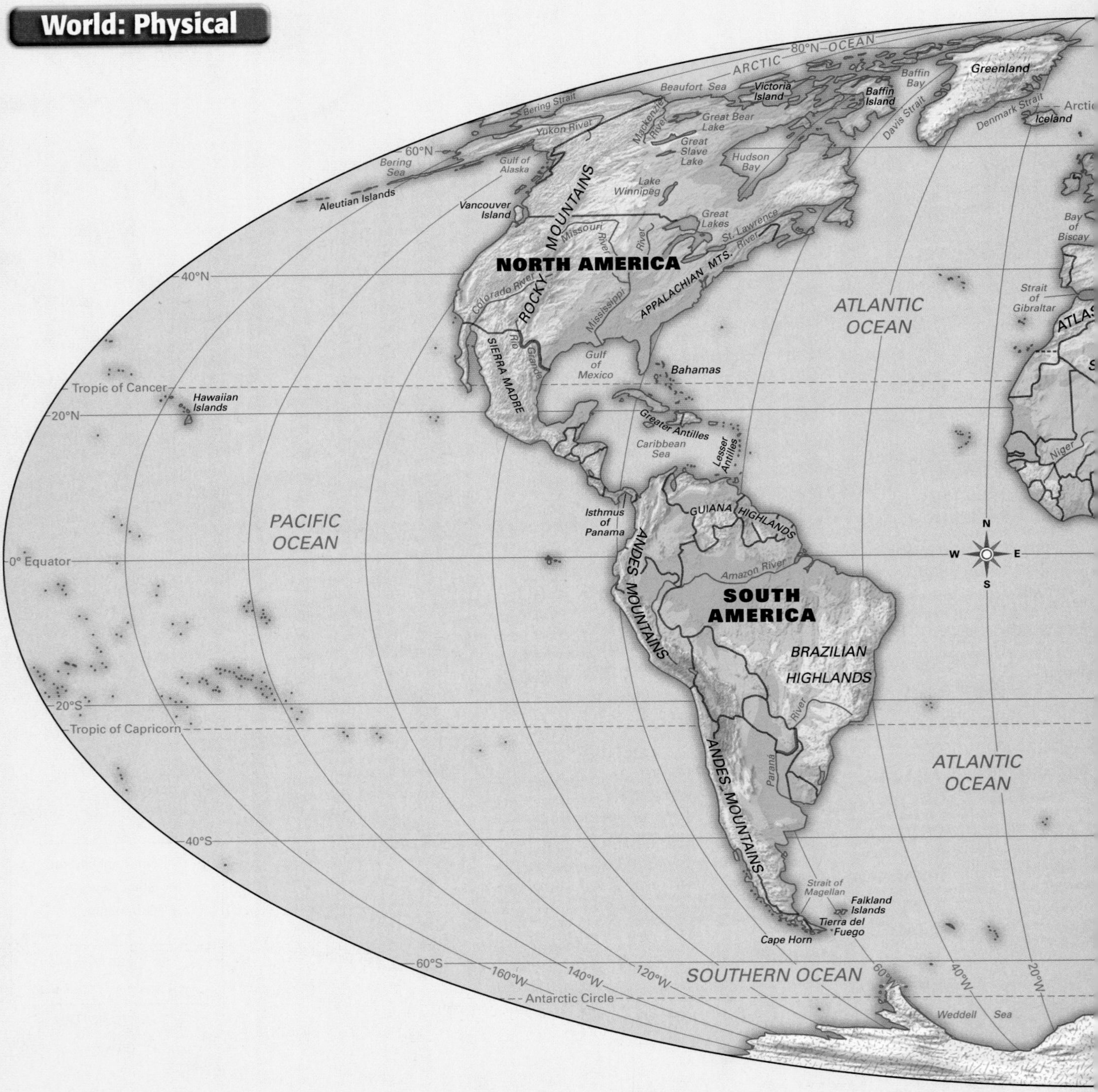

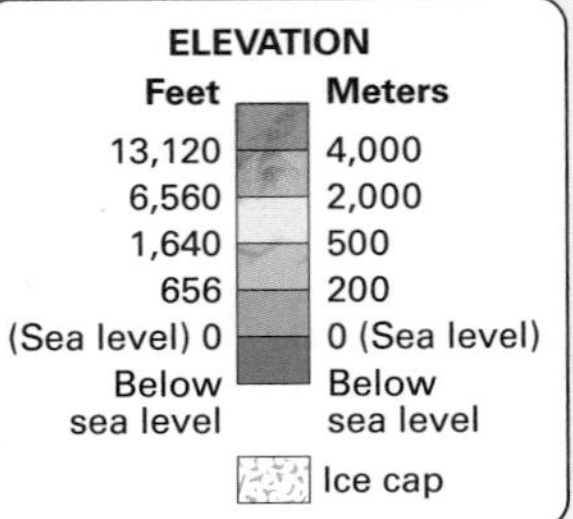

0 500 1,000 1,500 2,000 Miles
0 1,000 2,000 Kilometers
Projection: Mollweide

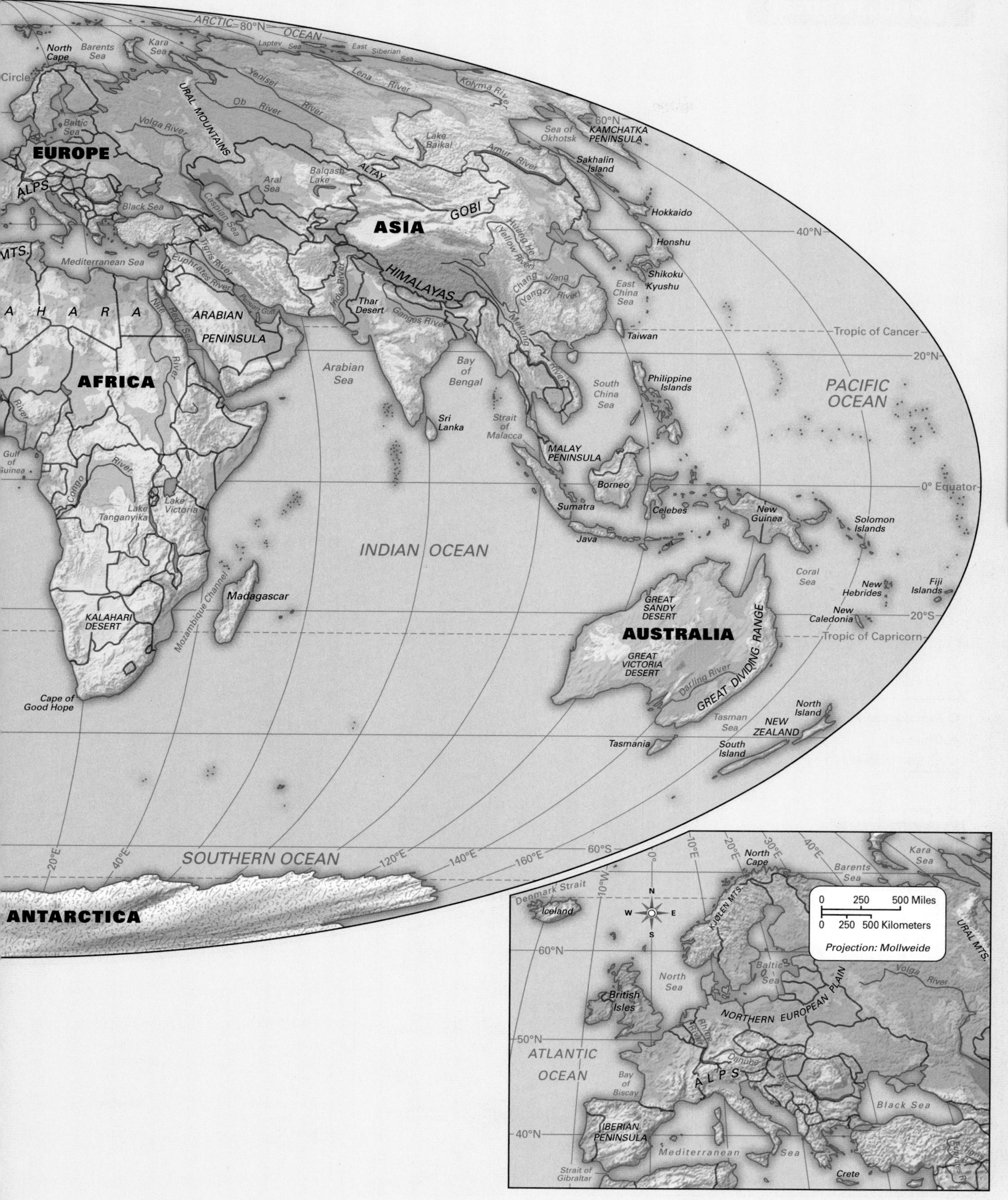
ARCTIC OCEAN
80°N
North Cape
Barents Sea
Kara Sea
Laptev Sea
East Siberian Sea
Circle
Yenisei River
Lena River
Kolyma River
URAL MOUNTAINS
Ob River
Baltic Sea
Volga River
60°N
Sea of Okhotsk
KAMCHATKA PENINSULA
Lake Baikal
Amur River
Sakhalin Island
EUROPE
ALPS
Aral Sea
Balqash Lake
ALTAY
Black Sea
Caspian Sea
GOBI
Hokkaido
ASIA
Huang He (Yellow River)
Honshu
40°N
MTS.
Mediterranean Sea
Tigris River
Euphrates River
Indus River
HIMALAYAS
Chang Jiang (Yangzi River)
Shikoku
Kyushu
East China Sea
S A H A R A
Nile
Red Sea
Persian Gulf
ARABIAN PENINSULA
Thar Desert
Ganges River
Mekong River
Taiwan
Tropic of Cancer
20°N
AFRICA
River
Arabian Sea
Bay of Bengal
South China Sea
Philippine Islands
PACIFIC OCEAN
Sri Lanka
Strait of Malacca
Gulf of Guinea
MALAY PENINSULA
Congo River
Lake Tanganyika
Lake Victoria
Borneo
0° Equator
Sumatra
Celebes
New Guinea
Solomon Islands
Java
INDIAN OCEAN
Coral Sea
Madagascar
Mozambique Channel
GREAT SANDY DESERT
New Hebrides
Fiji Islands
KALAHARI DESERT
New Caledonia
20°S
AUSTRALIA
GREAT DIVIDING RANGE
Tropic of Capricorn
GREAT VICTORIA DESERT
Darling River
Cape of Good Hope
North Island
Tasman Sea
NEW ZEALAND
Tasmania
South Island
20°E
40°E
SOUTHERN OCEAN
120°E
140°E
160°E
60°S
ANTARCTICA
10°E
0°
20°E
30°E
40°E
North Cape
Barents Sea
Kara Sea
Denmark Strait
10°W
Iceland
N
W
E
S
KJØLEN MTS.
0 250 500 Miles
0 250 500 Kilometers
Projection: Mollweide
URAL MTS.
60°N
North Sea
Baltic Sea
Volga River
British Isles
NORTHERN EUROPEAN PLAIN
50°N
Rhine
Danube
ATLANTIC OCEAN
Bay of Biscay
ALPS
Black Sea
IBERIAN PENINSULA
40°N
Mediterranean Sea
Strait of Gibraltar
Crete

World: Political

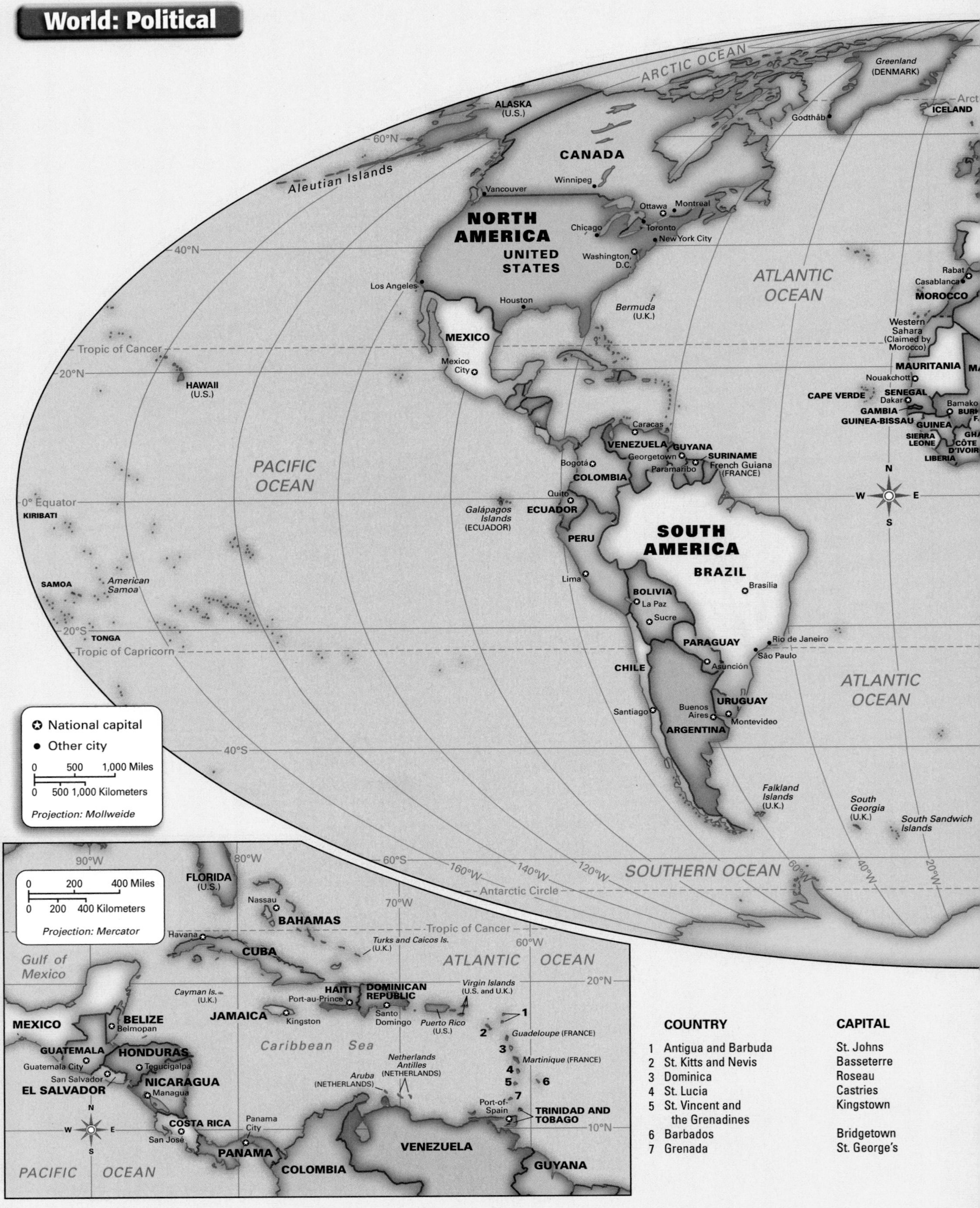

	COUNTRY	CAPITAL
1	Antigua and Barbuda	St. Johns
2	St. Kitts and Nevis	Basseterre
3	Dominica	Roseau
4	St. Lucia	Castries
5	St. Vincent and the Grenadines	Kingstown
6	Barbados	Bridgetown
7	Grenada	St. George's

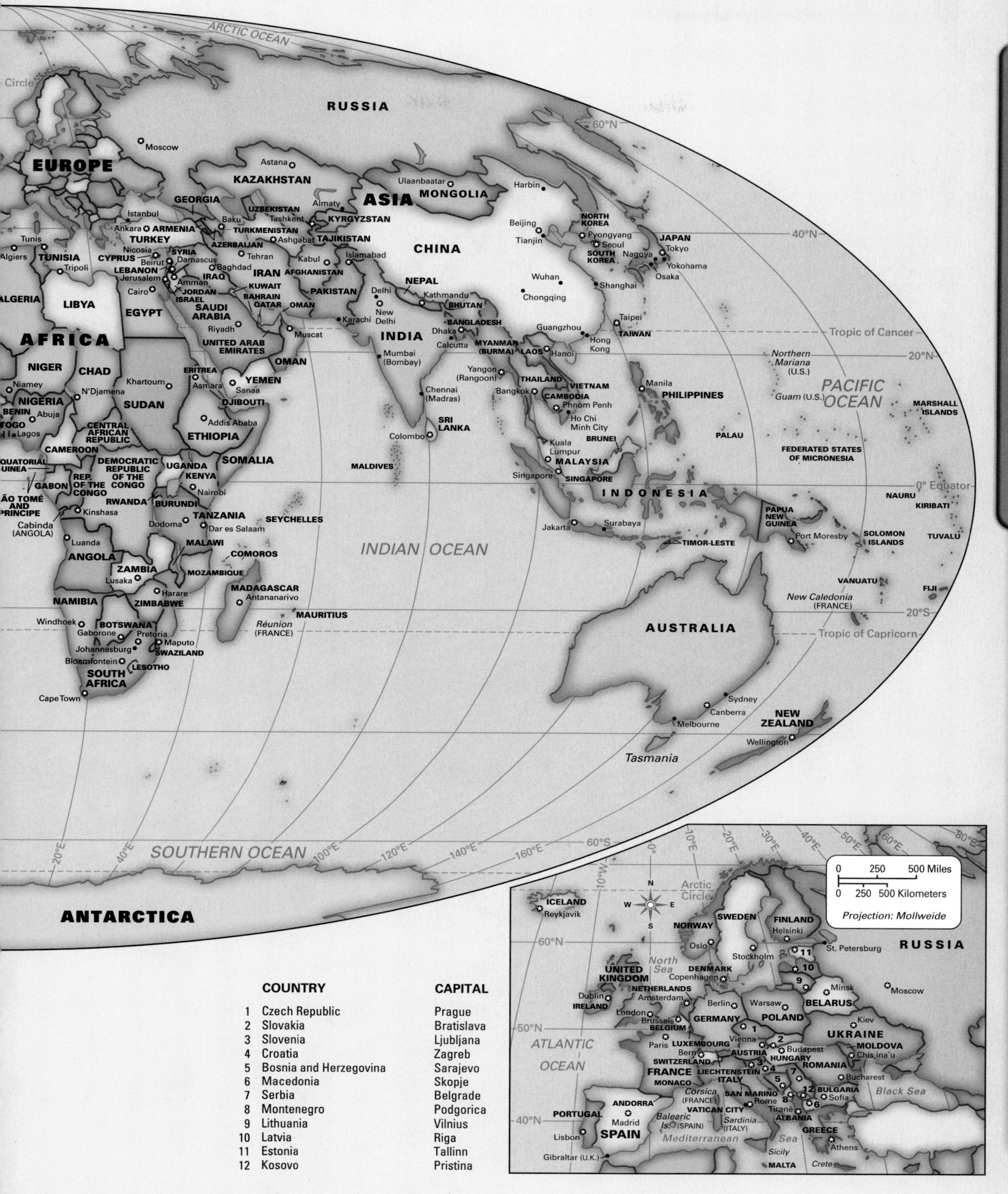

	COUNTRY	CAPITAL
1	Czech Republic	Prague
2	Slovakia	Bratislava
3	Slovenia	Ljubljana
4	Croatia	Zagreb
5	Bosnia and Herzegovina	Sarajevo
6	Macedonia	Skopje
7	Serbia	Belgrade
8	Montenegro	Podgorica
9	Lithuania	Vilnius
10	Latvia	Riga
11	Estonia	Tallinn
12	Kosovo	Pristina

North America: Physical

ARCTIC OCEAN
North Pole
POLAR ICE PACK
ASIA
EUROPE
St. Lawrence Island
Bering Sea
Bering Strait
Nunivak Island
BROOKS RANGE
Mt. McKinley 20,320 ft (6,194 m)
ALASKA RANGE
Yukon River
Beaufort Sea
Queen Elizabeth Islands
Ellesmere Island
Greenland
Denmark Strait
Arctic Circle
Baffin Bay
Banks Island
Victoria Island
Baffin Island
Davis Strait
Cape Farewell
Kodiak Island
Gulf of Alaska
YUKON PLATEAU
Great Bear Lake
Mackenzie River
Great Slave Lake
Southampton Island
Hudson Strait
Coats Island
Mansel Island
Labrador Sea
Hudson Bay
Alexander Archipelago
Queen Charlotte Islands
ROCKY MOUNTAINS
Peace River
Athabasca River
Lake Athabasca
CANADIAN SHIELD
Nelson River
Saskatchewan River
Lake Winnipeg
Anticosti Island
Newfoundland
Gulf of St. Lawrence
Prince Edward Island
Cape Breton Island
St. Lawrence River
PACIFIC OCEAN
Vancouver Island
Fraser River
Mount Rainier 14,410 ft (4,392 m)
CASCADE RANGE
COAST RANGES
Columbia River
GREAT PLAINS
Missouri River
Lake Superior
Lake Michigan
Lake Huron
Lake Ontario
Lake Erie
Mississippi River
Cape Cod
Long Island
ATLANTIC OCEAN
Cape Mendocino
Snake River
BLACK HILLS
Great Salt Lake
GREAT BASIN
SIERRA NEVADA
CENTRAL VALLEY
DEATH VALLEY
Mount Whitney 14,494 ft (4,418 m)
Colorado River
COLORADO PLATEAU
Platte River
INTERIOR PLAINS
Ohio River
Cumberland R.
Tennessee River
APPALACHIAN MOUNTAINS
PIEDMONT
ATLANTIC COASTAL PLAIN
OZARK PLATEAU
Arkansas River
Red River
Brazos River
Rio Grande
Cape Hatteras
Bermuda
Guadalupe Island
BAJA CALIFORNIA
Gulf of California
SIERRA MADRE OCCIDENTAL
SIERRA MADRE ORIENTAL
GULF COASTAL PLAIN
FLORIDA PENINSULA
Cape Canaveral
Tropic of Cancer
Bahamas
Gulf of Mexico
Florida Keys
Straits of Florida
Cuba
Greater Antilles
Hispaniola
Puerto Rico
Lesser Antilles
Jamaica
Popocatépetl 17,887 ft (5,452 m)
YUCATÁN PENINSULA
Caribbean Sea
Trinidad
SIERRA MADRE DEL SUR
Lake Nicaragua
CENTRAL AMERICA
ISTHMUS OF PANAMA
SOUTH AMERICA
0° Equator

ELEVATION

Feet	Meters
13,120	4,000
6,560	2,000
1,640	500
656	200
(Sea level) 0	0 (Sea level)
Below sea level	Below sea level

Ice cap

0 300 600 Miles
0 300 600 Kilometers

Projection: Azimuthal Equal Area

North America: Political

ARCTIC OCEAN
North Pole
ASIA
EUROPE
ICELAND
Greenland (DENMARK)
Arctic Circle
Denmark Strait
Bering Strait
Bering Sea
St. Lawrence Island
Nunivak Island
Point Barrow
Beaufort Sea
Queen Elizabeth Islands
Ellesmere Island
Banks Island
Victoria Island
Baffin Bay
Baffin Island
Davis Strait
Cape Farewell
ALASKA (U.S.)
Anchorage
Gulf of Alaska
Kodiak Island
Great Bear Lake
Great Slave Lake
Southampton Island
Coats Island
Mansel Island
Hudson Strait
Labrador Sea
Hudson Bay
Juneau
Alexander Archipelago
Queen Charlotte Islands
PACIFIC OCEAN
Vancouver Island
Edmonton
CANADA
Calgary
Lake Winnipeg
Anticosti Island
Newfoundland
Gulf of St. Lawrence
Prince Edward Island
Cape Breton Island
St. Pierre and Miquelon (FRANCE)
Vancouver
Seattle
Portland
Winnipeg
Lake Superior
Lake Huron
Quebec
Montreal
Ottawa
Toronto
Lake Ontario
Boston
Cape Cod
Minneapolis
Lake Michigan
Lake Erie
New York City
Philadelphia
Milwaukee
Detroit
Cleveland
Columbus
Chicago
Baltimore
Washington, D.C.
ATLANTIC OCEAN
San Francisco
San Jose
Great Salt Lake
Salt Lake City
Denver
Kansas City
Indianapolis
St. Louis
Norfolk
UNITED STATES
Los Angeles
San Diego
Tijuana
Phoenix
Memphis
Atlanta
Birmingham
Bermuda (U.K.)
Dallas
Jacksonville
Gulf of California
Austin
San Antonio
Houston
New Orleans
Tropic of Cancer
Miami
BAHAMAS
Nassau
Turks and Caicos Islands (U.K.)
Gulf of Mexico
Florida Keys
Straits of Florida
Monterrey
DOMINICAN REPUBLIC
Puerto Rico (U.S.)
ST. KITTS & NEVIS
ANTIGUA & BARBUDA
Guadeloupe (FRANCE)
San Juan
Havana
CUBA
MEXICO
DOMINICA
BARBADOS
Guadalajara
Mexico City
Mérida
HAITI
Santo Domingo
Virgin Is. (U.S., U.K.)
Martinique (FRANCE)
ST. LUCIA
ST. VINCENT AND THE GRENADINES
Cayman Is. (U.K.)
Kingston
Port-au-Prince
JAMAICA
Puebla
Belmopan
BELIZE
Caribbean Sea
Netherlands Antilles (NETHERLANDS)
GRENADA
GUATEMALA
HONDURAS
Guatemala City
Tegucigalpa
Aruba (NETHERLANDS)
TRINIDAD AND TOBAGO
San Salvador
NICARAGUA
Managua
EL SALVADOR
Panama Canal
San José
Panama City
COSTA RICA
PANAMA
SOUTH AMERICA
0° Equator

160°E
170°E
180°
170°W
160°W
150°W
140°W
130°W
120°W
110°W
100°W
90°W
80°N
70°N
60°N
50°N
40°N
30°N
20°N
10°N
10°E
0°
10°W
20°W
30°W
40°W
50°W

N
S
E
W

National capital
Other city
0 300 600 Miles
0 300 600 Kilometers
Projection: Azimuthal Equal-Area

ATLAS

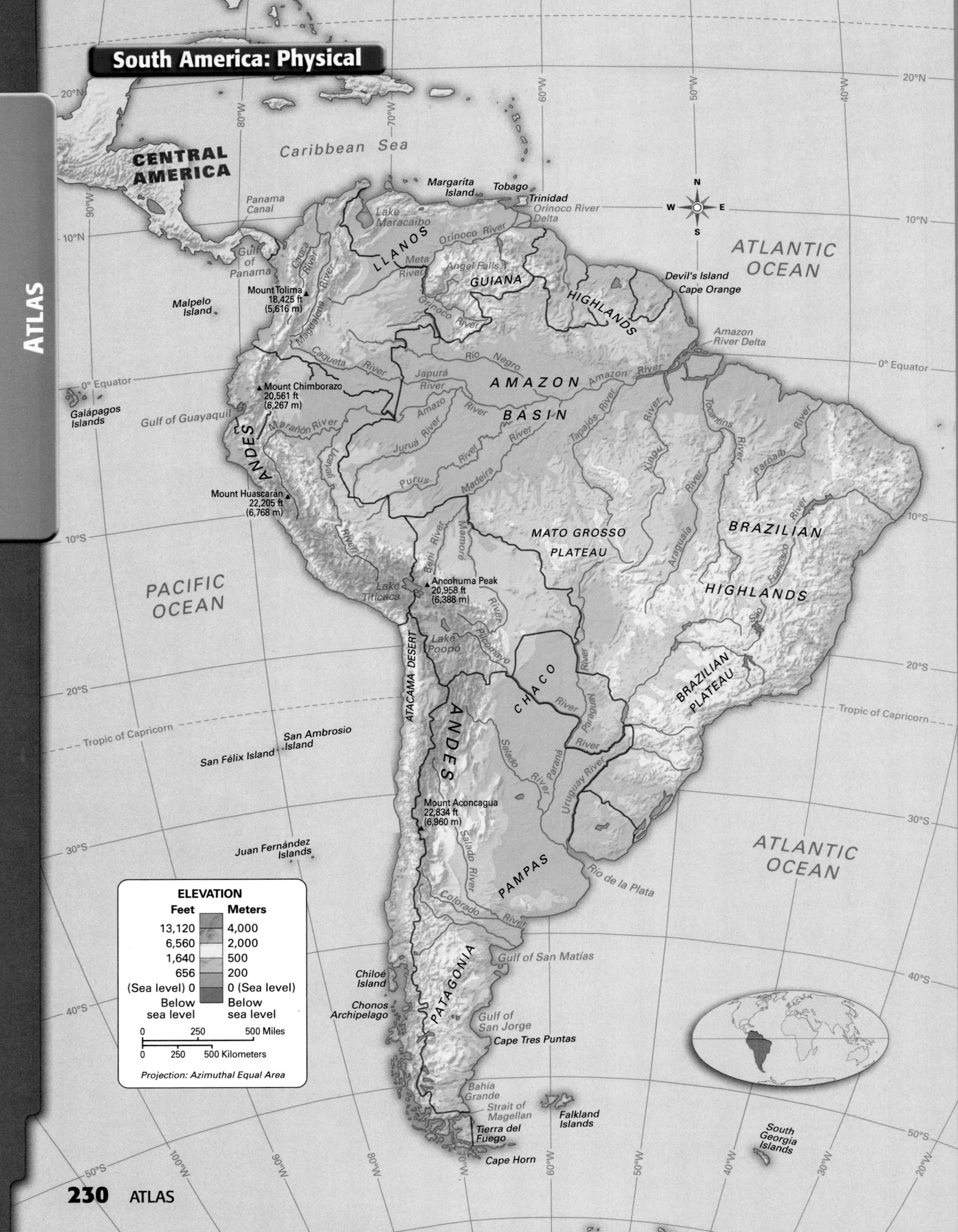
South America: Physical
ATLAS
CENTRAL AMERICA
Caribbean Sea
Panama Canal
Gulf of Panama
Margarita Island
Tobago
Trinidad
Orinoco River Delta
Lake Maracaibo
LLANOS
Orinoco River
Meta River
Angel Falls
GUIANA
HIGHLANDS
ATLANTIC OCEAN
Devil's Island
Cape Orange
Amazon River Delta
Mount Tolima 18,425 ft (5,616 m)
Malpelo Island
Cauca River
Magdalena River
Caqueta River
Japurá River
Río Negro
AMAZON
BASIN
Amazon River
0° Equator
Mount Chimborazo 20,561 ft (6,267 m)
Galápagos Islands
Gulf of Guayaquil
Marañón River
ANDES
Juruá River
Purus River
Madeira River
Tapajós River
Xingu River
Tocantins River
Araguaia River
Parnaíb River
Ucayali
Mount Huascarán 22,205 ft (6,768 m)
MATO GROSSO PLATEAU
BRAZILIAN HIGHLANDS
São Francisco River
Beni River
Mamoré
Lake Titicaca
Ancohuma Peak 20,958 ft (6,388 m)
PACIFIC OCEAN
Lake Poopó
Pilcomayo
ATACAMA DESERT
CHACO
Paraguay River
BRAZILIAN PLATEAU
Tropic of Capricorn
San Ambrosio Island
San Félix Island
Salado River
Paraná River
Uruguay River
Mount Aconcagua 22,834 ft (6,960 m)
Juan Fernández Islands
PAMPAS
Río de la Plata
Colorado River
ATLANTIC OCEAN
ELEVATION
Feet / Meters
13,120 / 4,000
6,560 / 2,000
1,640 / 500
656 / 200
(Sea level) 0 / 0 (Sea level)
Below sea level / Below sea level
0 250 500 Miles
0 250 500 Kilometers
Projection: Azimuthal Equal Area
Gulf of San Matías
Chiloé Island
Chonos Archipelago
PATAGONIA
Gulf of San Jorge
Cape Tres Puntas
Bahía Grande
Strait of Magellan
Falkland Islands
Tierra del Fuego
Cape Horn
South Georgia Islands
N S E W
20°N
10°N
10°S
20°S
30°S
40°S
50°S
90°W
80°W
70°W
60°W
50°W
40°W
30°W
20°W
100°W

South America: Political
Caribbean Sea
CENTRAL AMERICA
Barranquilla
Cartagena
Caracas
Lake Maracaibo
VENEZUELA
Georgetown
GUYANA
Paramaribo
SURINAME
Cayenne
French Guiana (FRANCE)
ATLANTIC OCEAN
Medellín
Bogotá
COLOMBIA
Cali
Malpelo Island (COLOMBIA)
Quito
ECUADOR
Guayaquil
Galápagos Islands (ECUADOR)
0° Equator
Belém
PERU
BRAZIL
Recife
Trujillo
Callao
Lima
Lake Titicaca
La Paz
Lake Poopó
BOLIVIA
Sucre
Arequipa
PACIFIC OCEAN
Brasília
Salvador
Belo Horizonte
PARAGUAY
Asunción
Campinas
São Paulo
Rio de Janeiro
Curitiba
Tropic of Capricorn
San Ambrosio Island (CHILE)
San Félix Island (CHILE)
CHILE
Pôrto Alegre
Córdoba
Rosario
URUGUAY
Valparaíso
Santiago
Juan Fernández Islands (CHILE)
Buenos Aires
Montevideo
ARGENTINA
ATLANTIC OCEAN
National capital
Other city
0 250 500 Miles
0 250 500 Kilometers
Projection: Azimuthal Equal-Area
Strait of Magellan
Falkland Islands (U.K.)
Tierra del Fuego
South Georgia Island (U.K.)
ATLAS

Europe: Physical

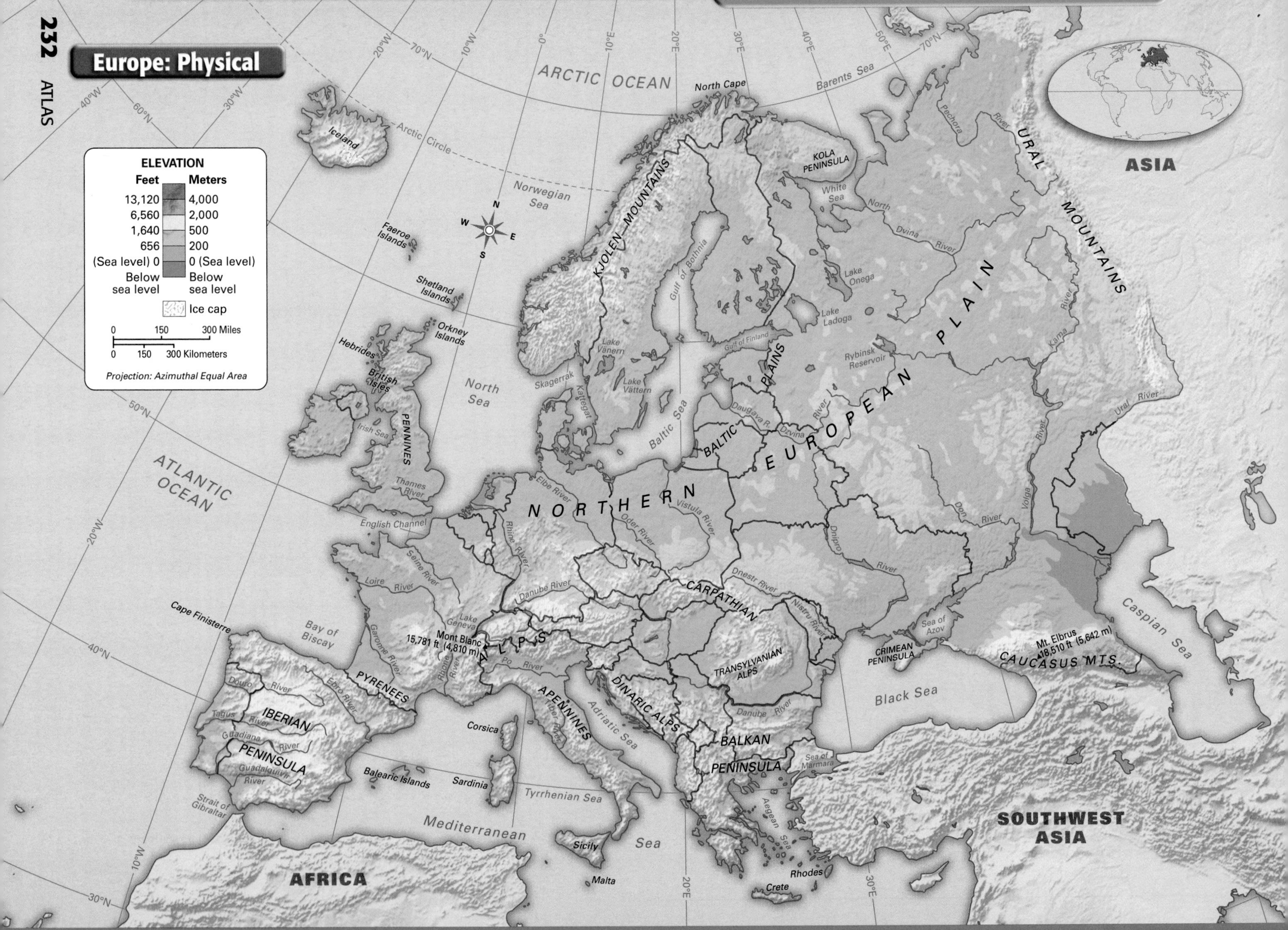

ELEVATION

Feet	Meters
13,120	4,000
6,560	2,000
1,640	500
656	200
(Sea level) 0	0 (Sea level)
Below sea level	Below sea level

Ice cap

0 150 300 Miles
0 150 300 Kilometers

Projection: Azimuthal Equal Area

ARCTIC OCEAN
Barents Sea
North Cape
Arctic Circle
Norwegian Sea
Iceland
Faeroe Islands
Shetland Islands
Orkney Islands
Hebrides
British Isles
Irish Sea
PENNINES
Thames River
North Sea
English Channel
ATLANTIC OCEAN
Bay of Biscay
Cape Finisterre
KOLA PENINSULA
White Sea
KJOLEN MOUNTAINS
Gulf of Bothnia
Gulf of Finland
Lake Vänern
Lake Vättern
Skagerrak
Kattegat
Baltic Sea
Lake Onega
Lake Ladoga
North Dvina River
Rybinsk Reservoir
Pechora River
URAL MOUNTAINS
Ural River
Kama River
Volga River
Don River
Dnipro River
Dnestr River
Nistru River
Daugava R.
Dvina River
BALTIC PLAINS
NORTHERN EUROPEAN PLAIN
ASIA
Elbe River
Oder River
Vistula River
Rhine River
Seine River
Loire River
Garonne River
Rhône River
Danube River
Lake Geneva
Mont Blanc 15,781 ft (4,810 m)
ALPS
Po River
CARPATHIAN
TRANSYLVANIAN ALPS
Sea of Azov
CRIMEAN PENINSULA
Black Sea
Mt. Elbrus 18,510 ft (5,642 m)
CAUCASUS MTS.
Caspian Sea
PYRENEES
Douro River
Ebro River
Tagus River
Guadiana River
Guadalquivir River
IBERIAN PENINSULA
Strait of Gibraltar
Balearic Islands
Corsica
Sardinia
APENNINES
Tiber River
Adriatic Sea
DINARIC ALPS
BALKAN PENINSULA
Sea of Marmara
Aegean Sea
Tyrrhenian Sea
Mediterranean Sea
Sicily
Malta
Crete
Rhodes
AFRICA
SOUTHWEST ASIA
70°N
60°N
50°N
40°N
30°N
40°W
30°W
20°W
10°W
0°
10°E
20°E
30°E
40°E
50°E

Europe: Political

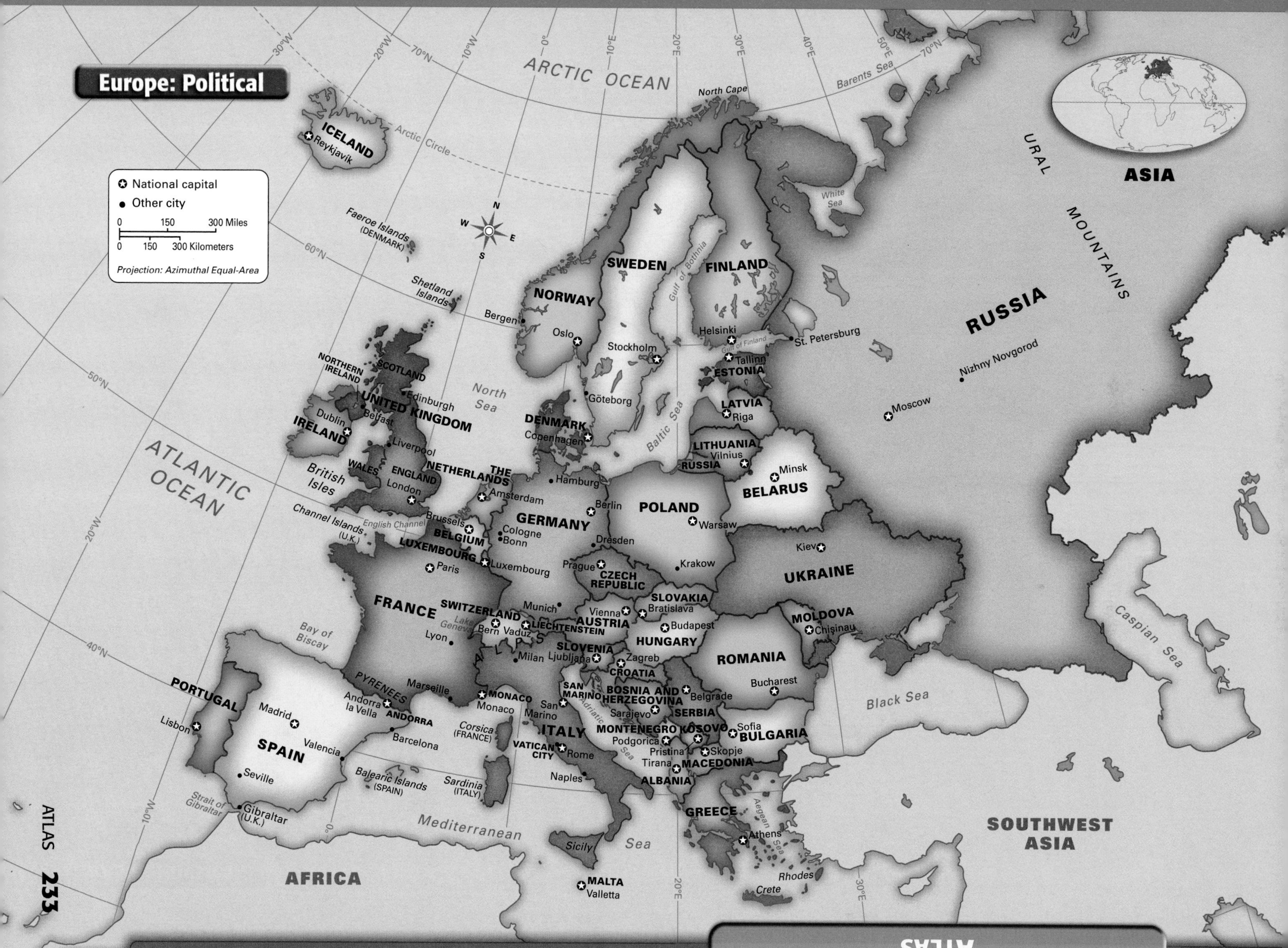

- ✪ National capital
- • Other city

0 150 300 Miles
0 150 300 Kilometers

Projection: Azimuthal Equal-Area

ARCTIC OCEAN
ATLANTIC OCEAN
North Sea
Baltic Sea
Gulf of Bothnia
Gulf of Finland
Barents Sea
White Sea
Bay of Biscay
Mediterranean Sea
Adriatic Sea
Aegean Sea
Black Sea
Caspian Sea
English Channel
Strait of Gibraltar
Arctic Circle
North Cape
URAL MOUNTAINS
PYRENEES
ALPS
ASIA
SOUTHWEST ASIA
AFRICA
British Isles

ICELAND
Reykjavik
Faeroe Islands (DENMARK)
Shetland Islands
NORWAY
Oslo
Bergen
SWEDEN
Stockholm
Göteborg
FINLAND
Helsinki
RUSSIA
St. Petersburg
Moscow
Nizhny Novgorod
ESTONIA
Tallinn
LATVIA
Riga
LITHUANIA
Vilnius
BELARUS
Minsk
UKRAINE
Kiev
MOLDOVA
Chișinau
DENMARK
Copenhagen
UNITED KINGDOM
SCOTLAND
NORTHERN IRELAND
ENGLAND
WALES
Edinburgh
Belfast
Liverpool
London
IRELAND
Dublin
Channel Islands (U.K.)
THE NETHERLANDS
Amsterdam
BELGIUM
Brussels
LUXEMBOURG
Luxembourg
GERMANY
Hamburg
Berlin
Cologne
Bonn
Dresden
Munich
POLAND
Warsaw
Krakow
CZECH REPUBLIC
Prague
SLOVAKIA
Bratislava
AUSTRIA
Vienna
HUNGARY
Budapest
ROMANIA
Bucharest
BULGARIA
Sofia
FRANCE
Paris
Lyon
Marseille
SWITZERLAND
Bern
Lake Geneva
LIECHTENSTEIN
Vaduz
MONACO
Monaco
ANDORRA
Andorra la Vella
SPAIN
Madrid
Barcelona
Valencia
Seville
Gibraltar (U.K.)
PORTUGAL
Lisbon
Balearic Islands (SPAIN)
Corsica (FRANCE)
Sardinia (ITALY)
ITALY
Milan
Rome
Naples
Sicily
SAN MARINO
San Marino
VATICAN CITY
MALTA
Valletta
SLOVENIA
Ljubljana
CROATIA
Zagreb
BOSNIA AND HERZEGOVINA
Sarajevo
SERBIA
Belgrade
MONTENEGRO
Podgorica
KOSOVO
Pristina
MACEDONIA
Skopje
ALBANIA
Tirana
GREECE
Athens
Crete
Rhodes

70°N
60°N
50°N
40°N
30°W
20°W
10°W
0°
10°E
20°E
30°E
40°E
50°E

ATLAS

Asia: Physical

ELEVATION

Feet	Meters
13,120	4,000
6,560	2,000
1,640	500
656	200
(Sea level) 0	0 (Sea level)
Below sea level	Below sea level

Ice cap

0 250 500 750 Miles
0 250 500 750 Kilometers

Projection: Two-Point Equidistant

North Pole
EUROPE
AFRICA
AUSTRALIA
PACIFIC OCEAN
INDIAN OCEAN
Arctic Circle
Tropic of Cancer
0° Equator
Mediterranean Sea
Black Sea
Bosporus
Caspian Sea
Red Sea
Persian Gulf
Strait of Hormuz
Gulf of Oman
Gulf of Aden
Arabian Sea
Bay of Bengal
Andaman Sea
Barents Sea
Kara Sea
Laptev Sea
Bering Sea
Sea of Okhotsk
Sea of Japan (East Sea)
Korea Strait
Yellow Sea
East China Sea
Luzon Strait
South China Sea
Gulf of Tonkin
Gulf of Thailand
Strait of Malacca
Java Sea
Celebes Sea
Banda Sea
Arafura Sea
Franz Josef Land
Novaya Zemlya
North Land
TAYMYR PENINSULA
New Siberian Islands
Wrangel Island
Aleutian Islands
KAMCHATKA PENINSULA
CENTRAL RANGE
Sakhalin Island
Kuril Islands
Hokkaido
Honshu
Shikoku
Kyushu
Ryukyu Islands
Okinawa
Taiwan
Luzon
Philippines
Mindanao
Hainan
Borneo
Celebes
Moluccas
New Guinea
MAOKE MOUNTAINS
Sumatra
Bangka
Java
Mentawai Islands
Andaman Islands
Nicobar Islands
Sri Lanka
Maldives
Lakshadweep Islands
Socotra Island
Cyprus
SINAI PENINSULA
ANATOLIAN PLATEAU
Mount Ararat 16,945 ft (5,165 m)
CAUCASUS MTS.
SYRIAN DESERT
AN-NAFUD
RUB' AL-KHALI
ZAGROS MTS.
GREAT SALT DESERT
Tigris River
Euphrates River
USTYURT PLATEAU
Aral Sea
Ural River
URAL MOUNTAINS
TURAN LOWLAND
KYZYL KUM
KARA KUM
Amu Darya
Syr Darya
KAZAKH UPLANDS
Balqash Lake
Ishim River
Irtysh River
Ob River
WEST SIBERIAN PLAIN
S I B E R I A
Yenisey River
Lower Tunguska River
Angara River
CENTRAL SIBERIAN PLATEAU
Lena River
Aldan River
VERKHOYANSKIY RANGE
CHERSKIY RANGE
KOLYMA MTS.
STANOVOY MOUNTAINS
Amur River
Lake Baykal
YABLONOVY RANGE
Shilka River
SAYAN MOUNTAINS
ALTAY MOUNTAINS
MONGOLIAN PLATEAU
GREATER KHINGAN RANGE
GOBI
TIAN SHAN
TARIM BASIN
TAKLIMAKAN DESERT
HINDU KUSH
KUNLUN MOUNTAINS
PLATEAU OF TIBET
H I M A L A Y A S
Mount Everest 29,035 ft (8,850 m)
Nu River
Brahmaputra River
Indus River
Sutlej River
Ganges River
INDO-GANGETIC PLAIN
THAR DESERT
DECCAN PLATEAU
Godavari River
EASTERN GHATS
WESTERN GHATS
Irrawaddy River
Huang He (Yellow River)
NORTH CHINA PLAIN
QIN LING
Chang Jiang (Yangzi River)
BOHEA HILLS
Xi River
Hong River
Mekong River
Chao Phraya River
INDOCHINA PENINSULA
MALAY PENINSULA
0° 10°E 20°E 30°E 40°E 50°E 60°E 70°E 80°E 90°E 100°E 110°E 120°E 130°E 140°E 150°E 160°E 170°E 180° 170°W
10°S 10°N 20°N 30°N 40°N 50°N 60°N 70°N 80°N
N S E W

Asia: Political

National capitals
Other cities
0 250 500 750 Miles
0 250 500 750 Kilometers
Projection: Two-Point Equidistant

North Pole
Arctic Circle
Tropic of Cancer
0° Equator

EUROPE
AFRICA
AUSTRALIA
PACIFIC OCEAN
INDIAN OCEAN
URAL MOUNTAINS

RUSSIA
Moscow
Chelyabinsk
Yekaterinburg
Omsk
Novosibirsk
Irkutsk
Yakutsk
Vladivostok
Sakhalin Island
Kuril Islands (RUSSIA)
Aleutian Islands
KAZAKHSTAN
Astana
Almaty
UZBEKISTAN
Tashkent
TURKMENISTAN
Ashgabat
KYRGYZSTAN
Bishkek
TAJIKISTAN
Dushanbe
AFGHANISTAN
Kabul
PAKISTAN
Islamabad
Lahore
Karachi
MONGOLIA
Ulaanbaatar
CHINA
Beijing
Harbin
Fushun
Dalian
Qingdao
Nanjing
Shanghai
Wuhan
Chengdu
Chongqing
Guangzhou
Hong Kong
Macao
Hainan (CHINA)
NORTH KOREA
Pyongyang
SOUTH KOREA
Seoul
Pusan
JAPAN
Tokyo
Yokohama
Sapporo
Kyoto
Osaka
Hiroshima
Nagasaki
Ryukyu Islands (JAPAN)
TAIWAN
Taipei
PHILIPPINES
Manila
INDIA
New Delhi
Delhi
Jaipur
Ahmadabad
Mumbai (Bombay)
Bangalore
Chennai (Madras)
Kolkata (Calcutta)
Lakshadweep Islands (INDIA)
Andaman Islands (INDIA)
Nicobar Islands (INDIA)
NEPAL
Kathmandu
BHUTAN
Thimphu
BANGLADESH
Dhaka
SRI LANKA
Colombo
MALDIVES
Male
MYANMAR (BURMA)
Mandalay
Yangon (Rangoon)
LAOS
Vientiane
THAILAND
Bangkok
CAMBODIA
Phnom Penh
VIETNAM
Hanoi
Ho Chi Minh City
MALAYSIA
Kuala Lumpur
SINGAPORE
Singapore
BRUNEI
Bandar Seri Begawan
INDONESIA
Jakarta
Bandung
Surabaya
Ujung Pandang
Medan
TIMOR-LESTE
Dili
New Guinea
TURKEY
Istanbul
Izmir
Ankara
GEORGIA
Tbilisi
ARMENIA
Yerevan
AZERBAIJAN
Baku
CYPRUS
Nicosia
SYRIA
Damascus
LEBANON
Beirut
ISRAEL
Tel Aviv
Jerusalem
JORDAN
Amman
IRAQ
Baghdad
Mosul
Basra
IRAN
Tehran
Shiraz
KUWAIT
Kuwait City
BAHRAIN
Manama
QATAR
Doha
UNITED ARAB EMIRATES
Abu Dhabi
OMAN
Masqat (Muscat)
SAUDI ARABIA
Riyadh
Mecca
Jidda
YEMEN
Sanaa
Socotra (YEMEN)

Mediterranean Sea
Black Sea
Caspian Sea
Aral Sea
Lake Balkhash
Lake Baykal
Barents Sea
Kara Sea
Laptev Sea
Bering Sea
Sea of Okhotsk
Yellow Sea
East China Sea
South China Sea
Luzon Strait
Celebes Sea
Java Sea
Arafura Sea
Gulf of Thailand
Andaman Sea
Bay of Bengal
Arabian Sea
Gulf of Aden
Red Sea
Persian Gulf

N
S
E
W

Africa: Physical

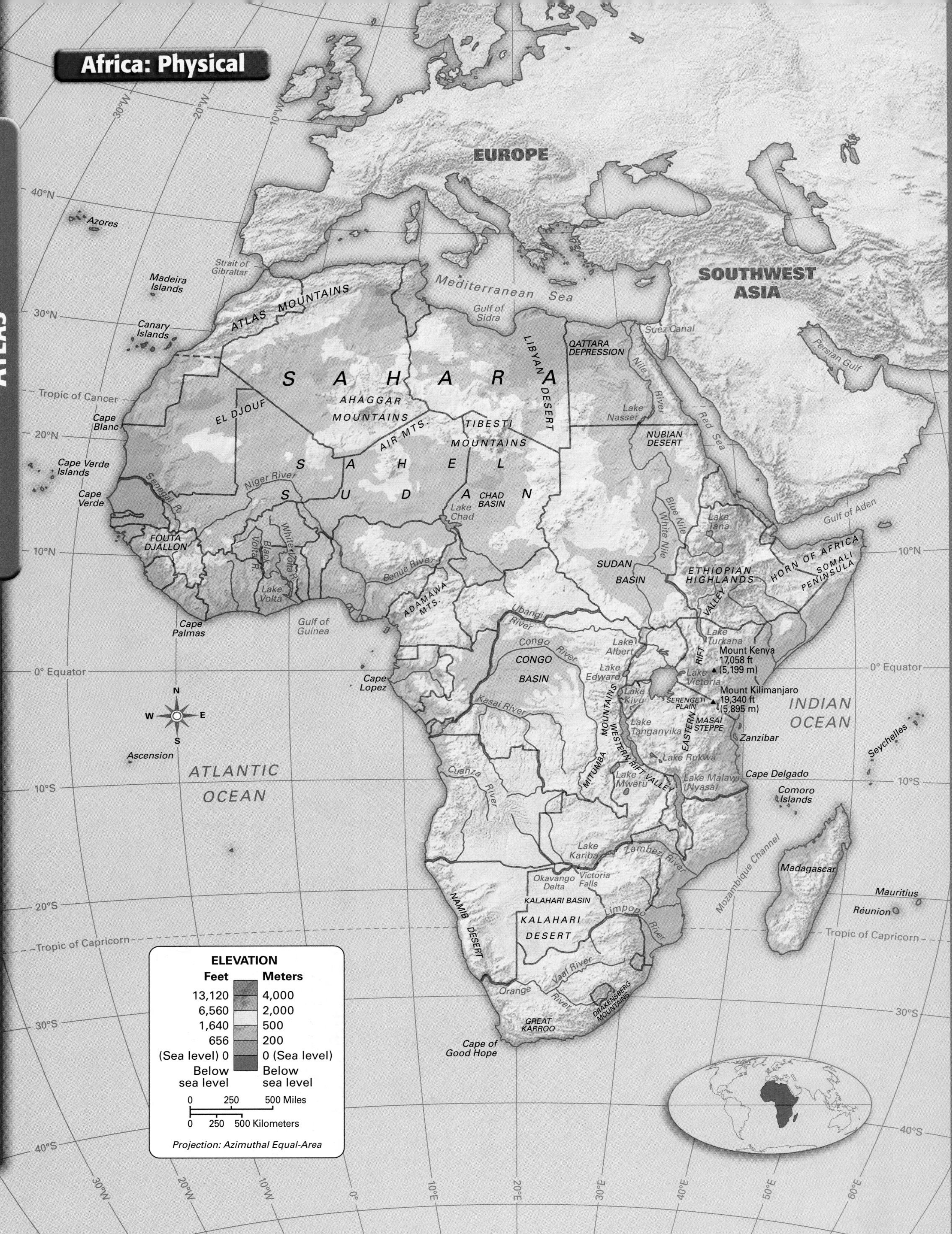

ATLAS

EUROPE
SOUTHWEST ASIA
Azores
Madeira Islands
Canary Islands
Strait of Gibraltar
Mediterranean Sea
Gulf of Sidra
Suez Canal
Persian Gulf
ATLAS MOUNTAINS
QATTARA DEPRESSION
LIBYAN DESERT
SAHARA
AHAGGAR MOUNTAINS
EL DJOUF
AIR MTS.
TIBESTI MOUNTAINS
Nile River
Lake Nasser
Red Sea
NUBIAN DESERT
Tropic of Cancer
Cape Blanc
Cape Verde Islands
Cape Verde
Senegal R.
Niger River
SAHEL
SUDAN
Lake Chad
CHAD BASIN
Blue Nile
White Nile
Lake Tana
Gulf of Aden
FOUTA DJALLON
Black Volta R.
White Volta R.
Lake Volta
Benue River
SUDAN BASIN
ETHIOPIAN HIGHLANDS
HORN OF AFRICA
SOMALI PENINSULA
RIFT VALLEY
ADAMAWA MTS.
Cape Palmas
Gulf of Guinea
Ubangi River
Congo River
CONGO BASIN
Lake Albert
Lake Turkana
Mount Kenya 17,058 ft (5,199 m)
Lake Edward
Lake Victoria
Cape Lopez
Lake Kivu
SERENGETI PLAIN
Mount Kilimanjaro 19,340 ft (5,895 m)
INDIAN OCEAN
Kasai River
MITUMBA MOUNTAINS
WESTERN RIFT VALLEY
Lake Tanganyika
EASTERN RIFT VALLEY
MASAI STEPPE
Zanzibar
Seychelles
Ascension
ATLANTIC OCEAN
Cuanza River
Lake Rukwa
Lake Mweru
Lake Malawi (Nyasa)
Cape Delgado
Comoro Islands
Lake Kariba
Zambezi River
Mozambique Channel
Madagascar
Okavango Delta
Victoria Falls
NAMIB DESERT
KALAHARI BASIN
KALAHARI DESERT
Limpopo River
Mauritius
Réunion
Tropic of Capricorn
Vaal River
Orange River
DRAKENSBERG MOUNTAINS
GREAT KARROO
Cape of Good Hope

40°N, 30°N, 20°N, 10°N, 0° Equator, 10°S, 20°S, 30°S, 40°S
30°W, 20°W, 10°W, 0°, 10°E, 20°E, 30°E, 40°E, 50°E, 60°E

N, S, E, W

ELEVATION

Feet	Meters
13,120	4,000
6,560	2,000
1,640	500
656	200
(Sea level) 0	0 (Sea level)
Below sea level	Below sea level

0 250 500 Miles
0 250 500 Kilometers

Projection: Azimuthal Equal-Area

Africa: Political

EUROPE

SOUTHWEST ASIA

Azores (PORTUGAL)
Madeira (PORTUGAL)
Canary Islands (SPAIN)
Strait of Gibraltar
Casablanca
Rabat
MOROCCO
Algiers
Tunis
TUNISIA
Mediterranean Sea
Tripoli
Alexandria
Giza
Cairo
El Aaiún
WESTERN SAHARA (Claimed by Morocco)
ALGERIA
LIBYA
EGYPT
Red Sea
Tropic of Cancer
MAURITANIA
Nouakchott
MALI
NIGER
CHAD
SUDAN
CAPE VERDE
Praia
SENEGAL
Dakar
GAMBIA
Banjul
Bissau
GUINEA-BISSAU
GUINEA
Conakry
Freetown
SIERRA LEONE
Monrovia
LIBERIA
Bamako
BURKINA FASO
Ouagadougou
Niamey
Lake Chad
N'Djamena
Khartoum
ERITREA
Asmara
Gulf of Aden
DJIBOUTI
Djibouti
ETHIOPIA
Addis Ababa
CÔTE D'IVOIRE
Yamoussoukro
Abidjan
GHANA
Accra
TOGO
Lomé
BENIN
Porto-Novo
NIGERIA
Abuja
Lagos
Gulf of Guinea
CENTRAL AFRICAN REPUBLIC
Bangui
CAMEROON
Yaoundé
Malabo
EQUATORIAL GUINEA
SÃO TOMÉ AND PRÍNCIPE
São Tomé
Libreville
GABON
REPUBLIC OF THE CONGO
Brazzaville
Kinshasa
CABINDA (ANGOLA)
DEMOCRATIC REPUBLIC OF THE CONGO
Kisangani
UGANDA
Kampala
KENYA
Nairobi
SOMALIA
Mogadishu
RWANDA
Kigali
Lake Victoria
Bujumbura
BURUNDI
TANZANIA
Dodoma
Lake Tanganyika
Mombasa
Pemba
Zanzibar
Dar es Salaam
Lake Malawi (Nyasa)
INDIAN OCEAN
Victoria
SEYCHELLES
COMOROS
Moroni
ATLANTIC OCEAN
Luanda
ANGOLA
Lubumbashi
ZAMBIA
Lusaka
MALAWI
Lilongwe
MOZAMBIQUE
Harare
ZIMBABWE
Bulawayo
St. Helena (U.K.)
NAMIBIA
Windhoek
BOTSWANA
Gaborone
Pretoria
Johannesburg
Maputo
Mbabane
SWAZILAND
Bloemfontein
Maseru
LESOTHO
SOUTH AFRICA
Cape Town
MADAGASCAR
Antananarivo
MAURITIUS
Port Louis
Réunion (FRANCE)
Tropic of Capricorn
0° Equator

40°N, 30°N, 20°N, 10°N, 0°, 10°S, 20°S, 30°S, 40°S
30°W, 20°W, 10°W, 0°, 10°E, 20°E, 30°E, 40°E, 50°E, 60°E

N, E, S, W

National capital
Other city
0 250 500 Miles
0 250 500 Kilometers
Projection: Azimuthal Equal-Area

ATLAS

The Pacific: Political

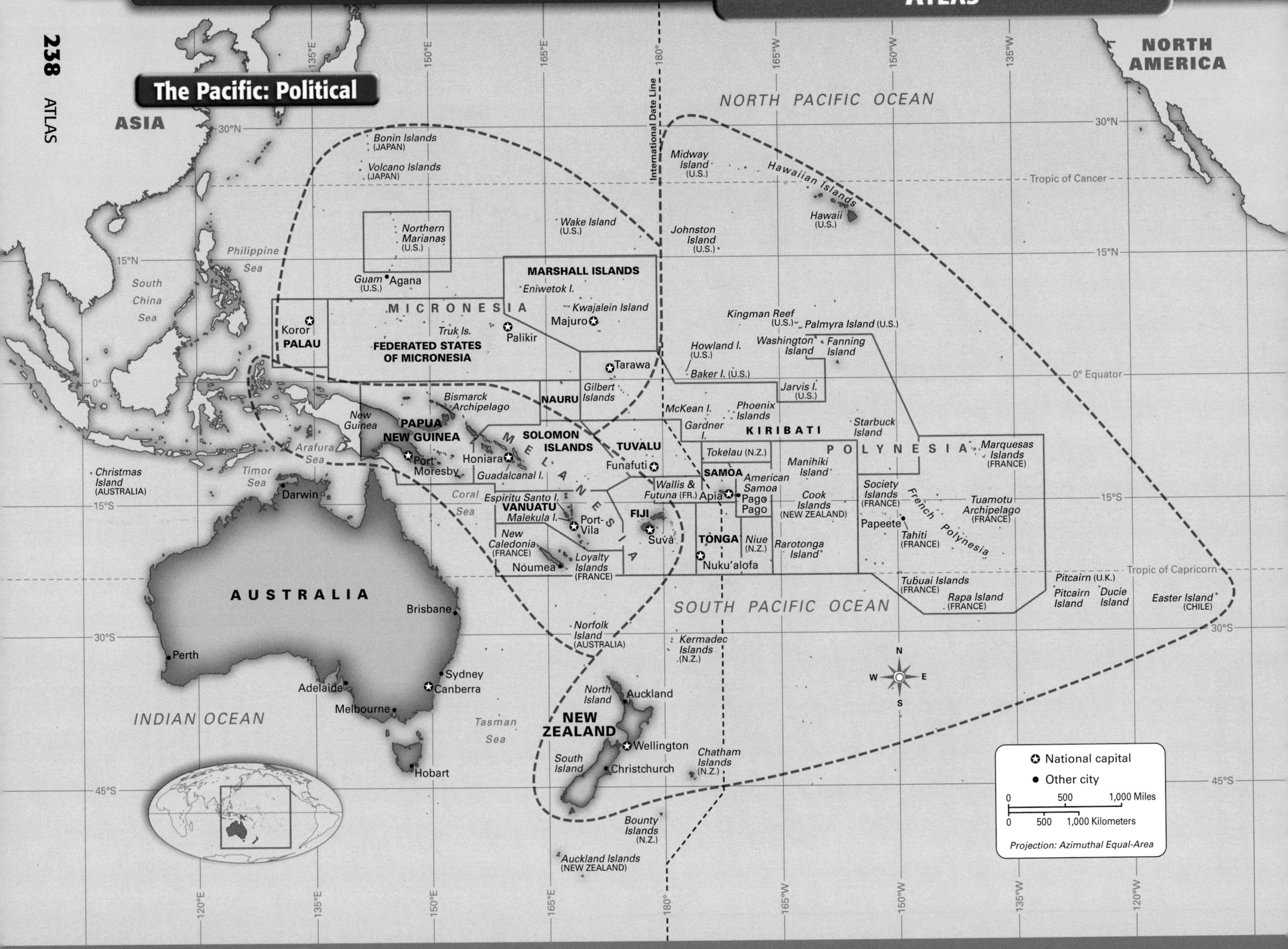

ASIA
NORTH AMERICA
NORTH PACIFIC OCEAN
SOUTH PACIFIC OCEAN
INDIAN OCEAN
Philippine Sea
South China Sea
Arafura Sea
Timor Sea
Coral Sea
Tasman Sea
Tropic of Cancer
Tropic of Capricorn
0° Equator
International Date Line
30°N
15°N
0°
15°S
30°S
45°S
120°E
135°E
150°E
165°E
180°
165°W
150°W
135°W
120°W
Bonin Islands (JAPAN)
Volcano Islands (JAPAN)
Northern Marianas (U.S.)
Guam (U.S.)
Agana
Wake Island (U.S.)
Midway Island (U.S.)
Hawaiian Islands
Hawaii (U.S.)
Johnston Island (U.S.)
MICRONESIA
MARSHALL ISLANDS
Eniwetok I.
Kwajalein Island
Majuro
Koror
PALAU
Truk Is.
Palikir
FEDERATED STATES OF MICRONESIA
Tarawa
Gilbert Islands
NAURU
Kingman Reef (U.S.)
Palmyra Island (U.S.)
Washington Island
Fanning Island
Howland I. (U.S.)
Baker I. (U.S.)
Jarvis I. (U.S.)
McKean I.
Phoenix Islands
Gardner I.
KIRIBATI
Starbuck Island
POLYNESIA
Marquesas Islands (FRANCE)
Bismarck Archipelago
New Guinea
PAPUA NEW GUINEA
Port Moresby
MELANESIA
SOLOMON ISLANDS
Honiara
Guadalcanal I.
TUVALU
Funafuti
Tokelau (N.Z.)
SAMOA
Apia
American Samoa
Pago Pago
Manihiki Island
Cook Islands (NEW ZEALAND)
Society Islands (FRANCE)
French Polynesia
Tuamotu Archipelago (FRANCE)
Papeete
Tahiti (FRANCE)
Wallis & Futuna (FR.)
FIJI
Suva
Espiritu Santo I.
VANUATU
Malekula I.
Port-Vila
New Caledonia (FRANCE)
Noumea
Loyalty Islands (FRANCE)
TONGA
Nuku'alofa
Niue (N.Z.)
Rarotonga Island
Tubuai Islands (FRANCE)
Rapa Island (FRANCE)
Pitcairn (U.K.)
Pitcairn Island
Ducie Island
Easter Island (CHILE)
Christmas Island (AUSTRALIA)
Darwin
AUSTRALIA
Brisbane
Perth
Sydney
Canberra
Adelaide
Melbourne
Hobart
Norfolk Island (AUSTRALIA)
Kermadec Islands (N.Z.)
North Island
Auckland
NEW ZEALAND
Wellington
South Island
Christchurch
Chatham Islands (N.Z.)
Bounty Islands (N.Z.)
Auckland Islands (NEW ZEALAND)
N
W
E
S
National capital
Other city
0 500 1,000 Miles
0 500 1,000 Kilometers
Projection: Azimuthal Equal-Area

The North Pole

0 200 400 Miles
0 200 400 Kilometers
Projection: Polar Azimuthal Equidistant

EUROPE
Barents Sea
Kara Sea
Norwegian Sea
Arctic Circle
Laptev Sea
ASIA
ARCTIC OCEAN
North Pole
Greenland Sea
Greenland (DENMARK)
ATLANTIC OCEAN
International Date Line
POLAR ICE PACK
North Magnetic Pole
Baffin Bay
Bering Sea
Beaufort Sea
NORTH AMERICA
90°E
60°E
30°E
0°
120°E
150°E
180°
80°N
70°N
60°N
50°N
150°W
120°W
90°W
60°W
30°W

ATLAS

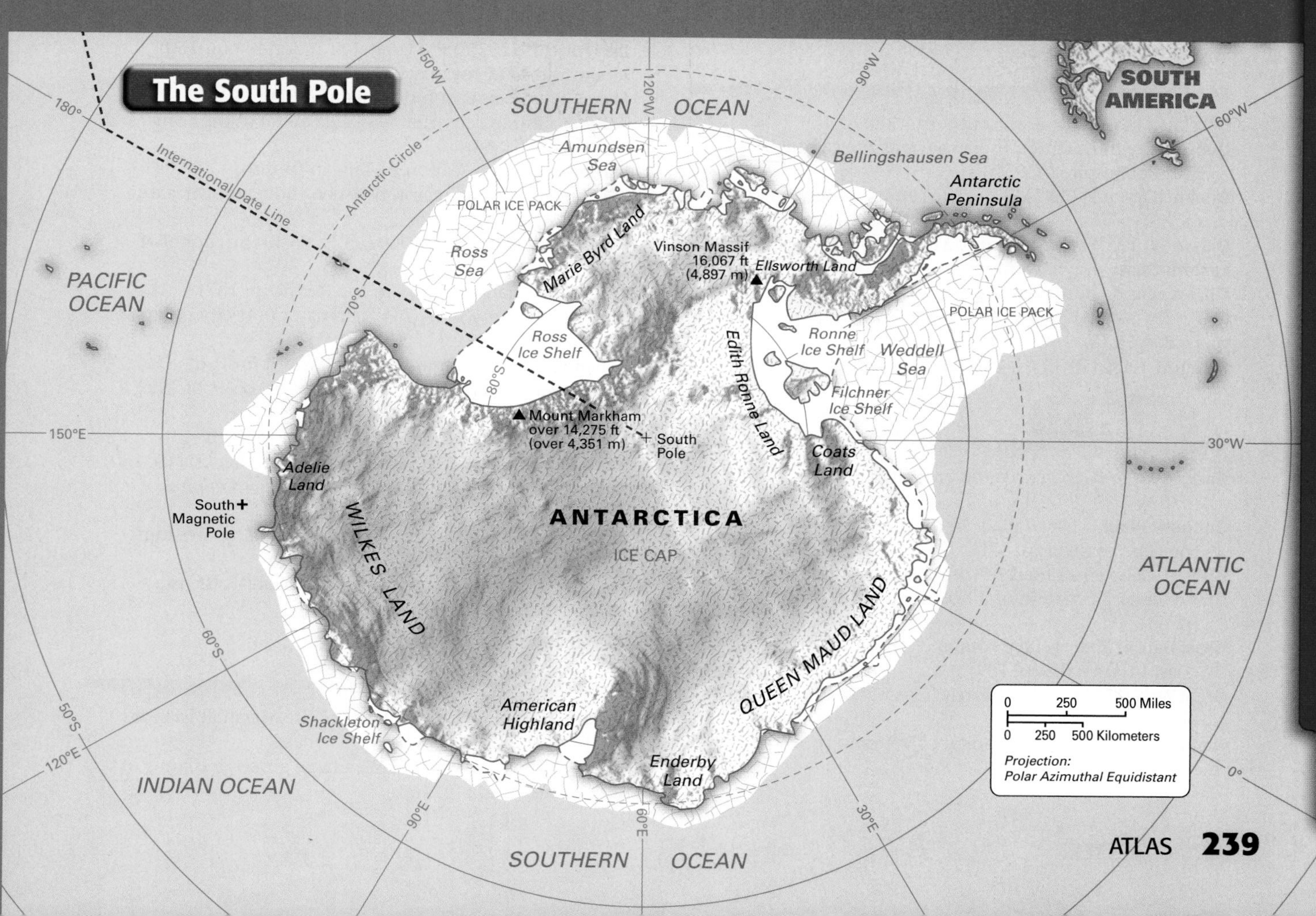

Gazetteer

A, B, C

Adelaide (35°S, 139°E) a city in southern Australia (p. 186)
Antarctica a continent around the South Pole (p. 187)
Antarctic Peninsula a large peninsula in Antarctica (p. 187)
Apia (14°S, 172°W) the capital of Western Samoa (p. 200)
Arabian Sea a large arm of the Indian Ocean between India and Arabia (p. 85)
Asia the world's largest continent, bounded by the Arctic, Pacific, and Indian oceans (p. 234)
Australia a country and continent in the Pacific (p. 186)
Bandar Seri Begawan (5°N, 115°E) capital of Brunei (p. 161)
Bangkok (14°N, 100°E) the capital of Thailand (p. 160)
Bangladesh a country in South Asia (p. 85)
Bay of Bengal a large bay of the Indian Ocean between India and Southeast Asia (p. 85)
Beijing (40°N, 116°E) the capital of China (p. 109)
Bhutan a country in South Asia north of India (p. 85)
Borneo the world's third-largest island; located in Southeast Asia (p. 163)
Brunei (brooh-NY) a country in Southeast Asia on the northern coast of Borneo (p. 161)
Cambodia a country in Southeast Asia (p. 160)
Canberra (35°S, 149°E) the capital of Australia (p. 186)
Chang Jiang (Yangzi River) a major river in China (p. 109)
Chao Phraya (chow PRY-uh) a river in Thailand (p. 234)
China a large country in East Asia (p. 109)
Colombo (7°N, 80°E) the capital of Sri Lanka (p. 85)

D, E, F

Deccan a large plateau in southern India (p. 87)
Delhi a city in northern India that was the capital of the Mughal Empire (p. 85)
Dhaka (DA-kuh) (24°N, 90°E) the capital of Bangladesh (p. 85)
Dili (8°N, 125°E) the capital of Timor-Leste (p. 161)
Eastern Ghats (gawts) a mountain range in India (p. 87)
Fiji an island country in the Pacific (p. 187)
Fuji (FOO-jee) (35°N, 135°E) a volcano and Japan's highest peak (p. 137)
Funafuti (9°S, 179°E) the capital of Tuvalu (p. 200)

G, H, I

Ganges River (GAN-jeez) a major river in northern India (p. 87)
Gangetic Plain a broad plain in northern India formed by the Ganges River (p. 87)
Gobi (GOH-bee) a desert in China and Mongolia (p. 111)
Grand Canal a canal linking northern and southern China (p. 63)
Great Barrier Reef a huge coral reef off the northeastern coast of Australia (p. 189)
Great Wall of China a long barrier near China's northern border (p. 51)
Hanoi (21°N, 106°E) the capital of Vietnam (p. 160)
Harappa (huh-RA-puh) an ancient city in the Indus Valley in modern Pakistan (p. 17)
Himalayas the highest mountains in the world; they separate the Indian Subcontinent from China (p. 87)
Hindu Kush a group of mountains that separates the Indian Subcontinent from Central Asia (p. 87)
Ho Chi Minh City a large city in southern Vietnam (p. 160)
Hokkaido (hoh-KY-doh) the northernmost of Japan's four major islands (p. 137)
Hong Kong (22°N, 115°E) a city in southern China (p. 109)
Honiara (9°S, 160°E) the capital of the Solomon Islands (p. 200)
Honshu (HAWN-shoo) the largest of Japan's four major islands (p. 137)
Huang He (Yellow River) a major river in northern China (p. 111)
India a country in South Asia (p. 85)
Indian Ocean the world's third-largest ocean; it is located between Asia and Antarctica (pp. 224–225)
Indochina Peninsula a large peninsula in Southeast Asia (p. 163)
Indonesia the largest country in Southeast Asia (p. 161)
Indus River a major river in Pakistan (p. 87)
Indus River Valley a river valley in Pakistan that was home to the ancient Harappan civilization (p. 87)
Islamabad (34°N, 73°E) the capital of Pakistan (p. 85)

J, K, L

Jakarta (6°S, 107°E) the capital of Indonesia (p. 160)
Japan an island country in East Asia (p. 135)
Java a large island in Indonesia (p. 161)
Kaifeng Chinese city that was the capital of the Song dynasty (p. 64)
Kao-hsiung main seaport of Taiwan (p. 128)
Kashmir a disputed region between India and Pakistan (p. 85)
Kathmandu (kat-man-DOO) (28°N, 85°E) the capital of Nepal (p. 85)
Kiribati an island country in the Pacific (p. 187)
Kobe (KOH-bay) (35°N, 135°E) a major port city in Japan (p. 138)
Kolkata (Calcutta) a major city in eastern India (p. 85)
Korean Peninsula a peninsula on the east coast of Asia (p. 135)
Koror (9°N, 138°E) the capital of Palau (p. 200)
Kuala Lumpur (3°N, 102°E) the capital of Malaysia (p. 160)
Kyoto (KYOH-toh) (35°N, 136°E) the ancient capital of Japan (p. 135)
Kyushu (KYOO-shoo) the southernmost of Japan's four major islands (p. 137)
Laos (LOWS) a landlocked country in Southeast Asia (p. 160)

M

Majuro (7°N, 171°E) the capital of the Marshall Islands (p. 200)
Malay Archipelago (muh-LAY) a large group of islands in Southeast Asia (p. 163)

Malay Peninsula (muh-LAY) a narrow peninsula in Southeast Asia (p. 163)
Malaysia a country in Southeast Asia (p. 160)
Maldives an island country south of India (p. 87)
Male (5°N, 72°E) the capital of the Maldives (p. 235)
Manila (15°N, 121°E) the capital of the Philippines (p. 161)
Marshall Islands an island country in the Pacific (p. 187)
Mekong River a major river in Southeast Asia (p. 163)
Melanesia a huge group of Pacific islands that stretches from New Guinea to Fiji (p. 200)
Melbourne (38°S, 145°E) a city in southeastern Australia (p. 186)
Micronesia a large group of Pacific islands located east of the Philippines (p. 200)
Micronesia, Federated States of an island country in the western Pacific (p. 186)
Mohenjo Daro (mo-HEN-joh DAR-oh) (27°N, 68°E) an ancient city of the Harappan civilization in modern Pakistan (p. 17)
Mongolia a landlocked country in East Asia (p. 109)
Mount Everest the highest mountain in the world at 29,035 feet (8,850 km); it is located in India and Nepal (p. 87)
Mumbai (Bombay) a major city in western India (p. 85)
Myanmar (Burma) (MYAHN-mahr) a country in Southeast Asia (p. 160)

N, O, P

Nauru an island country in the Pacific (p. 187)
Naypyidaw (20°N, 98°E) the administrative capital of Myanmar (Burma) (p.160)
Nepal a landlocked country in South Asia (p. 85)
New Delhi (29°N, 77°E) the capital of India (p. 85)
New Guinea the world's second-largest island; located in Southeast Asia (p. 163)
New Zealand an island country southeast of Australia (p. 187)
North China Plain a plains region of northeastern China (p. 111)
North Korea a country in East Asia (p. 135)
Nuku'alofa (21°N, 174°E) the capital of Tonga (p. 200)
Osaka (oh-SAH-kuh) (35°N, 135°E) a city in Japan (p. 135)
Outback the dry interior region of Australia (p. 189)
Pacific Ocean Earth's largest ocean; located between North and South America and Asia and Australia (p. 224–25)
Pakistan a country in South Asia northwest of India (p. 85)
Palau an island country in the Pacific (p. 186)
Palikir (6°N, 158°E) the capital of the Federated States of Micronesia (p. 200)
Papua New Guinea a country on the island of New Guinea (p. 186)
Perth (32°S, 116°E) a city in western Australia (p. 186)
Philippines an island country in Southeast Asia (p. 161)
Phnom Penh (puh-NAWM pen) (12°N, 105°E) the capital of Cambodia (p. 160)
Plateau of Tibet a high plateau in western China (p. 111)
Polynesia the largest group of islands in the Pacific Ocean (p. 200)
Port Moresby (10°S, 147°E) the capital of Papua New Guinea (p. 186)
Port-Vila (18°S, 169°E) the capital of Vanuatu (p. 200)
Pyongyang (pyuhng-YANG) (39°N, 126°E) the capital of North Korea (p. 135)

R, S

Ross Ice Shelf the largest ice shelf in Antarctica (p. 187)
Samoa an island country in the Pacific (p. 187)
Seoul (38°N, 127°E) the capital of South Korea (p. 135)
Shanghai (31°N, 121°E) a major port city in eastern China (p. 109)
Shikoku (shee-koh-koo) the smallest of Japan's four major islands (p. 137)
Singapore an island country at the tip of the Malay Peninsula in Southeast Asia (p. 160)
Solomon Islands an island country in the Pacific (p. 187)
South Korea a country in East Asia (p. 135)
Sri Lanka an island country located south of India (p. 85)
Sumatra a large island in Indonesia (p. 160)
Suva (19°S, 178°E) the capital of Fiji (p. 200)
Sydney (34°S, 151°E) the largest city in Australia (p. 186)

T, U, V

Taipei (25°N, 122°E) the capital of Taiwan (p. 109)
Taiwan (ty-wahn) an island country southeast of China (p. 109)
Tarawa the capital of Kiribati (p. 200)
Tasmania a large island off the southern coast of Australia (p. 186)
Thailand (TY-land) a country in Southeast Asia (p. 160)
Thar Desert (TAHR) a desert in western India and eastern Pakistan (p. 87)
Thimphu (28°N, 90°E) the capital of Bhutan (p. 85)
Tibet a plateau region in western China (p. 108)
Timor island in the Malay archipelago (p. 169)
Timor-Leste an island country in Southeast Asia (p. 161)
Tokyo (36°N, 140°E) the capital of Japan (p. 135)
Tonga an island country in the Pacific (p. 187)
Tuvalu an island country in the Pacific (p. 187)
Ulaanbaatar (oo-lahn-BAH-tawr) (48°N, 107°E) the capital of Mongolia (p. 109)
Uluru a huge natural rock formation in central Australia; also called Ayers Rock (p. 189)
Vanuatu an island country in the Pacific (p. 187)
Vientiane (vyen-THAN) (18°N, 103°E) the capital of Laos (p. 160)
Vietnam (vee-ET-NAHM) a country in Southeast Asia (p. 160)

W, X, Y

Wellington (41°S, 175°E) the capital of New Zealand (p. 187)
Western Ghats (GAWTS) a mountain range in India (p. 87)
Xi'an (34°N, 109°E) a city in China (p. 63)
Yangon (Rangoon) (17°N, 96°E) the capital of Myanmar (Burma) (p. 160)
Yellow Sea a body of water between northeastern China and the Korean Peninsula (p. 111)

English and Spanish Glossary

MARK	AS IN	RESPELLING	EXAMPLE
a	alphabet	a	*AL-fuh-bet
ā	Asia	ay	AY-zhuh
ä	cart, top	ah	KAHRT, TAHP
e	let, ten	e	LET, TEN
ē	even, leaf	ee	EE-vuhn, LEEF
i	it, tip, British	i	IT, TIP, BRIT-ish
ī	site, buy, Ohio	y	SYT, BY, oh-HY-oh
	iris	eye	EYE-ris
k	card	k	KAHRD
kw	quest	kw	KWEST
ō	over, rainbow	oh	OH-vuhr, RAYN-boh
ù	book, wood	ooh	BOOHK, WOOHD
ò	all, orchid	aw	AWL, AWR-kid
òi	foil, coin	oy	FOYL, KOYN
àu	out	ow	OWT
ə	cup, butter	uh	KUHP, BUHT-uhr
ü	rule, food	oo	ROOL, FOOD
yü	few	yoo	FYOO
zh	vision	zh	VIZH-uhn

*A syllable printed in small capital letters receives heavier emphasis than the other syllable(s) in a word.

Phonetic Respelling and Pronunciation Guide

Many of the key terms in this textbook have been respelled to help you pronounce them. The letter combinations used in the respelling throughout the narrative are explained in this phonetic respelling and pronunciation guide. The guide is adapted from Merriam-Webster's Collegiate Dictionary, Eleventh Edition; Merriam-Webster's Geographical Dictionary; and Merriam-Webster's Biographical Dictionary.

A

Aborigines (a-buh-rij-uh-nees) the original inhabitants of Australia (p. 191)
aborígenes habitantes originales de Australia (pág.191)

acupuncture (AK-yoo-punk-cher) the Chinese practice of inserting fine needles through the skin at specific points to cure disease or relieve pain (p. 59)
acupuntura práctica china de insertar agujas finas en la piel en puntos específicos para curar enfermedades o aliviar el dolor (pág. 59)

alloy a mixture of two or more metals (p. 42)
aleación mezcla de dos o más metales (pág. 42)

archipelago a large group of islands (p. 162)
archipiélago gran grupo de islas (pág. 162)

Association of Southeast Asian Nations (ASEAN) an organization that promotes economic development and social and cultural cooperation among the countries of Southeast Asia (p. 173)
Asociación de Naciones de Asia del Sudeste (ASEAN por sus siglas en inglés) organización que promueve el desarrollo económico y social y la cooperación cultural entre los países del sureste asiático (pág.173)

astronomy the study of stars and planets (p. 43)
astronomía estudio de las estrellas y los planetas (pág. 43)

atoll a ring-shaped coral island that surrounds a lagoon (p. 198)
atolón isla de coral en forma de anillo que rodea una laguna (pág.198)

B

Buddhism a religion based on the teachings of the Buddha that developed in India in the 500s BC (p. 94)
budismo religión basada en las enseñanzas de Buda, originada en la India en el siglo VI a. C. (pág. 94)

bureaucracy a body of unelected government officials (p. 70)
burocracia grupo de empleados no electos del gobierno (pág. 70)

caste system the division of Indian society into groups based on birth or occupation (p. 94)
sistema de castas división de la sociedad india en grupos basados en el nacimiento o la profesión (pág. 94)

civil service service as a government official (p. 70)
servicio público servicio como empleado del gobierno (pág. 70)

colony a territory inhabited and controlled by people from a foreign land (p. 92)
colonia territorio habitado y controlado por personas de otro país (pág. 92)

command economy an economic system in which the central government makes all economic decisions (p. 121)
economía autoritaria sistema económico en el que el gobierno central toma todas las decisiones económicas (pág. 121)

compass an instrument that uses Earth's magnetic field to indicate direction (p. 66)
brújula instrumento que utiliza el campo magnético de la Tierra para indicar la dirección (pág. 66)

Confucianism a philosophy based on the ideas of Confucius that focuses on morality, family order, social harmony, and government (p. 118)
confucianismo filosofía basada en las ideas de Confucio que se concentra en la moralidad, el orden familiar, la armonía social y el gobierno (pág. 118)

coral reef a chain of rocky material found in shallow tropical waters (p. 189)
arrecife de coral cadena de material rocoso que se encuentra en aguas tropicales de poca profundidad (p. 189)

Daoism a philosophy that developed in China and stressed the belief that one should live in harmony with the Dao, the guiding force of all reality (p. 118)
taoísmo filosofía que se desarrolló en China y que enfatizaba la creencia de que se debe vivir en armonía con el Tao, la fuerza que guía toda la realidad (pág. 118)

delta a landform at the mouth of a river created by sediment deposits (p. 87)
delta accidente geográfico que se forma en la desembocadura de un río, creado por depósitos de sedimento (pág. 87)

demilitarized zone an empty buffer zone created to keep two countries from fighting (p. 153)
zona desmilitarizada zona vacía que se crea como barrera entre dos países para evitar que luchen (pág. 153)

dialect a regional version of a language (p. 117)
dialecto versión regional de una lengua (pág. 117)

Diet the name for Japan's elected legislature (p. 146)
Dieta nombre de la asamblea legislativa electa de Japón (pág. 146)

domino theory the idea that if one country fell to Communism, neighboring countries would follow like falling dominoes (p. 170)
teoría del efecto dominó idea de que si un país cae en manos del comunismo, los países vecinos lo seguirán como fichas de dominó que caen una tras otra (pág. 170)

dynasty a series of rulers from the same family (p. 115)
dinastía serie de gobernantes de la misma familia (pág. 115)

edicts laws (p. 35)
edictos leyes (pág. 35)

fasting going without food for a period of time (p. 29)
ayunar dejar de comer durante un período de tiempo (pág. 29)

fishery a place where lots of fish and other seafood can be caught (p. 139)
pesquería lugar donde suele haber muchos peces y mariscos para pescar (pág. 139)

Forbidden City a huge palace complex built by China's Ming emperors that included hundreds of imperial residences, temples, and other government buildings (p. 76)
Ciudad Prohibida enorme complejo de palacios construido por orden de los emperadores Ming de China que incluía cientos de residencias imperiales, templos y otros edificios del gobierno (pág. 76)

free port a city in which almost no taxes are placed on goods (p. 180)
puerto libre ciudad donde hay muy pocos impuestos sobre los bienes (pág. 180)

ger a large, circular, felt tent used in Mongolia and Central Asia (p. 127)
ger gran tienda circular de fieltro usada en Mongolia y Asia Central (pág. 127)

Grand Canal a canal linking northern and southern China (p. 62)
Gran Canal canal que conecta el norte y el sur de China (pág. 62)

ENGLISH AND SPANISH GLOSSARY

Great Wall a barrier built to protect China from invasion that stood near China's northern border (p. 53)
Gran Muralla barrera construida cerca de la frontera norte de China para proteger a China de las invasiones (pág. 53)

green revolution a program that encouraged farmers to adopt modern agricultural methods to produce more food (p. 99)
revolución verde programa que animó a los agricultores a adoptar métodos de agricultura modernos para producir más alimentos (pág. 99)

gunpowder a mixture of powders used in guns and explosives (p. 66)
pólvora mezcla de polvos utilizada en las armas de fuego y los explosivos (pág. 66)

Hindu-Arabic numerals the number system we use today; it was created by Indian scholars during the Gupta dynasty (p. 42)
numerales indoarábigos sistema numérico que usamos hoy en día; fue creado por estudiosos de la India durante la dinastía Gupta (pág. 42)

Hinduism the main religion of India; it teaches that everything is part of a universal spirit called Brahman (p. 94)
hinduismo religión principal de la India; sus enseñanzas dicen que todo forma parte de un espíritu universal llamado Brahma (pág. 94)

human rights rights that all people deserve, such as rights to equality and justice (p. 174)
derechos humanos derechos que toda la gente merece como derechos a la igualdad y la justicia (pág. 174)

iceberg a floating mass of ice that has broken off a glacier (p. 203)
iceberg masa de hielo flotante que se ha desprendido de un glaciar (pág. 203)

ice shelf a ledge of ice that extends over the water (p. 203)
banco de hielo saliente de hielo que se extiende sobre el agua (pág. 203)

inoculation (i-nah-kyuh-LAY-shuhn) injecting a person with a small dose of a virus to help build up defenses to a disease (p. 42)
inoculación inyectarle una pequeña dosis de un virus a una persona para ayudarla a crear defensas contra una enfermedad (pág. 42)

isolationism a policy of avoiding contact with other countries (p. 78)
aislacionismo política de evitar el contacto con otros países (pág. 78)

kampong a traditional village in Indonesia; also the term for crowded slums around Indonesia's large cities (p. 179)
kampong aldea tradicional de Indonesia; término que también se usa para los barrios pobres y superpoblados que rodean las grandes ciudades de Indonesia (pág. 179)

karma in Buddhism and Hinduism, the effects that good or bad actions have on a person's soul (p. 26)
karma en el budismo y el hinduismo, efectos que las buenas o malas acciones producen en el alma de una persona (pág. 26)

kimchi a traditional Korean food made from pickled cabbage and spices (p. 145)
kimchi comida tradicional coreana hecha con repollo en vinagre y especias (pág. 145)

kimono a traditional robe worn in Japan (p. 144)
kimono bata tradicional usada en Japón (pág. 144)

klong a canal in Bangkok (p. 174)
klong canal de Bangkok (pág. 174)

loess (LES) fertile, yellowish soil (p. 112)
loess suelo amarillento y fértil (pág. 112)

mandate of heaven the idea that heaven chose China's ruler and gave him or her power (p. 52)
mandato divino idea de que el cielo elegía al gobernante de China y le daba el poder (pág. 52)

Maori (mowr-ee) the original inhabitants of New Zealand (p. 191)
maoríes primeros habitantes de Nueva Zelanda (pág. 191)

meditation deep continued thought that focuses the mind on spiritual ideas (p. 29)
meditación concentración profunda y continua que enfoca la mente en ideas espirituales (pág. 29)

mercenary a hired soldier (p. 34)
mercenario soldado a sueldo (pág. 34)

metallurgy (MET-uhl-uhr-jee) the science of working with metals (p. 42)
metalurgia ciencia de trabajar los metales (pág. 42)

missionary someone who works to spread religious beliefs (p. 32)
misionero alguien que trabaja para difundir creencias religiosas (pág. 32)

monsoons seasonal winds that bring either dry or moist air to an area (p. 89)
monzones vientos estacionales que traen aire seco o húmedo a una región (pág. 89)

N

nirvana in Buddhism, a state of perfect peace (p. 30)
nirvana en el budismo, estado de paz perfecta (pág. 30)

nonviolence the avoidance of violent actions (p. 27)
no violencia rechazo de las acciones violentas (pág. 27)

O

ozone layer a layer of Earth's atmosphere that protects living things from the harmful effects of the sun's ultraviolet rays (p. 204)
capa de ozono capa de la atmósfera de la Tierra que protege a los seres vivos de los efectos dañinos de los rayos ultravioleta del sol (pág. 204)

P

pagoda a Buddhist temple based on Indian designs (p. 119)
pagoda templo budista basado en diseños de la India (pág. 119)

partition division (p. 93)
partición división (pág. 93)

polar desert a high-latitude region that receives little precipitation (p. 203)
desierto polar región a una latitud alta que recibe pocas precipitaciones (pág. 203)

porcelain a thin, beautiful pottery invented in China (p. 65)
porcelana cerámica bella y fina creada en China (pág. 65)

R

reincarnation a Hindu and Buddhist belief that souls are born and reborn many times, each time into a new body (p. 25)
reencarnación creencia hindú y budista de que las almas nacen y renacen muchas veces, cada vez en un cuerpo nuevo (pág. 25)

S

samurai (SA-muh-ry) a trained professional warrior in feudal Japan (p. 142)
samurai guerrero profesional entrenado del Japón feudal (pág. 142)

Sanskrit the most important language of ancient India (p. 21)
sánscrito el idioma más importante de la antigua India (pág. 21)

scholar-official an educated member of China's government who passed a series of written examinations (p. 70)
funcionario erudito miembro culto del gobierno de China que aprobaba una serie de exámenes escritos (pág. 70)

seismograph a device that measures the strength of an earthquake (p. 58)
sismógrafo aparato que mide la fuerza de un terremoto (pág. 58)

Sherpas an ethnic group from the mountains of Nepal (p. 100)
sherpas grupo étnico de las montañas de Nepal (pág. 100)

shogun a general who ruled Japan in the emperor's name (p. 142)
shogun general que gobernaba a Japón en nombre del emperador (pág. 142)

subcontinent a large landmass that is smaller than a continent (p. 86)
subcontinente gran masa de tierra, más pequeña que un continente (pág. 86)

sultan the supreme ruler of a Muslim country (p. 181)
sultán gobernante supremo de un país musulmán (pág. 181)

sundial a device that uses the position of shadows cast by the sun to tell the time of day (p. 58)
reloj de sol aparato que utiliza la posición de las sombras que proyecta el sol para indicar las horas del día (pág. 58)

T

tariff a fee that a country charges on imports or exports (p. 147)
arancel tarifa que impone un país a las importaciones y exportaciones (pág. 147)

territory an area that is under the authority of another government (p. 199)
territorio zona que está bajo el control de otro gobierno (pág. 199)

trade surplus when a country exports more goods than it imports (p. 147)
excedente comercial cuando un país exporta más bienes de los que importa (pág. 147)

tsunami (sooh-NAH-mee) a destructive and fast-moving wave (p. 138)
tsunami ola rápida y destructiva (pág. 138)

U

urbanization the increase in the percentage of people who live in cities (p. 98)
urbanización aumento del porcentaje de personas que vive en las ciudades (pág. 98)

W

wat a Buddhist temple that also serves as a monastery (p. 170)
wat templo budista que sirve también como monasterio (pág. 170)

woodblock printing a form of printing in which an entire page is carved into a block of wood, covered with ink, and pressed to a piece of paper to create a printed page (p. 66)
xilografía forma de impresión en la que una página completa se talla en una plancha de madera, se cubre de tinta y se presiona sobre un papel para crear una página impresa (pág. 66)

work ethic a belief that work in itself is worthwhile (p. 147)
ética de trabajo creencia de que el trabajo tiene valor propio (pág. 147)

Index

KEY TO INDEX

c = chart	*m* = map
f = feature	*p* = photo

INDEX

Q

R

S

Z

Credits and Acknowledgments

For permission to reproduce copyrighted material, grateful acknowledgment is made to the following sources:

Bantam Books, a division of Random House, Inc., www.randomhouse.com: From *The Bhagavad-Gita*, translated by Barbara Stoler Miller. Copyright © 1986 by Barbara Stoler Miller.

CNN: From "Taiwan: War bill a big provocation," from *CNN.com* Web site, March 14, 2005. Copyright © 2005 by Cable News Network LP, LLLP. Accessed September 22, 2005, at http://edition.cnn.com/2005/WORLD/asiapcf/03/14/china.npc.law/

Foreign Affairs: From: "A Conversation With Lee Kuan Yew" by Fareed Zakaria from *Foreign Affairs*, March/April 1994, vol. 73, issue 2. Copyright © 2004 by Council on Foreign Relations. All rights reserved.

Alfred A. Knopf, Inc., a division of Random House, Inc., www.randomhouse.com: From *Shabanu: Daughter of Wind* by Suzanne Fisher Staples. Copyright ©1989 by Suzanne Fisher Staples. From *Crossing Antarctica* by Will Steger. Copyright © 1991 by Will Steger.

Penguin Books Ltd.: "Quiet Night Thoughts" by Li Po from *Li Po and Tu Fu: Poems*, translated by Arthur Cooper. Copyright © 1973 by Arthur Cooper.

Sources used by The World Almanac® for charts and graphs:

Geographical Extremes: South and East Asia: *The World Almanac and Book of Facts, 2005; The World Factbook, 2005;* U.S. Bureau of the Census; Food and Agriculture Organization of the United Nations—Forestry, Global Forest Watch; Geographical Extremes: The Pacific World: *The World Almanac and Book of Facts, 2005; The World Factbook, 2005;* U.S. Bureau of the Census; Marine Education Society of Australia; Food and Agriculture Organization of the United Nations—Forestry; South and East Asia and the Pacific: *The World Factbook, 2005;* U.S. Bureau of the Census, International Database; United Nations Statistical Yearbook; World's Largest Populations: International Programs Center, U.S. Census Bureau; Percent of World Population: International Programs Center, U.S. Census Bureau; Economic Powers: Japan and China: *The World Factbook, 2005;* Religions of the Indian Subcontinent: www.worldchristiandatabase.org; China's Projected Urban Population: United Nations Population Division; Population Growth in Japan: International Programs Center, U.S. Census Bureau; United Nations Population Division; Current Per Capita GDP in Island Southeast Asia and the United States: *The World Factbook, 2005;* Ethnic Groups in Australia and New Zealand: *The World Factbook, 2005*

Illustrations and Photo Credits

Cover: (l), James Nelson/Getty Images; (r), Jon Arnold/Getty Images.

Frontmatter: ii, Victoria Smith/HMH; iv, imagebroker/Alamy; (v) br, Jeremy Horner/Corbis; vi (tl), Associated Press/AP; vi (b), David Gray/Reuters/Corbis; vii, David Alan Parker/Image State; viii (br), Courtesy of NASA; H16 (t), Earth Satellite Corporation/Photo Researchers, Inc.; H16 (tc), Frans Lemmens/Getty Images; H16 (c), London Aerial Photo Library/Corbis; H16 (bc), Harvey Schwartz/Index Stock Imagery/Fotosearch; H16 (b), Tom Nebbia/Corbis.

Introduction: A, Bushnell/Soifer/Stone/Getty Images; B (bkgd), Planetary Visions; B (t), Ed Darack/Taxi/Getty Images; B (bl), Alanie/Life File/Photodisc/Getty Images; 1 (cl), Tim Davis/Stone/Getty Images; 3, Alison Wright/Photo Researchers, Inc.; 9 (c), Theo Allofs/Corbis; 12, Neil Rabinowitz/Corbis; 13 (bl), Tom Wagner/Corbis Saba; 13 (br), Macduff Everton/Corbis.

Chapter 1: 14 (b), DEA/A. Dagli Orti/Getty Images; 15 (bl), Jacob Halaska/Index Stock Imagery, Inc.; 15 (br), Richard A. Cooke/CORBIS; 20 (bl), Borromeo/Art Resource, NY; 24 (tr), Burstein Collection/Corbis; 25 (tr), Victoria & Albert Museum, London/Art Resource, NY; 25 (tl), Borromeo/Government Museum and National Art Gallery India/Art Resource, NY; 27 (tr), Manan Vatsyayana/AFP/Getty Images; 29 (t), HIP/Art Resource, NY; 30 (c), Dinodia Photo Library/age fotostock; 33 (tr), Sena Vidanagama/AFP/Getty Images; 37 SEF/Art Resource, NY; 38 (br), Christophe Boisvieux/Corbis; 40 (t), Sheldan Collins/CORBIS; 40 (tr), Lindsay Hebberd/CORBIS; 41 (br), Philadelphia Museum of Art/CORBIS; 42 (tr), PARIS PIERCE/Alamy; 42 (tl), C. M. Dixon Colour Photo Library/Ancient Art & Architecture Collection Ltd.; 43 (tl), Dinodia Photo Library RF/Age FotoStock; 43 (tr), Museum of the History of Science, University of Oxford; 45 (l), Borromeo/Art Resource, NY; 45 (cl), Dinodia Photo Library/age footstock; 45 (cr), Borromeo/Government Museum and National Art Gallery India/Art Resource, NY; 45 (r), C. M. Dixon Colour Photo Library/Ancient Art & Architecture Collection Ltd.

Chapter 2: 48 (br), O. Louis Mazzatenta/National Geographic Image Collection; 49 (tr), 2010 A&E Television Networks, LLC. All rights reserved; 49 (br), Free Agents Ltd./Corbis; 49 (bl), Otto Rogge/CORBIS; 52 (b), FSG/age fotostock/Photolibrary; 56 (b), Asian Art & Archaeology, Inc./Corbis; 57 (t), The Trustees Of/The British Museum (Detail); 58 (tl), Science & Society Picture Library; 59 (tr), Erich Lessing/Art Resource, NY; 59 (tl), Wellcome Library, London; 60 (bl), Tiziana and Gianni Baldizzone/CORBIS; 60 (bc), Araldo de Luca/CORBIS; 60 (cl), Elio Ciol/CORBIS; 61 (tr), Reza; Webistan/CORBIS; 61 (tl), Asian Art & Archaeology, Inc./CORBIS; 61 (tc), Bettmann/CORBIS; 64 (b), Carl & Ann Purcell/Corbis; 65 (cl), Keren Su/China Span/Alamy; 66 (tl), Paul Freeman/Private Collection/Bridgeman Art Library; 66 (cl), China Photo/Reuters/Corbis; 66 (bl), Liu Liqun/Corbis; 67 (tc), Private Collection/Bridgeman Art Library; 67 (tr), Tom Stewart/CORBIS; 68-69, Traditionally attributed to: Yan Liben, Chinese, died in 673. Northern Qi Scholar's Collating Classic Texts (detail). Chinese, Northern Song dynasty, 11th century. Object place: China. Ink and color on silk. 27.6 x 114 cm (10 7/8 x 44 7/8 in.). Museum of Fine Arts, Boston. Denman Waldo Ross Collection. 31.123/Museum of Fine Arts, Boston; 70-71 (tc), Snark/Art Resource, NY; 79 (br), National Palace Museum, Taipei, Taiwan/Bridgeman Art Library, 81 (t), Asian Art & Archaeology, Inc./Corbis.

Chapter 3: 84 (br), Anthony Cassidy/Stone/Getty Images; 85 (tr), 2010 A&E Television Networks, LLC. All rights reserved; 85 (bl), imagebroker/Alamy; 85 (br), Jon Arnold Images Ltd/Alamy; 87 (c), Ric Ergenbright/Corbis; 88 (b), Steve McCurry/Magnum Photos; 88 (t), Steve McCurry/Magnum Photos; 90, DEA/A. Dagli Orti/Getty Images; 91 (bl), Victoria & Albert Museum, London, UK/Bridgeman Art Library; 92 (tl), Hulton-Deutsch Collection/Corbis; 93 (b), Bettmann/Corbis; 98 (br), Mark Edwards/Photolibrary; 99 (cr), Henry Wilson/Robert Harding; 102 (tr), Sheldan Collins/Corbis; 103 (tr), Jeremy Horner/Corbis; 104 (tl), AFP/Getty Images; 105 (tr), Sheldan Collins/Corbis; 105 (tl), Ric Ergenbright/Corbis; 105 (tc), imagebroker/Alamy.

Chapter 4: 108 (br), Setboun/Corbis; 109 (tr), 2010 A&E Television Networks, LLC. All rights reserved; 109 (bl), Steve Vidler/eStock Photo; 109 (br), Michael Yamashita/Corbis; 111 (tr), Pal Teravagimov Photography/Getty Images; 111 (b), Panorama Media (Beijing), Ltd./Alamy; 113 (tr), CNES, 1998 Distribution Spot Image/Science Photo Library; 113 (tc), CNES, 1998 Distribution Spot Image/Science Photo Library; 114 (bl), DEA/G. Dagli Orti/Getty Images; 115 (br), Asian Art & Archaeology, Inc./Corbis; 115 (bl), O. Louis Mazzatenta/National Geographic Image Collection; 117 (br), Keren Su/Taxi/Getty Images; 117 (cr), David Sanger Photography; 117 (tr), Jack Hollingsworth/Corbis; 120 (tr), Associated Press, AP; 121 (b), Yann Layma/Getty Images; 122-123 (b), Mark Henley/Sinopix; 125 (cl), Adrian Bradshaw/Liaison/Getty Images; 125 (tl), Reportage/Getty Images; 127 (tr), Bruno Morandi/Robert Harding; 127 (t), Nik Wheeler/Corbis; 129 (t), AP Photo/Wally Santana; 131 (tr), AP Photo/Wally Santana; 131 (tc), Bruno Morandi/Robert Harding; 131 (tl), Mark Henley/Sinopix; 133 MC1-MC2, Ilya Terentyev/Getty Images.

Chapter 5: 134 (br), Werner Foreman/Art Resource, NY; 135 (tr), 2010 A&E Television Networks, LLC. All rights reserved; 135 (br), Tony Waltham/Robert Harding/Getty Images; 135 (bl), Roberto M. Arakaki/International Stock/Image State; 137 (br), Catherine Karnow/Corbis; 138 (tr), Michael S. Yamashita/Corbis; 139 (tr), AFP/Getty Images; 141 (bl), age fotostock/SuperStock; 142 (bl), Bettmann/Corbis; 143 (t), Kenneth Hamm/Photo Japan; 144 (t), David Gray/Reuters/Corbis; 145 (tl), R. Creation/amanaimages/Corbis; 147 (tr), AFP/Getty Images; 148 (bc), Chad Ehlers/Alamy; 149 (cr), Barry Lewis/Alamy; 151 (tr), TWPhoto/Corbis; 153 (t), Setboun/Corbis; 154 (bl), Royalty-Free/Getty Images; 155 (bl), David Humme Kennerly/Getty Images; 156 (tl), Reuters/Corbis; 157 (tr), Royalty Free/Getty Images; 157 (tl), Roberto M. Arakaki/International Stock/Image State; 157 (tc), TWPhoto/Corbis; 159 MC1-MC2, Burstein Collection/Corbis.

Chapter 6: 160 (br), Royalty-Free/Getty Images; 161 (bl), Free Agents Limited/Corbis; 161 (br), Christophe Loviny/Corbis; 163 (cr), Michael Yamashita/Corbis; 164 (tr), Louise Murray/Robert Harding; 165 (tl), Age Fotostock/SuperStock; 167 (tr), AFP/Getty Images; 169 (b), John Elk Photography; 171 (cr), Kevin R. Morris/Corbis; 172, Bruno De Hogues/Getty Images; 174 (bl), Alison Wright/Corbis; 175, Maxine Cass Photography; 176 (br), John Banagan/Lonely Planet Images; 176 (bl), Robert Francis/Robert Harding; 179 (br), Neil Rabinowitz/Corbis; 179 (bl), Paul Almasy/Corbis; 180 (t), Shoot PTY/Taxi/Getty Images; 181 (br), Steve Vidler/Image State; 183 (tr), Shoot PTY/Taxi/Getty Images; 183 (tc), Maxine Cass Photography; 183 (tl), John Elk Photography.

Chapter 7: 186 (br), Catherine Karnow/Corbis; 187 (tr), 2010 A&E Television Networks, LLC. All rights reserved; 187 (br), Age Fotostock/SuperStock; 187 (bl), Kevin Schafer/Corbis; 189 (cr), Richard Hamilton Smith/Corbis; 189 (cl), Oliver Strewe/Lonely Planet Images; 192 (cl), Reportage/Getty Images; 194 (bl), Heritage Image Partnership, Ltd./Image State; 198 (bl), David Alan Parker/Image State; 198 (cl), Greg Vaughn/Alamy; 201 (tr), Richard I'Anson/Lonely Planet Images; 202-203 (b), Digital Vision/Getty Images; 204 (tr), Hulton-Deutsch Collection/Corbis; 204 (tl), Bettmann/Corbis; 205 (tr), Courtesy of NASA; 206 (tl), Hugh Rose/DanitaDelimont.com; 207 (tr), Digital Vision/Getty Images; 207 (tl), Oliver Strewe/Lonely Planet Images; 207 (tc), Greg Vaughn/Alamy.

Staff Credits

The people who contributed to ***Holt McDougal: South and East Asia and the Pacific*** are listed below. They represent editorial, design, production, emedia, and permissions.

Melanie Baccus, Angela Beckmann, Julie Beckman-Key, Genick Blaise, Ed Blake, Jennifer Campbell, Henry Clark, Grant Davidson, Nina Degollado, Rose Degollado, Christine Devall, Michelle Dike, Lydia Doty, Chase Edmond, Mescal Evler, Susan Franques, Stephanie Friedman, Bob Fullilove, Matthew Gierhart, Bill Gillis, Ann Gorbett, Janet Harrington, Betsy Harris, Wendy Hodge, Tim Hovde, Cathy Jenevein, Carrie Jones, Kadonna Knape, Laura Lasley, Sarah Lee, Sean McCormick, Joe Melomo, Richard Metzger, Andrew Miles, Debra O'Shields, Jarred Prejean, Paul Provence, Shelly Ramos, Curtis Riker, Michael Rinella, Michelle Rimsa, Jennifer Rockwood, Carole Rollins, Beth Sample, Annette Saunders, Jenny Schaeffer, Kay Selke, Chris Smith, Jeremy Strykul, Jeannie Taylor, Terri Taylor, Joni Wackwitz, Mary Wages, Diana Holman Walker, Nadyne Wood, Robin Zaback